WELCOME TO THE BALLROOM no. 7

TOMO TAKEUCH

Contents

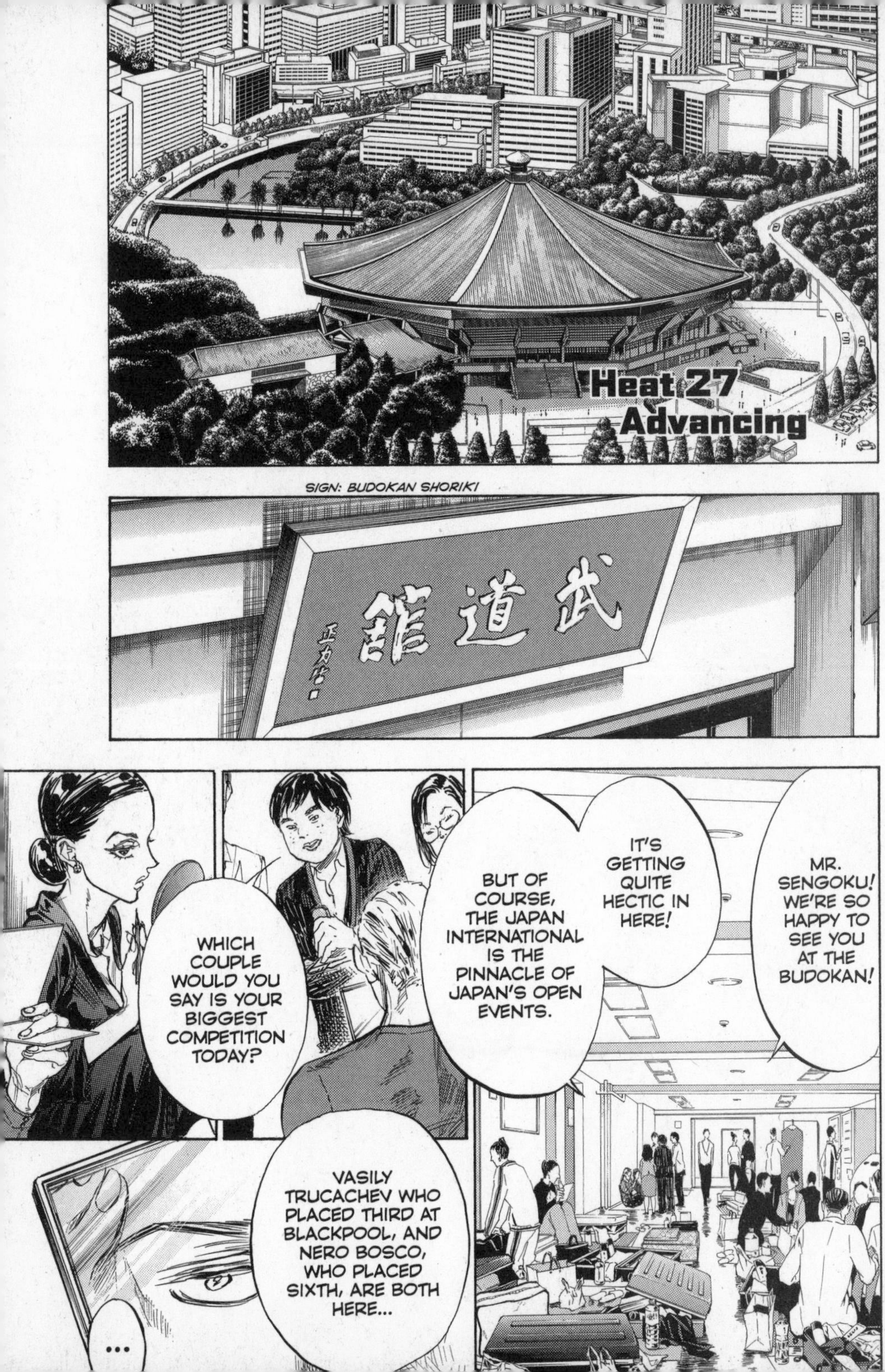
Heat 27
Advancing
SIGN: BUDOKAN SHORIKI
MR. SENGOKU! WE'RE SO HAPPY TO SEE YOU AT THE BUDOKAN!
IT'S GETTING QUITE HECTIC IN HERE!
BUT OF COURSE, THE JAPAN INTERNATIONAL IS THE PINNACLE OF JAPAN'S OPEN EVENTS.
WHICH COUPLE WOULD YOU SAY IS YOUR BIGGEST COMPETITION TODAY?
VASILY TRUCACHEV WHO PLACED THIRD AT BLACKPOOL, AND NERO BOSCO, WHO PLACED SIXTH, ARE BOTH HERE...
...

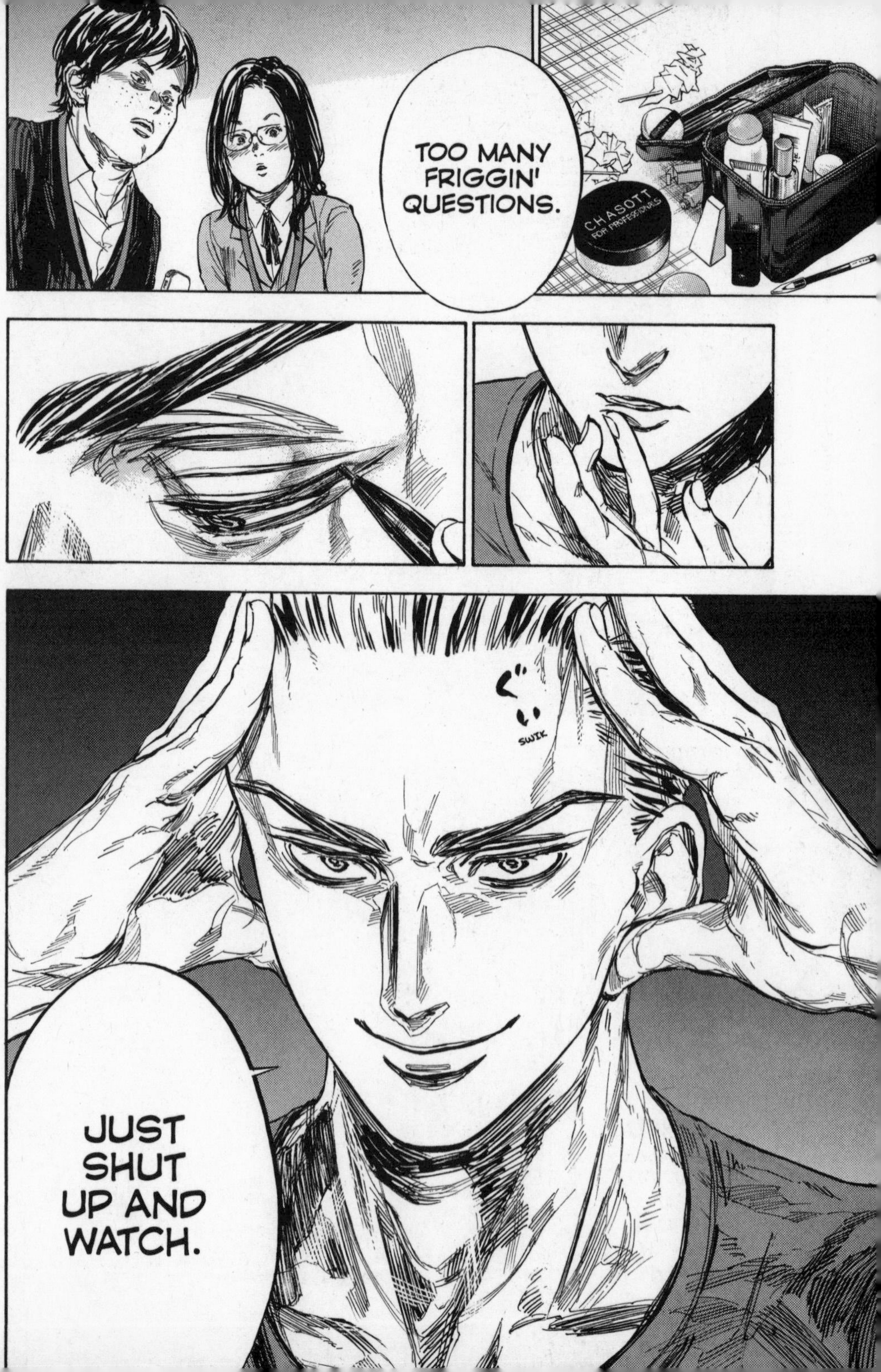
CHASOTT FOR PROFESSIONALS
TOO MANY FRIGGIN' QUESTIONS.
ぐい
SWIK
JUST SHUT UP AND WATCH.

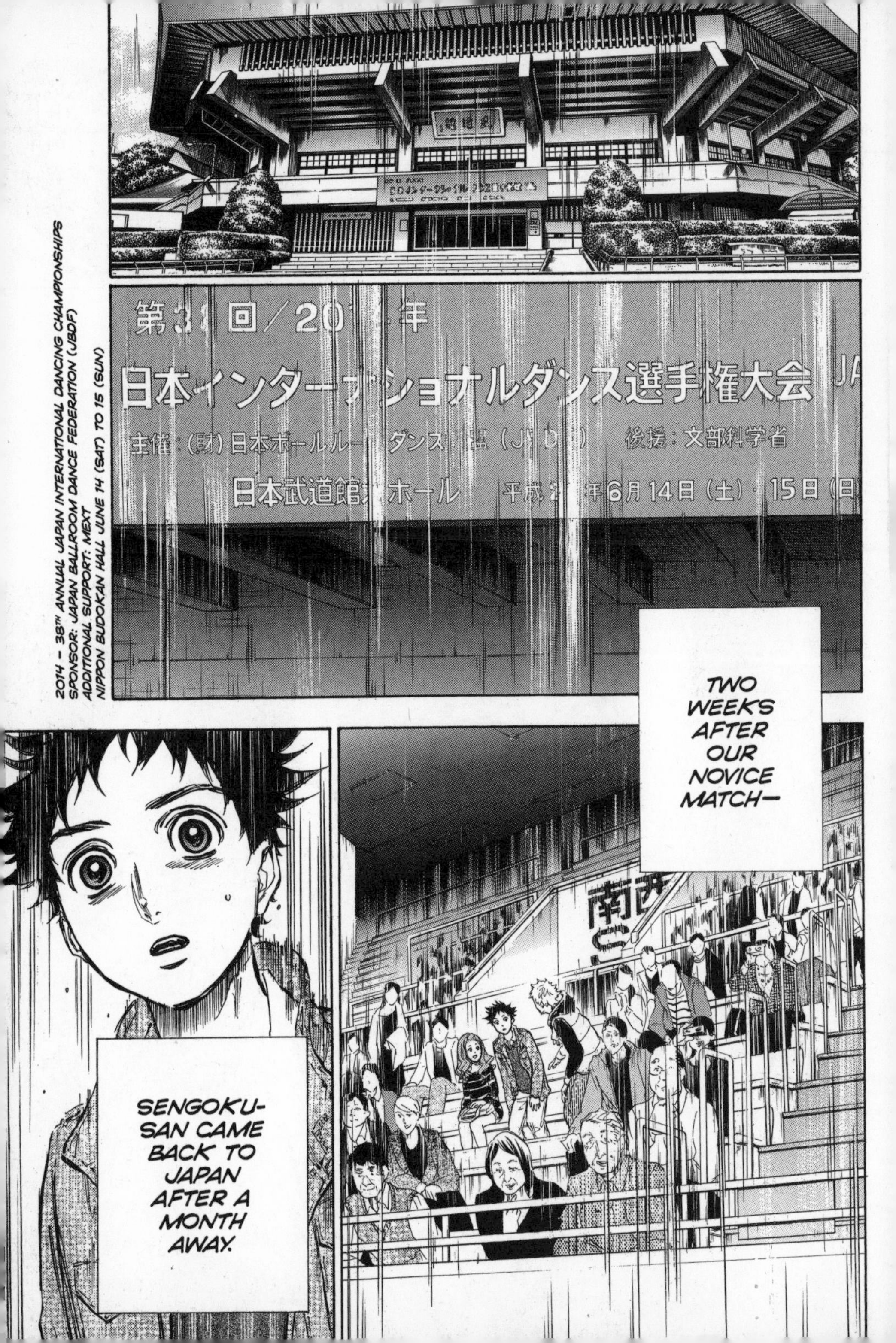
2014 - 38TH ANNUAL JAPAN INTERNATIONAL DANCING CHAMPIONSHIPS
SPONSOR: JAPAN BALLROOM DANCE FEDERATION (JBDF)
ADDITIONAL SUPPORT: MEXT
NIPPON BUDOKAN HALL JUNE 14 (SAT) TO 15 (SUN)
日本インターナショナルダンス選手権大会
TWO WEEKS AFTER OUR NOVICE MATCH—
SENGOKU-SAN CAME BACK TO JAPAN AFTER A MONTH AWAY.

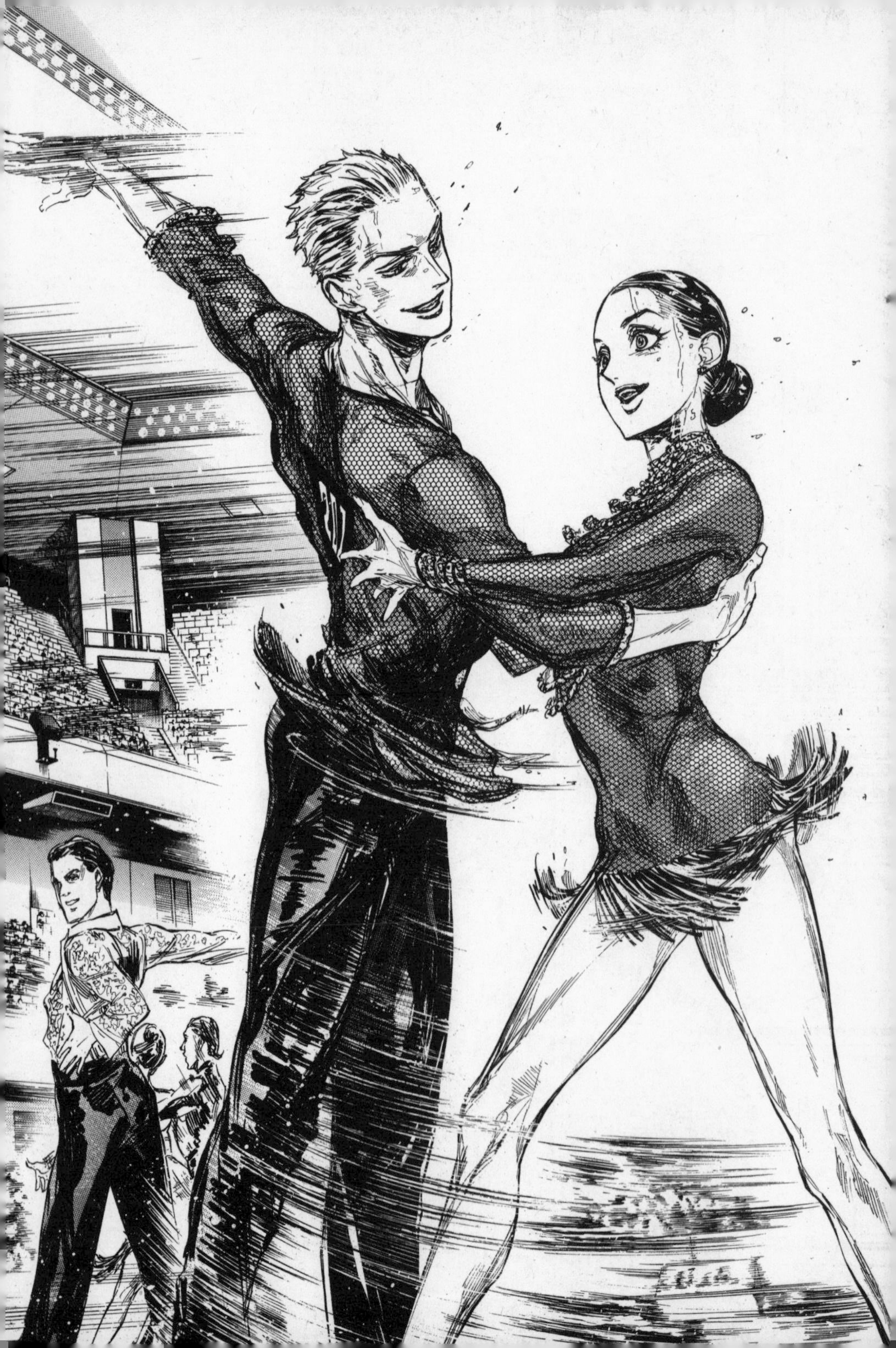

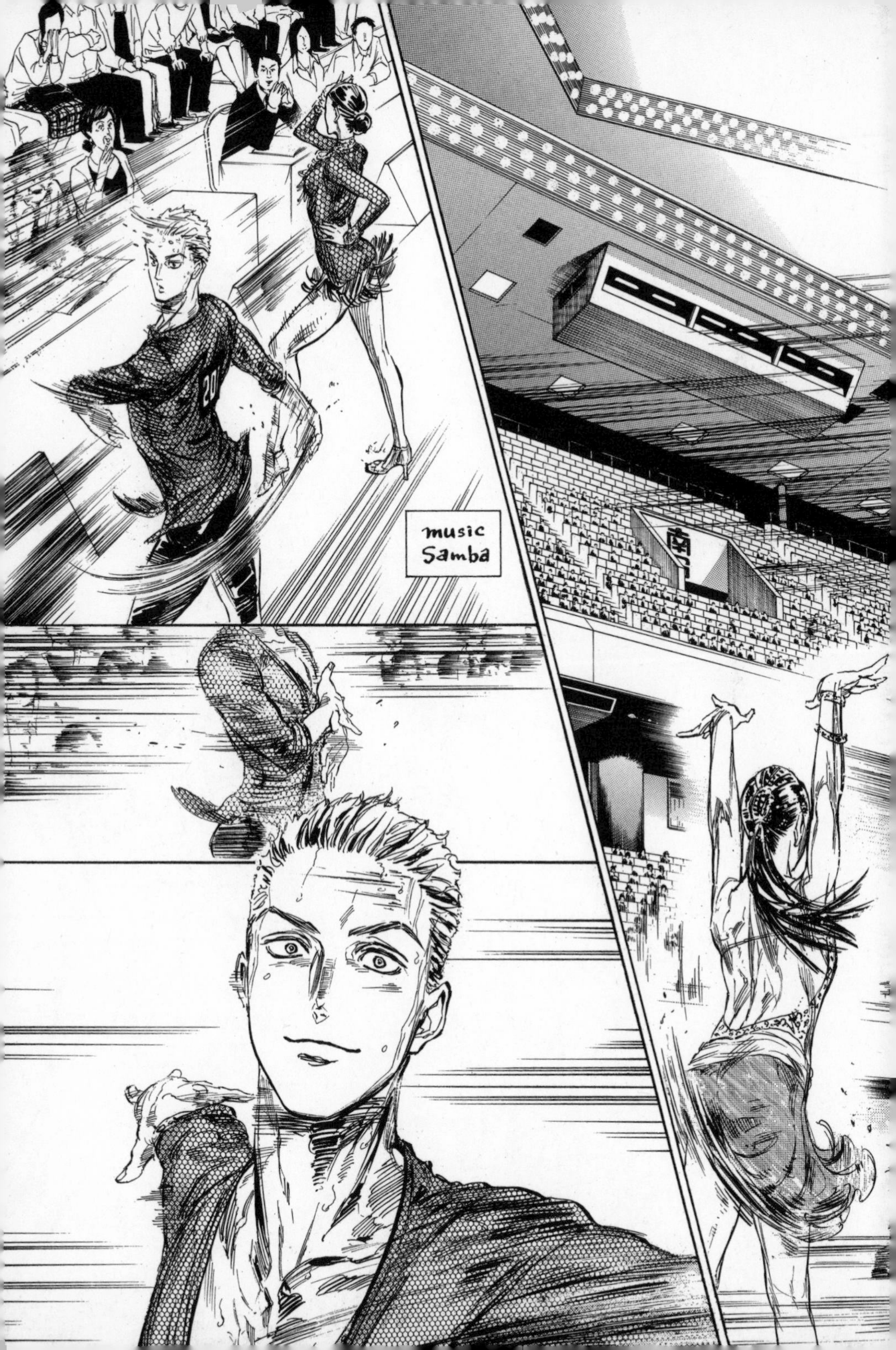
music
Samba

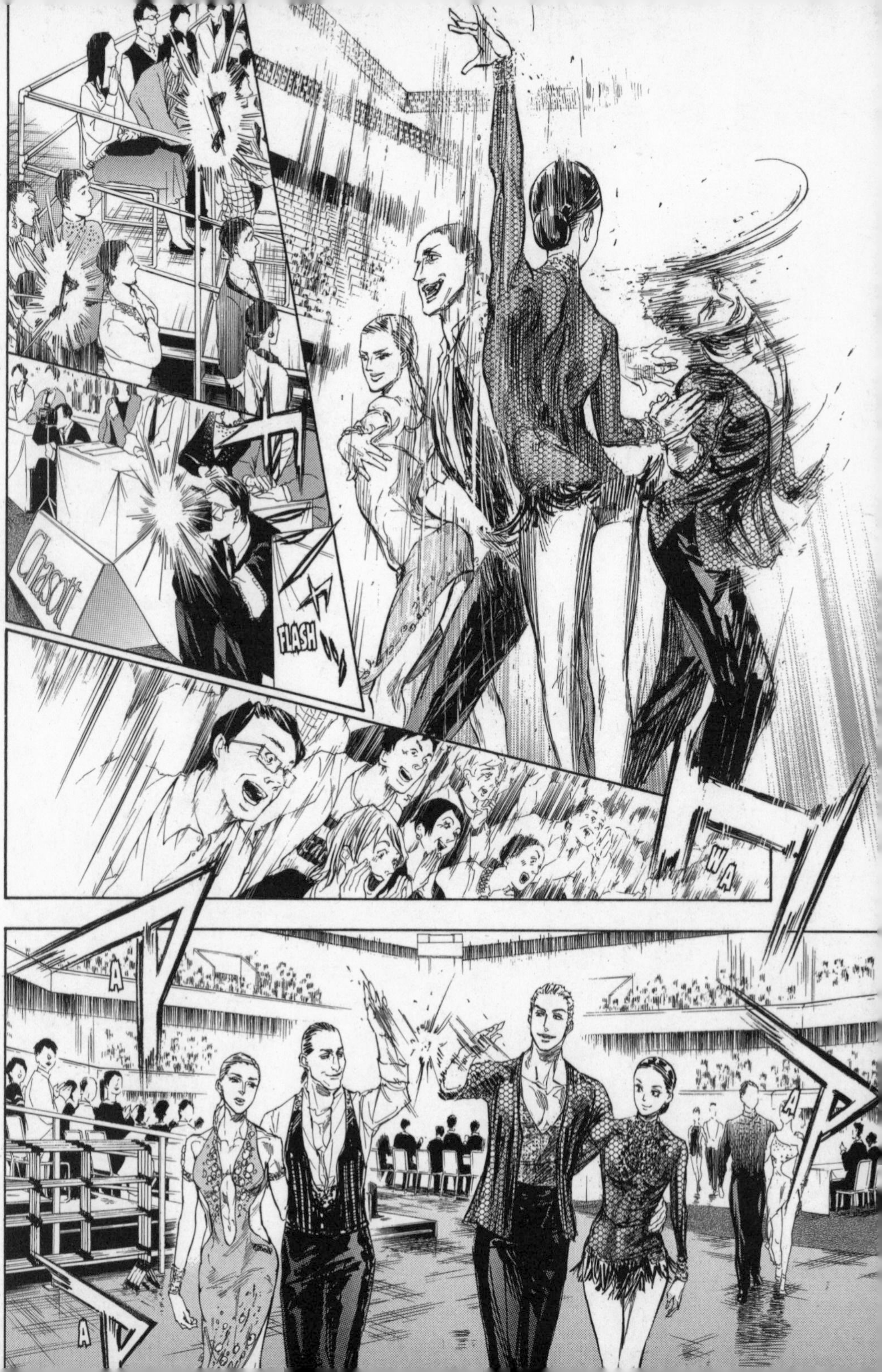
FLASH
Chasott
WA
A
A
A

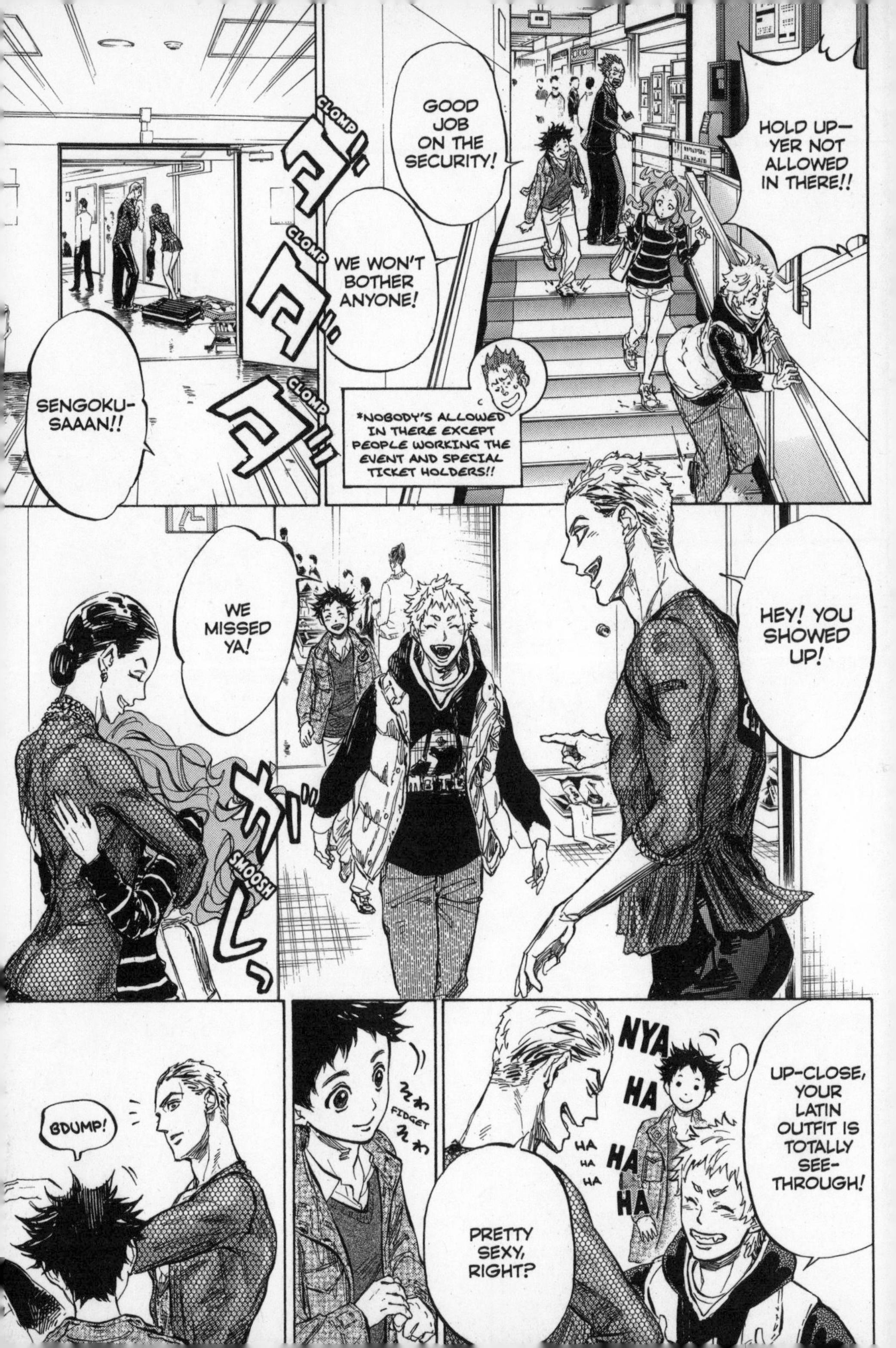
HOLD UP— YER NOT ALLOWED IN THERE!!
GOOD JOB ON THE SECURITY!
WE WON'T BOTHER ANYONE!
*NOBODY'S ALLOWED IN THERE EXCEPT PEOPLE WORKING THE EVENT AND SPECIAL TICKET HOLDERS!!
CLOMP
CLOMP
CLOMP
SENGOKU-SAAAN!!
HEY! YOU SHOWED UP!
WE MISSED YA!
SMOOSH
UP-CLOSE, YOUR LATIN OUTFIT IS TOTALLY SEE-THROUGH!
NYA HA HA HA HA
HA HA HA
PRETTY SEXY, RIGHT?
FIDGET
BDUMP!

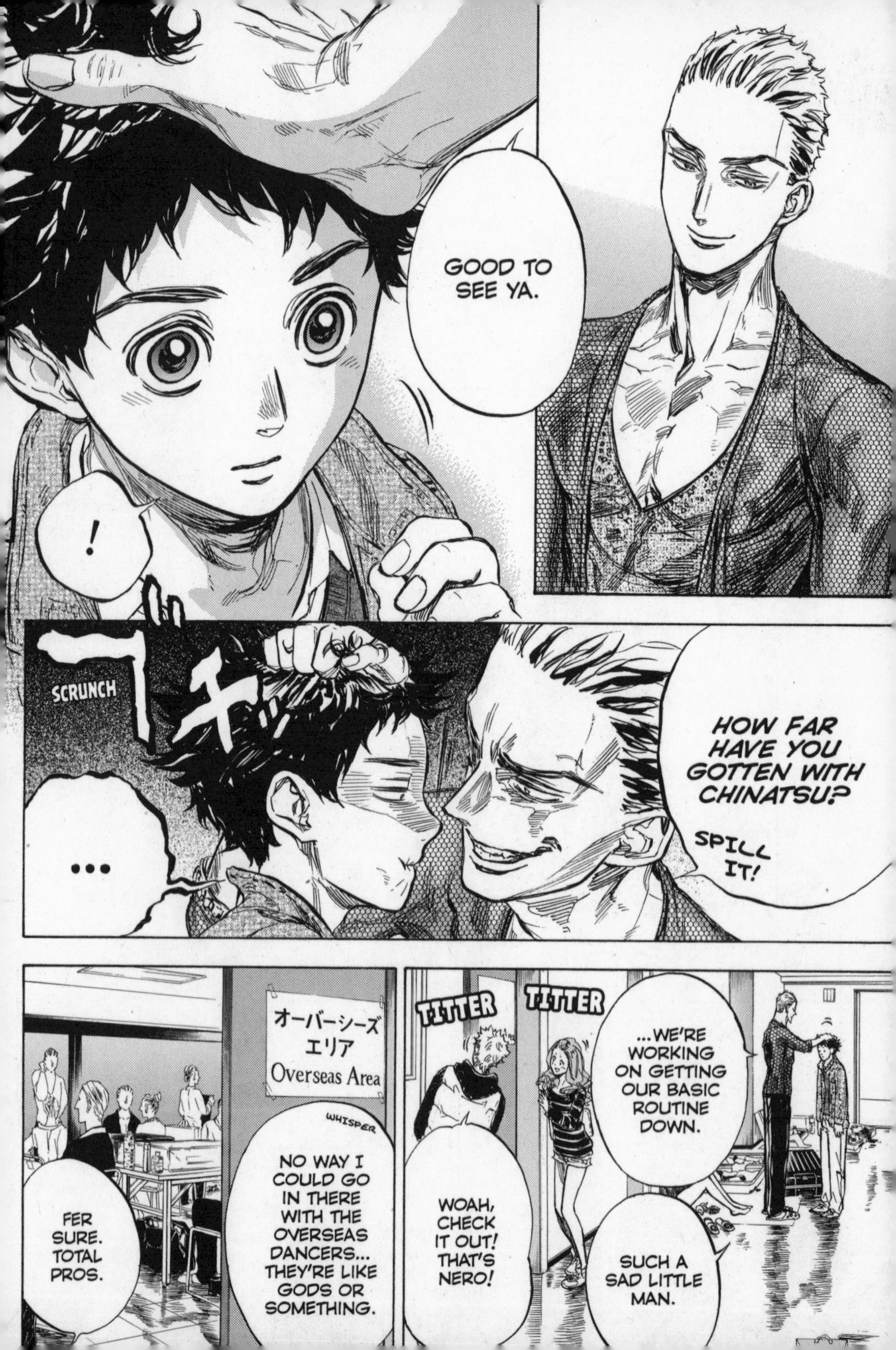

GOOD TO SEE YA.
!
HOW FAR HAVE YOU GOTTEN WITH CHINATSU?
SPILL IT!
SCRUNCH
...
TITTER
TITTER
...WE'RE WORKING ON GETTING OUR BASIC ROUTINE DOWN.
SUCH A SAD LITTLE MAN.
WOAH, CHECK IT OUT! THAT'S NERO!
オーバーシーズ
エリア
Overseas Area
WHISPER
NO WAY I COULD GO IN THERE WITH THE OVERSEAS DANCERS... THEY'RE LIKE GODS OR SOMETHING.
FER SURE. TOTAL PROS.

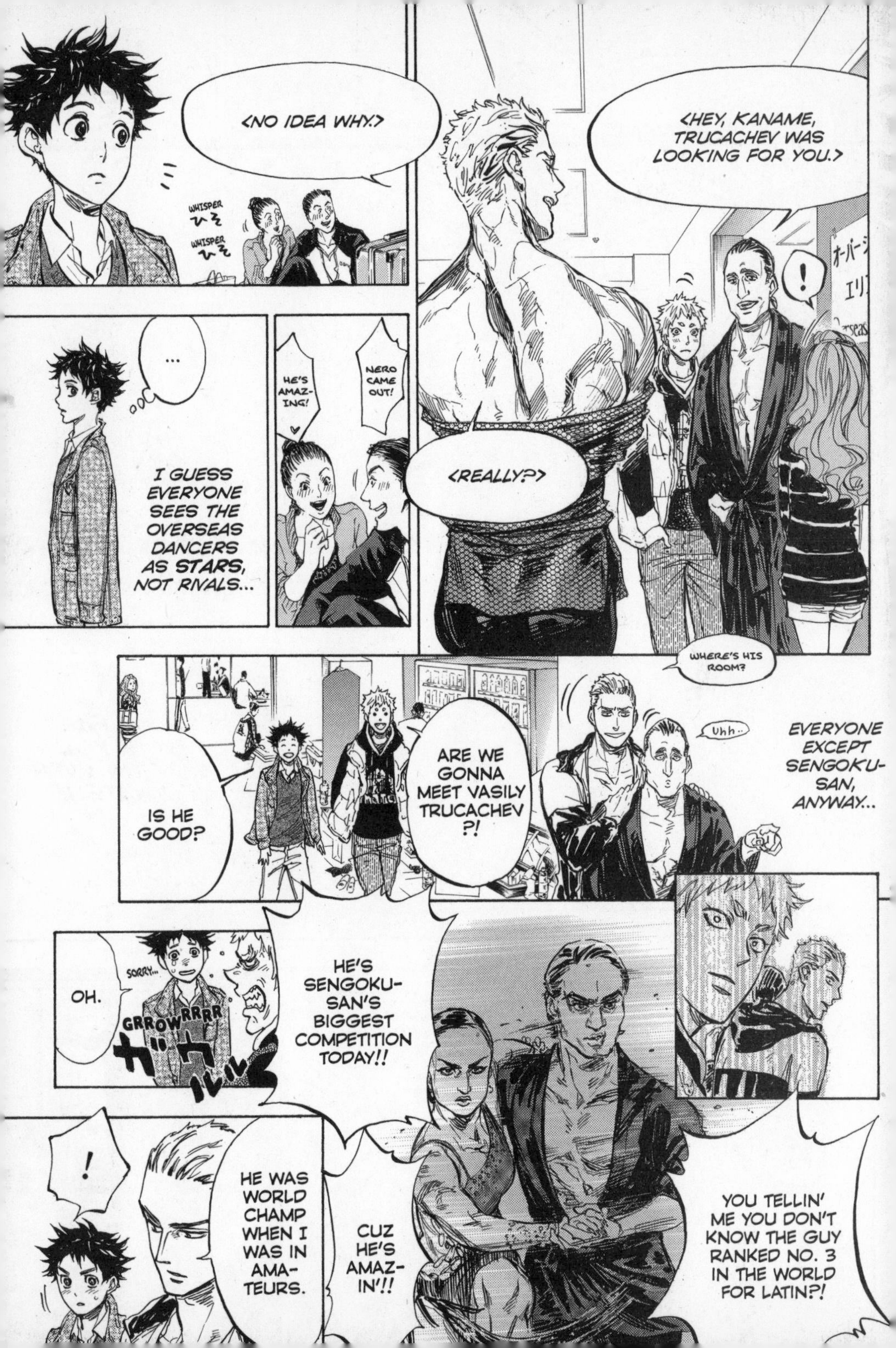

<HEY, KANAME, TRUCACHEV WAS LOOKING FOR YOU.>
!
<REALLY?>
<NO IDEA WHY.>
WHISPER
WHISPER
NERO CAME OUT!
HE'S AMAZ-ING!
...
I GUESS EVERYONE SEES THE OVERSEAS DANCERS AS STARS, NOT RIVALS...
EVERYONE EXCEPT SENGOKU-SAN, ANYWAY...
WHERE'S HIS ROOM?
Uhh..
ARE WE GONNA MEET VASILY TRUCACHEV?!
IS HE GOOD?
HE'S SENGOKU-SAN'S BIGGEST COMPETITION TODAY!!
SORRY...
OH.
GRROWRRRR
YOU TELLIN' ME YOU DON'T KNOW THE GUY RANKED NO. 3 IN THE WORLD FOR LATIN?!
CUZ HE'S AMAZ-IN'!!
HE WAS WORLD CHAMP WHEN I WAS IN AMA-TEURS.
!

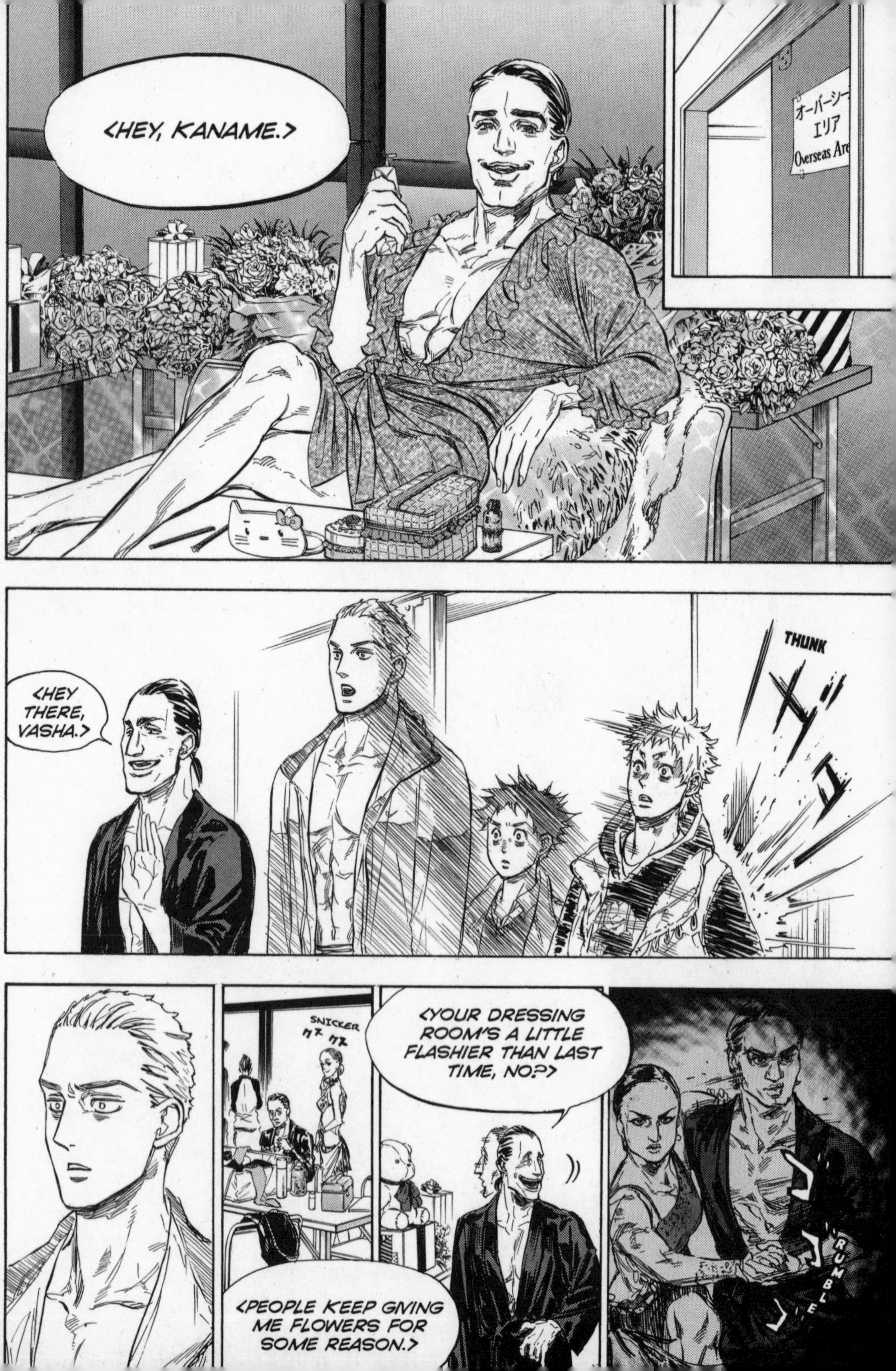
<HEY, KANAME.>
オーバーシー
エリア
Overseas Are
THUNK
<HEY THERE, VASHA.>
RUMBLE
<YOUR DRESSING ROOM'S A LITTLE FLASHIER THAN LAST TIME, NO?>
<PEOPLE KEEP GIVING ME FLOWERS FOR SOME REASON.>
SNICKER
クス クス

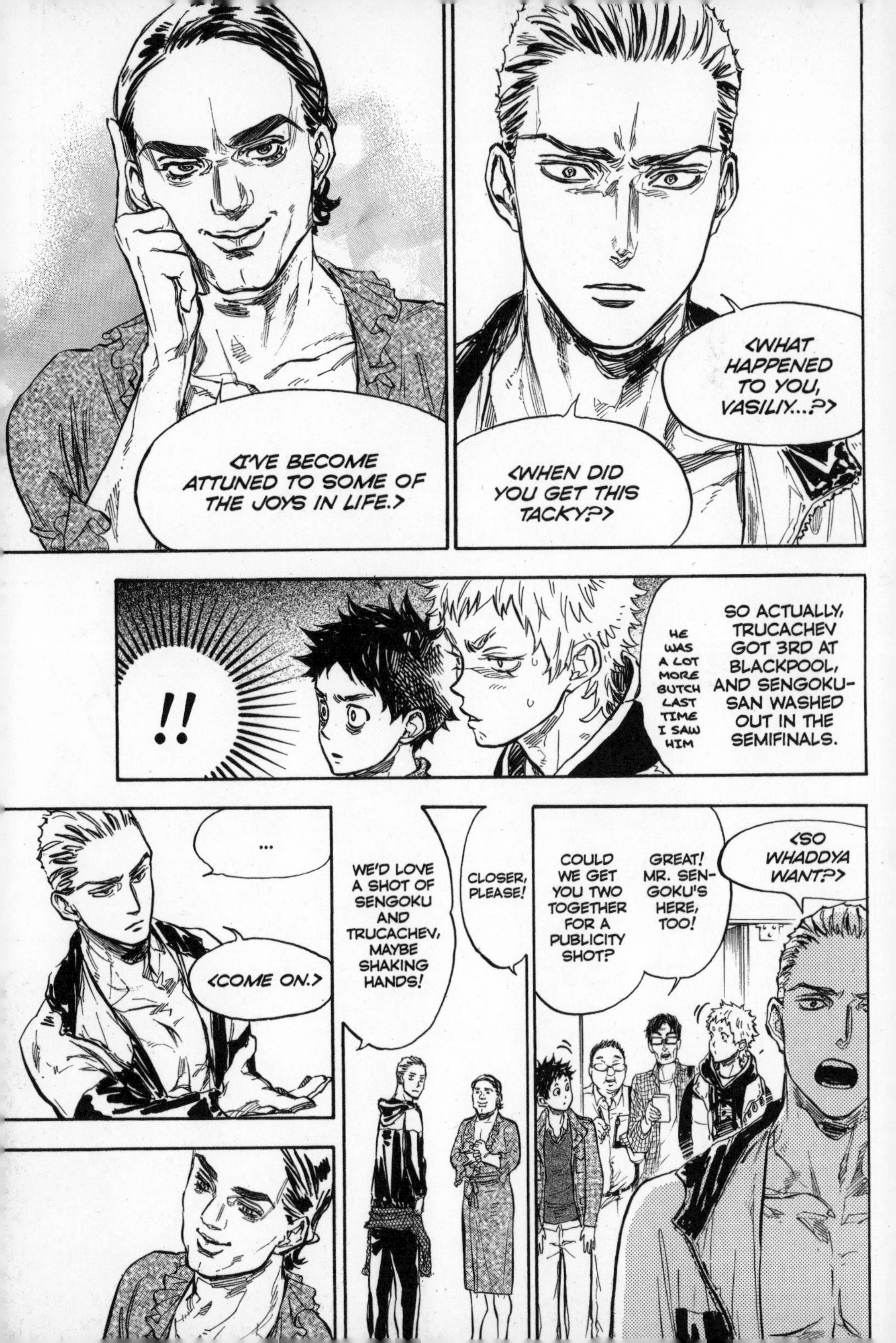
<WHAT HAPPENED TO YOU, VASILIY...?>
<WHEN DID YOU GET THIS TACKY?>
<I'VE BECOME ATTUNED TO SOME OF THE JOYS IN LIFE.>
SO ACTUALLY, TRUCACHEV GOT 3RD AT BLACKPOOL, AND SENGOKU-SAN WASHED OUT IN THE SEMIFINALS.
HE WAS A LOT MORE BUTCH LAST TIME I SAW HIM
!!
<SO WHADDYA WANT?>
GREAT! MR. SENGOKU'S HERE, TOO!
COULD WE GET YOU TWO TOGETHER FOR A PUBLICITY SHOT?
CLOSER, PLEASE!
WE'D LOVE A SHOT OF SENGOKU AND TRUCACHEV, MAYBE SHAKING HANDS!
...
<COME ON.>

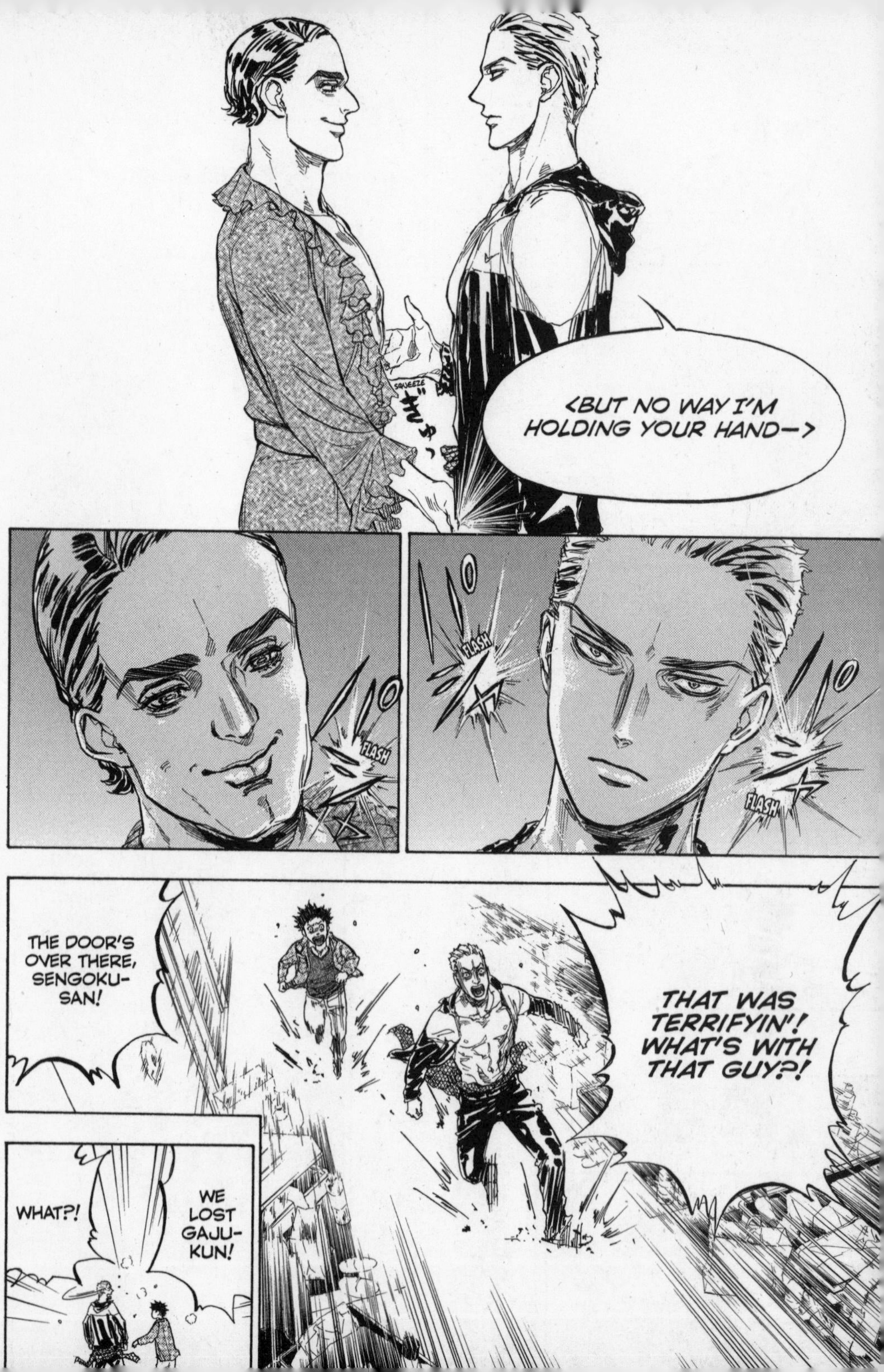
SQUEEZE
ぎゅっ
<BUT NO WAY I'M HOLDING YOUR HAND—>
FLASH
FLASH
FLASH
THAT WAS TERRIFYIN'! WHAT'S WITH THAT GUY?!
THE DOOR'S OVER THERE, SENGOKU-SAN!
WE LOST GAJU-KUN!
WHAT?!

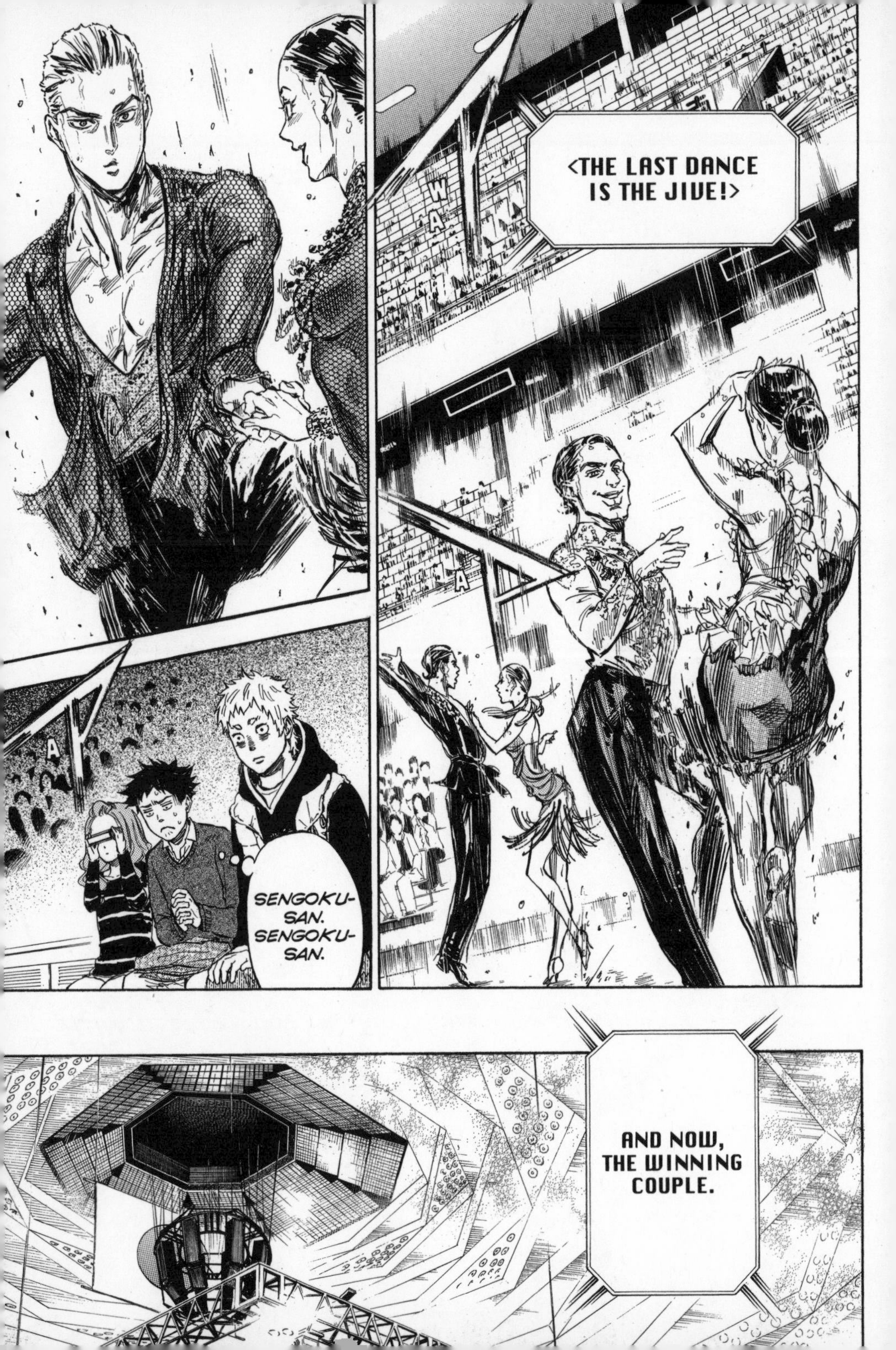
<THE LAST DANCE IS THE JIVE!>
SENGOKU-SAN. SENGOKU-SAN.
AND NOW, THE WINNING COUPLE.

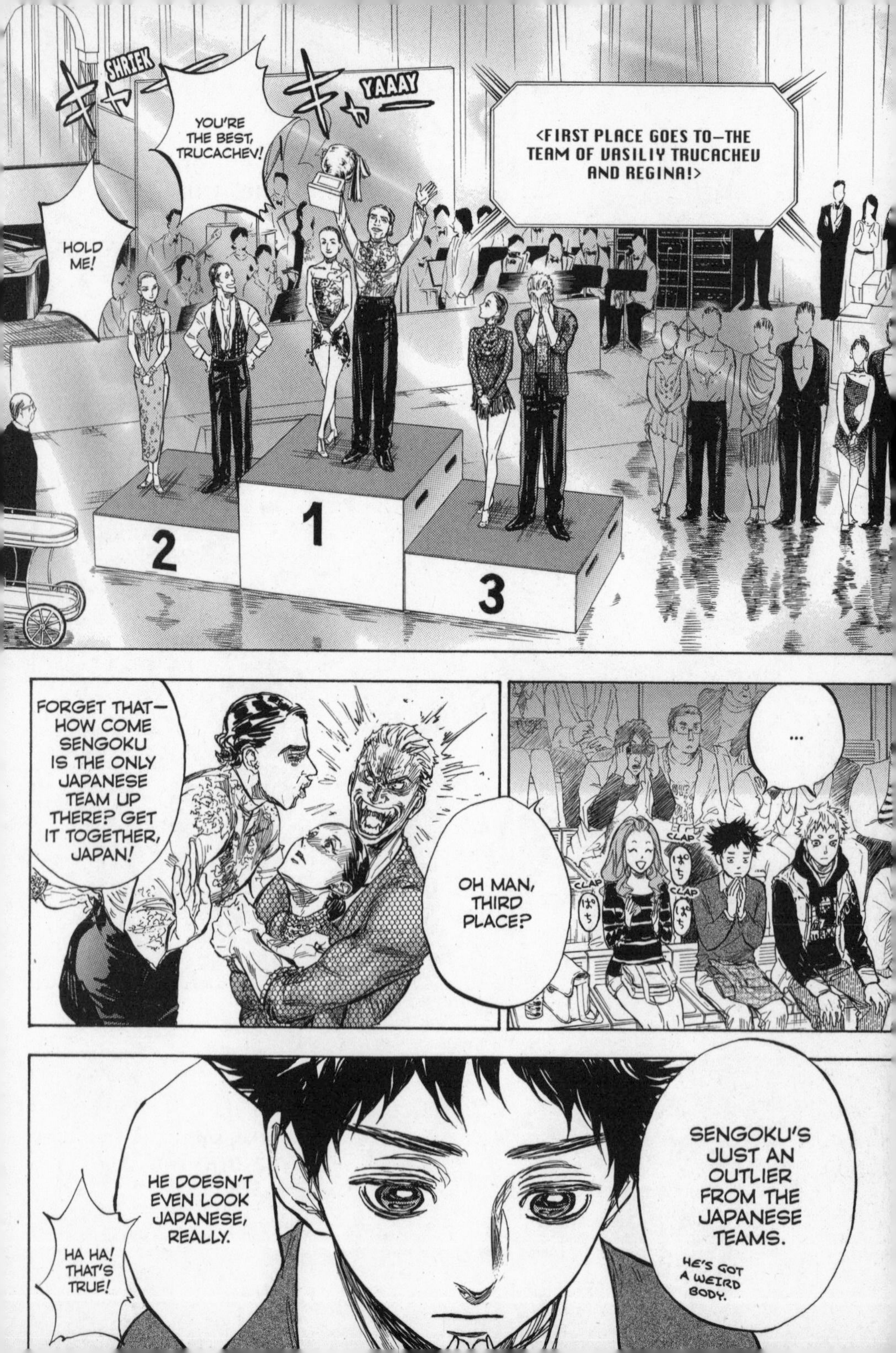
<FIRST PLACE GOES TO—THE TEAM OF VASILIY TRUCACHEV AND REGINA!>
YAAAY
YOU'RE THE BEST, TRUCACHEV!
SHRIEK
HOLD ME!
1
2
3
...
CLAP ぱち
CLAP ぱち
OH MAN, THIRD PLACE?
FORGET THAT—HOW COME SENGOKU IS THE ONLY JAPANESE TEAM UP THERE? GET IT TOGETHER, JAPAN!
SENGOKU'S JUST AN OUTLIER FROM THE JAPANESE TEAMS.
HE'S GOT A WEIRD BODY.
HE DOESN'T EVEN LOOK JAPANESE, REALLY.
HA HA! THAT'S TRUE!

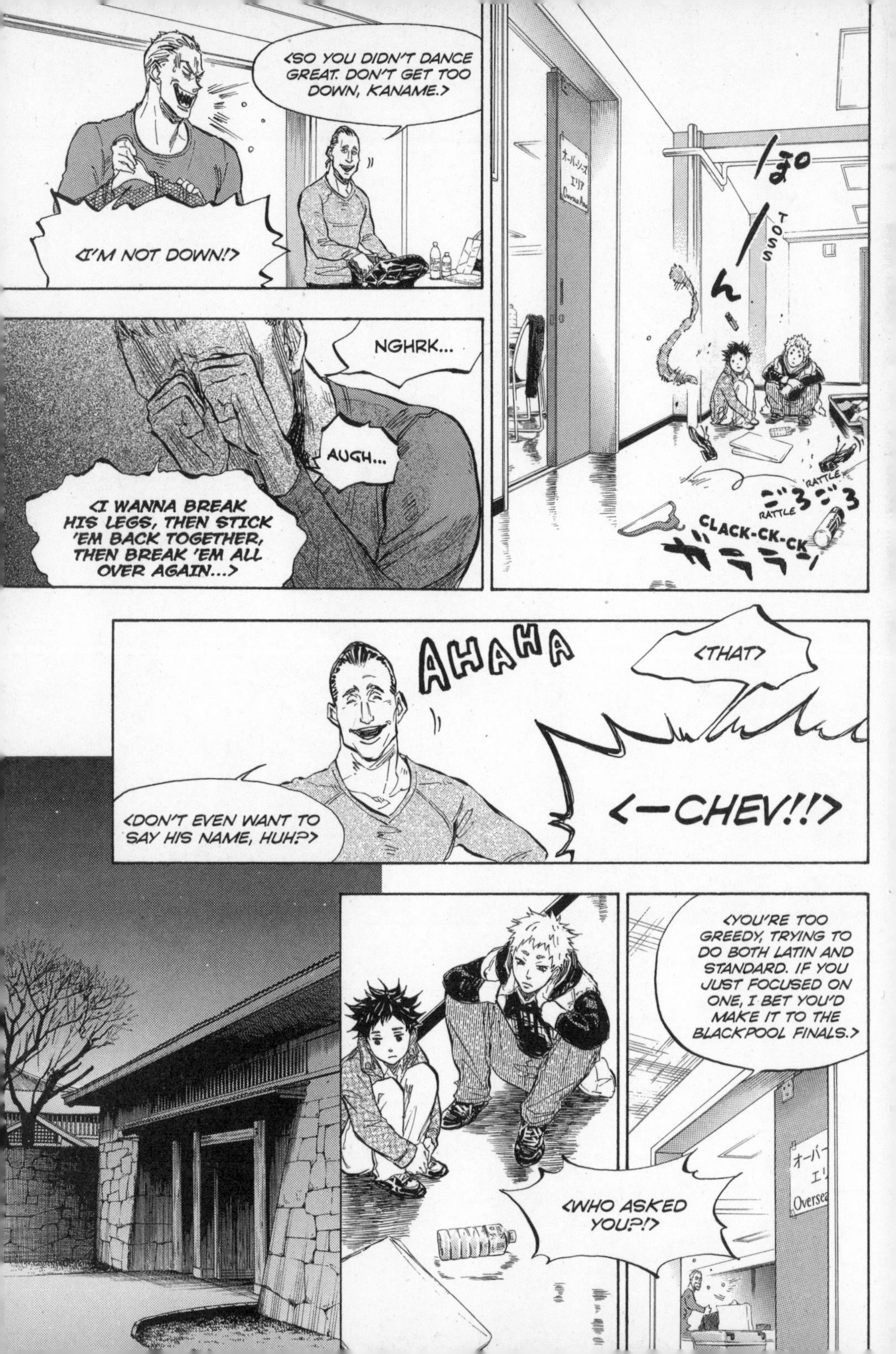
ぽーん
TOSS
RATTLE RATTLE
ごろごろ
CLACK-CK-CK
ガラララ
<SO YOU DIDN'T DANCE GREAT. DON'T GET TOO DOWN, KANAME.>
<I'M NOT DOWN!>
NGHRK...
AUGH...
<I WANNA BREAK HIS LEGS, THEN STICK 'EM BACK TOGETHER, THEN BREAK 'EM ALL OVER AGAIN...>
<THAT>
<—CHEV!!>
AHAHA
<DON'T EVEN WANT TO SAY HIS NAME, HUH?>
<YOU'RE TOO GREEDY, TRYING TO DO BOTH LATIN AND STANDARD. IF YOU JUST FOCUSED ON ONE, I BET YOU'D MAKE IT TO THE BLACKPOOL FINALS.>
<WHO ASKED YOU?!>

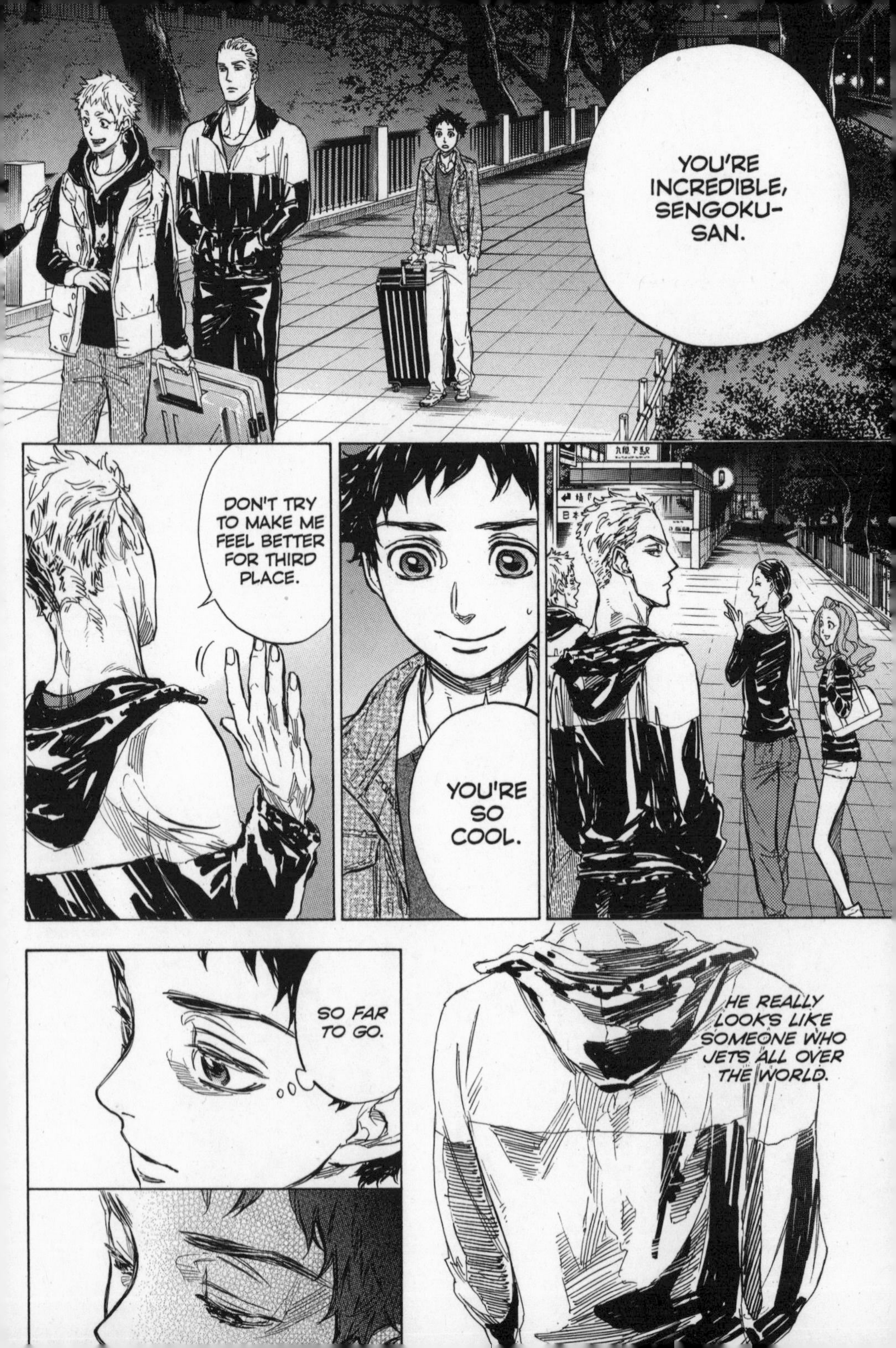
YOU'RE INCREDIBLE, SENGOKU-SAN.
九段下駅
YOU'RE SO COOL.
DON'T TRY TO MAKE ME FEEL BETTER FOR THIRD PLACE.
HE REALLY LOOKS LIKE SOMEONE WHO JETS ALL OVER THE WORLD.
SO FAR TO GO.

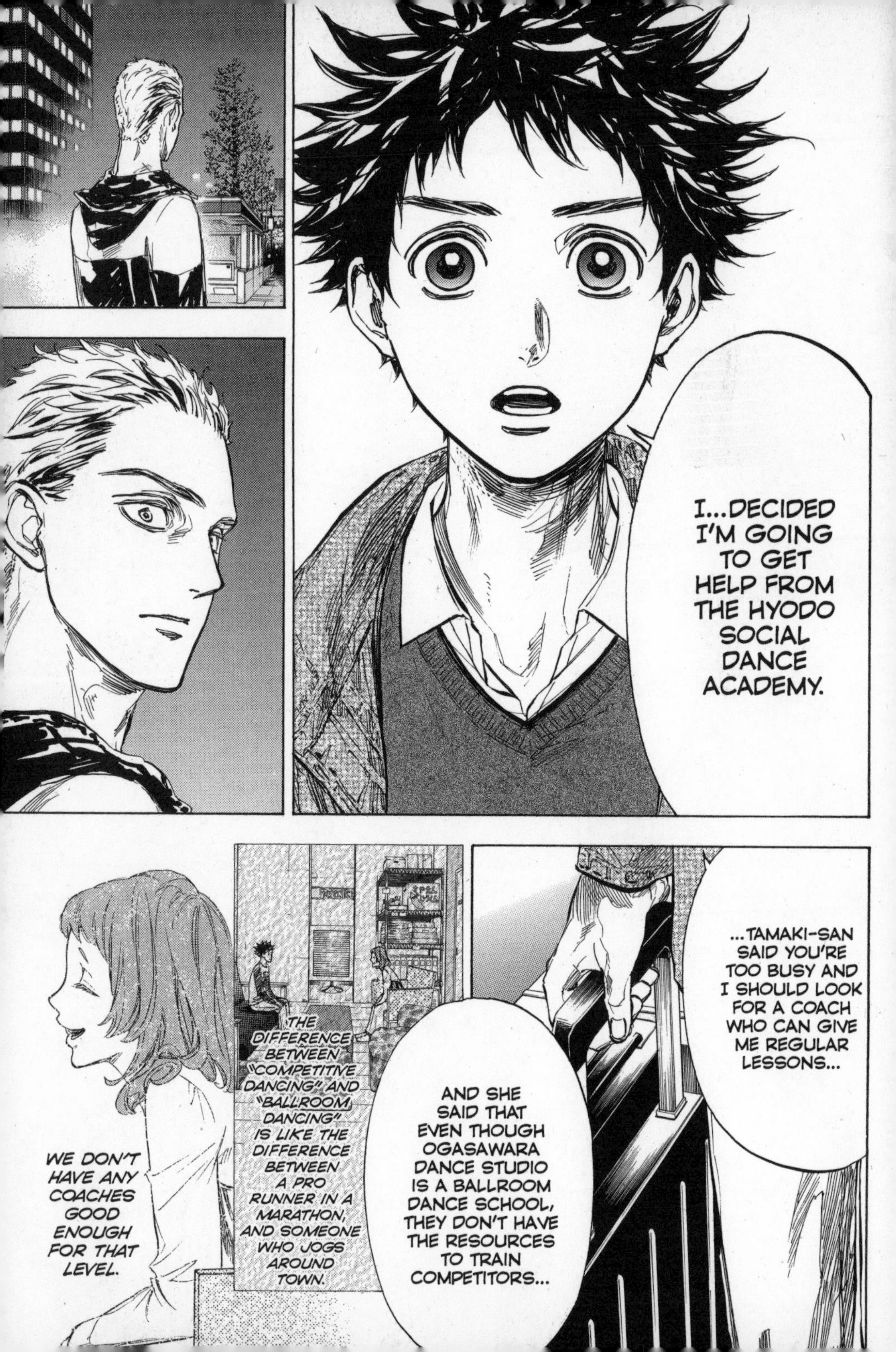
I...DECIDED I'M GOING TO GET HELP FROM THE HYODO SOCIAL DANCE ACADEMY.
...TAMAKI-SAN SAID YOU'RE TOO BUSY AND I SHOULD LOOK FOR A COACH WHO CAN GIVE ME REGULAR LESSONS...
AND SHE SAID THAT EVEN THOUGH OGASAWARA DANCE STUDIO IS A BALLROOM DANCE SCHOOL, THEY DON'T HAVE THE RESOURCES TO TRAIN COMPETITORS...
THE DIFFERENCE BETWEEN "COMPETITIVE DANCING" AND "BALLROOM DANCING" IS LIKE THE DIFFERENCE BETWEEN A PRO RUNNER IN A MARATHON, AND SOMEONE WHO JOGS AROUND TOWN.
WE DON'T HAVE ANY COACHES GOOD ENOUGH FOR THAT LEVEL.

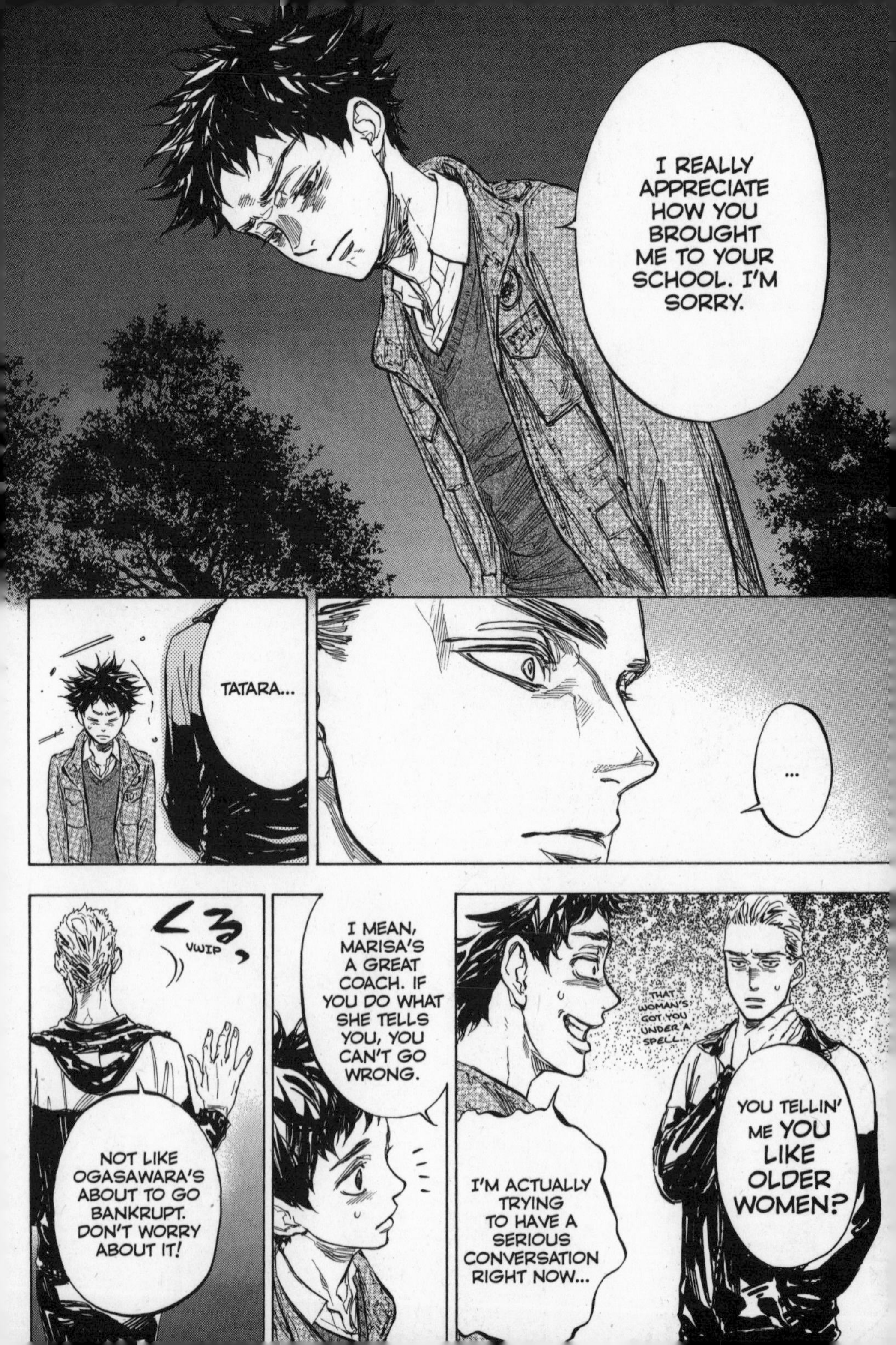
I REALLY APPRECIATE HOW YOU BROUGHT ME TO YOUR SCHOOL. I'M SORRY.
...
TATARA...
THAT WOMAN'S GOT YOU UNDER A SPELL...
YOU TELLIN' ME YOU LIKE OLDER WOMEN?
I'M ACTUALLY TRYING TO HAVE A SERIOUS CONVERSATION RIGHT NOW...
I MEAN, MARISA'S A GREAT COACH. IF YOU DO WHAT SHE TELLS YOU, YOU CAN'T GO WRONG.
くる
VWIP
NOT LIKE OGASAWARA'S ABOUT TO GO BANKRUPT. DON'T WORRY ABOUT IT!

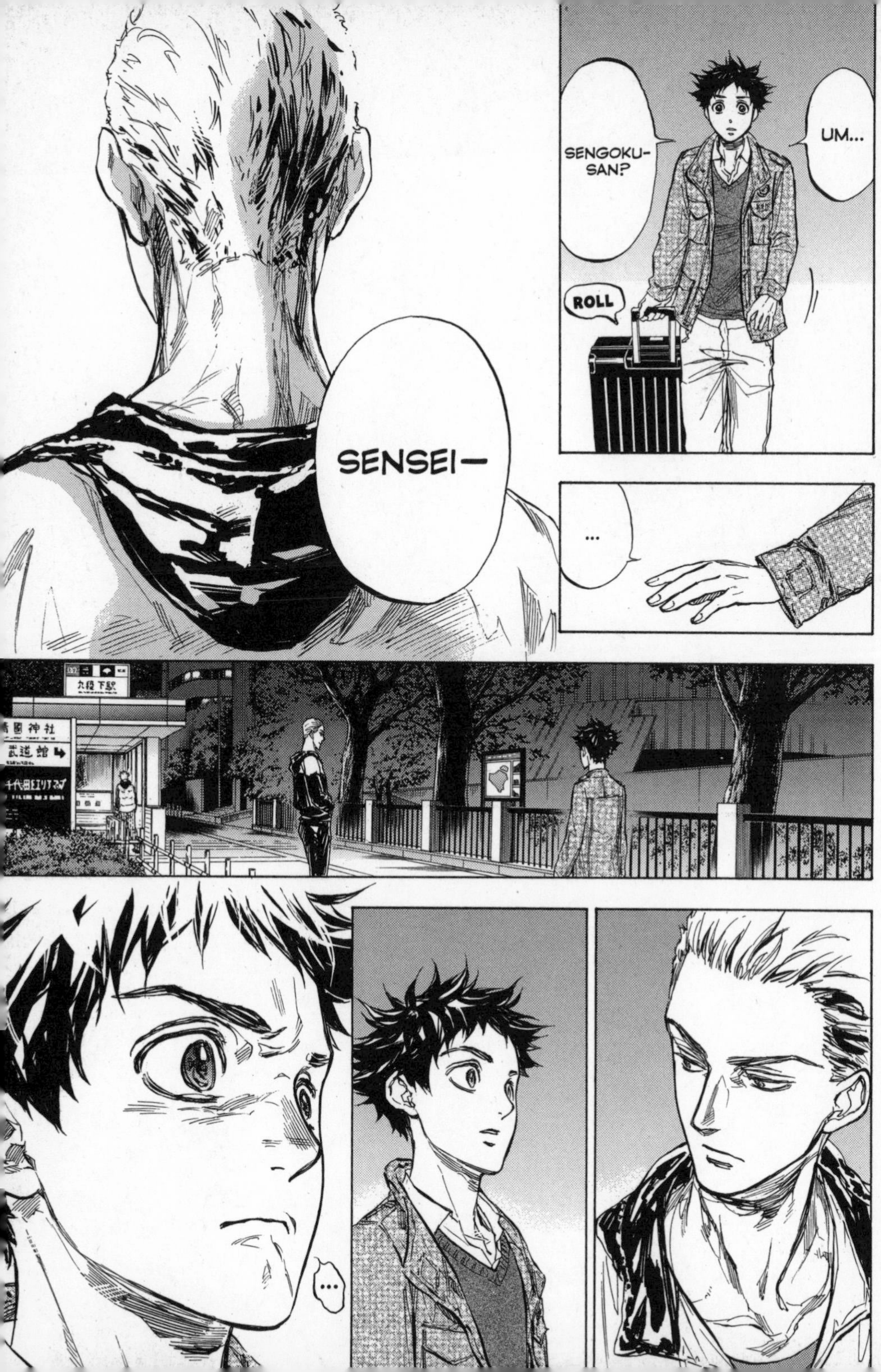
UM...
SENGOKU-SAN?
ROLL
...
SENSEI—
九段下駅
武道館
...

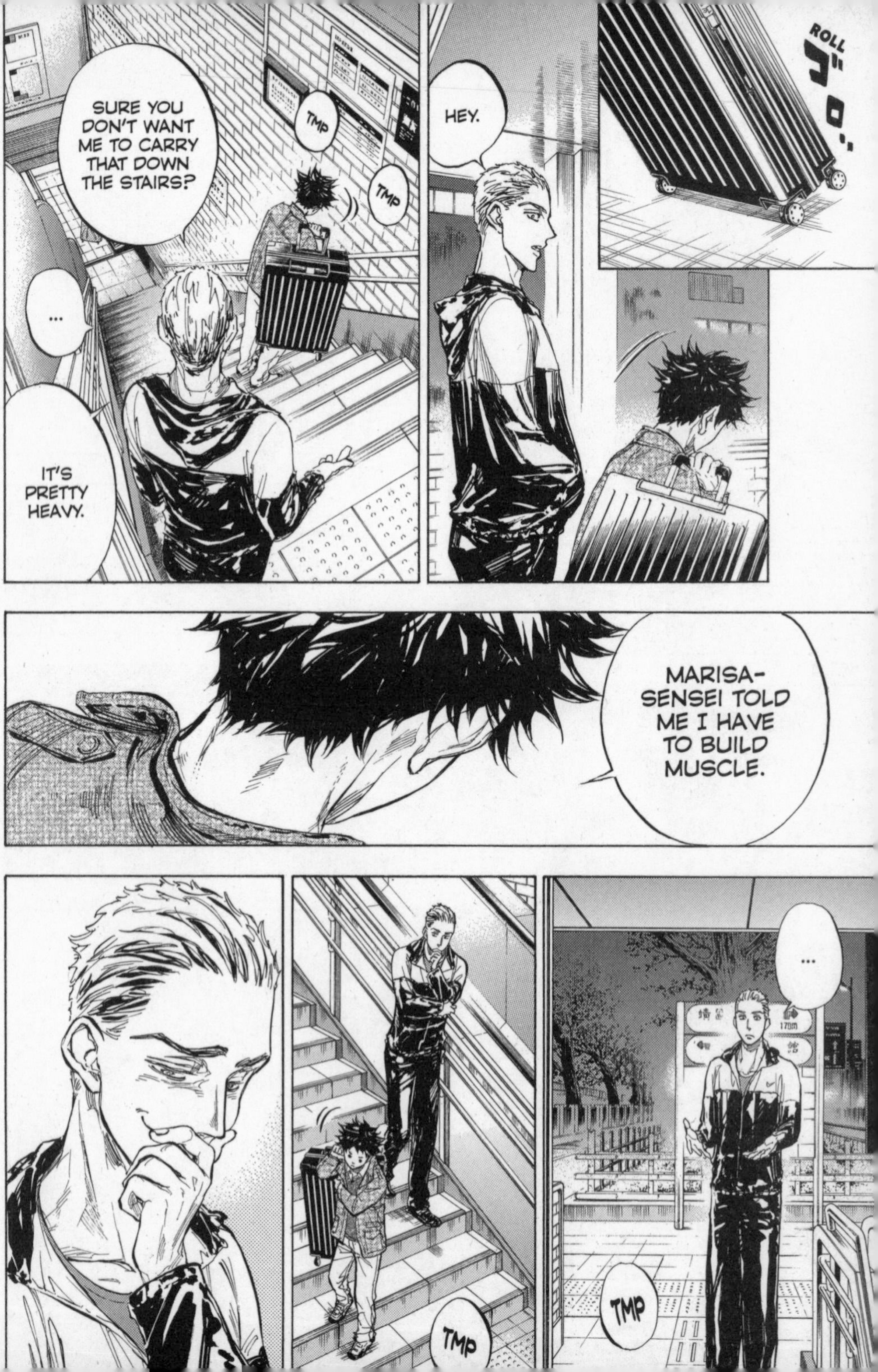
ROLL
ゴロ..
HEY.
TMP
TMP
SURE YOU DON'T WANT ME TO CARRY THAT DOWN THE STAIRS?
...
IT'S PRETTY HEAVY.
MARISA-SENSEI TOLD ME I HAVE TO BUILD MUSCLE.
...
TMP
TMP

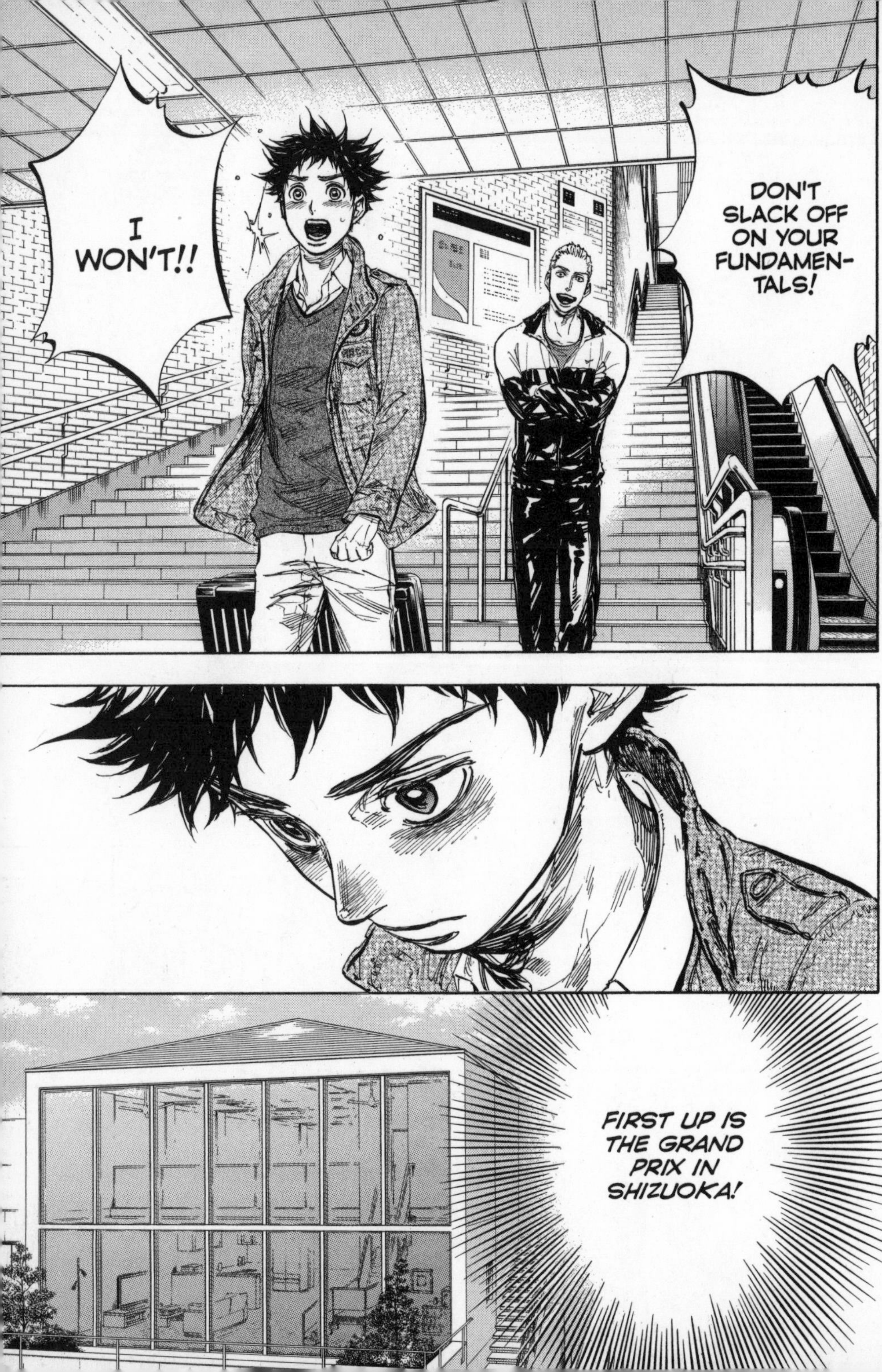
DON'T SLACK OFF ON YOUR FUNDAMENTALS!
I WON'T!!
FIRST UP IS THE GRAND PRIX IN SHIZUOKA!

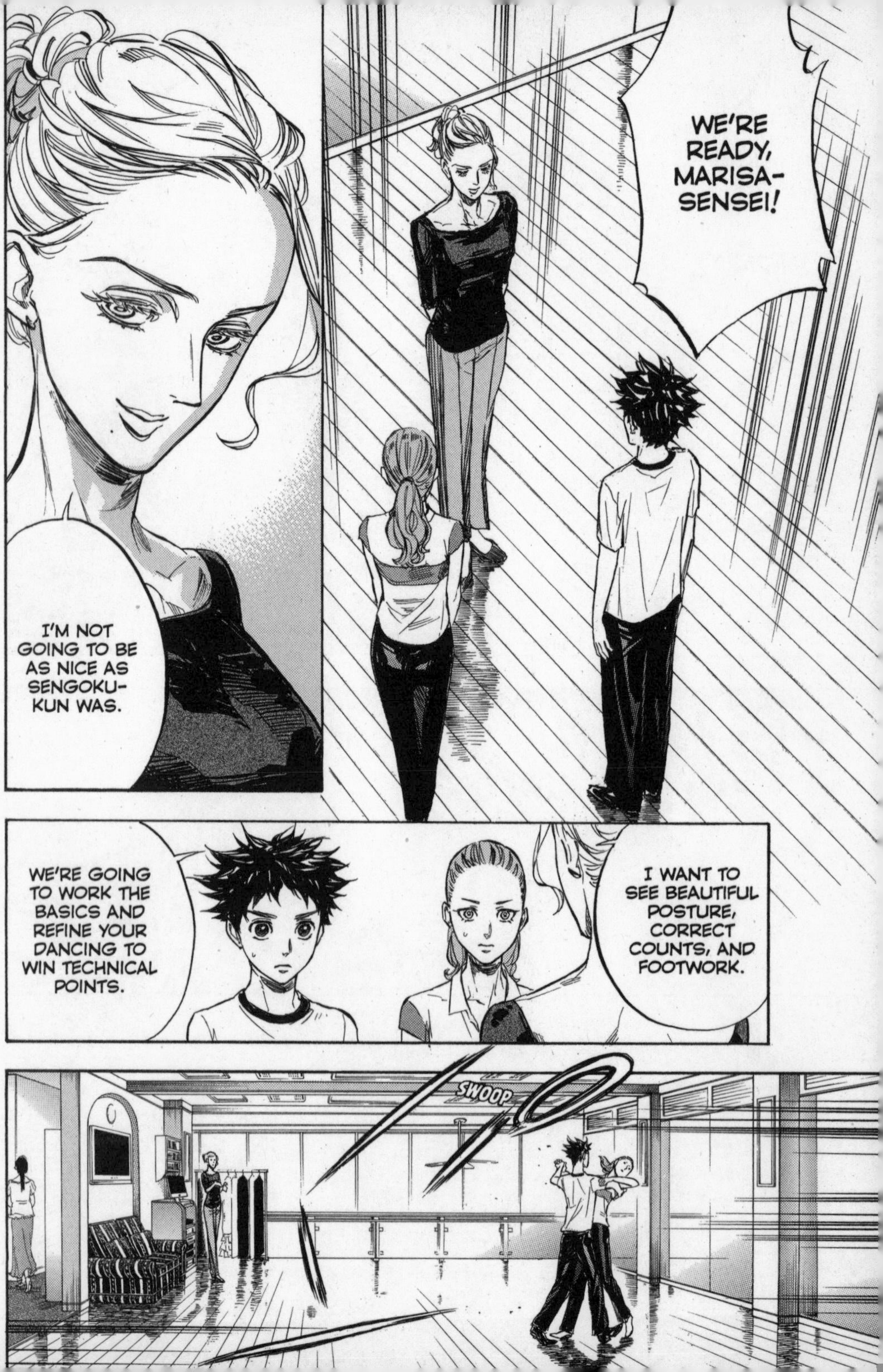
WE'RE READY, MARISA-SENSEI!
I'M NOT GOING TO BE AS NICE AS SENGOKU-KUN WAS.
I WANT TO SEE BEAUTIFUL POSTURE, CORRECT COUNTS, AND FOOTWORK.
WE'RE GOING TO WORK THE BASICS AND REFINE YOUR DANCING TO WIN TECHNICAL POINTS.
SWOOP

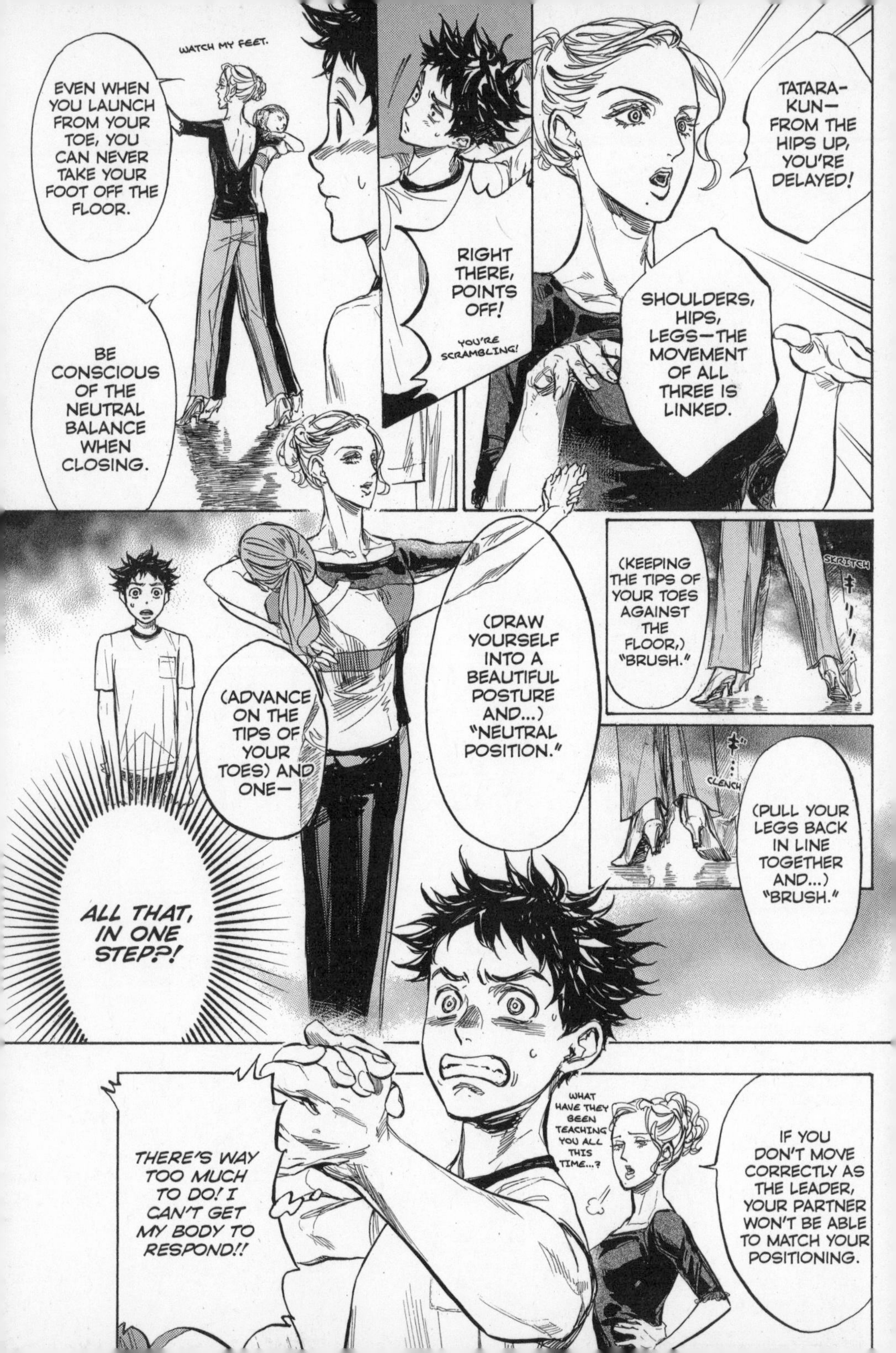
TATARA-KUN—FROM THE HIPS UP, YOU'RE DELAYED!
SHOULDERS, HIPS, LEGS—THE MOVEMENT OF ALL THREE IS LINKED.
RIGHT THERE, POINTS OFF!
YOU'RE SCRAMBLING!
WATCH MY FEET.
EVEN WHEN YOU LAUNCH FROM YOUR TOE, YOU CAN NEVER TAKE YOUR FOOT OFF THE FLOOR.
BE CONSCIOUS OF THE NEUTRAL BALANCE WHEN CLOSING.
SKRITCH
(KEEPING THE TIPS OF YOUR TOES AGAINST THE FLOOR,) "BRUSH."
CLENCH
(PULL YOUR LEGS BACK IN LINE TOGETHER AND...) "BRUSH."
(DRAW YOURSELF INTO A BEAUTIFUL POSTURE AND...) "NEUTRAL POSITION."
(ADVANCE ON THE TIPS OF YOUR TOES) AND ONE—
ALL THAT, IN ONE STEP?!
IF YOU DON'T MOVE CORRECTLY AS THE LEADER, YOUR PARTNER WON'T BE ABLE TO MATCH YOUR POSITIONING.
WHAT HAVE THEY BEEN TEACHING YOU ALL THIS TIME...?
THERE'S WAY TOO MUCH TO DO! I CAN'T GET MY BODY TO RESPOND!!

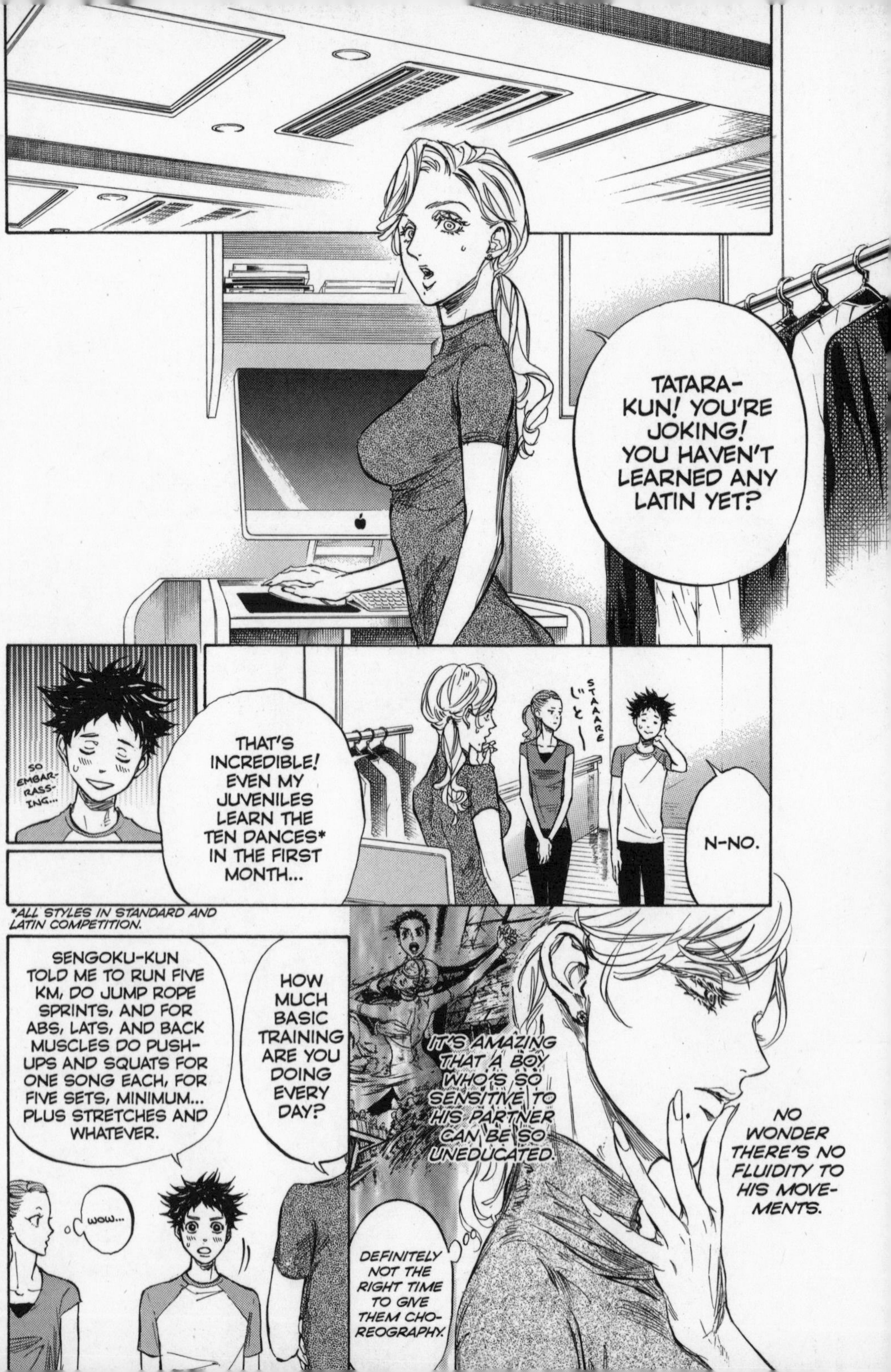
TATARA-KUN! YOU'RE JOKING! YOU HAVEN'T LEARNED ANY LATIN YET?
N-NO.
STAAARE
じとー
THAT'S INCREDIBLE! EVEN MY JUVENILES LEARN THE TEN DANCES* IN THE FIRST MONTH...
SO EMBARRASSING...
*ALL STYLES IN STANDARD AND LATIN COMPETITION.
NO WONDER THERE'S NO FLUIDITY TO HIS MOVEMENTS.
IT'S AMAZING THAT A BOY WHO'S SO SENSITIVE TO HIS PARTNER CAN BE SO UNEDUCATED.
DEFINITELY NOT THE RIGHT TIME TO GIVE THEM CHOREOGRAPHY.
HOW MUCH BASIC TRAINING ARE YOU DOING EVERY DAY?
SENGOKU-KUN TOLD ME TO RUN FIVE KM, DO JUMP ROPE SPRINTS, AND FOR ABS, LATS, AND BACK MUSCLES DO PUSH-UPS AND SQUATS FOR ONE SONG EACH, FOR FIVE SETS, MINIMUM... PLUS STRETCHES AND WHATEVER.
WOW...

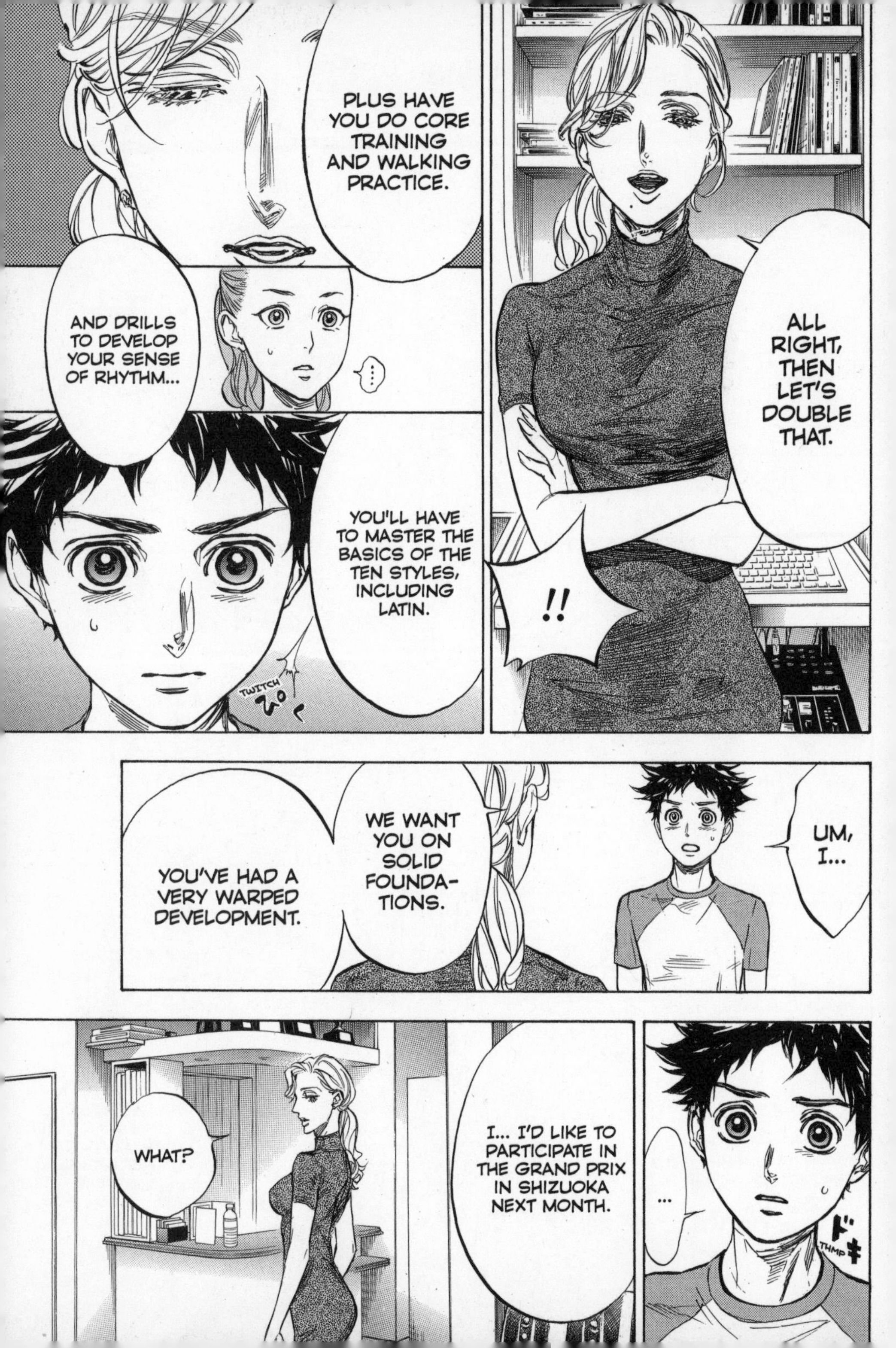
ALL RIGHT, THEN LET'S DOUBLE THAT.
!!
PLUS HAVE YOU DO CORE TRAINING AND WALKING PRACTICE.
AND DRILLS TO DEVELOP YOUR SENSE OF RHYTHM...
...
YOU'LL HAVE TO MASTER THE BASICS OF THE TEN STYLES, INCLUDING LATIN.
TWITCH
UM, I...
WE WANT YOU ON SOLID FOUNDA-TIONS.
YOU'VE HAD A VERY WARPED DEVELOPMENT.
...
THMP
I... I'D LIKE TO PARTICIPATE IN THE GRAND PRIX IN SHIZUOKA NEXT MONTH.
WHAT?

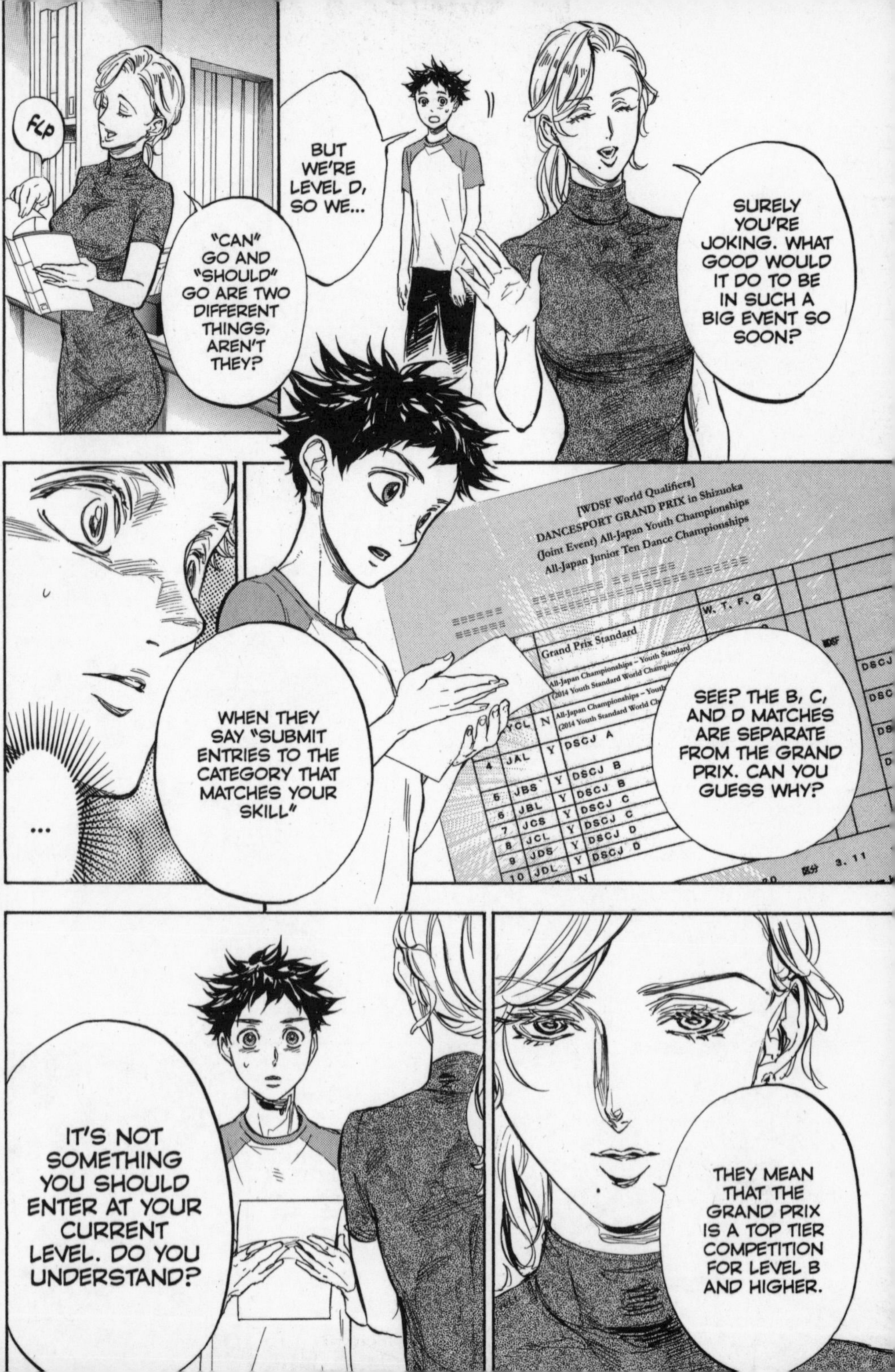
SURELY YOU'RE JOKING. WHAT GOOD WOULD IT DO TO BE IN SUCH A BIG EVENT SO SOON?
BUT WE'RE LEVEL D, SO WE...
FLP
"CAN" GO AND "SHOULD" GO ARE TWO DIFFERENT THINGS, AREN'T THEY?
SEE? THE B, C, AND D MATCHES ARE SEPARATE FROM THE GRAND PRIX. CAN YOU GUESS WHY?
[WDSF World Qualifiers]
DANCESPORT GRAND PRIX in Shizuoka
(Joint Event) All-Japan Youth Championships
All-Japan Junior Ten Dance Championships
W. T. F. Q
Grand Prix Standard
All-Japan Championships – Youth Standard
(2014 Youth Standard World Champion
YCL N DSCJ A
4 JAL Y DSCJ B
5 JBS Y DSCJ B
6 JBL Y DSCJ C
7 JCS Y DSCJ C
8 JCL Y DSCJ D
9 JDS Y DSCJ D
10 JDL N
WHEN THEY SAY "SUBMIT ENTRIES TO THE CATEGORY THAT MATCHES YOUR SKILL"
...
THEY MEAN THAT THE GRAND PRIX IS A TOP TIER COMPETITION FOR LEVEL B AND HIGHER.
IT'S NOT SOMETHING YOU SHOULD ENTER AT YOUR CURRENT LEVEL. DO YOU UNDERSTAND?

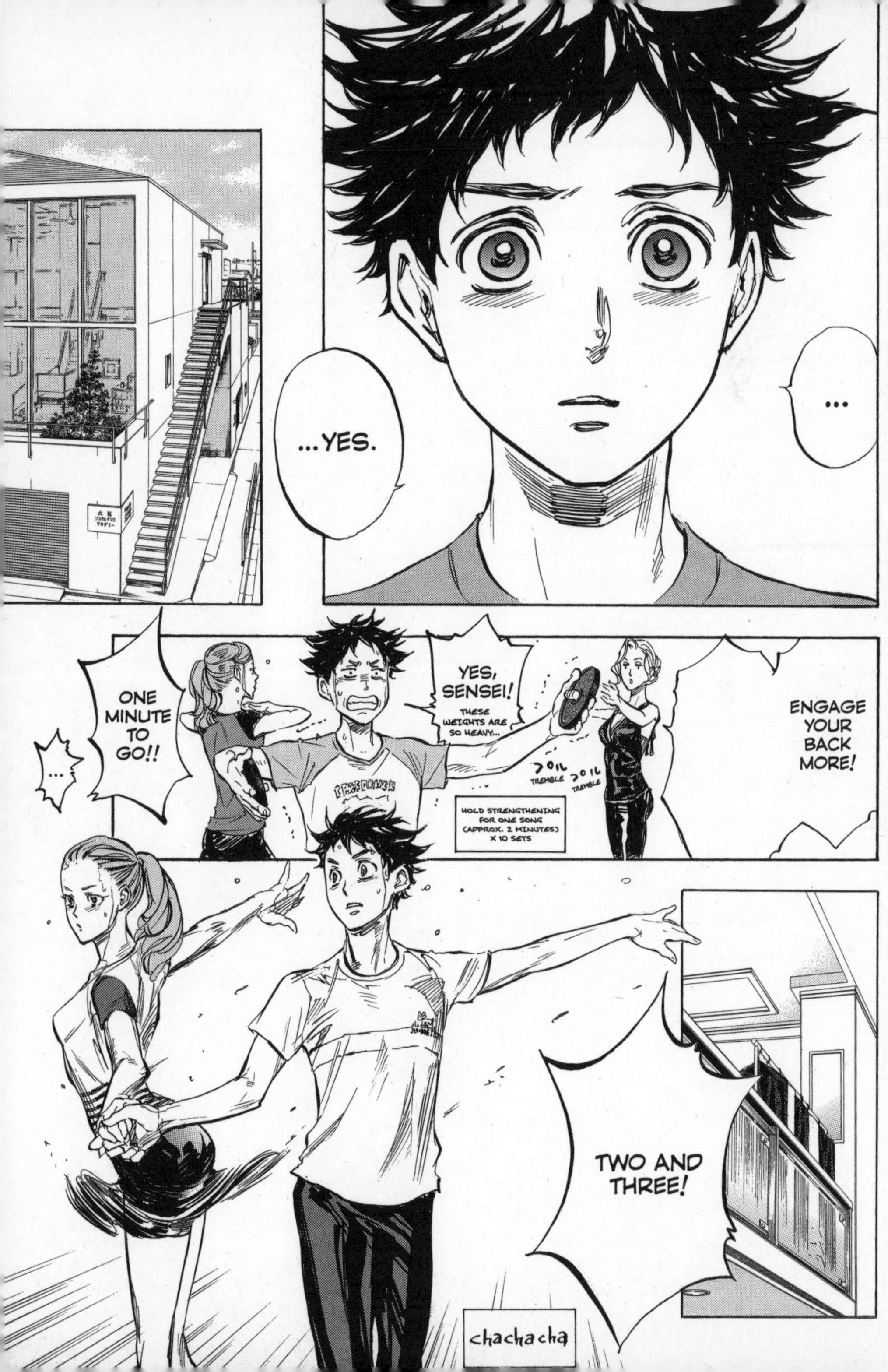
...
...YES.
ENGAGE YOUR BACK MORE!
YES, SENSEI!
THESE WEIGHTS ARE SO HEAVY...
TREMBLE
TREMBLE
HOLD STRENGTHENING FOR ONE SONG (APPROX. 2 MINUTES) X 10 SETS
ONE MINUTE TO GO!!
...
TWO AND THREE!
chachacha

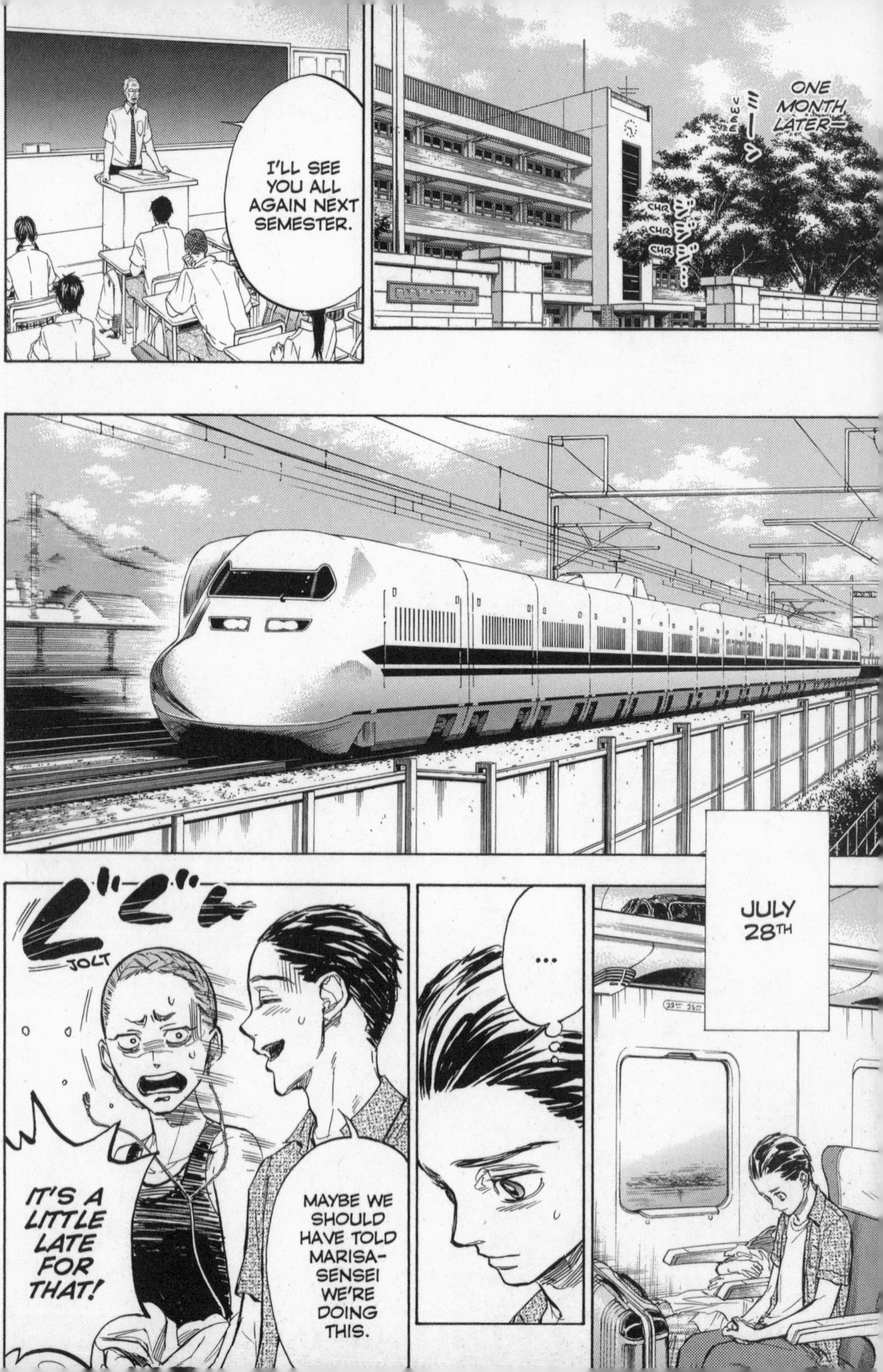
ONE MONTH LATER—
VWEE
CHR CHR CHR
I'LL SEE YOU ALL AGAIN NEXT SEMESTER.
JULY 28TH
...
JOLT
MAYBE WE SHOULD HAVE TOLD MARISA-SENSEI WE'RE DOING THIS.
IT'S A LITTLE LATE FOR THAT!

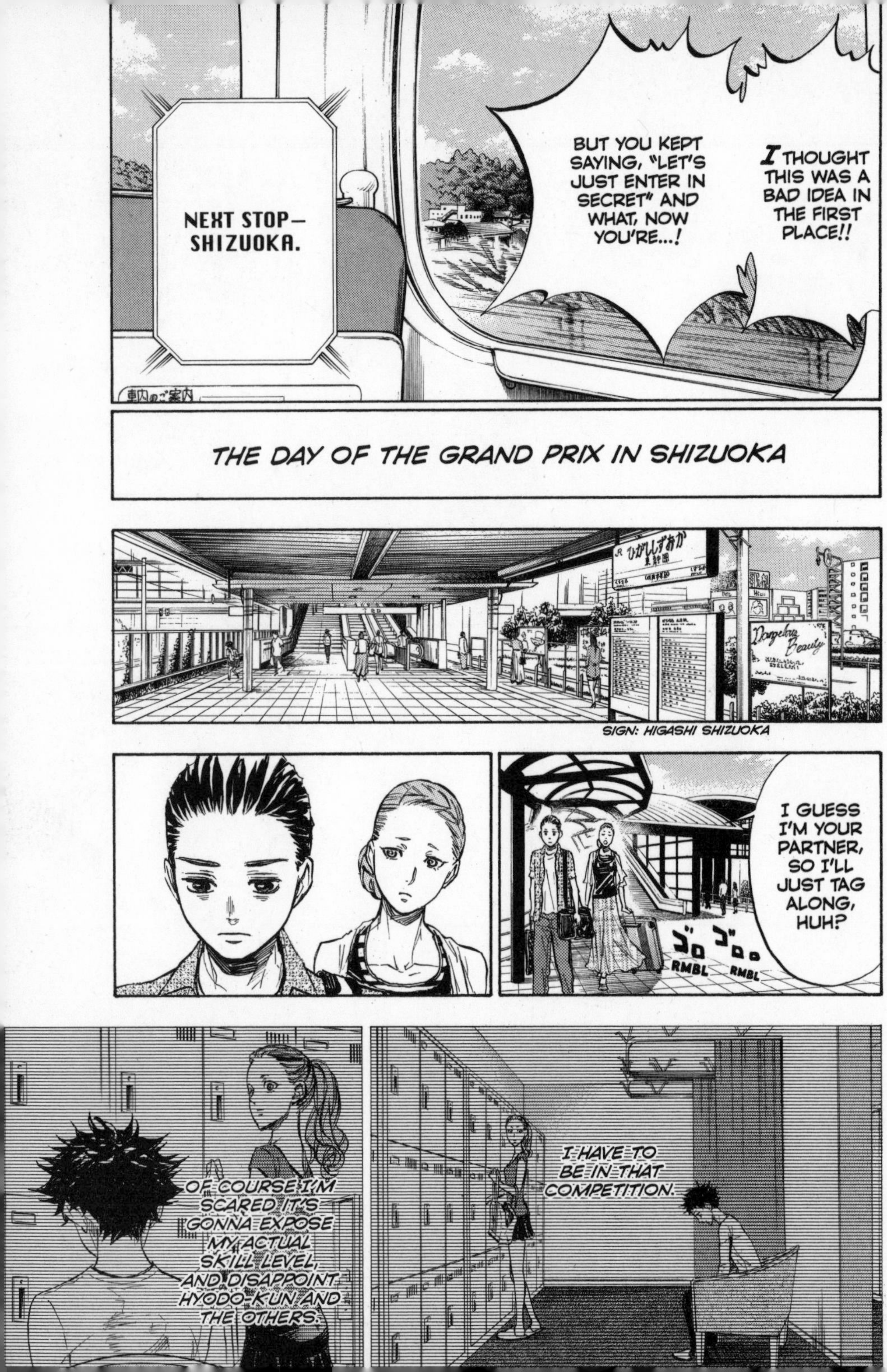
I THOUGHT THIS WAS A BAD IDEA IN THE FIRST PLACE!!
BUT YOU KEPT SAYING, "LET'S JUST ENTER IN SECRET" AND WHAT, NOW YOU'RE...!
NEXT STOP— SHIZUOKA.
THE DAY OF THE GRAND PRIX IN SHIZUOKA
SIGN: HIGASHI SHIZUOKA
I GUESS I'M YOUR PARTNER, SO I'LL JUST TAG ALONG, HUH?
RMBL
RMBL
I HAVE TO BE IN THAT COMPETITION.
OF COURSE I'M SCARED IT'S GONNA EXPOSE MY ACTUAL SKILL LEVEL AND DISAPPOINT HYODO-KUN AND THE OTHERS.

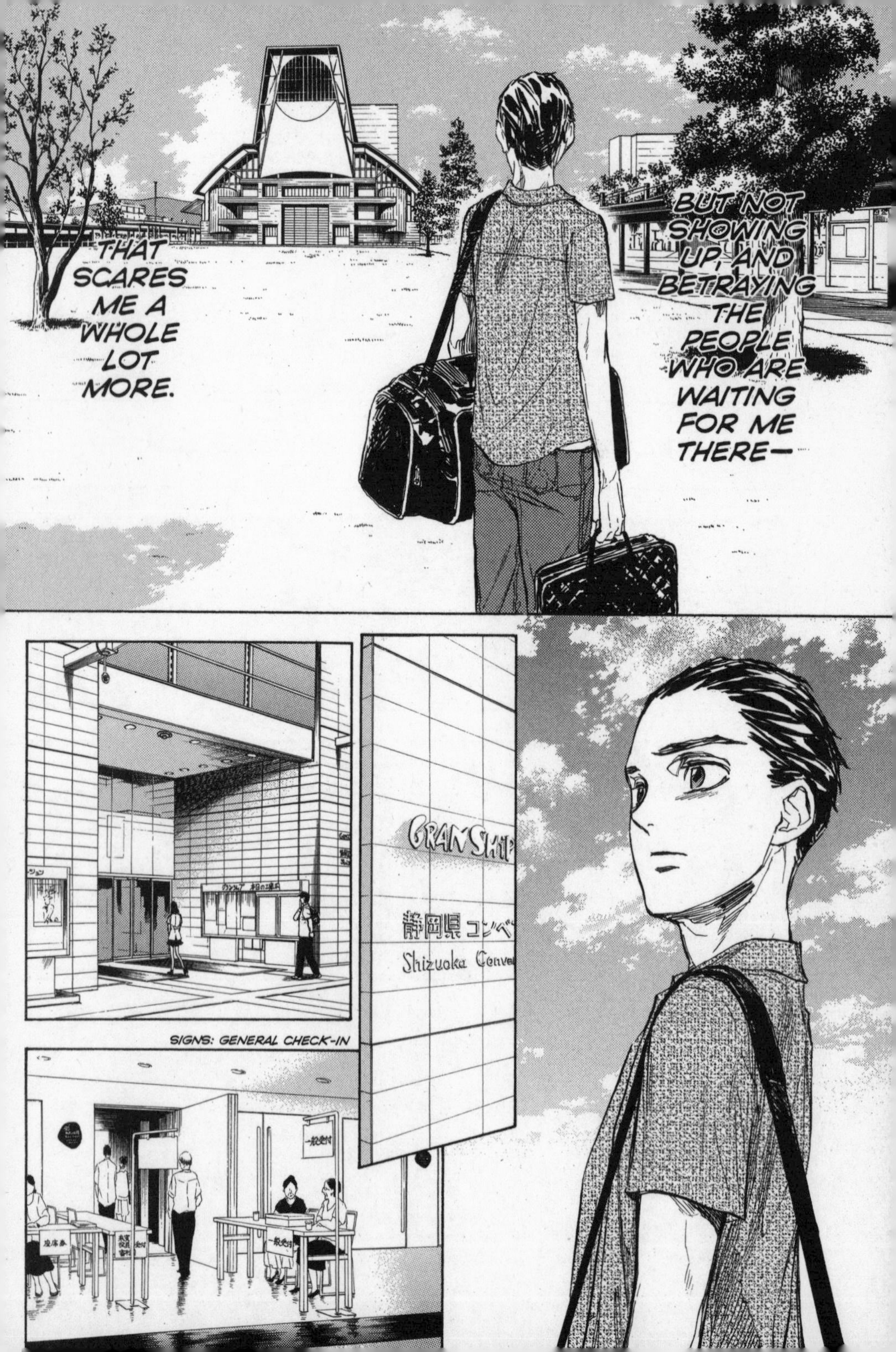
BUT NOT SHOWING UP, AND BETRAYING THE PEOPLE WHO ARE WAITING FOR ME THERE—
THAT SCARES ME A WHOLE LOT MORE.
GRANSHIP
静岡県コンベ
Shizuoka Conve
一般受付
SIGNS: GENERAL CHECK-IN

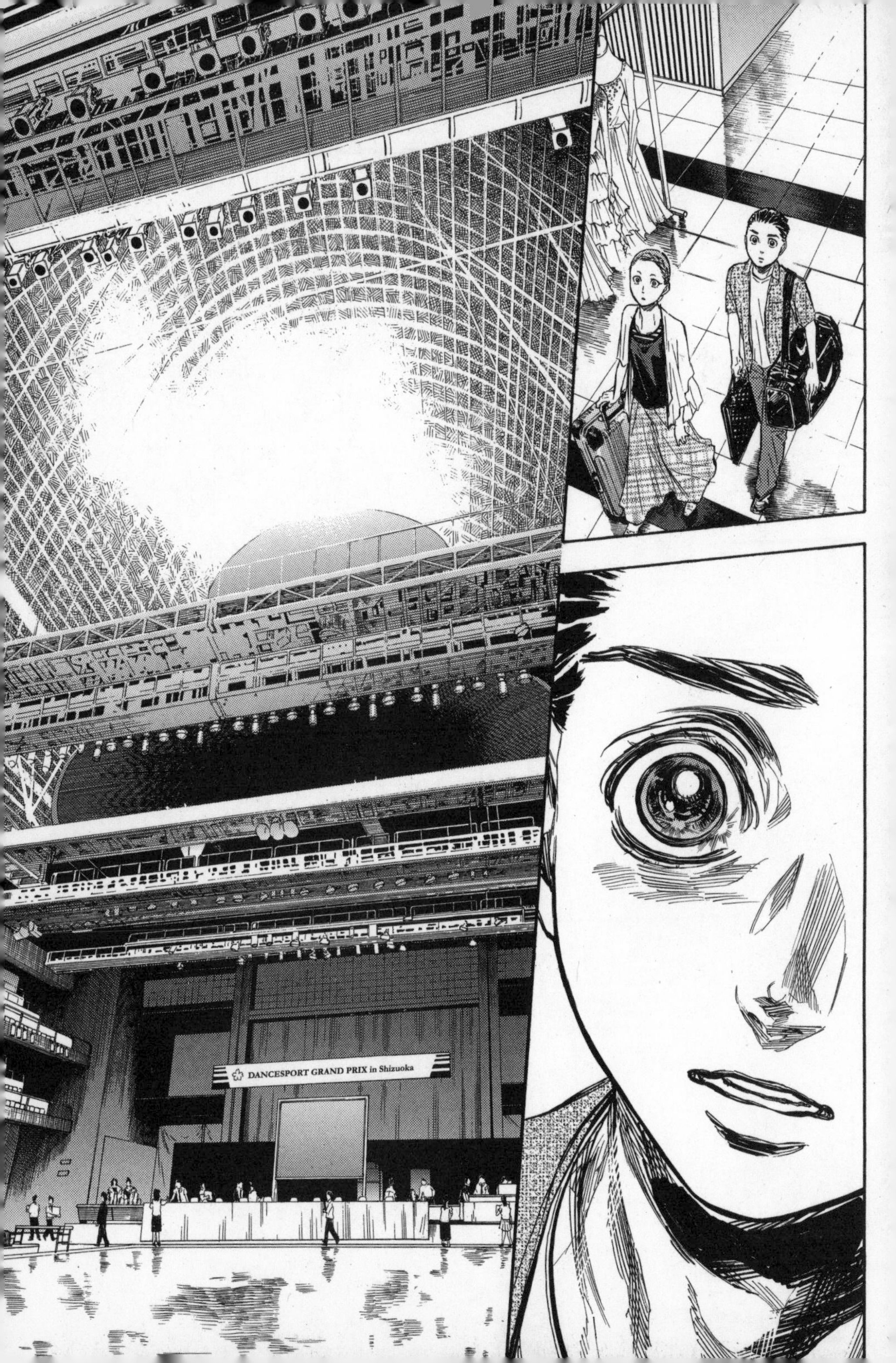
DANCESPORT GRAND PRIX in Shizuoka

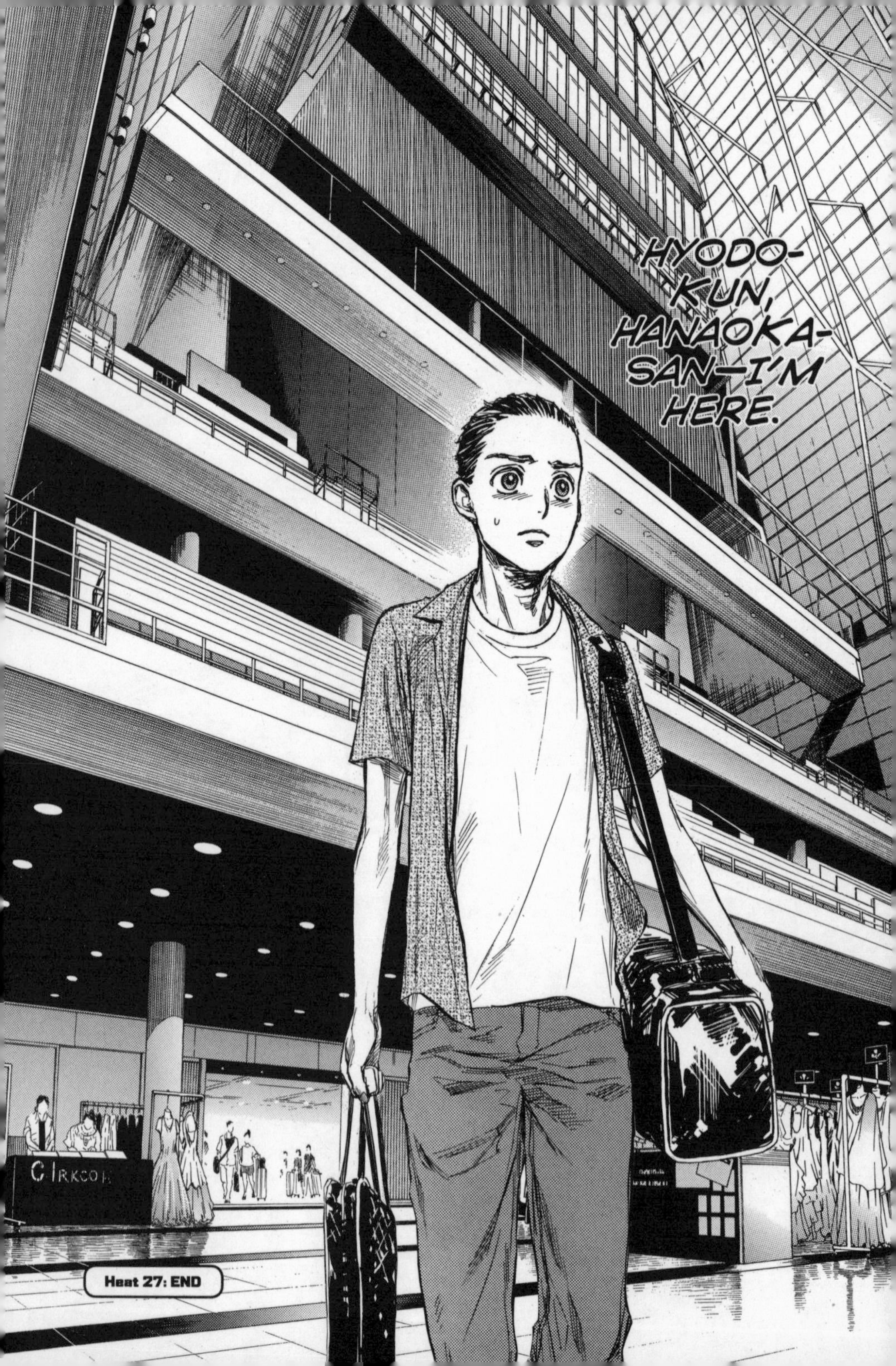
HYODO-KUN, HANAOKA-SAN—I'M HERE.
GIRKCOE
Heat 27: END

WELCOME TO THE BALLROOM

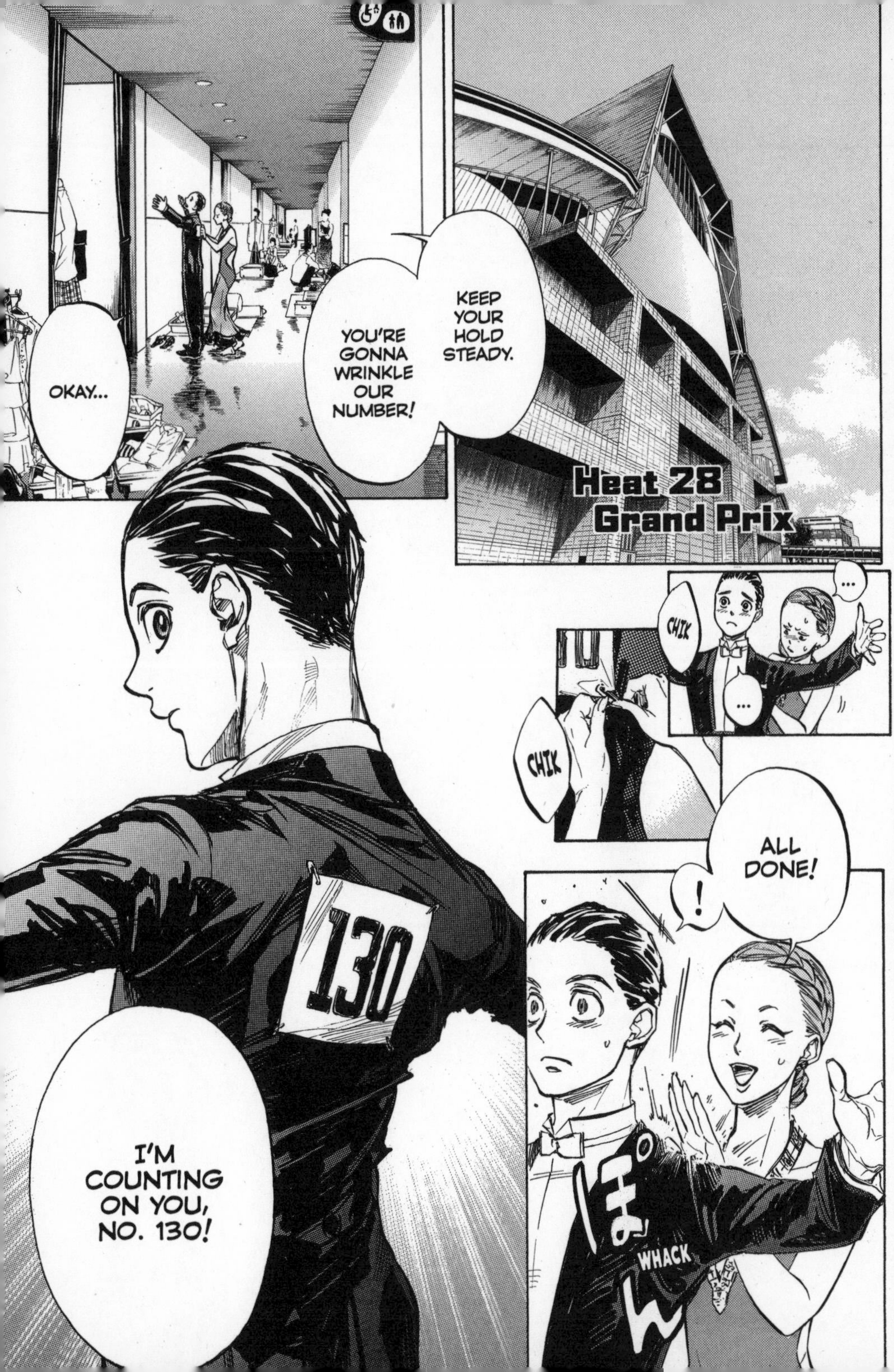
Heat 28
Grand Prix
KEEP YOUR HOLD STEADY.
YOU'RE GONNA WRINKLE OUR NUMBER!
OKAY...
...
CHIK
...
CHIK
ALL DONE!
!
WHACK
130
I'M COUNTING ON YOU, NO. 130!

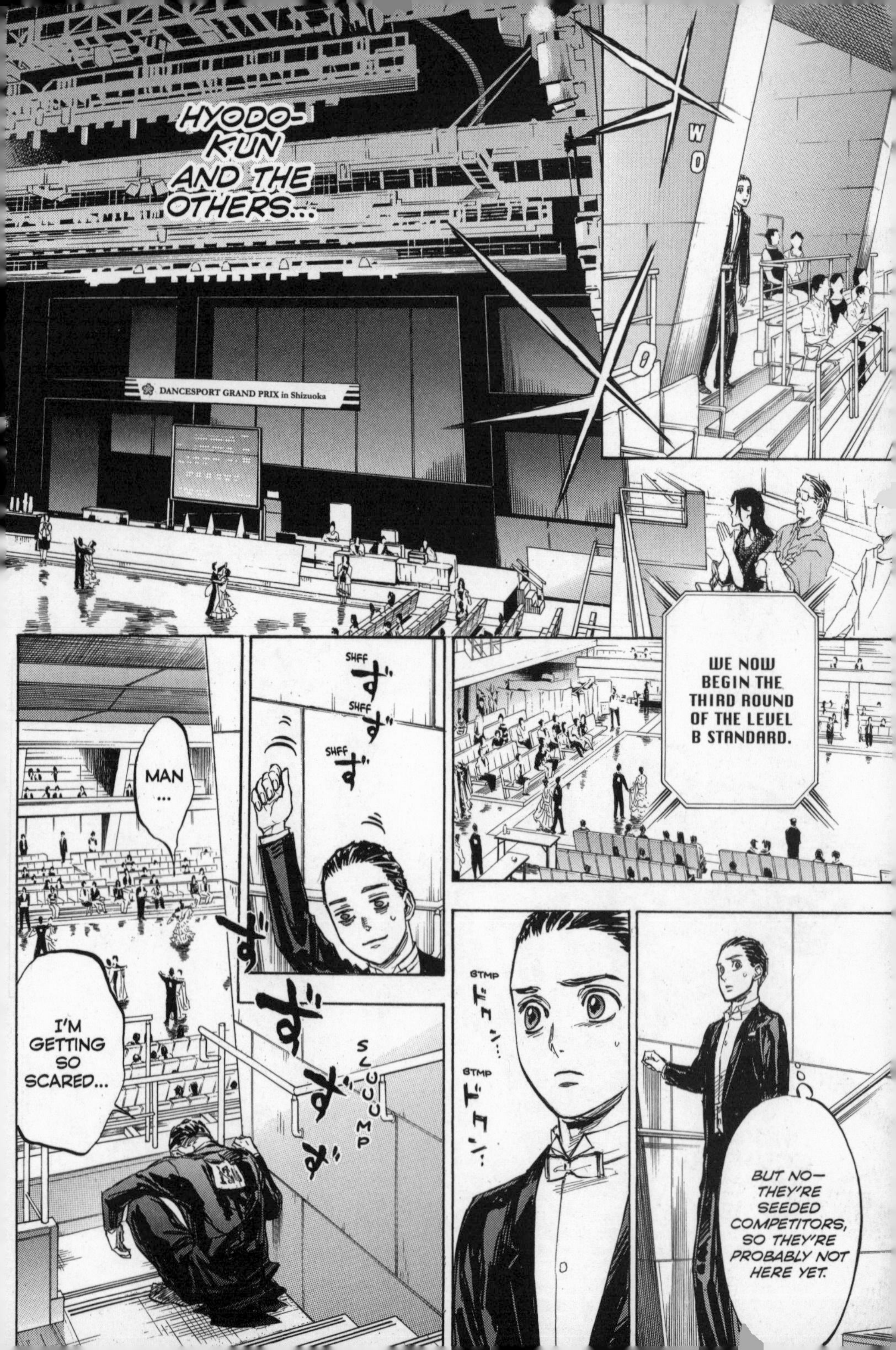

WO
O
HYODO-KUN AND THE OTHERS...
DANCESPORT GRAND PRIX in Shizuoka
WE NOW BEGIN THE THIRD ROUND OF THE LEVEL B STANDARD.
SHFF
SHFF
SHFF
MAN ...
I'M GETTING SO SCARED...
SLUUUMP
BUT NO— THEY'RE SEEDED COMPETITORS, SO THEY'RE PROBABLY NOT HERE YET.
BTMP
BTMP

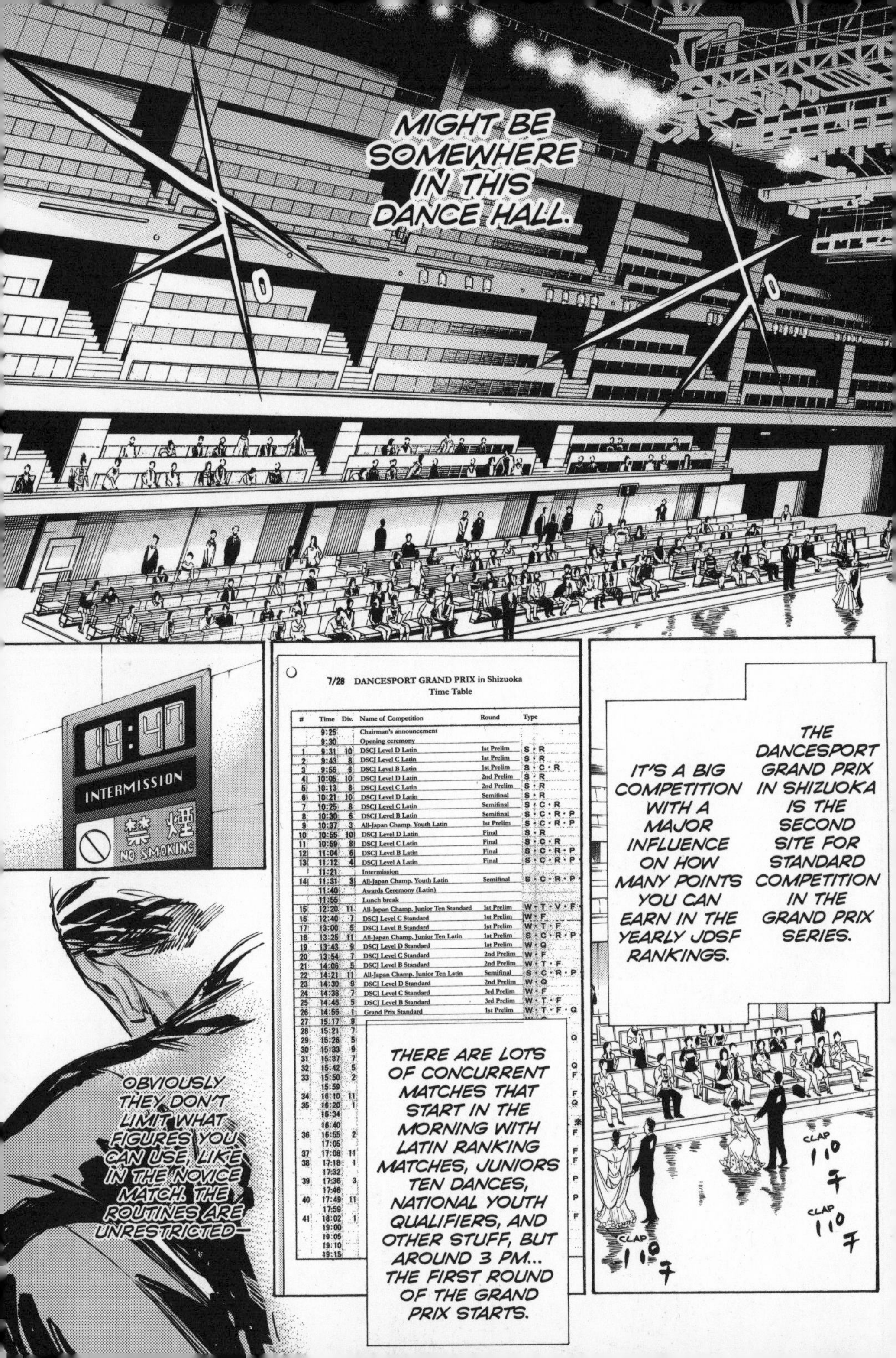
MIGHT BE SOMEWHERE IN THIS DANCE HALL.
THE DANCESPORT GRAND PRIX IN SHIZUOKA IS THE SECOND SITE FOR STANDARD COMPETITION IN THE GRAND PRIX SERIES.
IT'S A BIG COMPETITION WITH A MAJOR INFLUENCE ON HOW MANY POINTS YOU CAN EARN IN THE YEARLY JDSF RANKINGS.
CLAP
CLAP
CLAP
THERE ARE LOTS OF CONCURRENT MATCHES THAT START IN THE MORNING WITH LATIN RANKING MATCHES, JUNIORS TEN DANCES, NATIONAL YOUTH QUALIFIERS, AND OTHER STUFF, BUT AROUND 3 PM... THE FIRST ROUND OF THE GRAND PRIX STARTS.
14:47
INTERMISSION
禁煙
NO SMOKING
OBVIOUSLY THEY DON'T LIMIT WHAT FIGURES YOU CAN USE, LIKE IN THE NOVICE MATCH. THE ROUTINES ARE UNRESTRICTED—

7/28 DANCESPORT GRAND PRIX in Shizuoka
Time Table

#	Time	Div.	Name of Competition	Round	Type
	9:25		Chairman's announcement		
	9:30		Opening ceremony		
1	9:31	10	DSCJ Level D Latin	1st Prelim	S • R
2	9:43	8	DSCJ Level C Latin	1st Prelim	S • R
3	9:55	6	DSCJ Level B Latin	1st Prelim	S • C • R
4	10:05	10	DSCJ Level D Latin	2nd Prelim	S • R
5	10:13	8	DSCJ Level C Latin	2nd Prelim	S • R
6	10:21	10	DSCJ Level D Latin	Semifinal	S • R
7	10:25	8	DSCJ Level C Latin	Semifinal	S • C • R
8	10:30	6	DSCJ Level B Latin	Semifinal	S • C • R • P
9	10:37	3	All-Japan Champ. Youth Latin	1st Prelim	S • C • R • P
10	10:55	10	DSCJ Level D Latin	Final	S • R
11	10:59	8	DSCJ Level C Latin	Final	S • C • R
12	11:04	6	DSCJ Level B Latin	Final	S • C • R • P
13	11:12	4	DSCJ Level A Latin	Final	S • C • R • P
	11:21		Intermission		
14	11:31	3	All-Japan Champ. Youth Latin	Semifinal	S • C • R • P
	11:40		Awards Ceremony (Latin)		
	11:55		Lunch break		
15	12:20	11	All-Japan Champ. Junior Ten Standard	1st Prelim	W • T • V • F
16	12:40	7	DSCJ Level C Standard	1st Prelim	W • F
17	13:00	5	DSCJ Level B Standard	1st Prelim	W • T • F
18	13:25	11	All-Japan Champ. Junior Ten Latin	1st Prelim	S • C • R • P
19	13:43	9	DSCJ Level D Standard	1st Prelim	W • Q
20	13:54	7	DSCJ Level C Standard	2nd Prelim	W • F
21	14:06	5	DSCJ Level B Standard	2nd Prelim	W • T • F
22	14:21	11	All-Japan Champ. Junior Ten Latin	Semifinal	S • C • R • P
23	14:30	9	DSCJ Level D Standard	2nd Prelim	W • Q
24	14:38	7	DSCJ Level C Standard	3rd Prelim	W • F
25	14:46	5	DSCJ Level B Standard	3rd Prelim	W • T • F
26	14:56	1	Grand Prix Standard	1st Prelim	W • T • F • Q
27	15:17	9			
28	15:21	7			
29	15:26	5			Q
30	15:33	9			
31	15:37	7			
32	15:42	5			Q
33	15:50	2			F
	15:59				
34	16:10	11			F
35	16:20	1			Q
	16:34				
	16:40				来
36	16:55	2			F
	17:05				
37	17:08	11			F
38	17:18	1			F
	17:32				
39	17:36	3			P
	17:46				
40	17:49	11			P
	17:59				
41	18:02	1			F
	19:00				
	19:05				
	19:10				
	19:15				

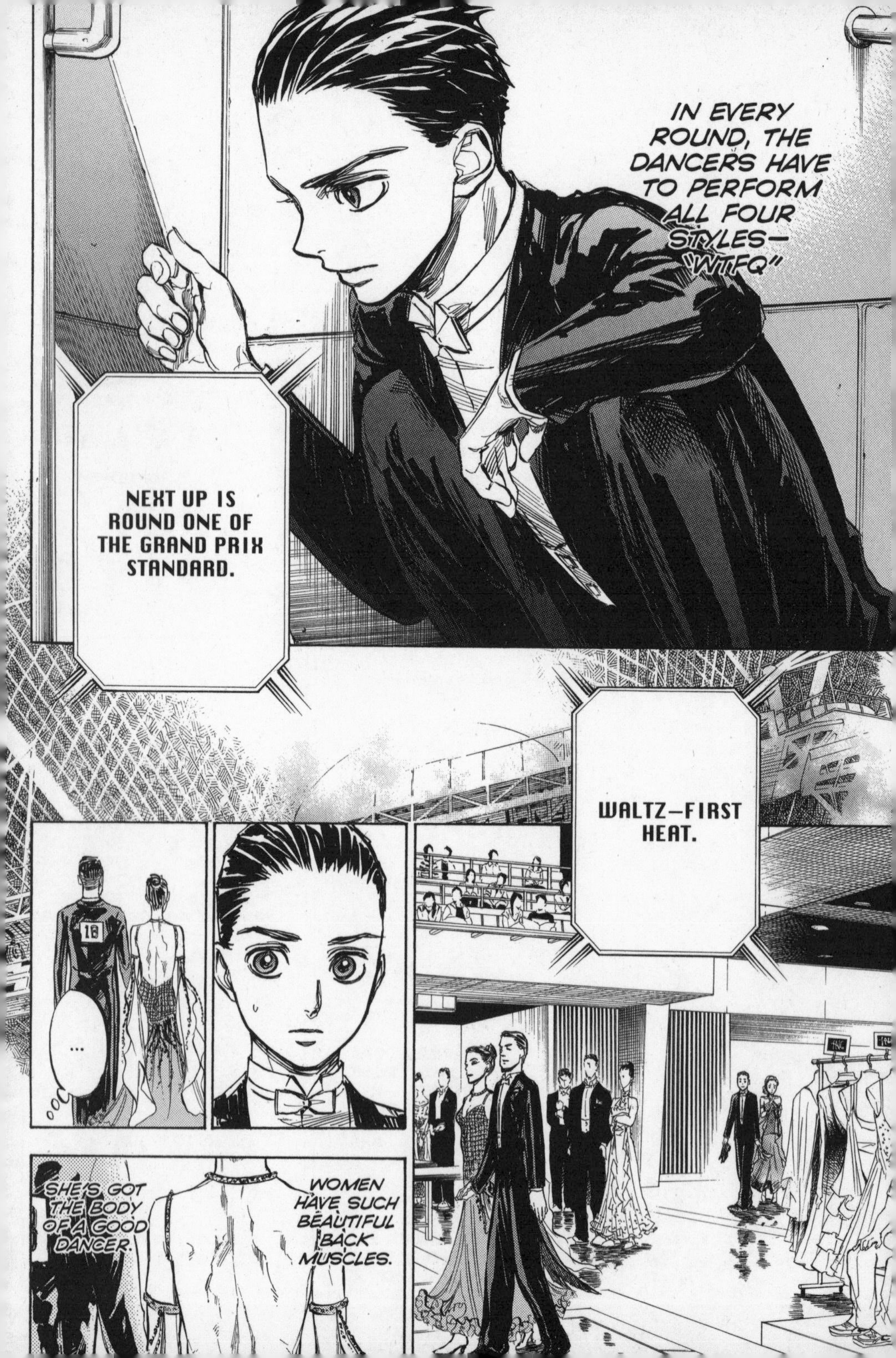
IN EVERY ROUND, THE DANCERS HAVE TO PERFORM ALL FOUR STYLES— "WTFQ"
NEXT UP IS ROUND ONE OF THE GRAND PRIX STANDARD.
WALTZ—FIRST HEAT.
...
WOMEN HAVE SUCH BEAUTIFUL BACK MUSCLES.
SHE'S GOT THE BODY OF A GOOD DANCER.

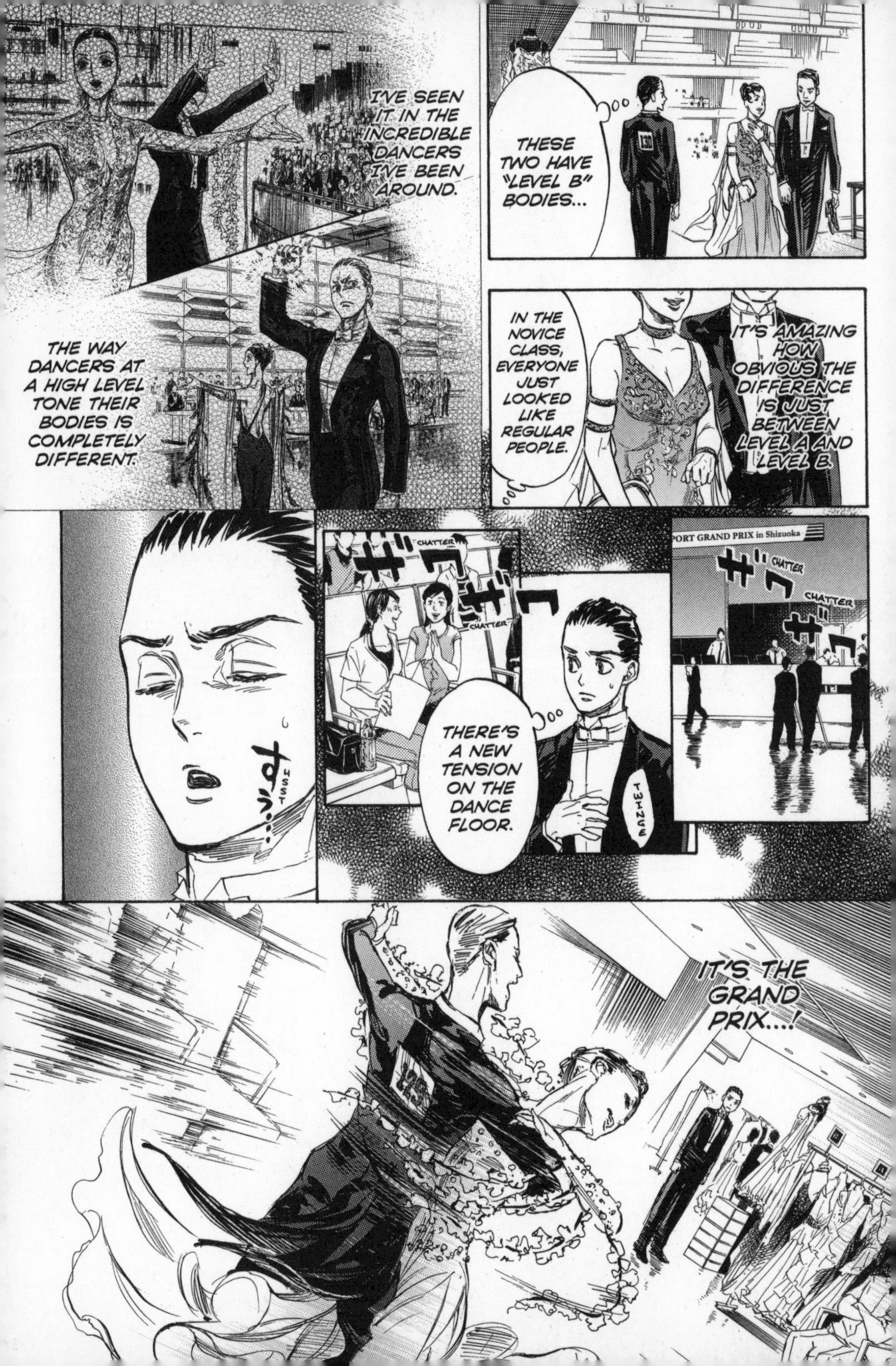
THESE TWO HAVE "LEVEL B" BODIES...
IT'S AMAZING HOW OBVIOUS THE DIFFERENCE IS JUST BETWEEN LEVEL A AND LEVEL B.
IN THE NOVICE CLASS, EVERYONE JUST LOOKED LIKE REGULAR PEOPLE.
I'VE SEEN IT IN THE INCREDIBLE DANCERS I'VE BEEN AROUND.
THE WAY DANCERS AT A HIGH LEVEL TONE THEIR BODIES IS COMPLETELY DIFFERENT.
PORT GRAND PRIX in Shizuoka
ザワ
CHATTER
ザワ
CHATTER
ザワ
CHATTER
ザワ
CHATTER
THERE'S A NEW TENSION ON THE DANCE FLOOR.
TWINGE
すぅ…
HSST
IT'S THE GRAND PRIX...!

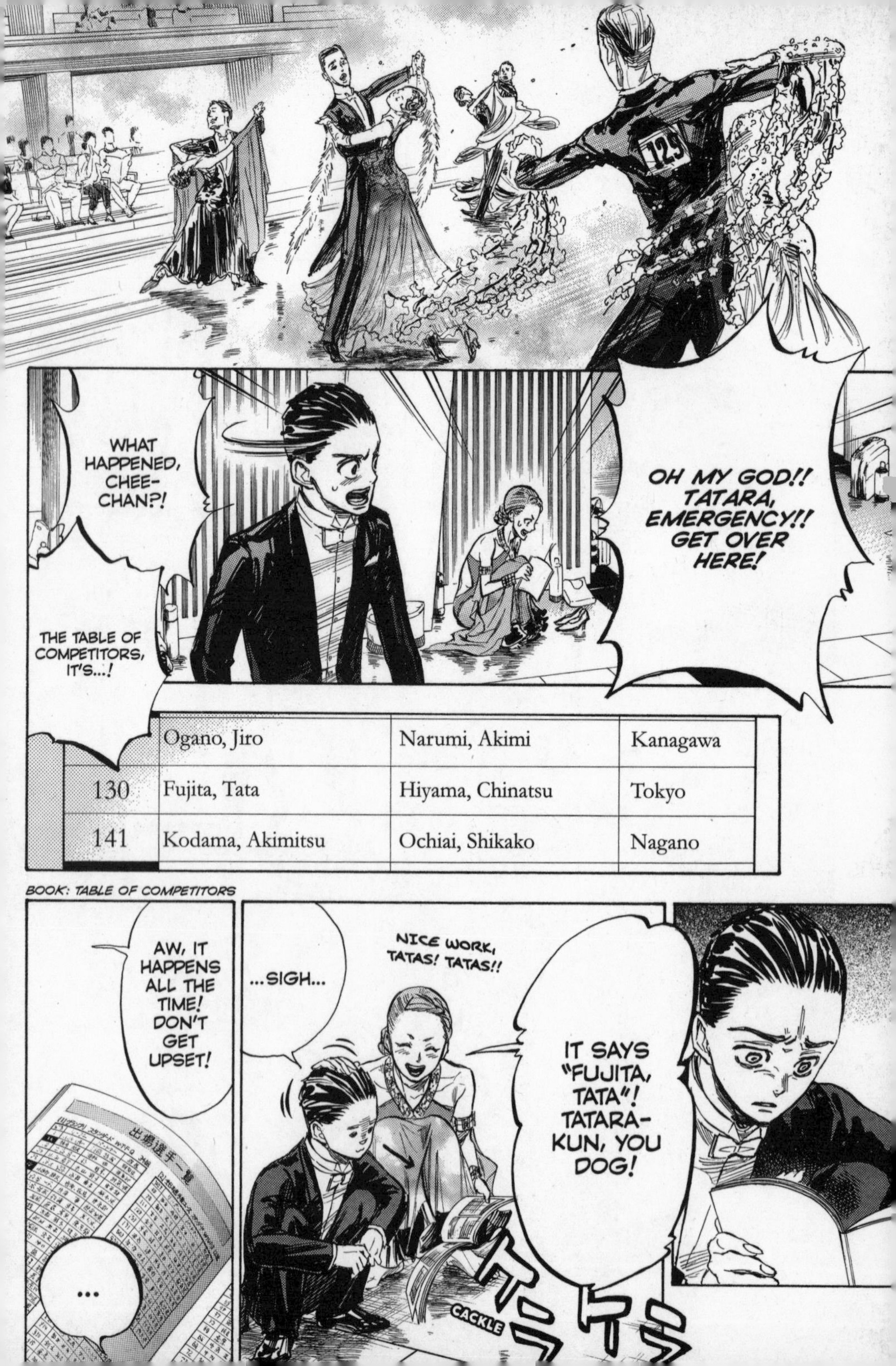
OH MY GOD!! TATARA, EMERGENCY!! GET OVER HERE!
WHAT HAPPENED, CHEE-CHAN?!
THE TABLE OF COMPETITORS, IT'S...!
Ogano, Jiro | Narumi, Akimi | Kanagawa
130 | Fujita, Tata | Hiyama, Chinatsu | Tokyo
141 | Kodama, Akimitsu | Ochiai, Shikako | Nagano
BOOK: TABLE OF COMPETITORS
IT SAYS "FUJITA, TATA"! TATARA-KUN, YOU DOG!
CACKLE
NICE WORK, TATAS! TATAS!!
...SIGH...
AW, IT HAPPENS ALL THE TIME! DON'T GET UPSET!
...

THERE'S NO "HYODO" OR "AKAGI" LISTED HERE...

WHY NOT?!

SERIOUSLY? GAJU-SAN DIDN'T TELL YOU?

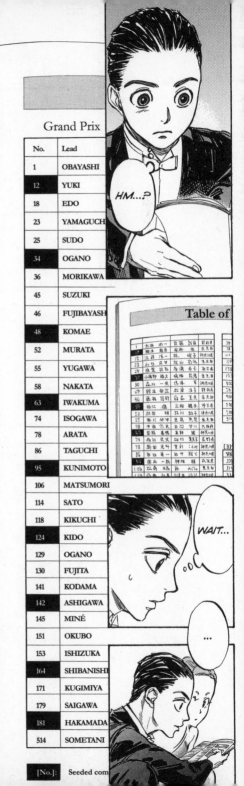

HM...?

Grand Prix

No.	Lead
1	OBAYASHI
12	YUKI
18	EDO
23	YAMAGUCHI
25	SUDO
34	OGANO
36	MORIKAWA
45	SUZUKI
46	FUJIBAYASHI
48	KOMAE
52	MURATA
55	YUGAWA
58	NAKATA
63	IWAKUMA
74	ISOGAWA
78	ARATA
86	TAGUCHI
95	KUNIMOTO
106	MATSUMORI
114	SATO
118	KIKUCHI
124	KIDO
129	OGANO
130	FUJITA
141	KODAMA
142	ASHIGAWA
145	MINÉ
151	OKUBO
153	ISHIZUKA
164	SHIBANISHI
171	KUGIMIYA
179	SAIGAWA
181	HAKAMADA
514	SOMETANI

Table of

WAIT...

...

[No.]: Seeded com

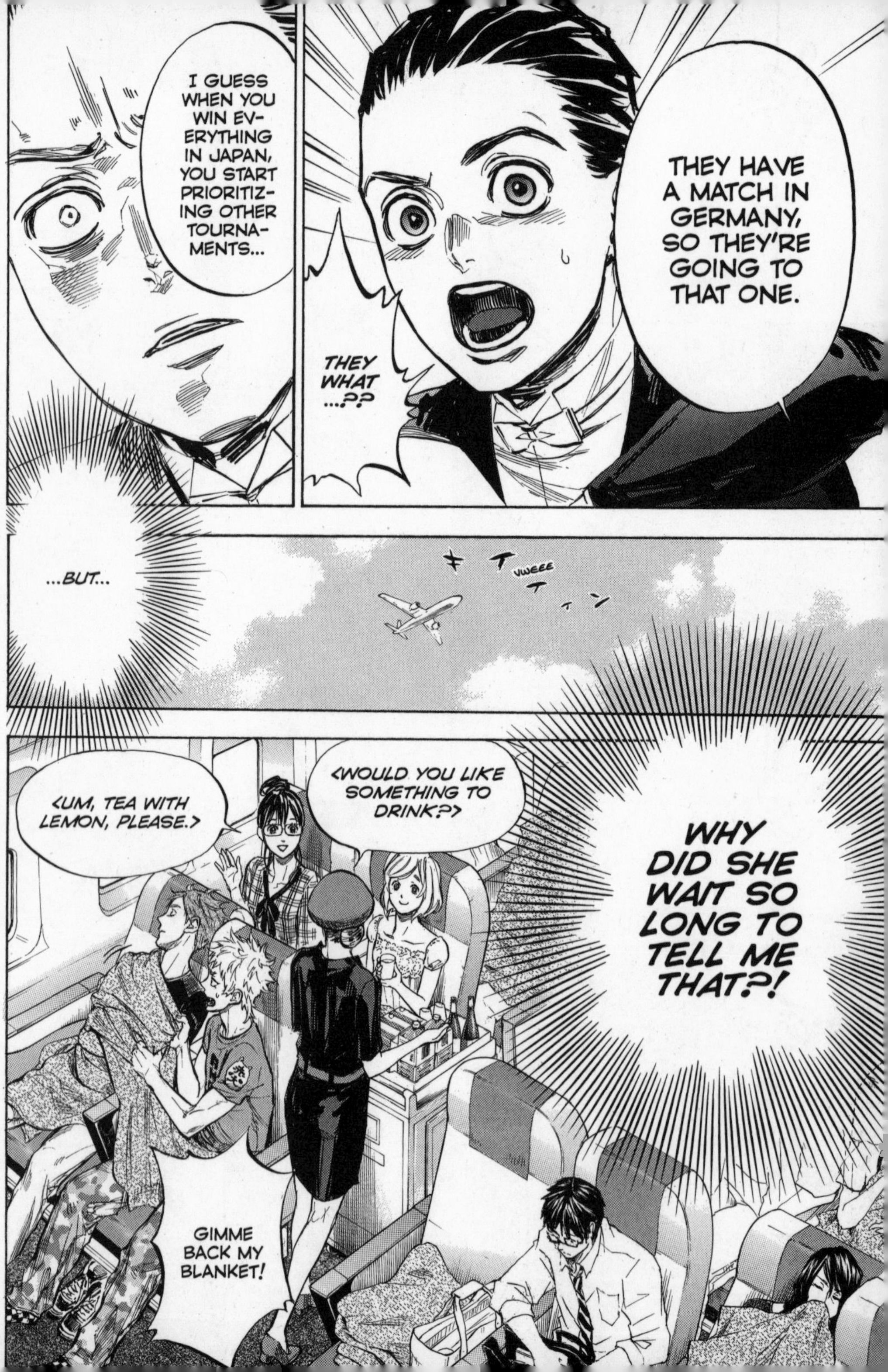
THEY HAVE A MATCH IN GERMANY, SO THEY'RE GOING TO THAT ONE.
THEY WHAT ...??
I GUESS WHEN YOU WIN EV-ERYTHING IN JAPAN, YOU START PRIORITIZ-ING OTHER TOURNA-MENTS...
VWEEE
...BUT...
WHY DID SHE WAIT SO LONG TO TELL ME THAT?!
<WOULD YOU LIKE SOMETHING TO DRINK?>
<UM, TEA WITH LEMON, PLEASE.>
GIMME BACK MY BLANKET!

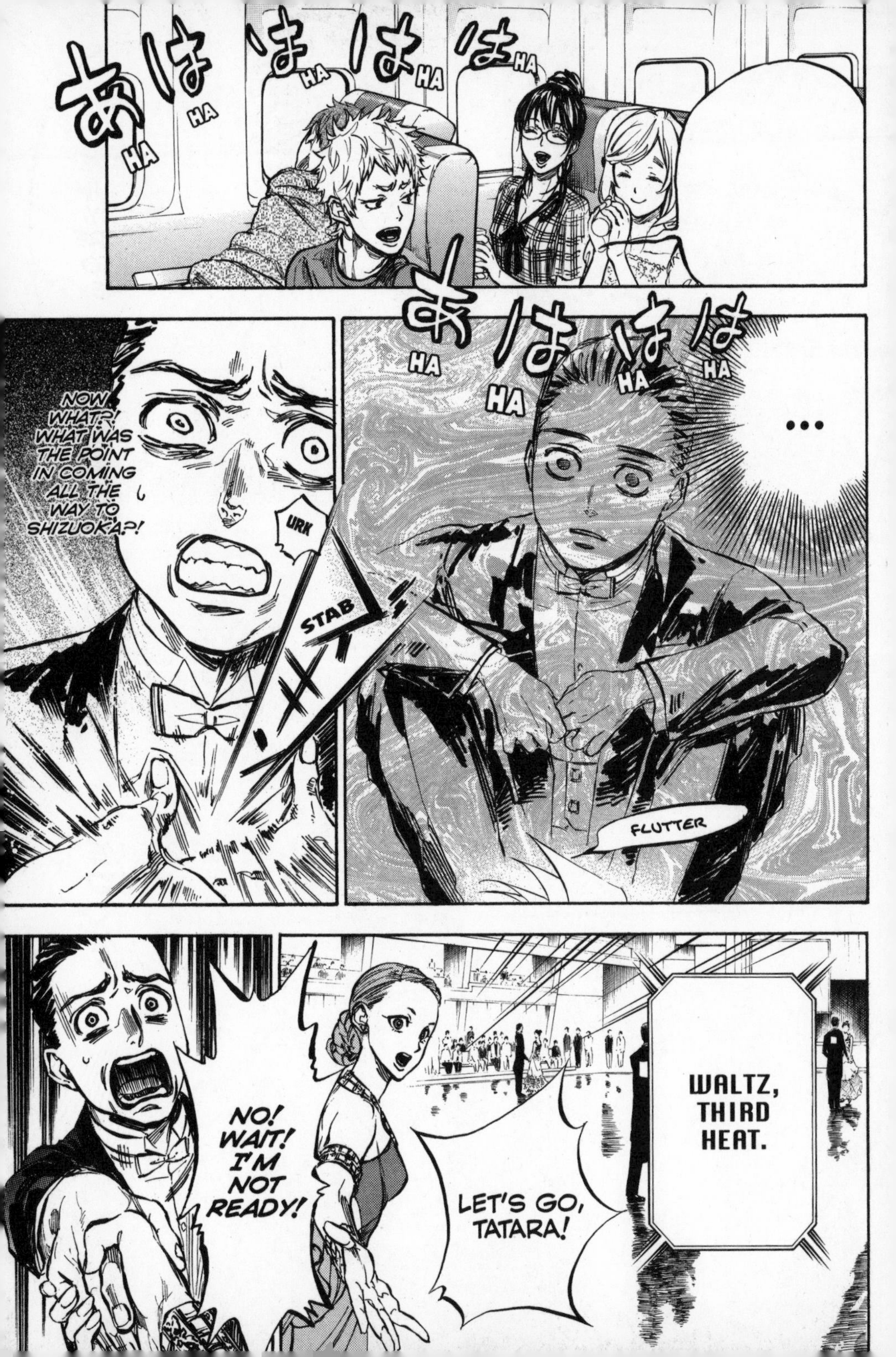

あはははは
HA HA HA HA HA
あははは
HA HA HA HA
...
FLUTTER
NOW WHAT?! WHAT WAS THE POINT IN COMING ALL THE WAY TO SHIZUOKA?!
URK
STAB
WALTZ, THIRD HEAT.
LET'S GO, TATARA!
NO! WAIT! I'M NOT READY!

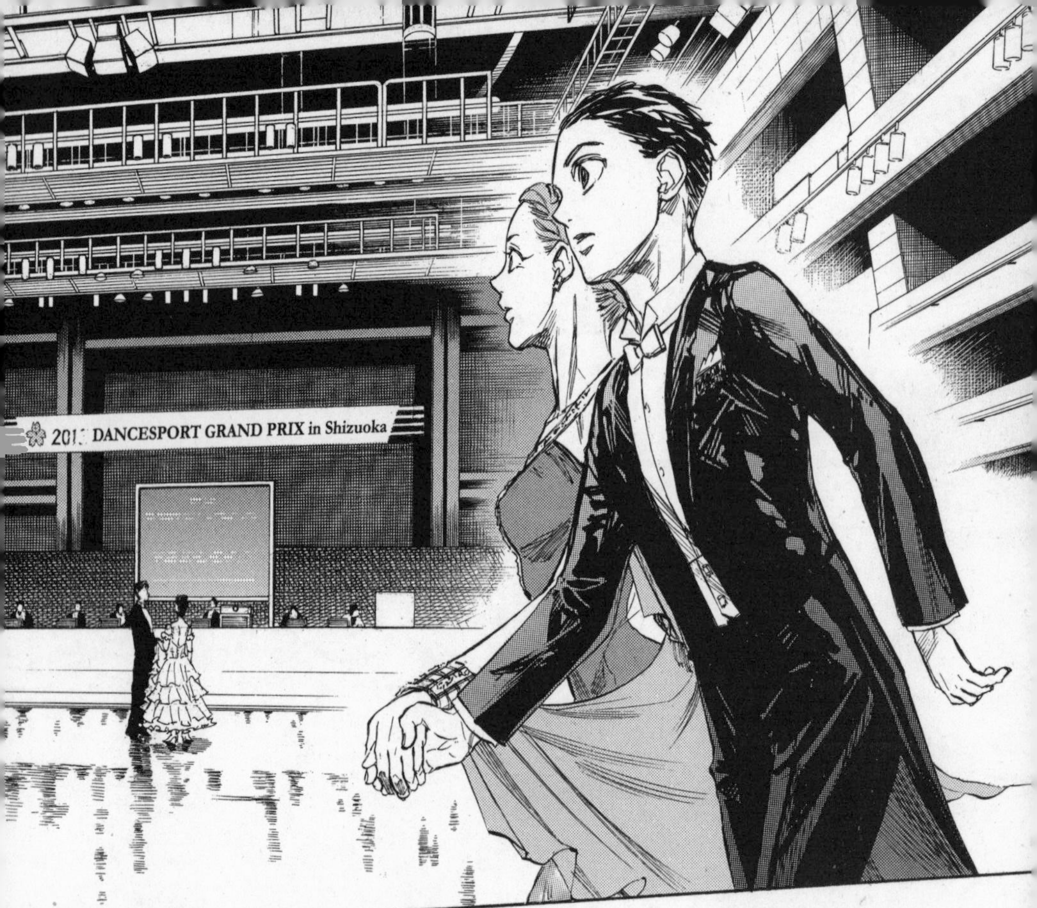
DANCESPORT GRAND PRIX in Shizuoka
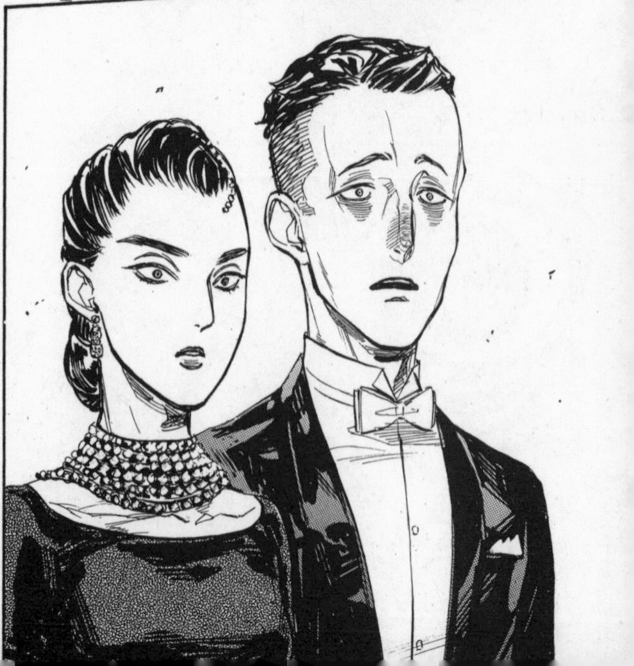
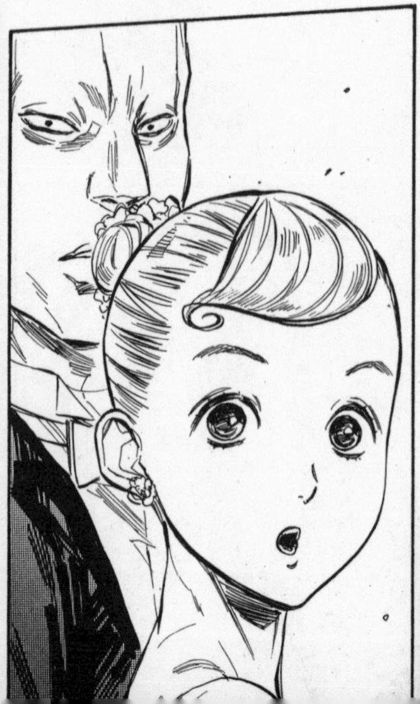

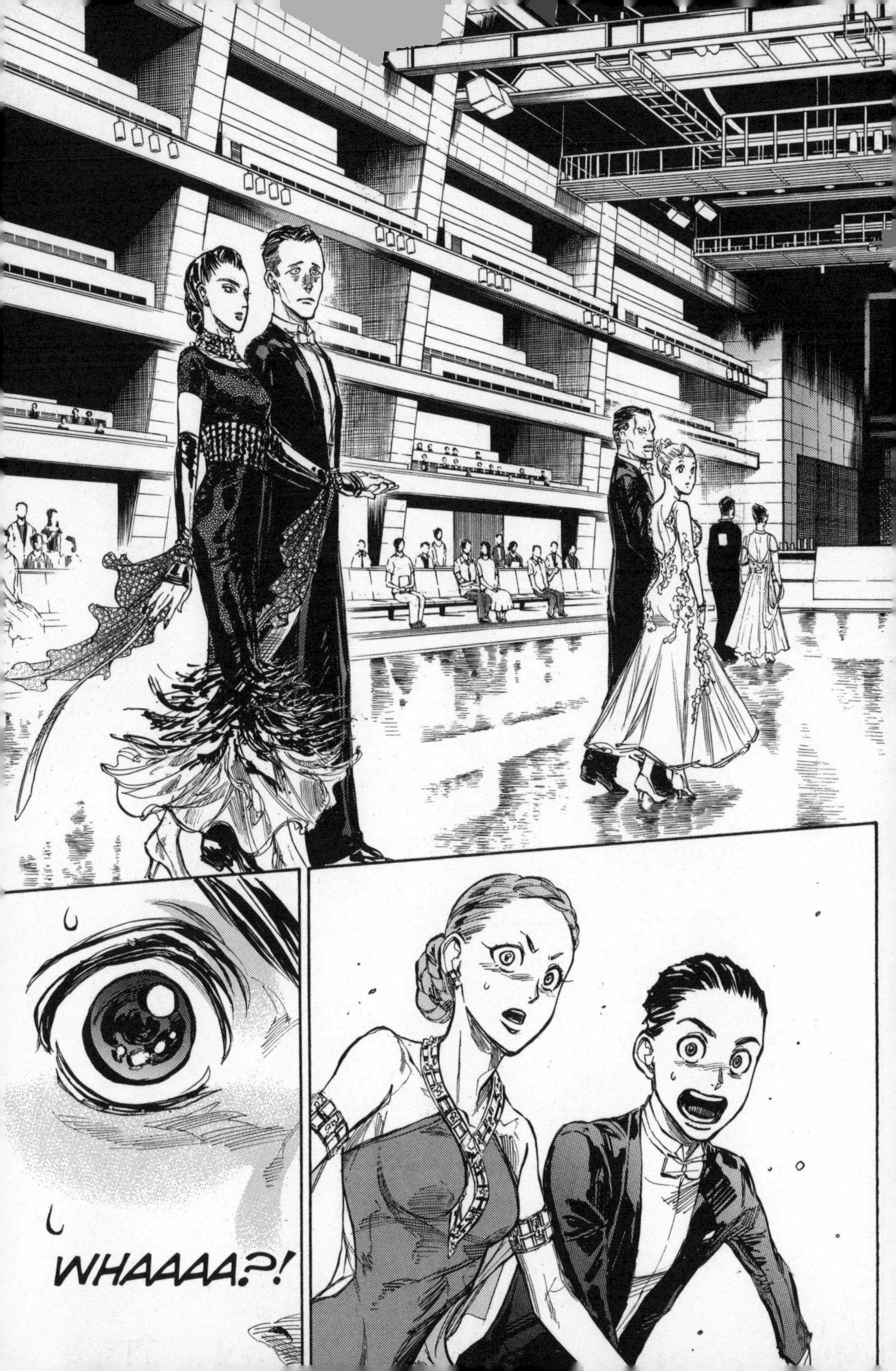
WHAAAA?!

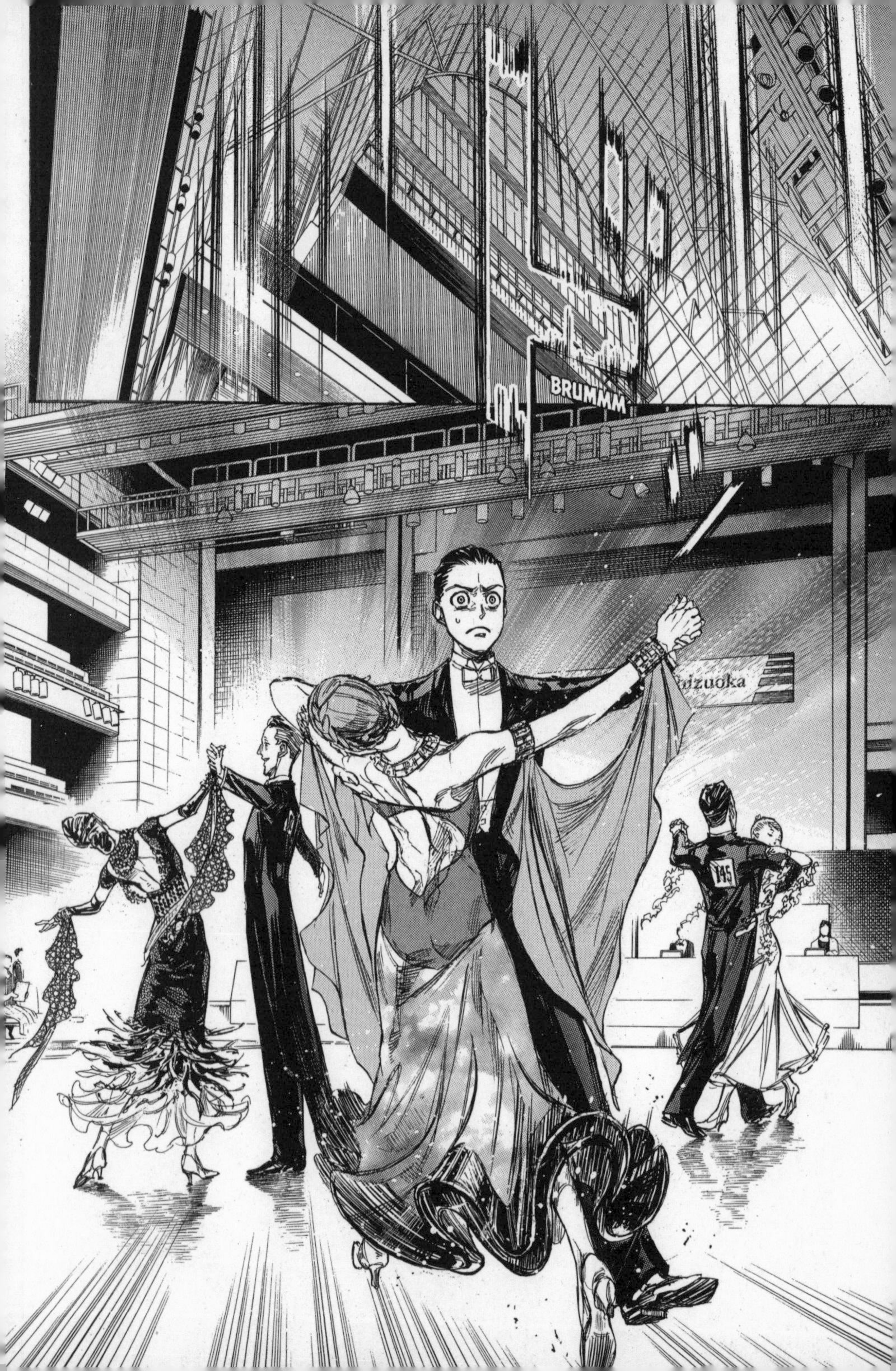
BRUMMM

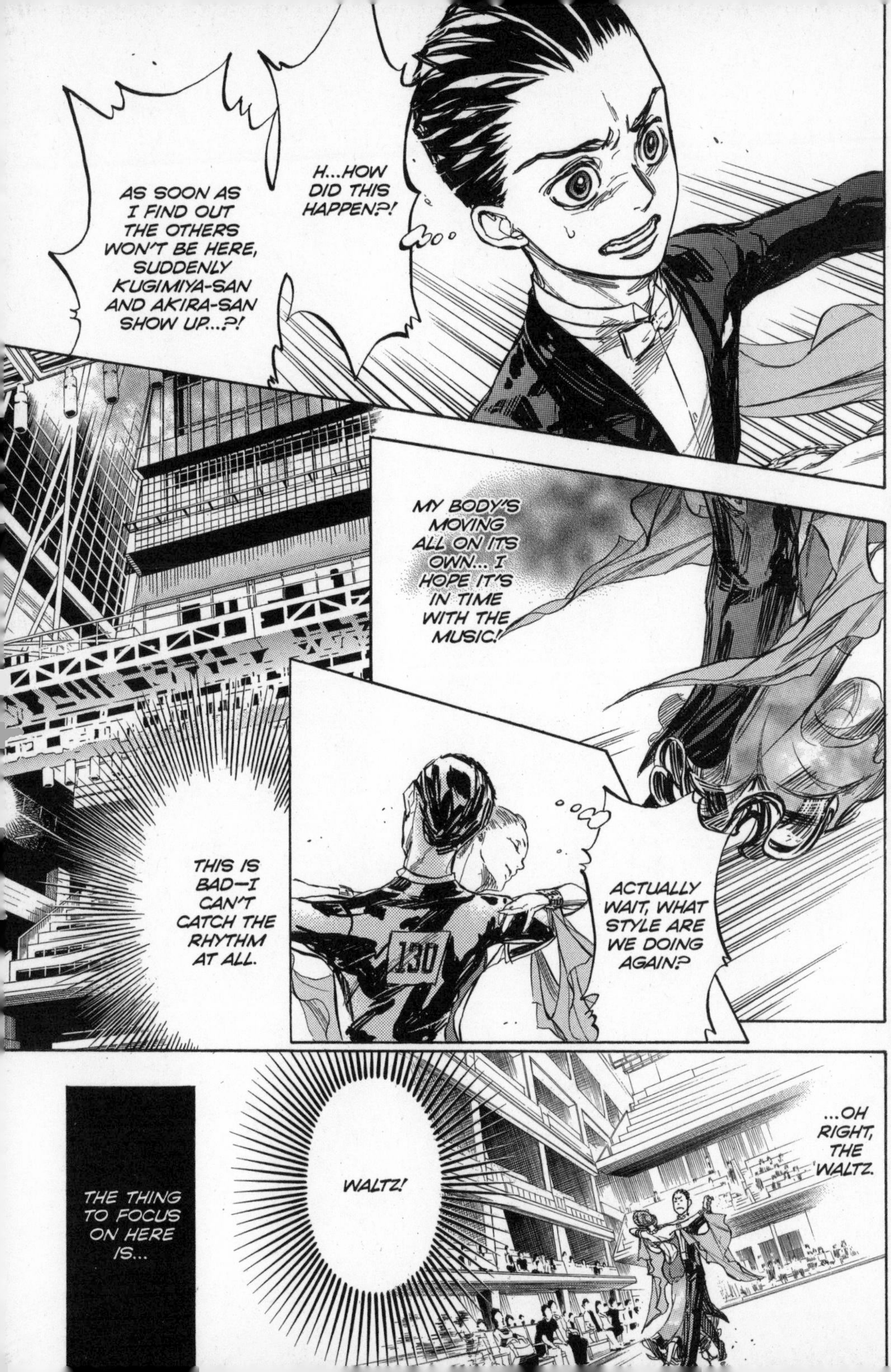
H...HOW DID THIS HAPPEN?!
AS SOON AS I FIND OUT THE OTHERS WON'T BE HERE, SUDDENLY KUGIMIYA-SAN AND AKIRA-SAN SHOW UP...?!
MY BODY'S MOVING ALL ON ITS OWN... I HOPE IT'S IN TIME WITH THE MUSIC!
ACTUALLY WAIT, WHAT STYLE ARE WE DOING AGAIN?
THIS IS BAD—I CAN'T CATCH THE RHYTHM AT ALL.
130
...OH RIGHT, THE WALTZ.
WALTZ!
THE THING TO FOCUS ON HERE IS...

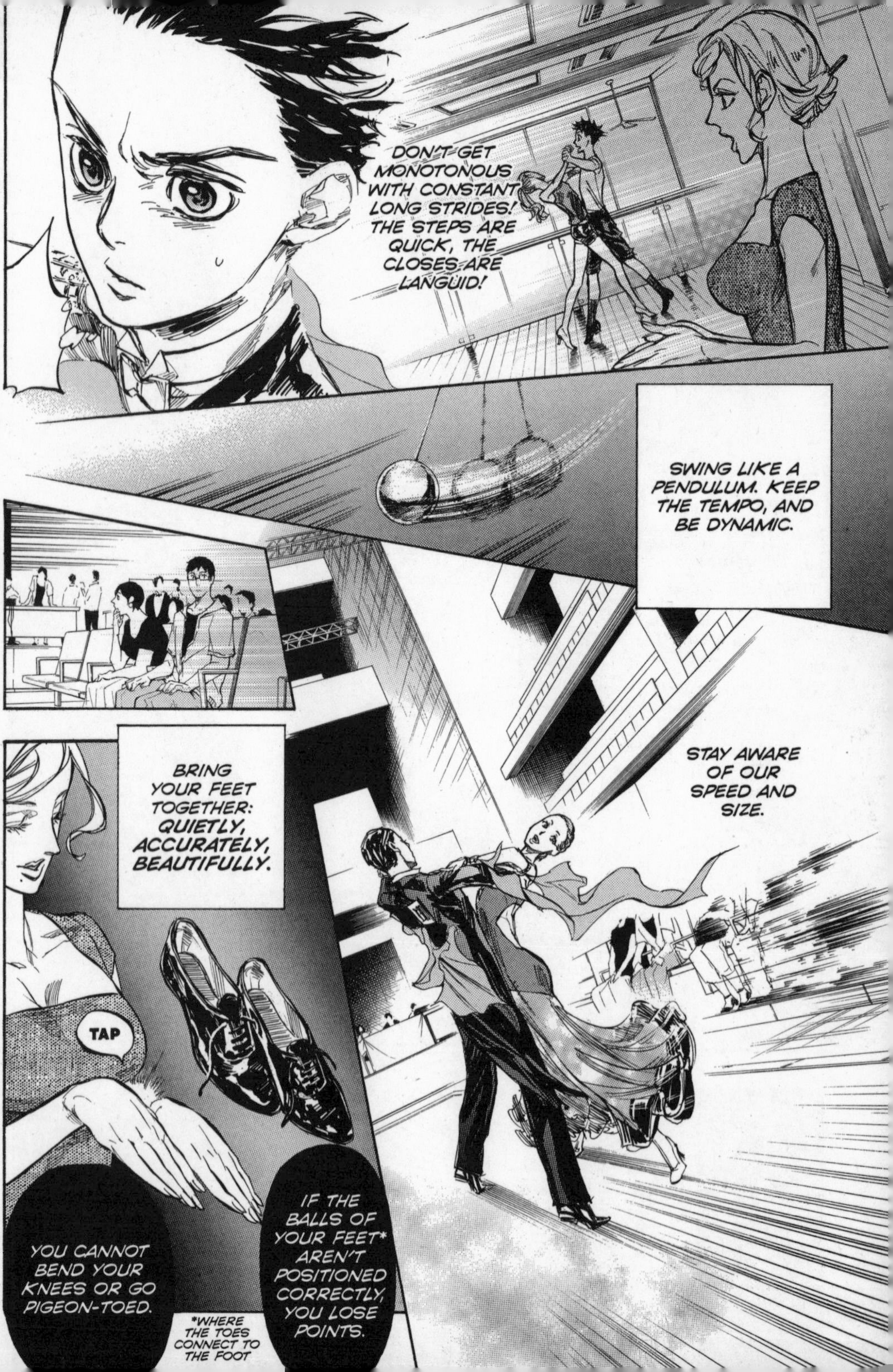
DON'T GET MONOTONOUS WITH CONSTANT LONG STRIDES! THE STEPS ARE QUICK, THE CLOSES ARE LANGUID!
SWING LIKE A PENDULUM. KEEP THE TEMPO, AND BE DYNAMIC.
STAY AWARE OF OUR SPEED AND SIZE.
BRING YOUR FEET TOGETHER: QUIETLY, ACCURATELY, BEAUTIFULLY.
TAP
IF THE BALLS OF YOUR FEET* AREN'T POSITIONED CORRECTLY, YOU LOSE POINTS.
YOU CANNOT BEND YOUR KNEES OR GO PIGEON-TOED.
*WHERE THE TOES CONNECT TO THE FOOT

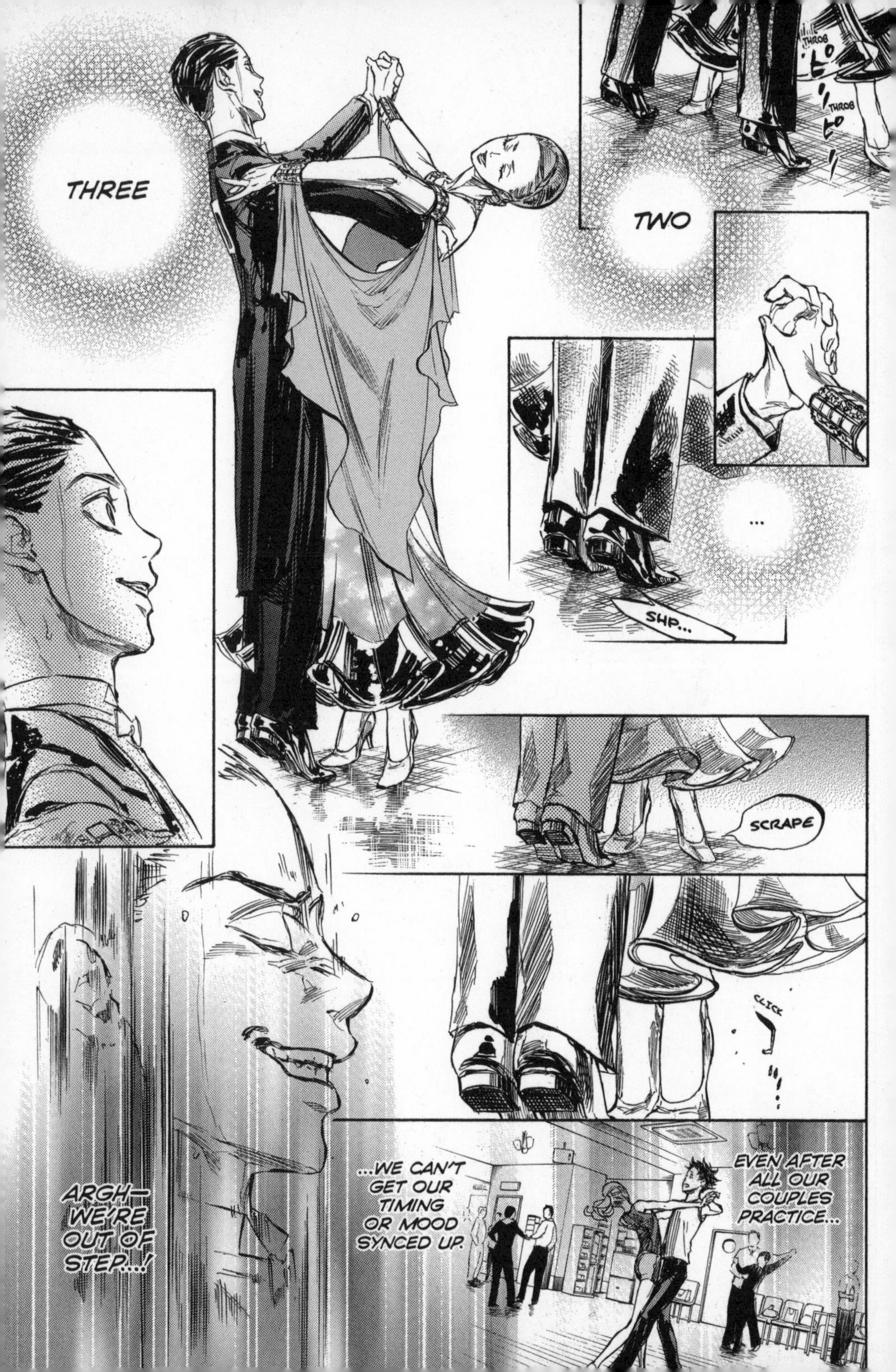
THROB
THROB
TWO
...
SHP...
THREE
SCRAPE
CLICK
EVEN AFTER ALL OUR COUPLES PRACTICE...
...WE CAN'T GET OUR TIMING OR MOOD SYNCED UP.
ARGH— WE'RE OUT OF STEP...!

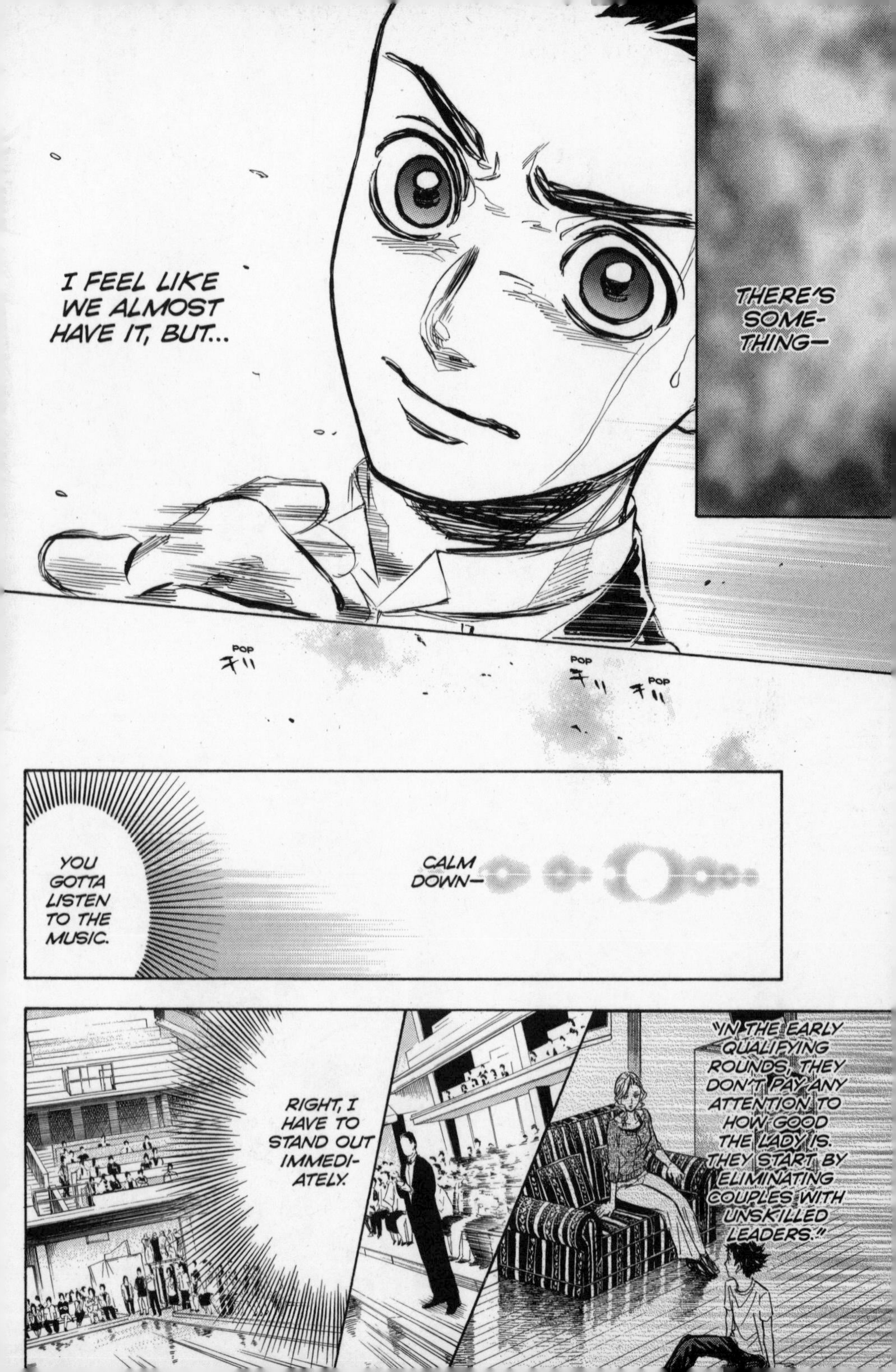
THERE'S SOMETHING—
I FEEL LIKE WE ALMOST HAVE IT, BUT...
POP
POP
POP
CALM DOWN—
YOU GOTTA LISTEN TO THE MUSIC.
"IN THE EARLY QUALIFYING ROUNDS, THEY DON'T PAY ANY ATTENTION TO HOW GOOD THE LADY IS. THEY START BY ELIMINATING COUPLES WITH UNSKILLED LEADERS."
RIGHT, I HAVE TO STAND OUT IMMEDIATELY.

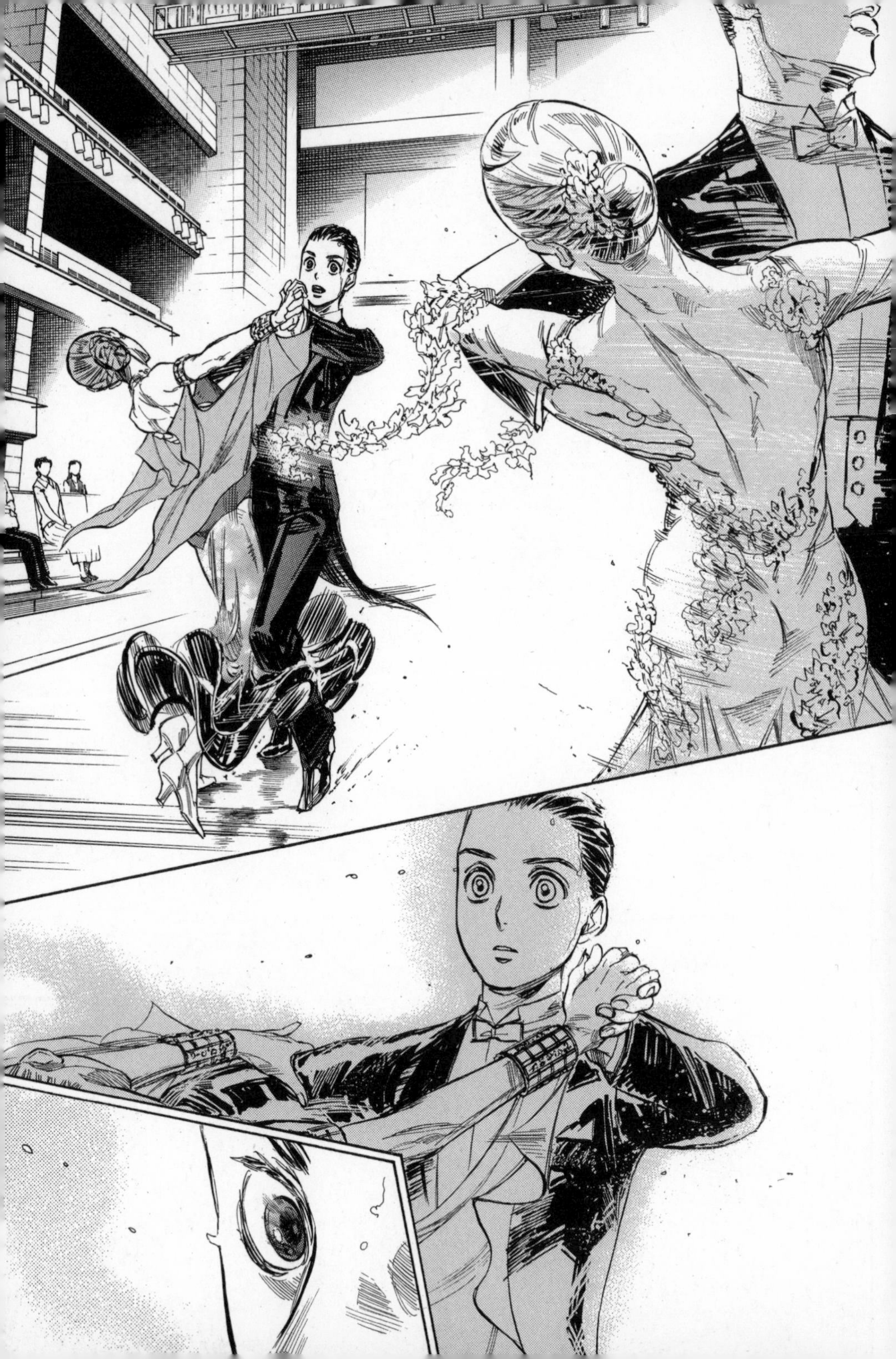

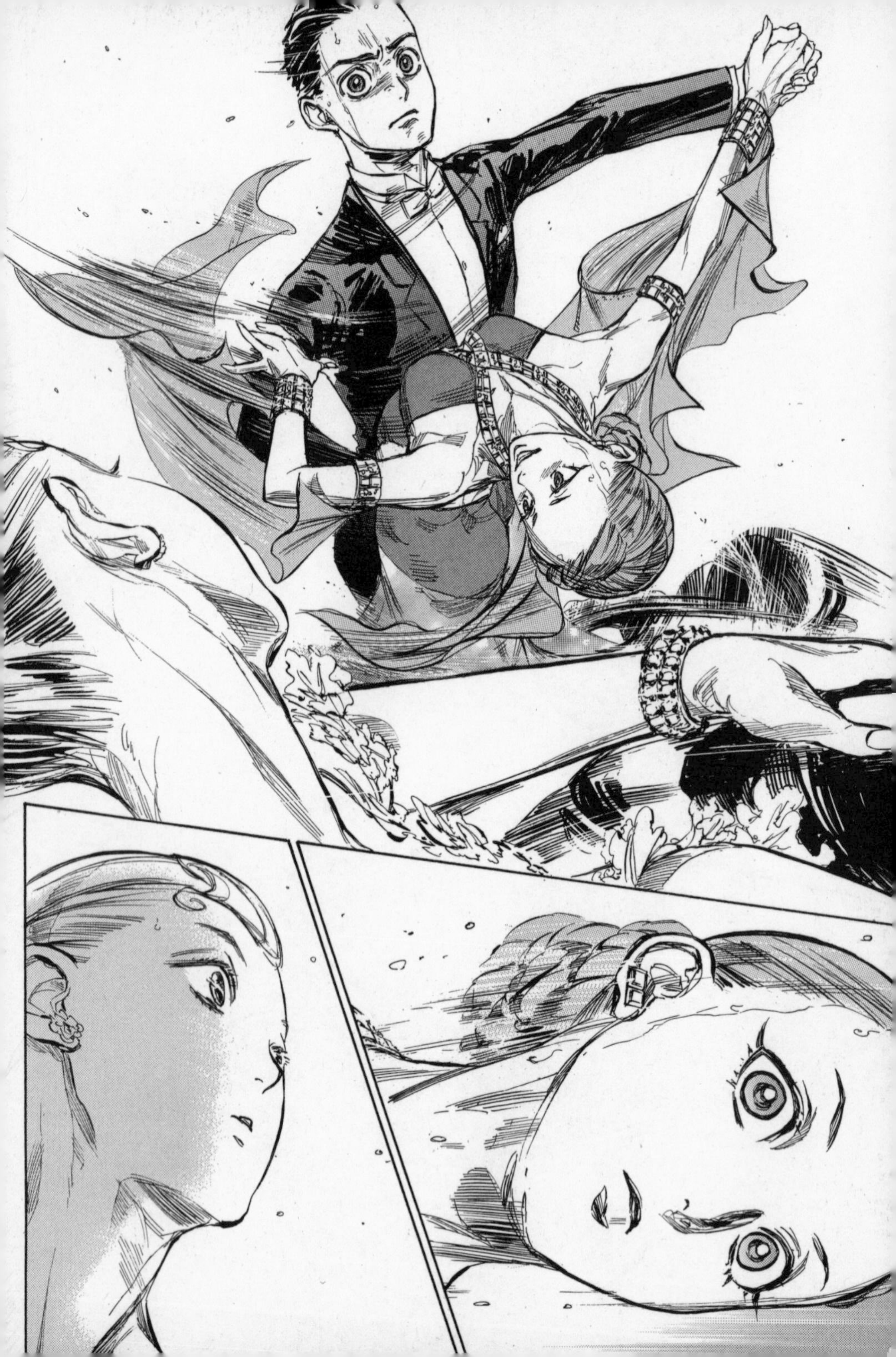

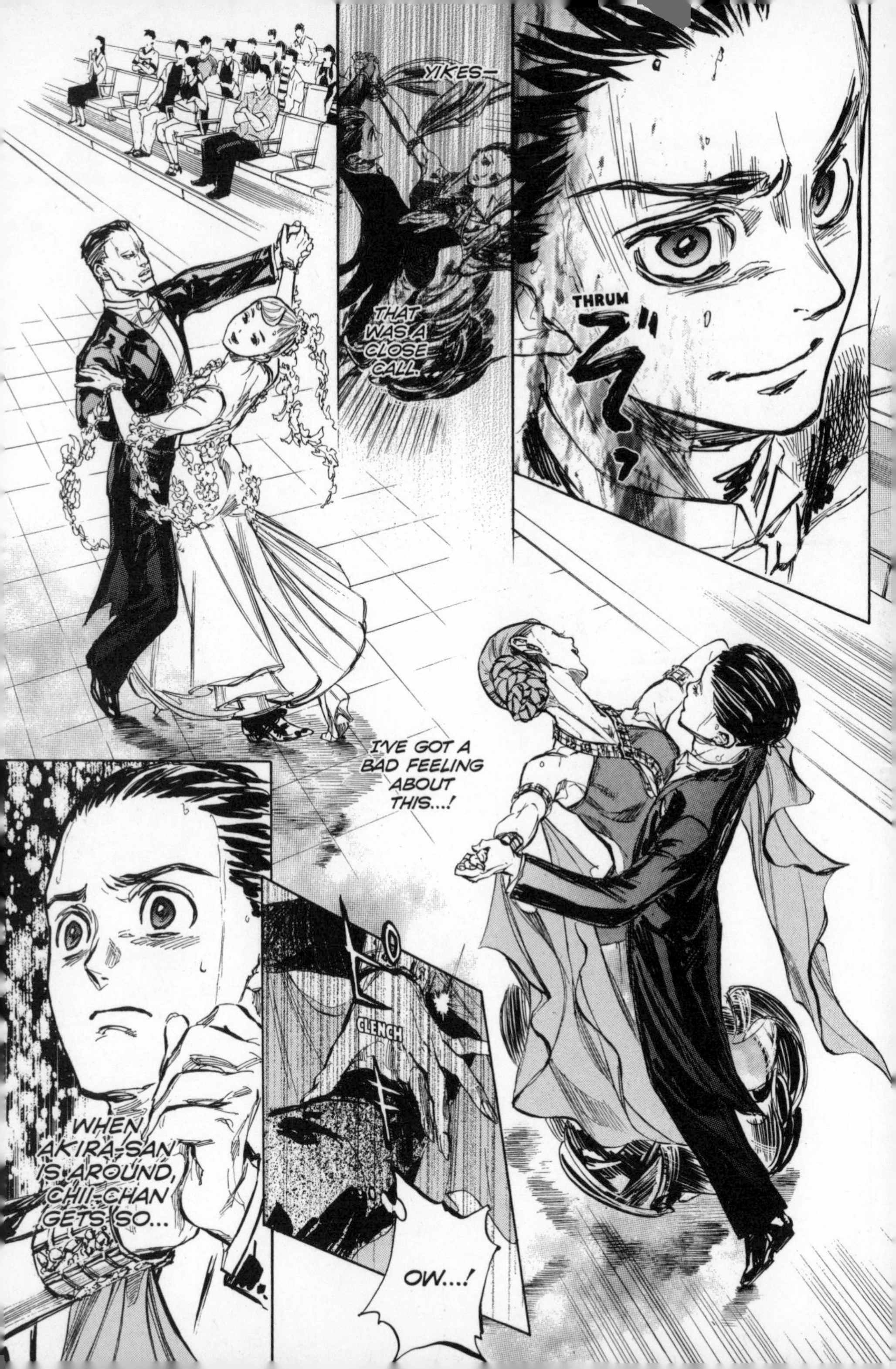
THRUM
YIKES—
THAT WAS A CLOSE CALL...
I'VE GOT A BAD FEELING ABOUT THIS...!
OW...!
CLENCH
WHEN AKIRA-SAN IS AROUND, CHII-CHAN GETS SO...

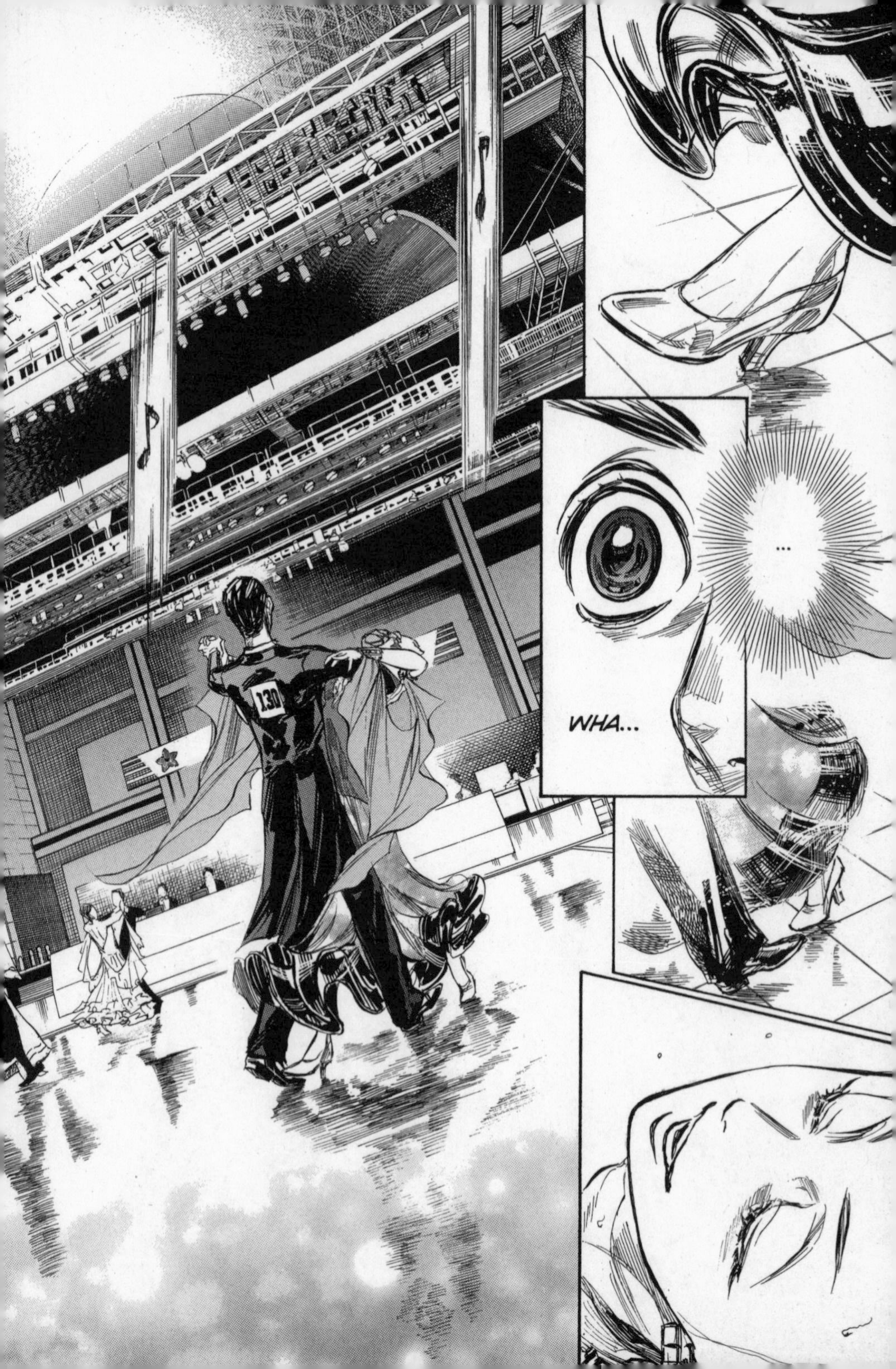
...
WHA...
130

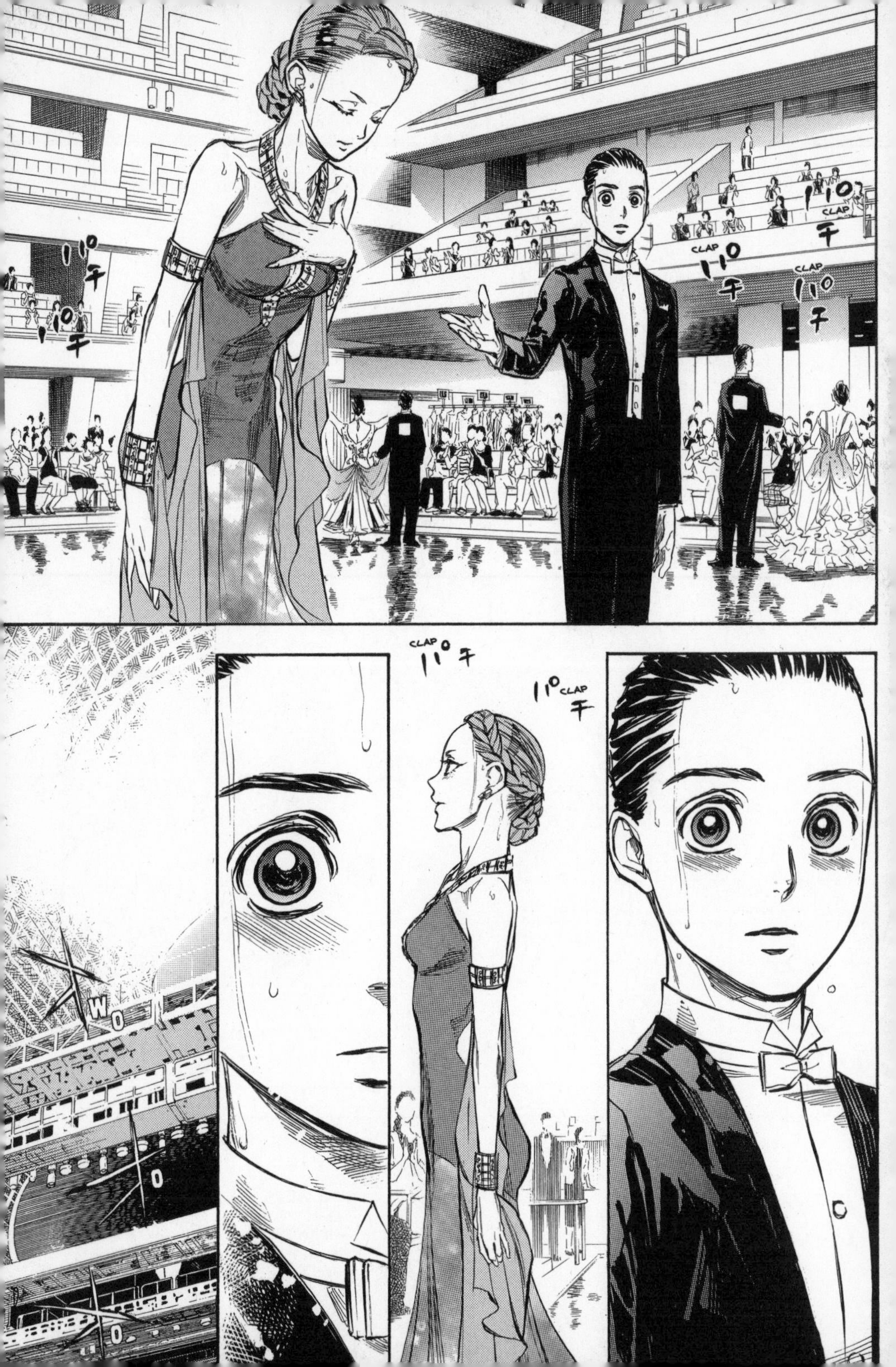

CLAP
パチ
CLAP
パチ
CLAP
パチ
パチ
パチ
CLAP
パチ
CLAP
パチ

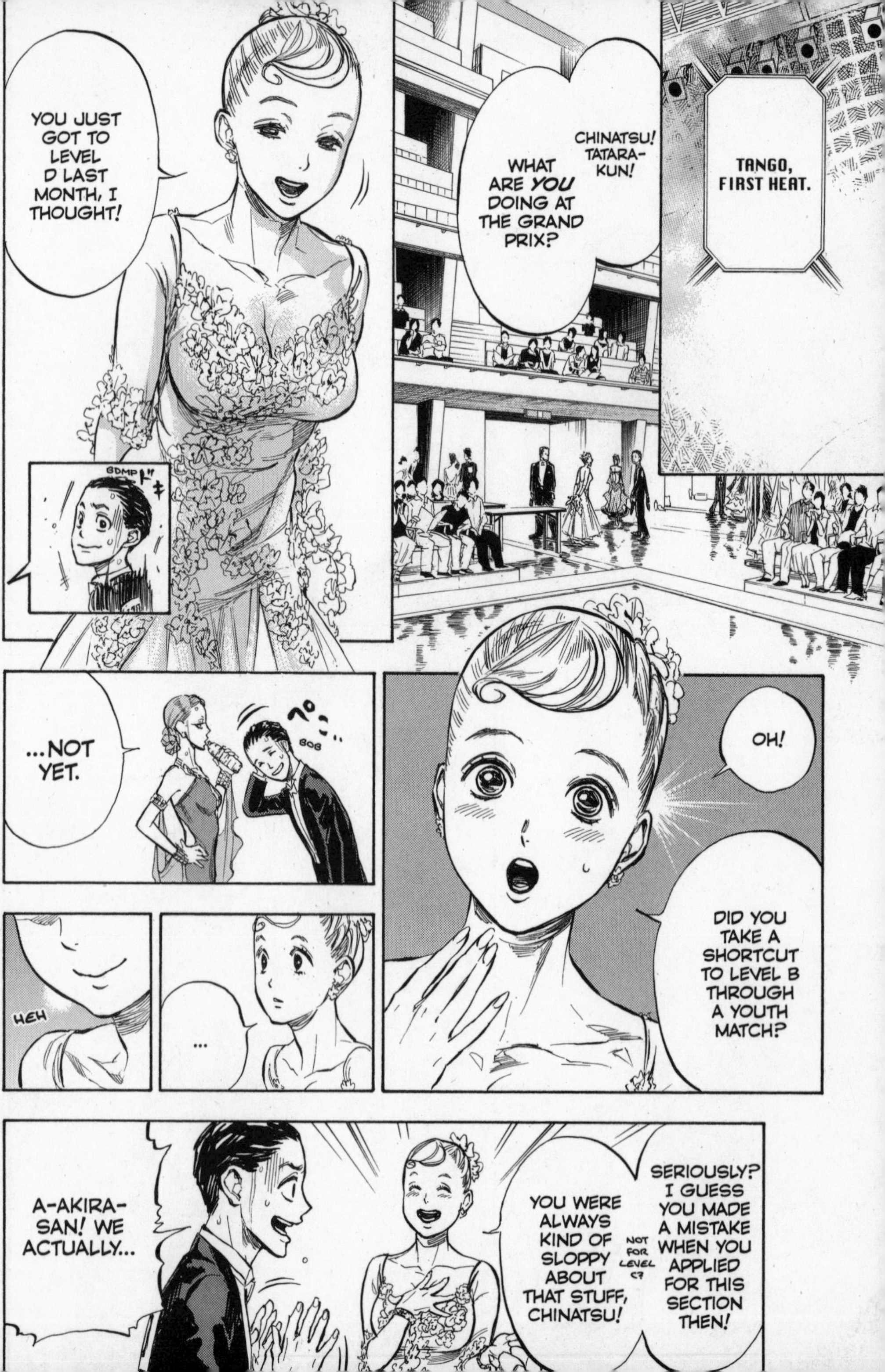
TANGO, FIRST HEAT.
CHINATSU! TATARA-KUN!
WHAT ARE *YOU* DOING AT THE GRAND PRIX?
YOU JUST GOT TO LEVEL D LAST MONTH, I THOUGHT!
BDMP
OH!
DID YOU TAKE A SHORTCUT TO LEVEL B THROUGH A YOUTH MATCH?
...NOT YET.
BOB
...
HEH
SERIOUSLY? I GUESS YOU MADE A MISTAKE WHEN YOU APPLIED FOR THIS SECTION THEN!
NOT FOR LEVEL C?
YOU WERE ALWAYS KIND OF SLOPPY ABOUT THAT STUFF, CHINATSU!
A-AKIRA-SAN! WE ACTUALLY...

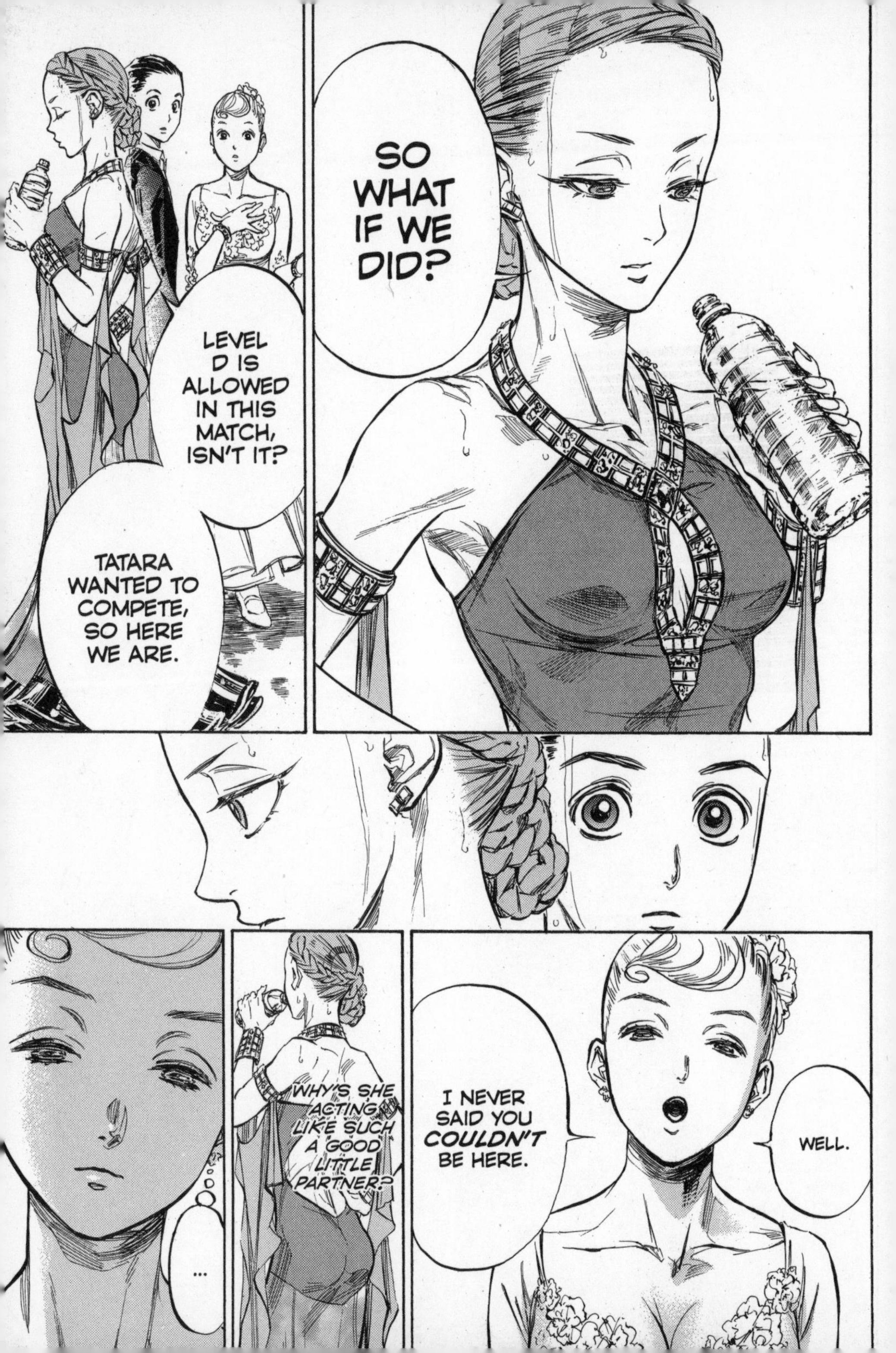
SO WHAT IF WE DID?
LEVEL D IS ALLOWED IN THIS MATCH, ISN'T IT?
TATARA WANTED TO COMPETE, SO HERE WE ARE.
WELL.
I NEVER SAID YOU COULDN'T BE HERE.
WHY'S SHE ACTING LIKE SUCH A GOOD LITTLE PARTNER?
...

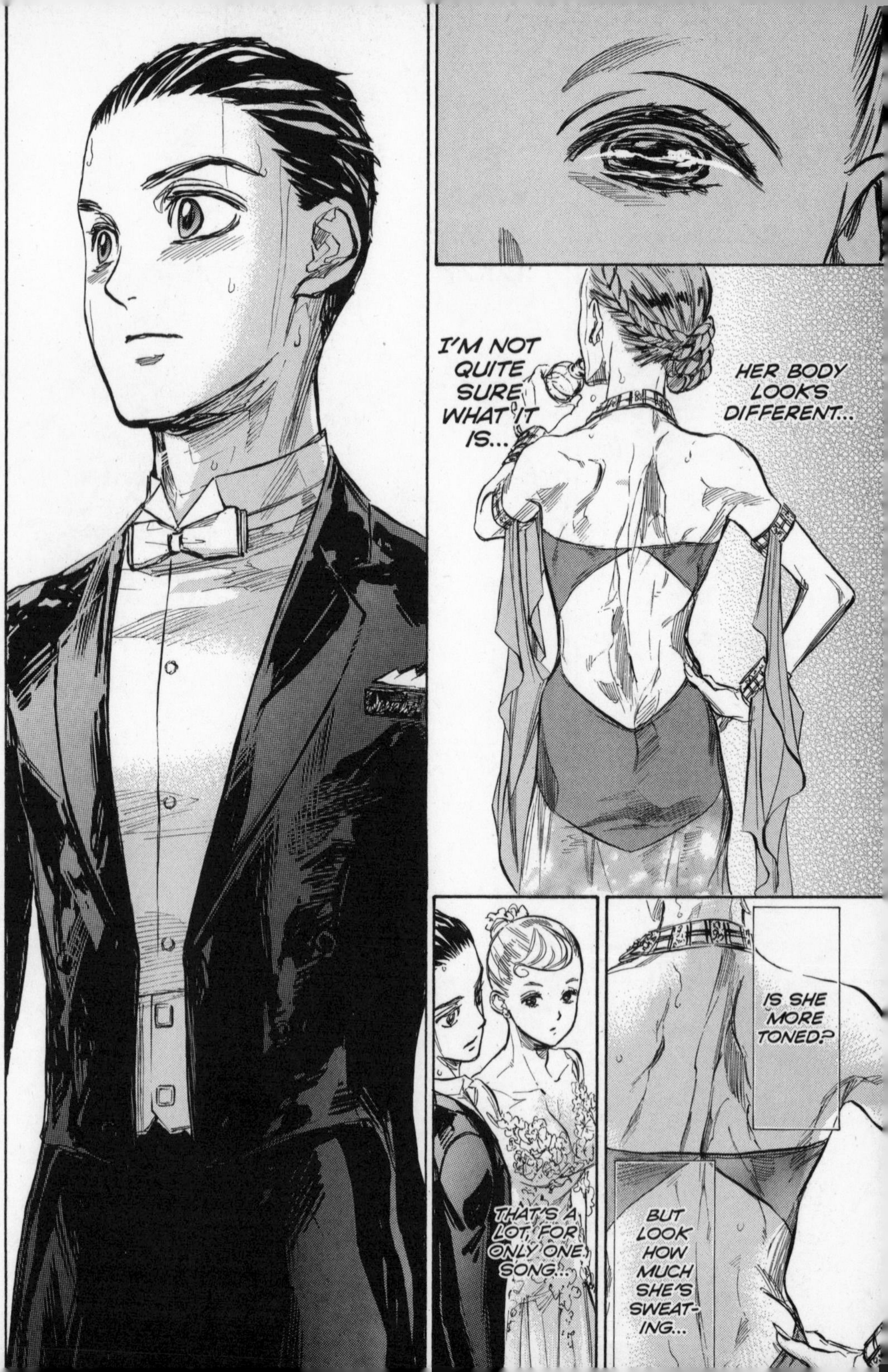
HER BODY LOOKS DIFFERENT...
I'M NOT QUITE SURE WHAT IT IS...
IS SHE MORE TONED?
BUT LOOK HOW MUCH SHE'S SWEAT-ING...
THAT'S A LOT, FOR ONLY ONE SONG...

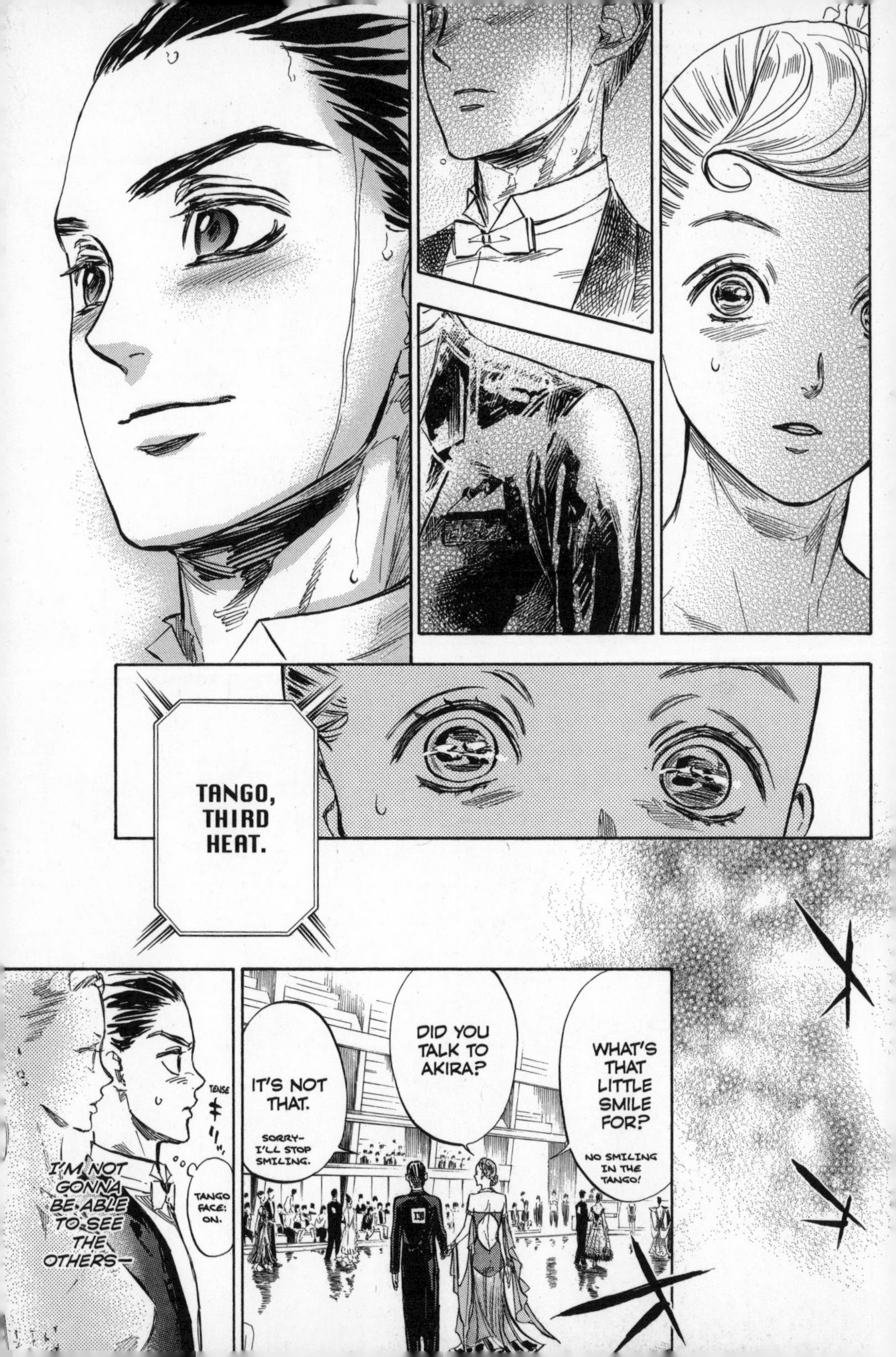
TANGO, THIRD HEAT.
WHAT'S THAT LITTLE SMILE FOR?
NO SMILING IN THE TANGO!
DID YOU TALK TO AKIRA?
IT'S NOT THAT.
SORRY— I'LL STOP SMILING.
TENSE
TANGO FACE: ON.
I'M NOT GONNA BE ABLE TO SEE THE OTHERS—

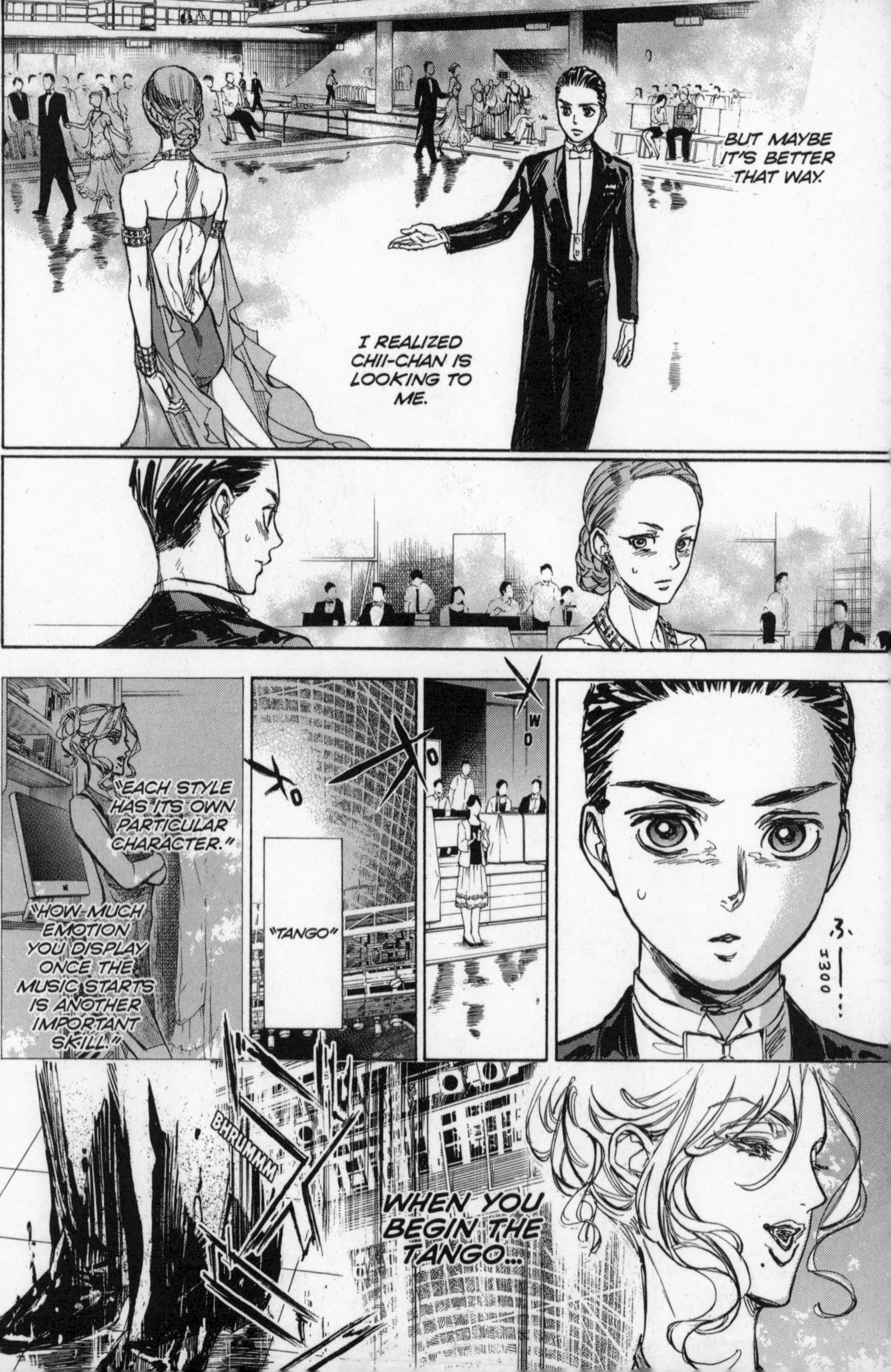
BUT MAYBE IT'S BETTER THAT WAY.
I REALIZED CHII-CHAN IS LOOKING TO ME.
"TANGO"
"EACH STYLE HAS ITS OWN PARTICULAR CHARACTER."
"HOW MUCH EMOTION YOU DISPLAY ONCE THE MUSIC STARTS IS ANOTHER IMPORTANT SKILL."
WHEN YOU BEGIN THE TANGO...
BHRUMMM

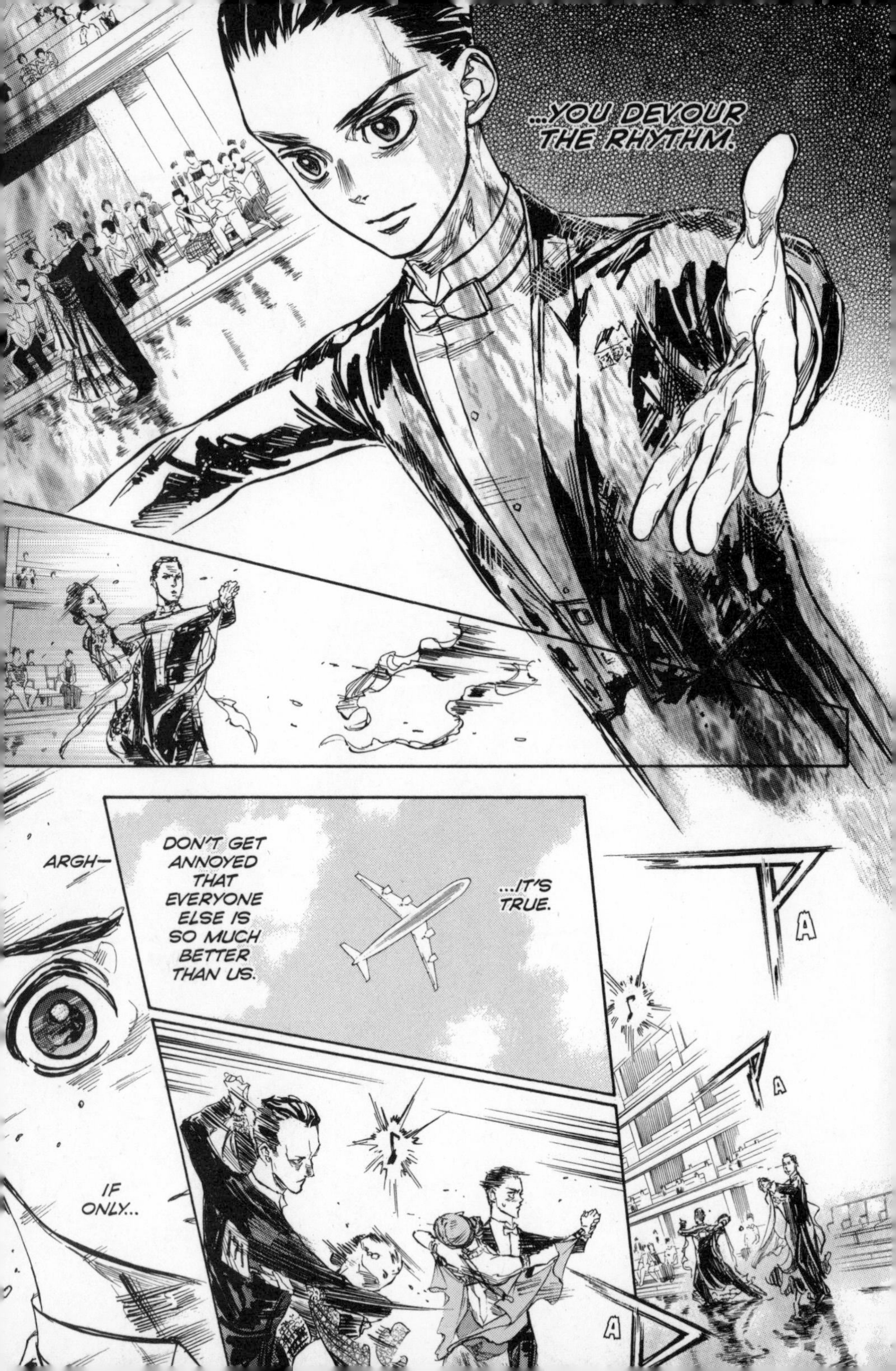
...YOU DEVOUR THE RHYTHM.
PA
...IT'S TRUE.
DON'T GET ANNOYED THAT EVERYONE ELSE IS SO MUCH BETTER THAN US.
ARGH—
PA
IF ONLY...
PA

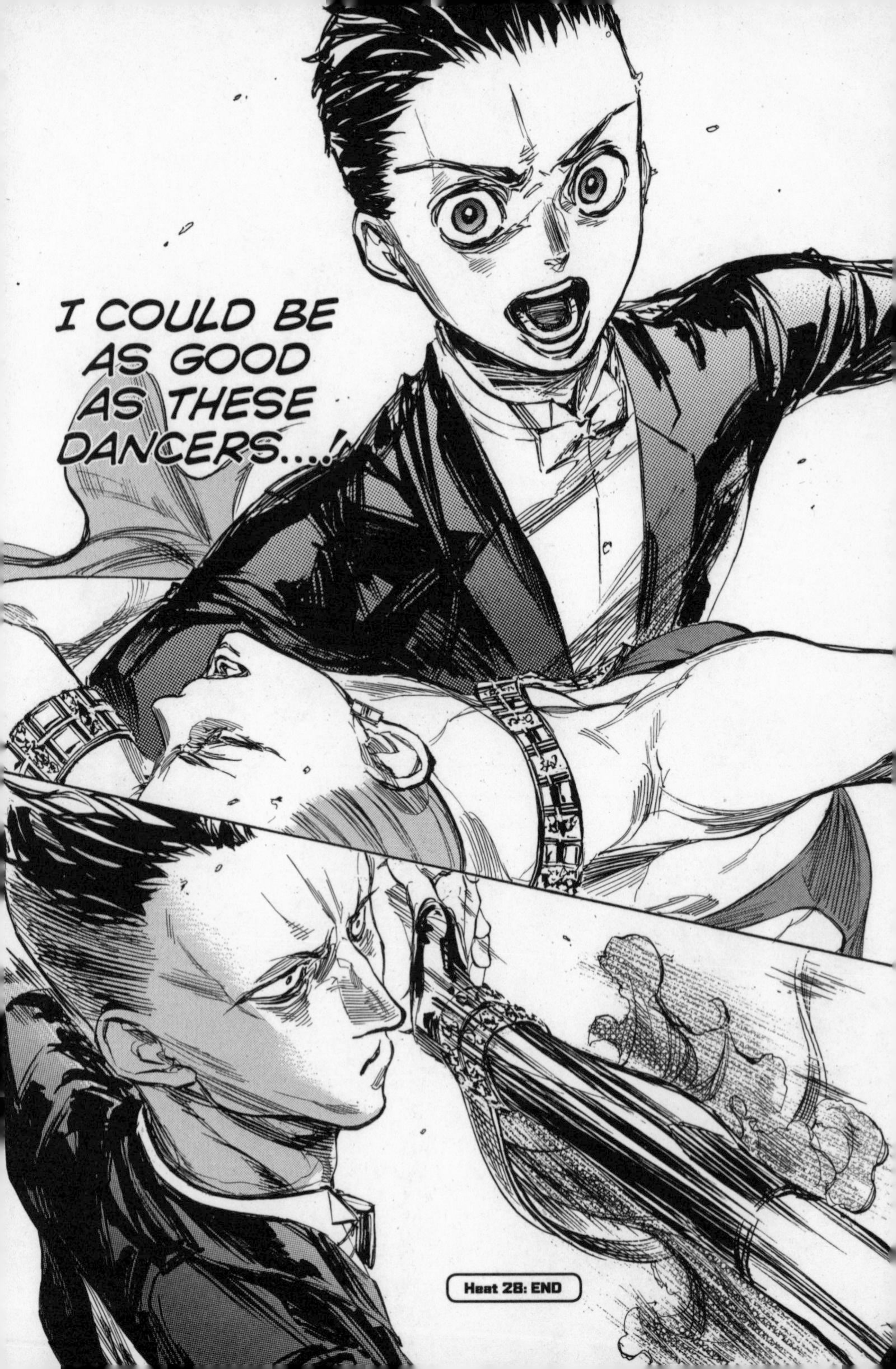

I COULD BE AS GOOD AS THESE DANCERS...!
Heat 28: END

WELCOME TO THE BALLROOM

Heat 29
Strange

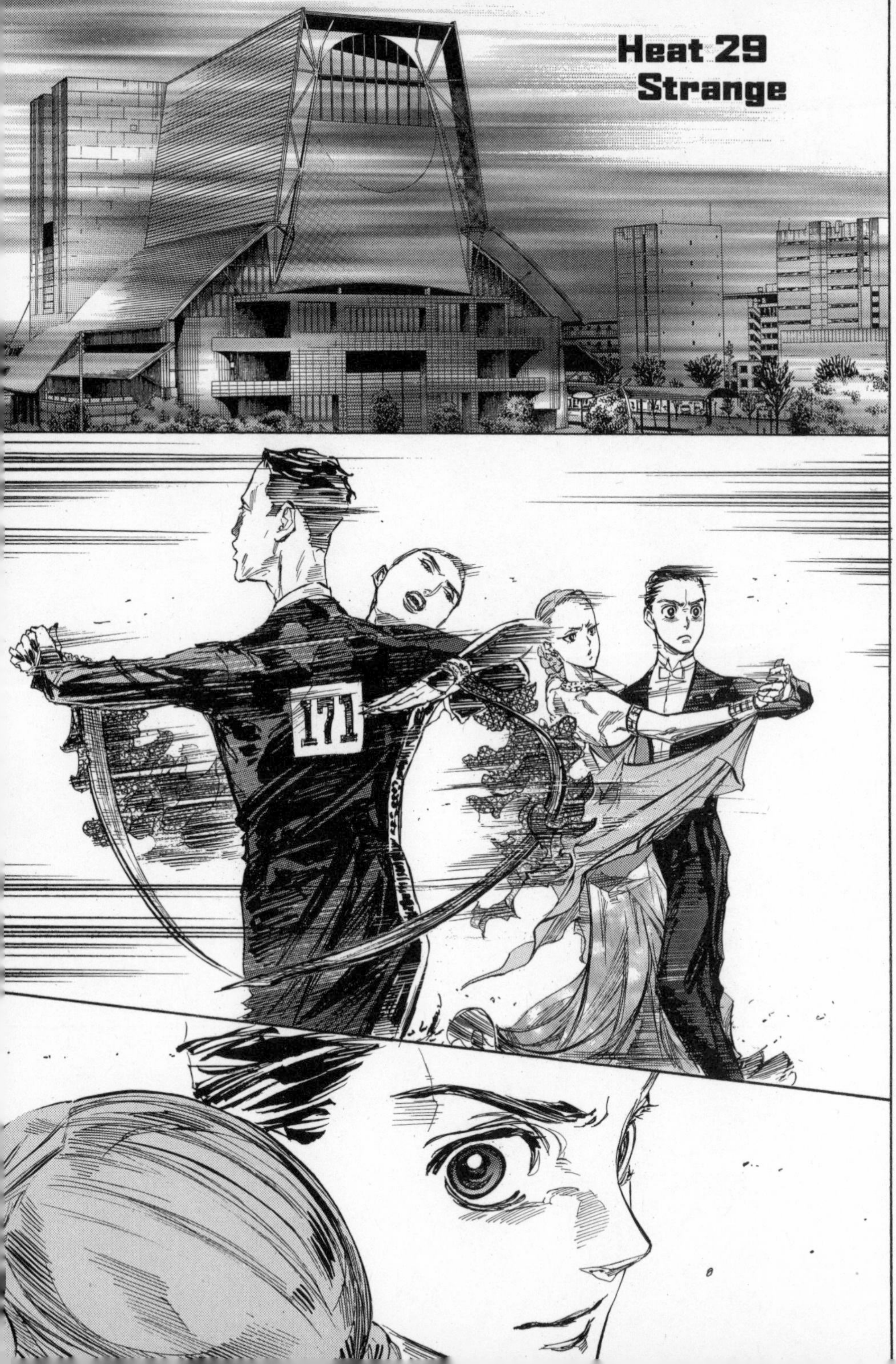
171

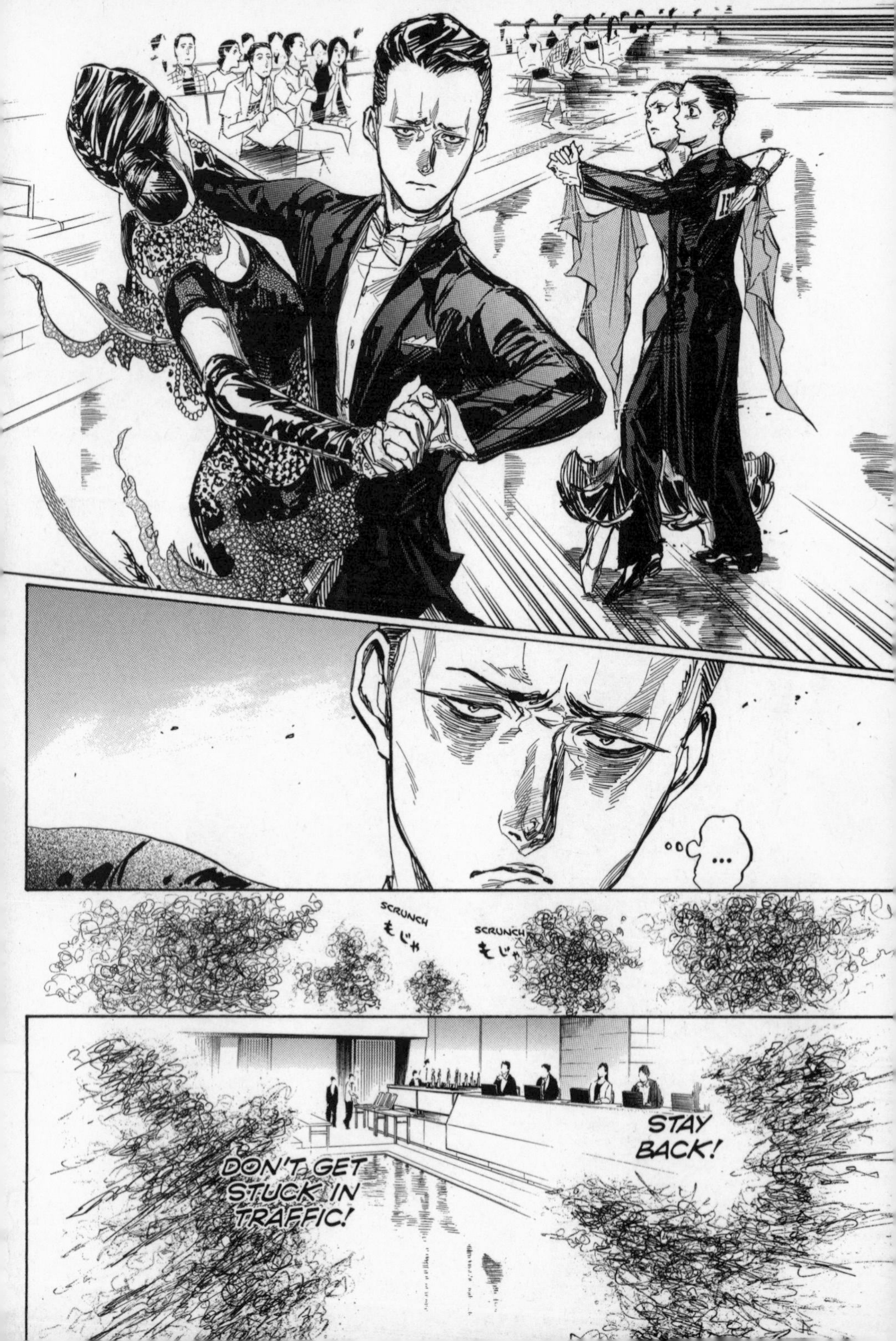
...
SCRUNCH もじゃ
SCRUNCH もじゃ
STAY BACK!
DON'T GET STUCK IN TRAFFIC!

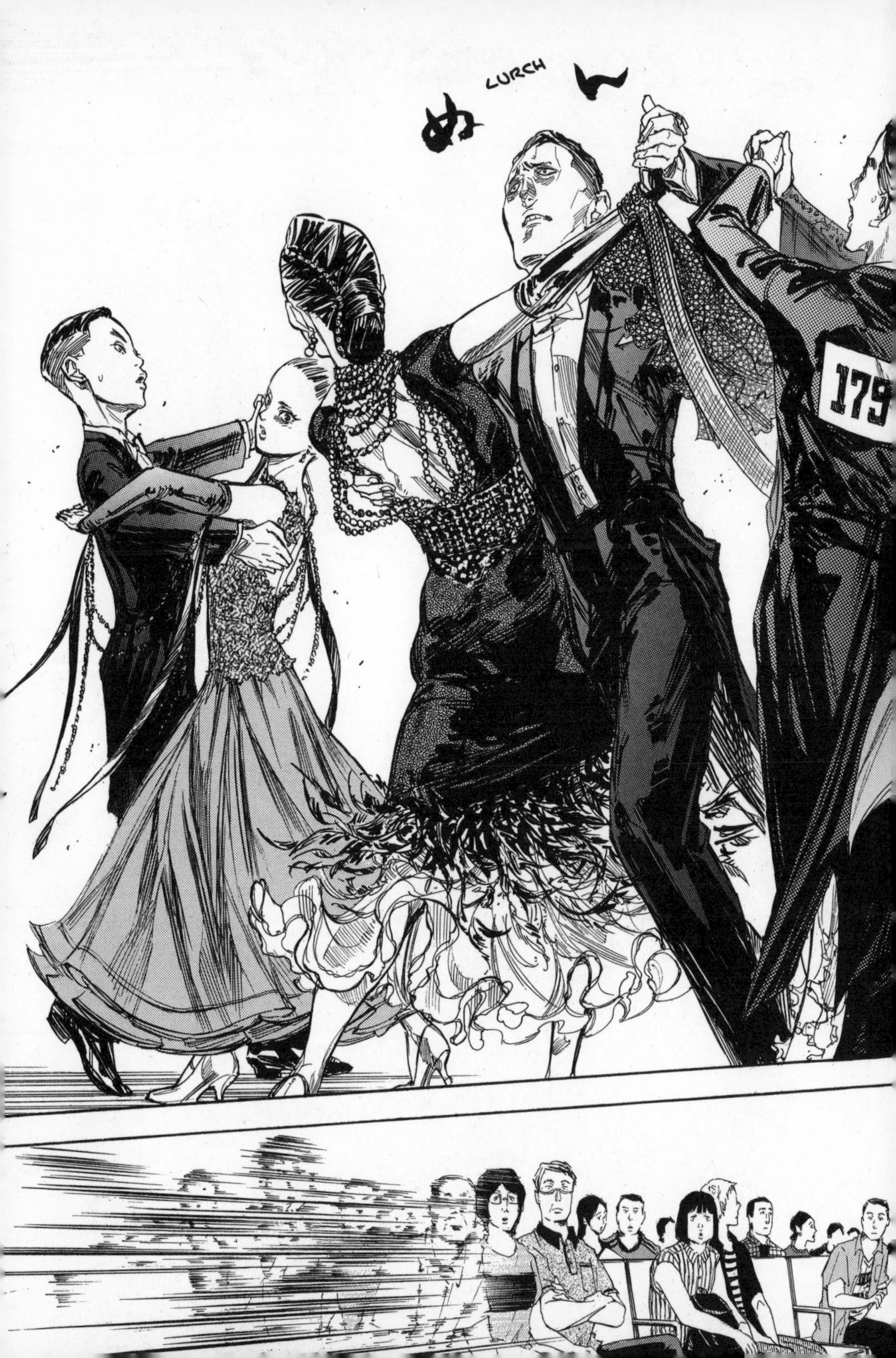

ぬん
LURCH
179

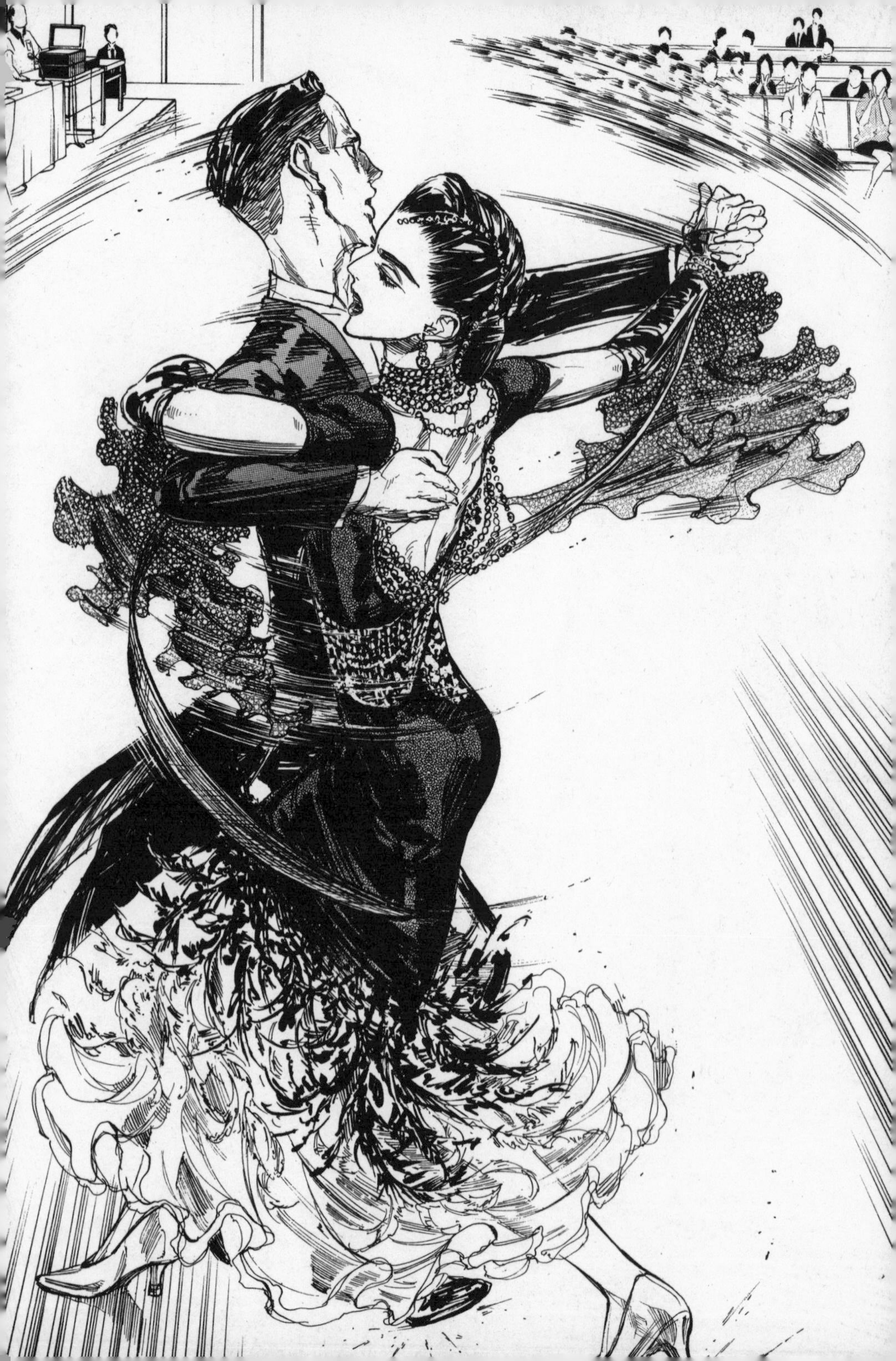

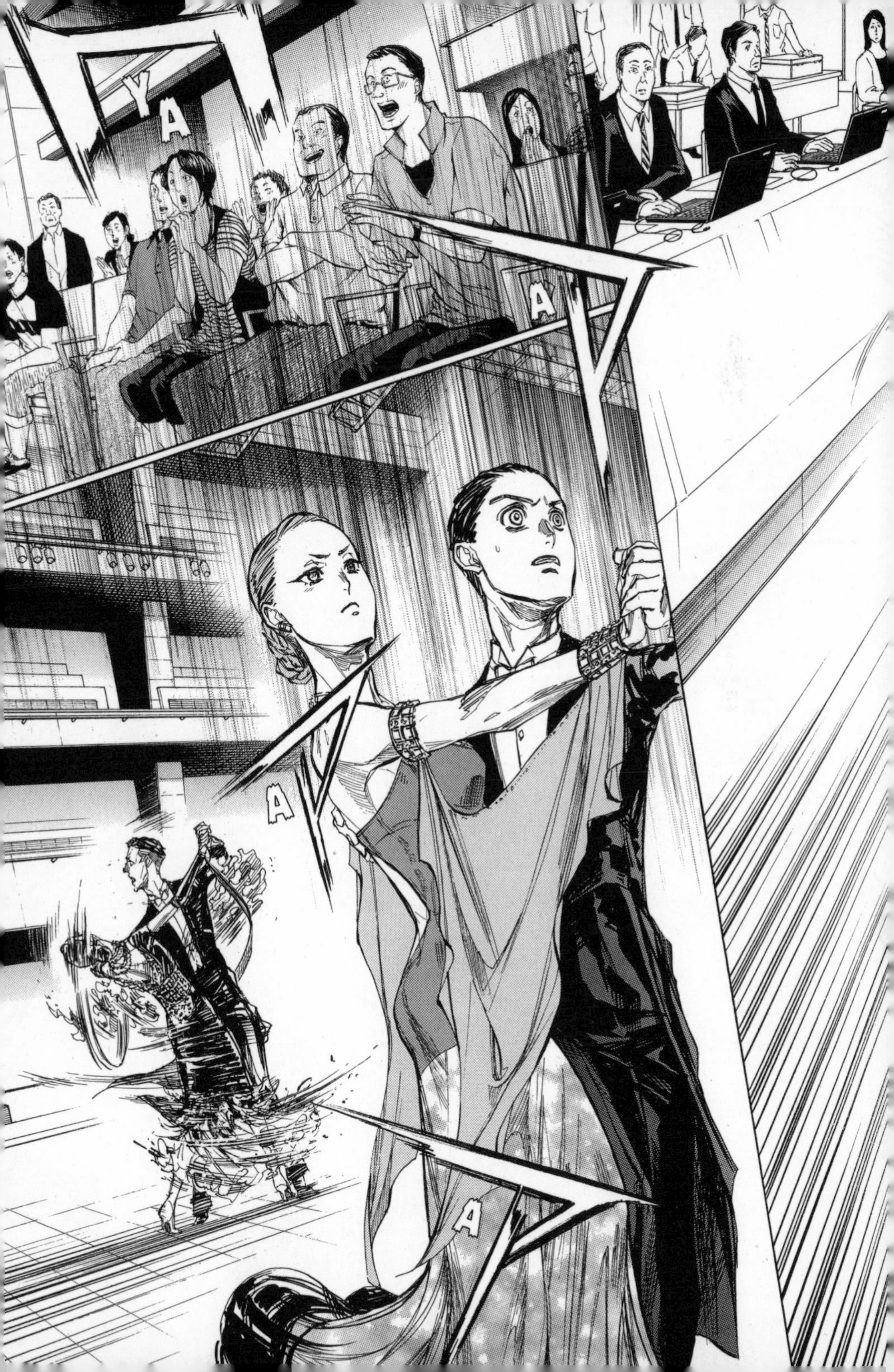
YA
A
A
A

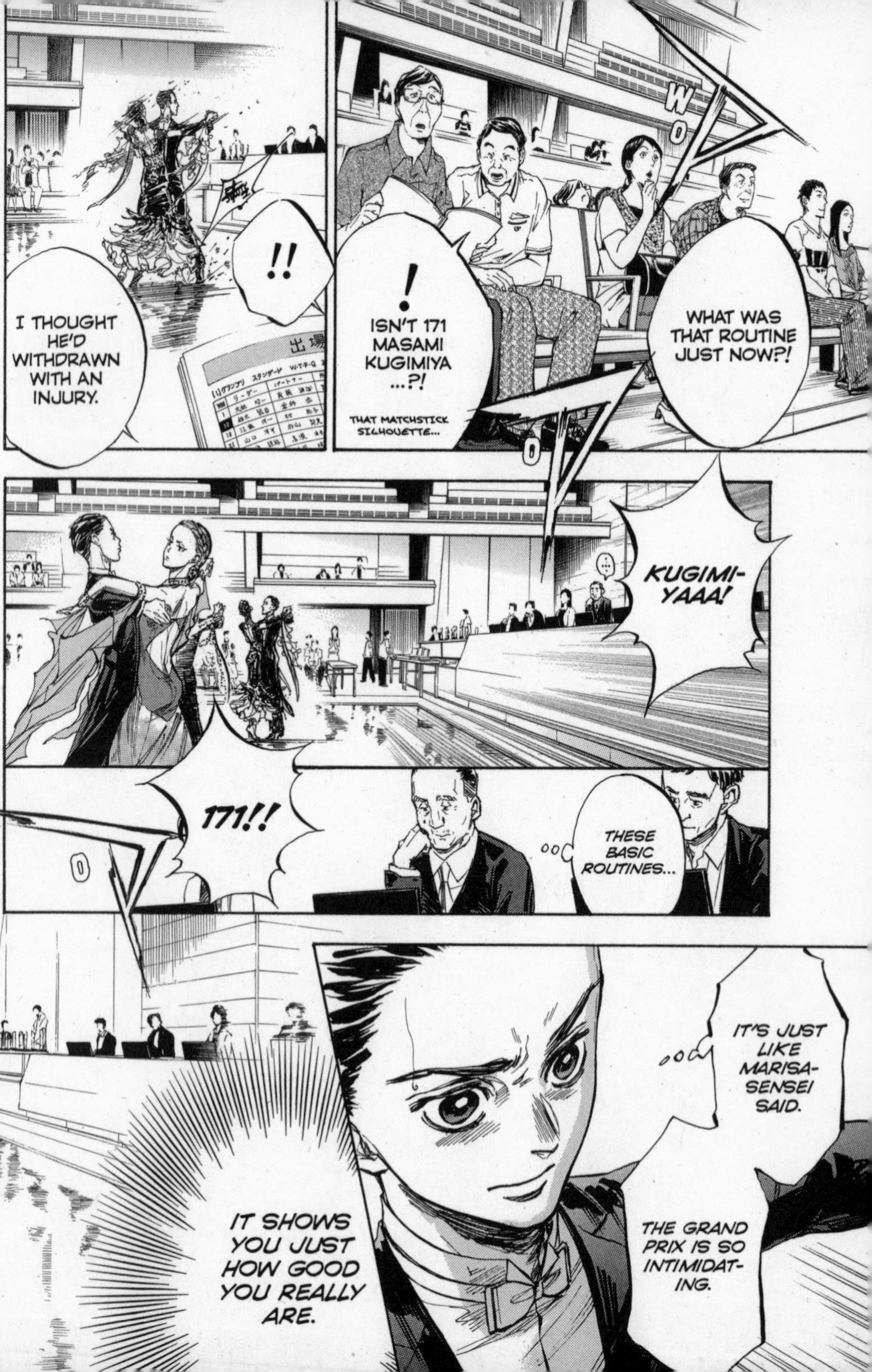
WHAT WAS THAT ROUTINE JUST NOW?!
WO
O
!
ISN'T 171 MASAMI KUGIMIYA ...?!
THAT MATCHSTICK SILHOUETTE...
!!
I THOUGHT HE'D WITHDRAWN WITH AN INJURY.
KUGIMI-YAAA!
THESE BASIC ROUTINES...
171!!
O
IT'S JUST LIKE MARISA-SENSEI SAID.
THE GRAND PRIX IS SO INTIMIDAT-ING.
IT SHOWS YOU JUST HOW GOOD YOU REALLY ARE.

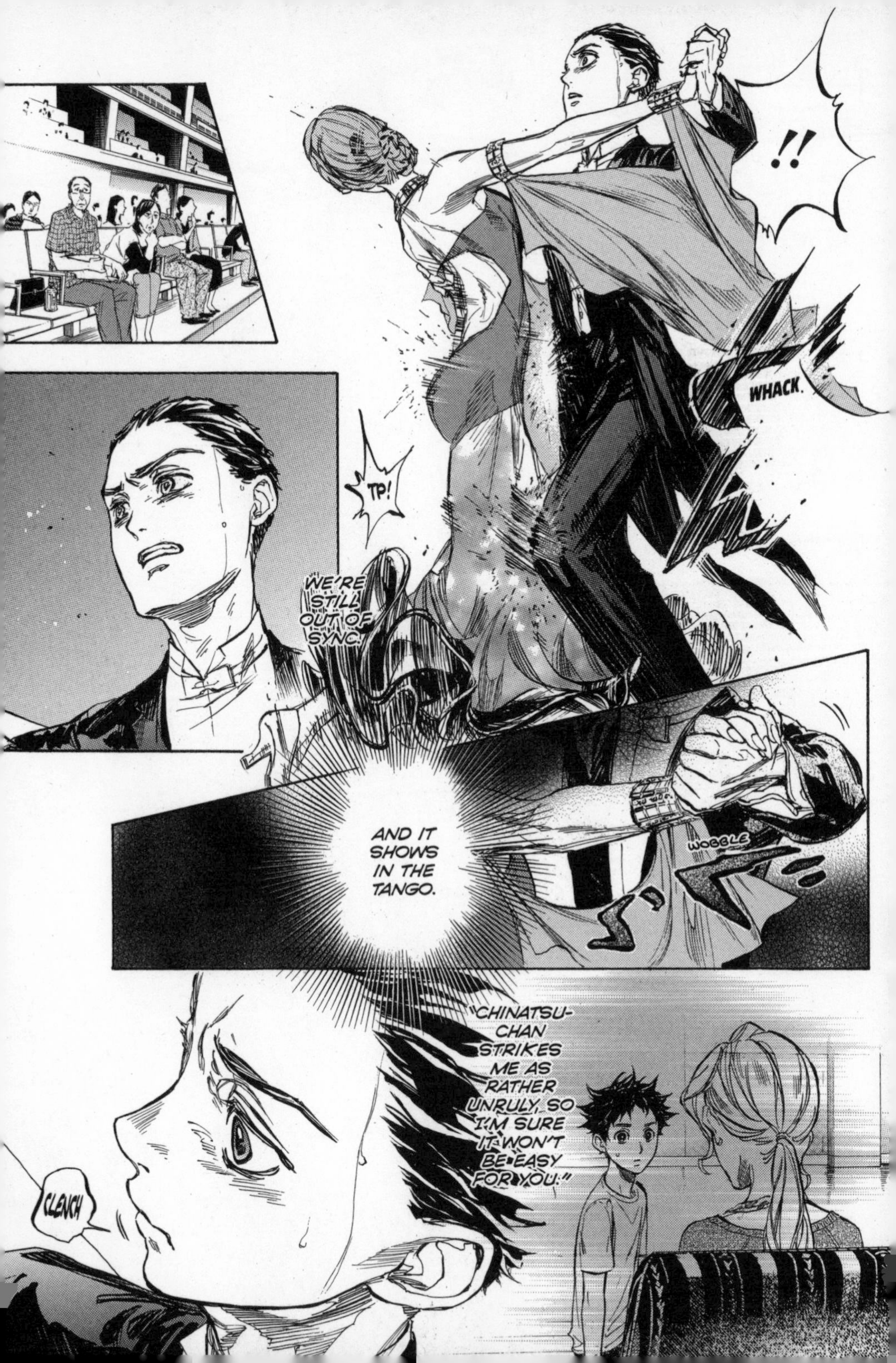
!!
WHACK
TP!
WE'RE STILL OUT OF SYNC.
WOBBLE
AND IT SHOWS IN THE TANGO.
"CHINATSU-CHAN STRIKES ME AS RATHER UNRULY, SO I'M SURE IT WON'T BE EASY FOR YOU."
CLENCH

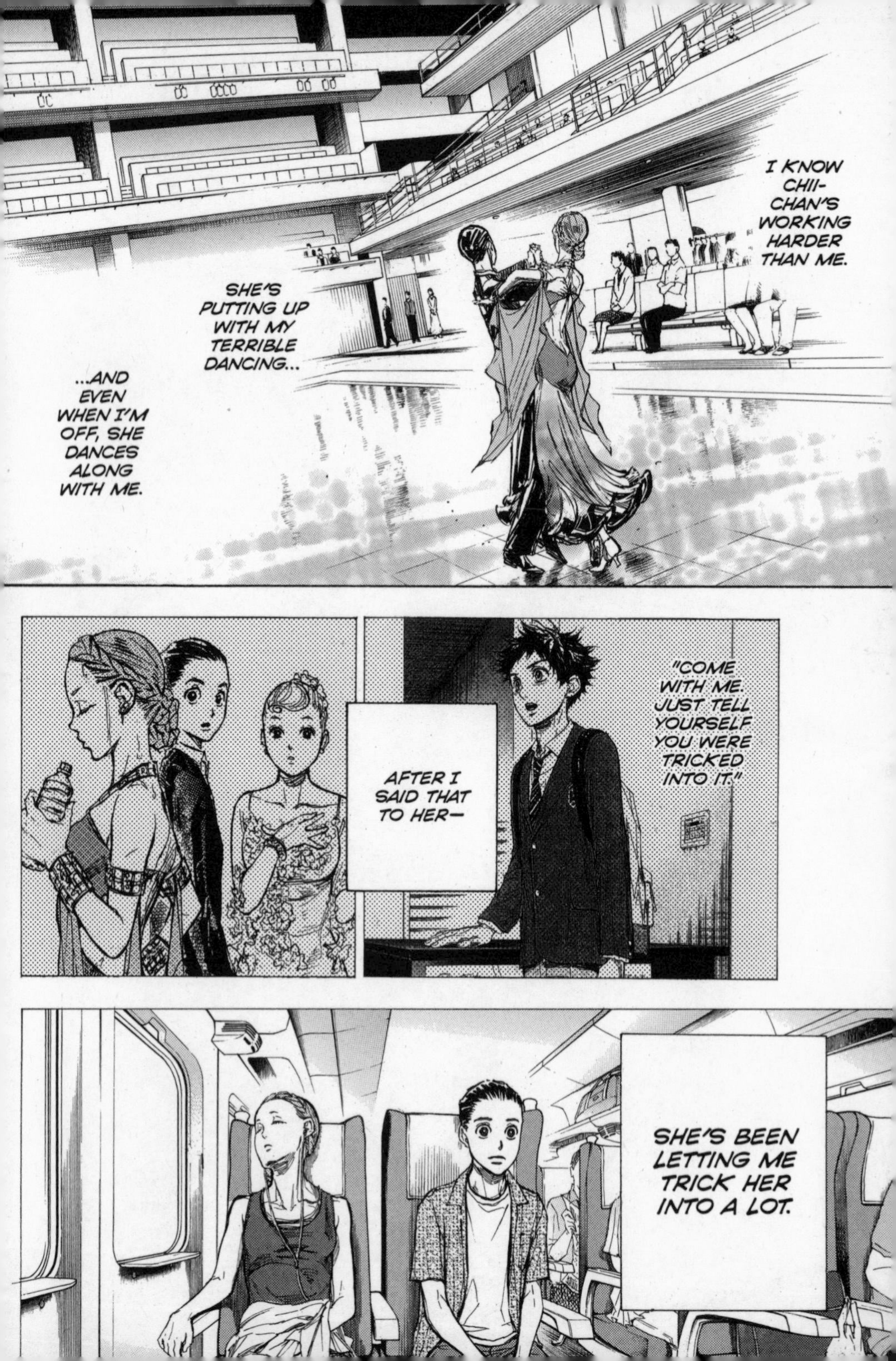
I KNOW CHII-CHAN'S WORKING HARDER THAN ME.
SHE'S PUTTING UP WITH MY TERRIBLE DANCING...
...AND EVEN WHEN I'M OFF, SHE DANCES ALONG WITH ME.
"COME WITH ME. JUST TELL YOURSELF YOU WERE TRICKED INTO IT."
AFTER I SAID THAT TO HER—
SHE'S BEEN LETTING ME TRICK HER INTO A LOT.

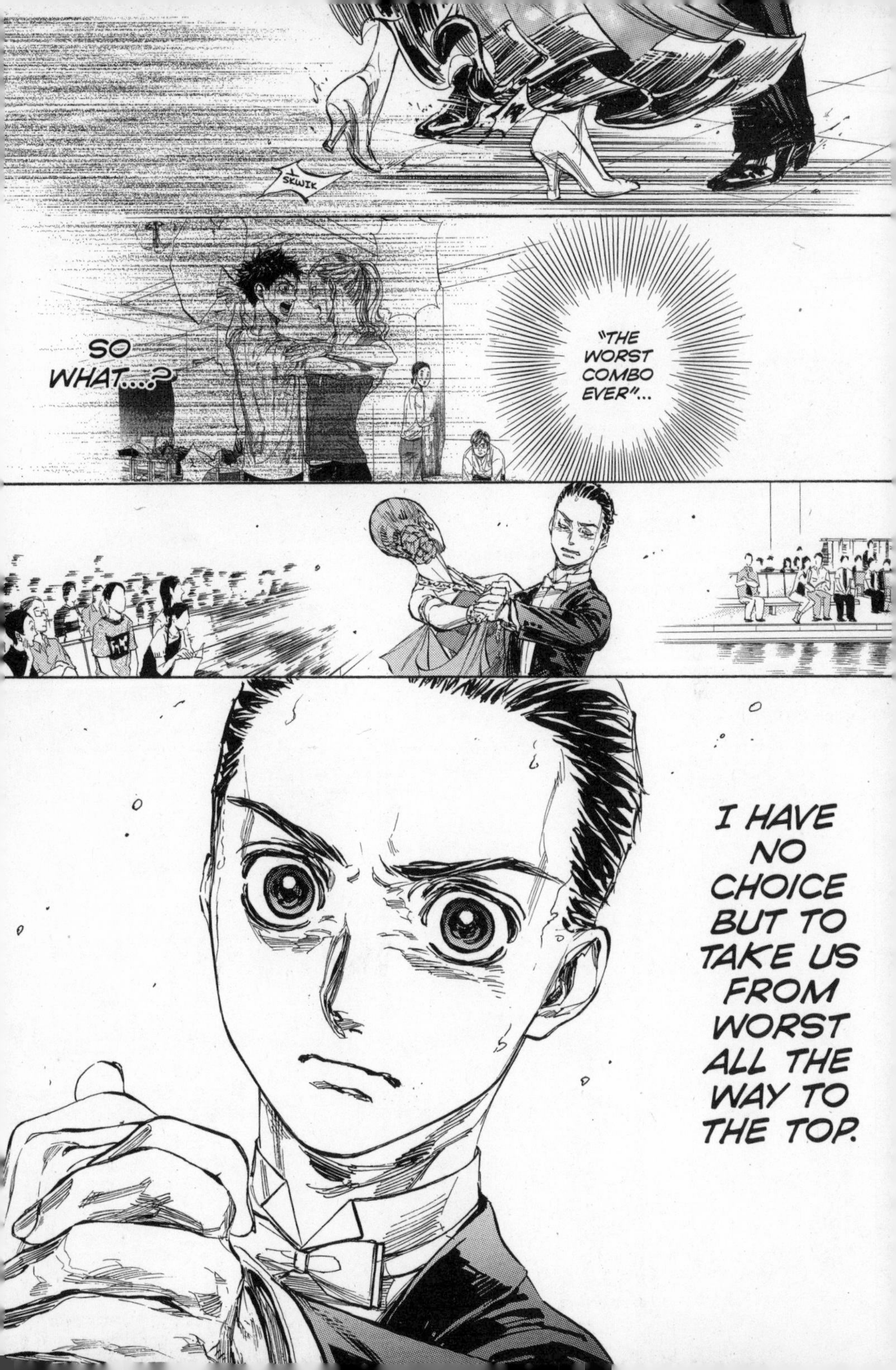
SKWIK
"THE WORST COMBO EVER"...
SO WHAT...?
I HAVE NO CHOICE BUT TO TAKE US FROM WORST ALL THE WAY TO THE TOP.

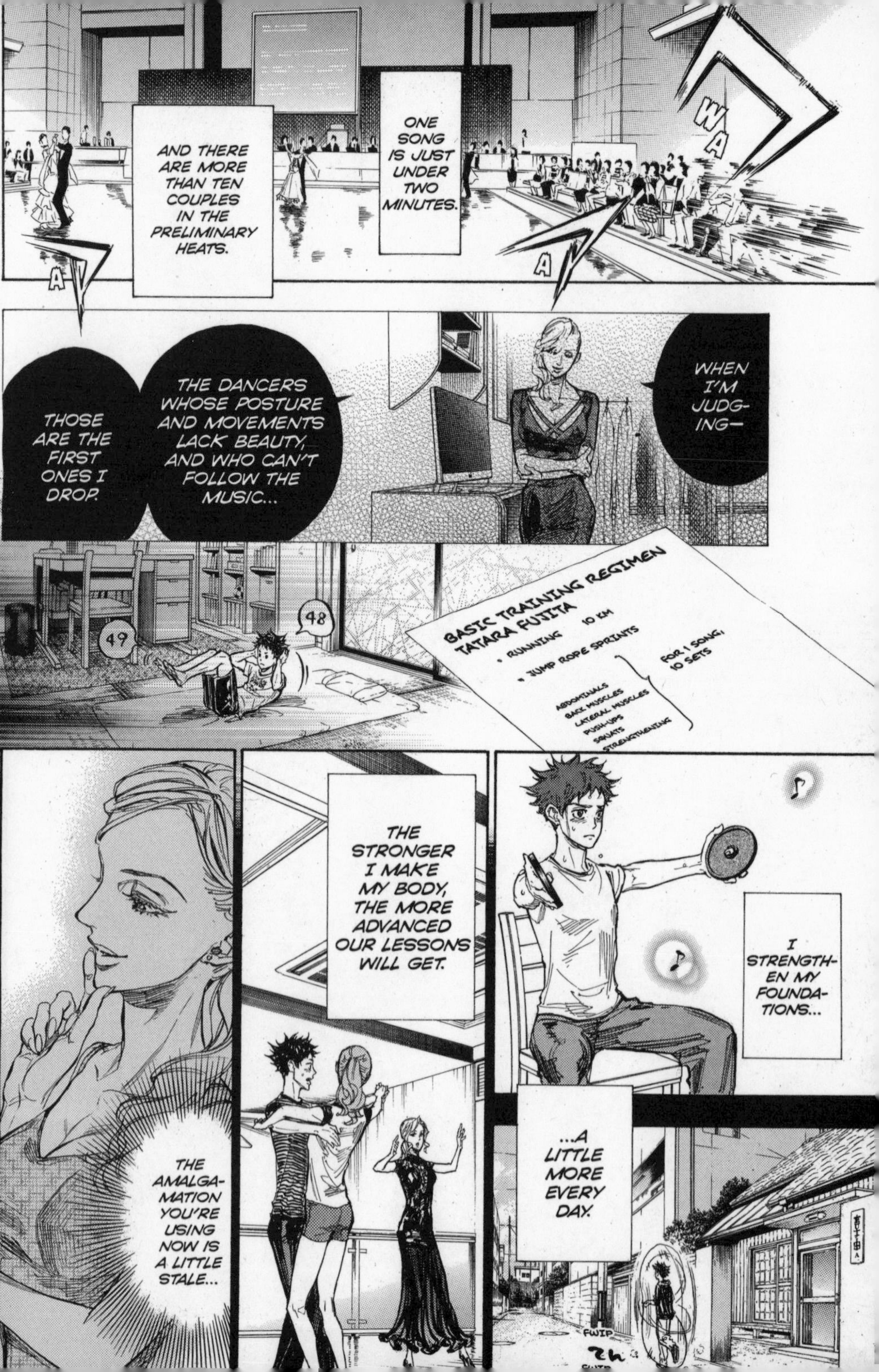
WA
ONE SONG IS JUST UNDER TWO MINUTES.
AND THERE ARE MORE THAN TEN COUPLES IN THE PRELIMINARY HEATS.
A
A
WHEN I'M JUDGING—
THE DANCERS WHOSE POSTURE AND MOVEMENTS LACK BEAUTY, AND WHO CAN'T FOLLOW THE MUSIC...
THOSE ARE THE FIRST ONES I DROP.
BASIC TRAINING REGIMEN
TATARA FUJITA
• RUNNING 10 KM
• JUMP ROPE SPRINTS
ABDOMINALS
BACK MUSCLES
LATERAL MUSCLES
PUSH-UPS
SQUATS
STRENGTHENING
FOR 1 SONG, 10 SETS
48
49
I STRENGTHEN MY FOUNDATIONS...
...A LITTLE MORE EVERY DAY.
FWIP
THE STRONGER I MAKE MY BODY, THE MORE ADVANCED OUR LESSONS WILL GET.
THE AMALGAMATION YOU'RE USING NOW IS A LITTLE STALE...

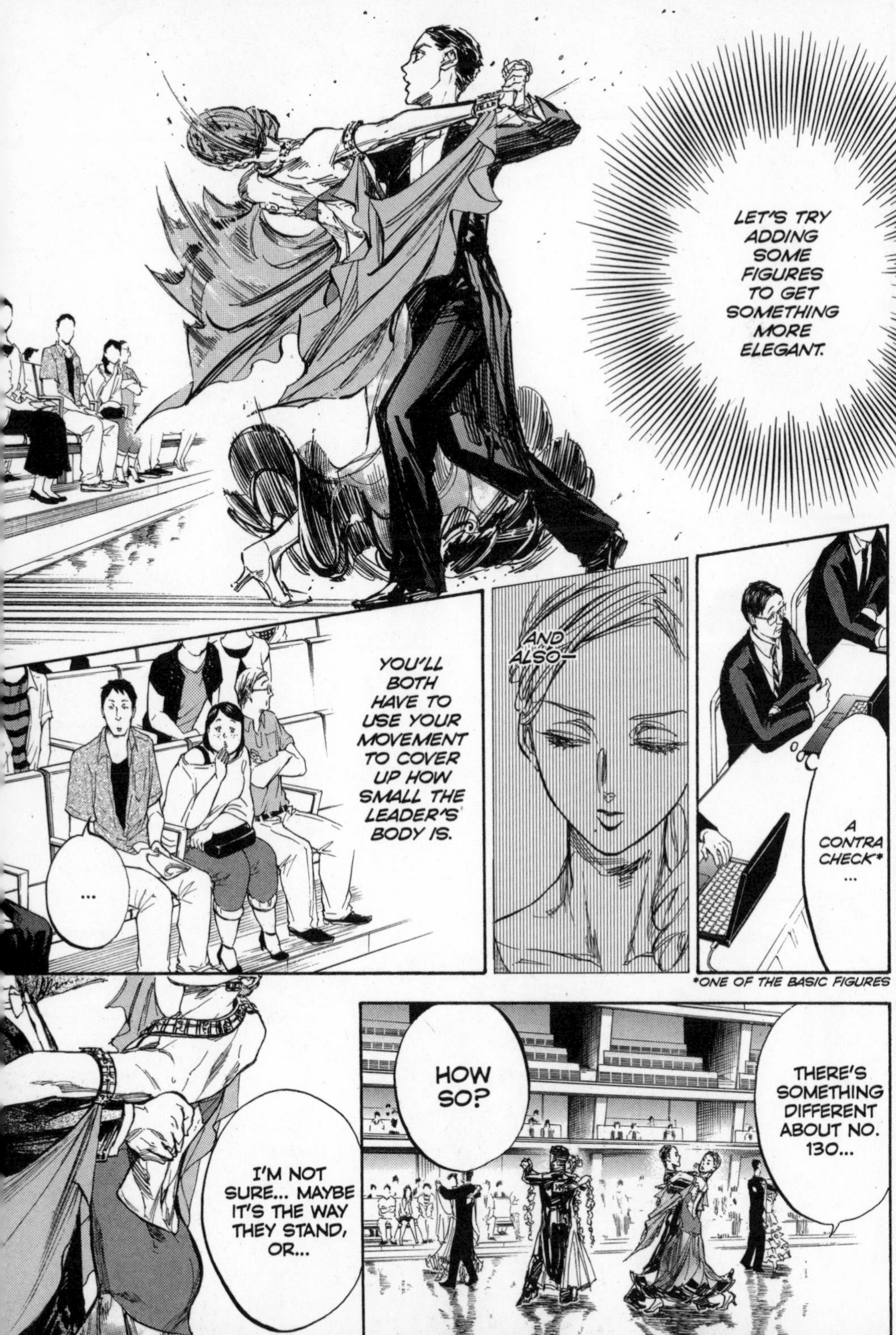
LET'S TRY ADDING SOME FIGURES TO GET SOMETHING MORE ELEGANT.
A CONTRA CHECK* ...
AND ALSO—
YOU'LL BOTH HAVE TO USE YOUR MOVEMENT TO COVER UP HOW SMALL THE LEADER'S BODY IS.
...
*ONE OF THE BASIC FIGURES
THERE'S SOMETHING DIFFERENT ABOUT NO. 130...
HOW SO?
I'M NOT SURE... MAYBE IT'S THE WAY THEY STAND, OR...

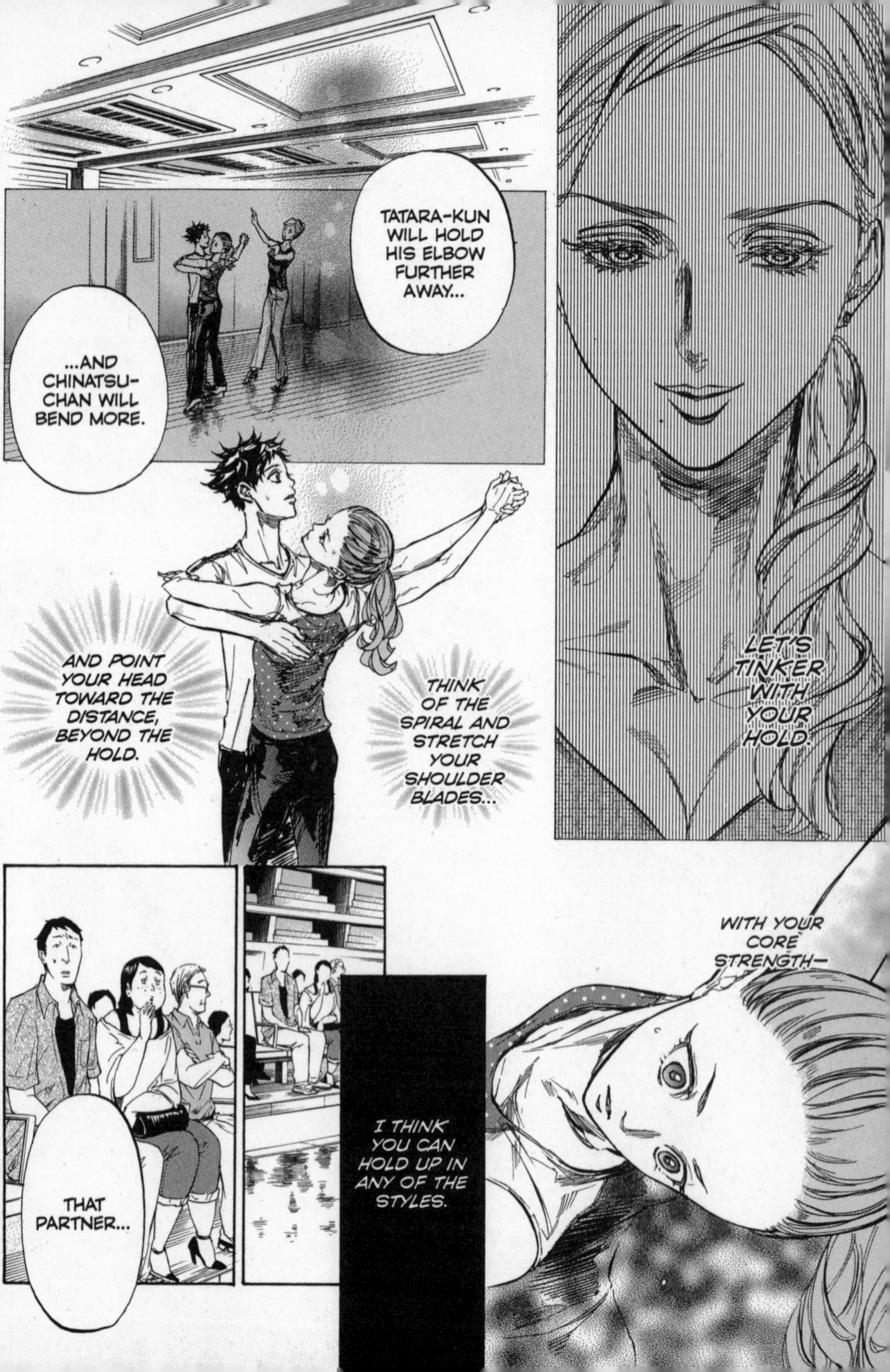

LET'S TINKER WITH YOUR HOLD.
TATARA-KUN WILL HOLD HIS ELBOW FURTHER AWAY...
...AND CHINATSU-CHAN WILL BEND MORE.
THINK OF THE SPIRAL AND STRETCH YOUR SHOULDER BLADES...
AND POINT YOUR HEAD TOWARD THE DISTANCE, BEYOND THE HOLD.
WITH YOUR CORE STRENGTH—
I THINK YOU CAN HOLD UP IN ANY OF THE STYLES.
THAT PARTNER...

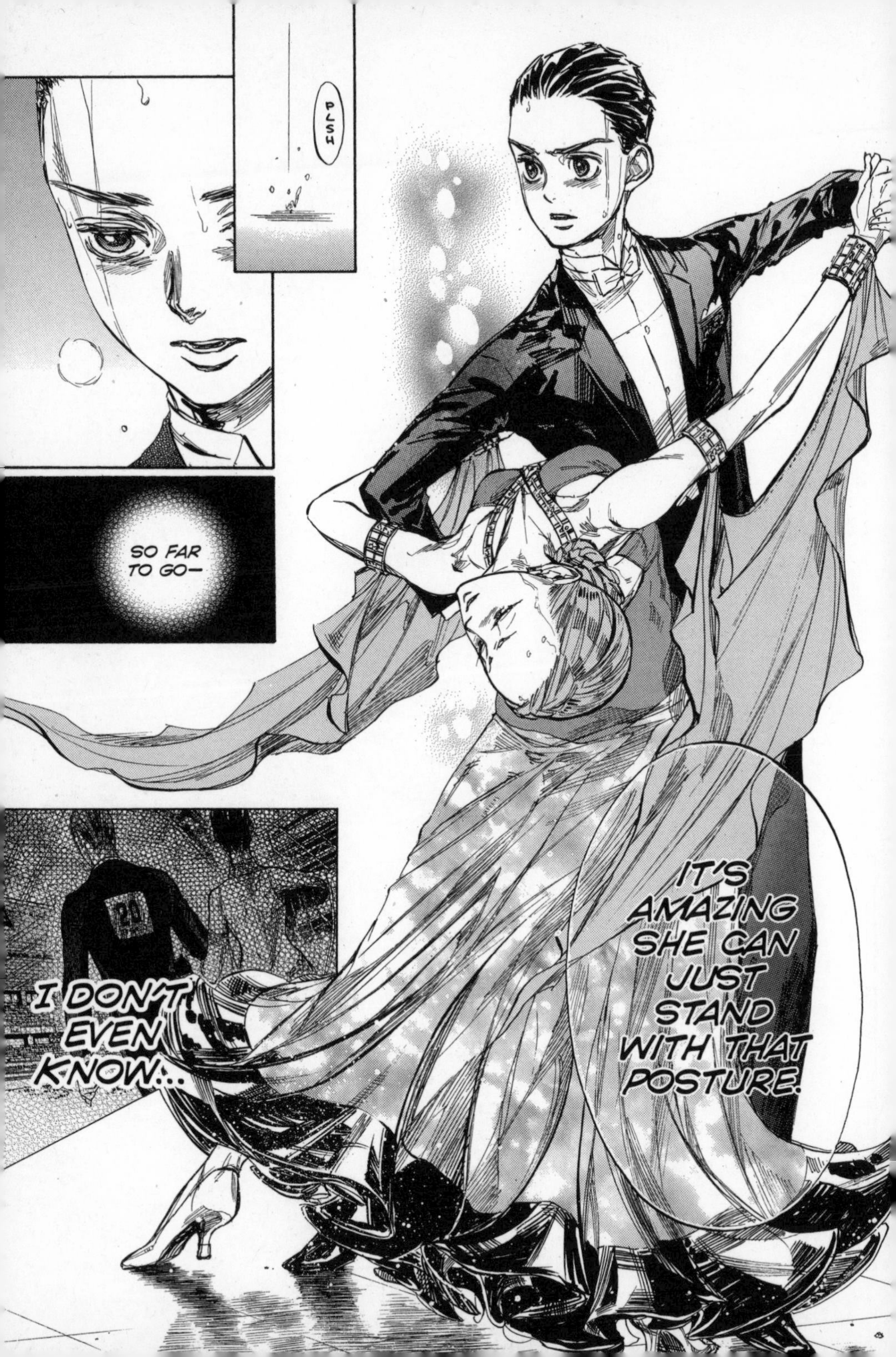
PLSH
SO FAR TO GO—
IT'S AMAZING SHE CAN JUST STAND WITH THAT POSTURE.
I DON'T EVEN KNOW...

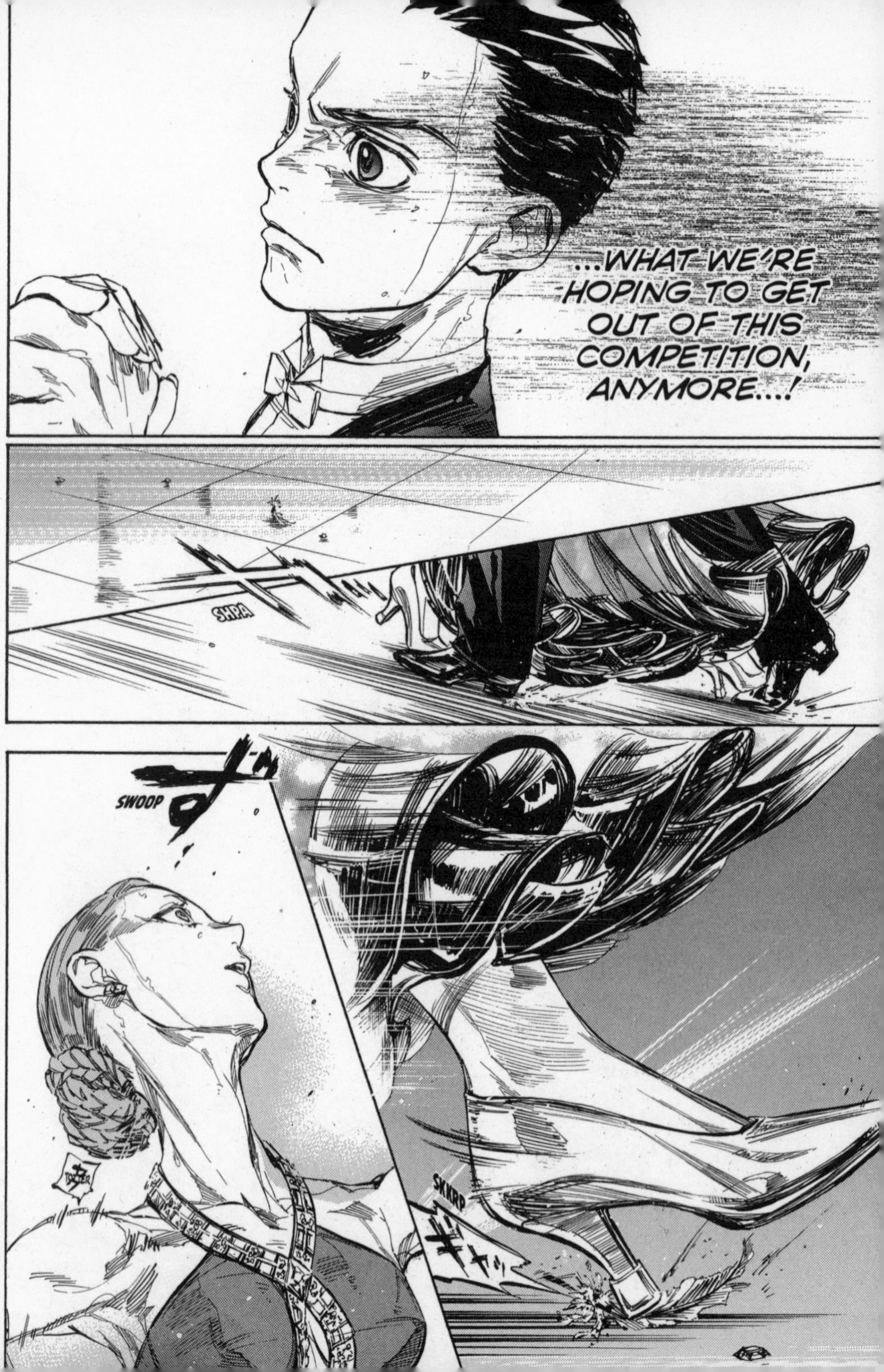
...WHAT WE'RE HOPING TO GET OUT OF THIS COMPETITION, ANYMORE...!
SHPA
SWOOP
SKKRP

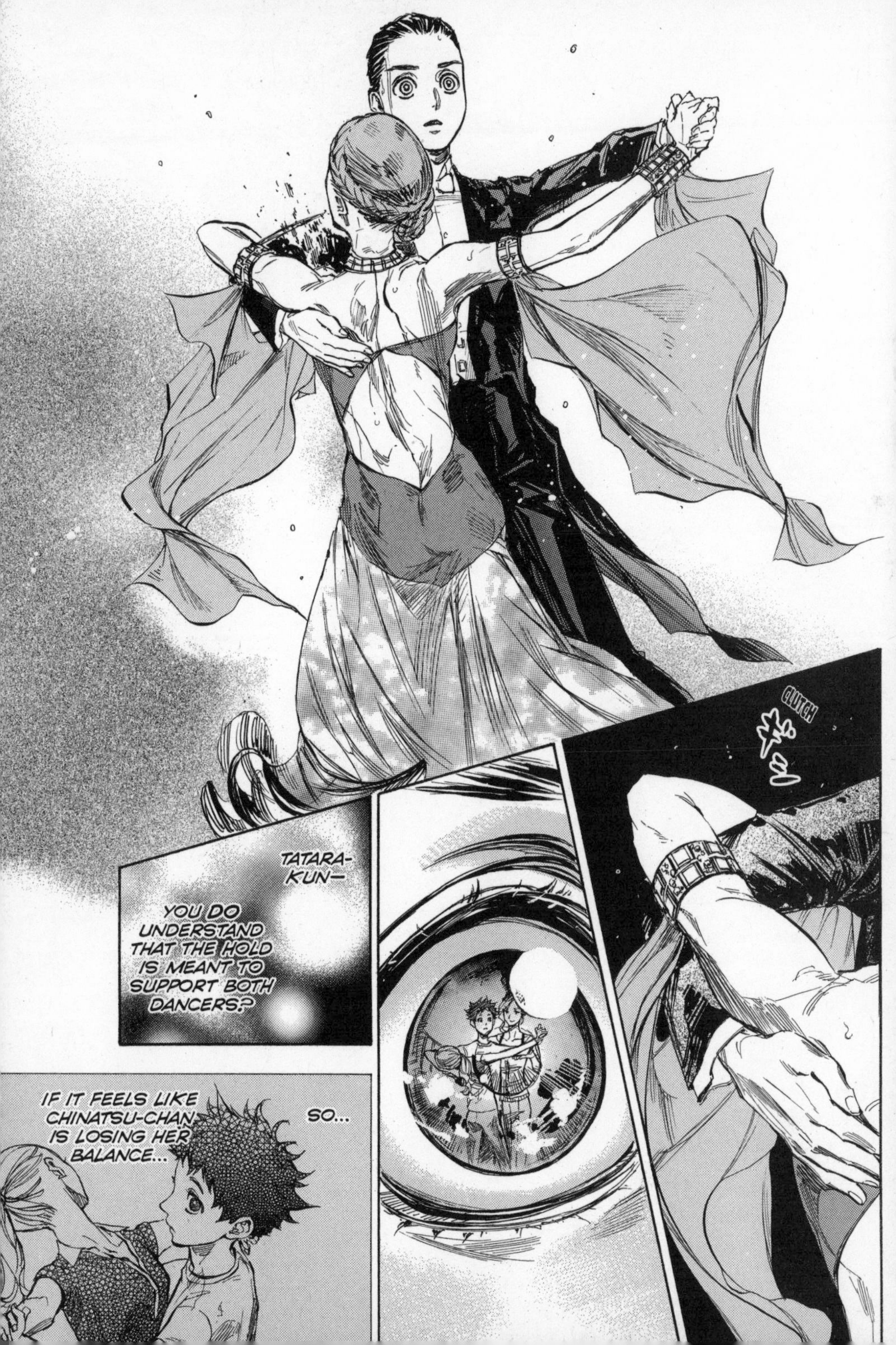
CLUTCH
TATARA-KUN—
YOU DO UNDERSTAND THAT THE HOLD IS MEANT TO SUPPORT BOTH DANCERS?
SO...
IF IT FEELS LIKE CHINATSU-CHAN IS LOSING HER BALANCE...

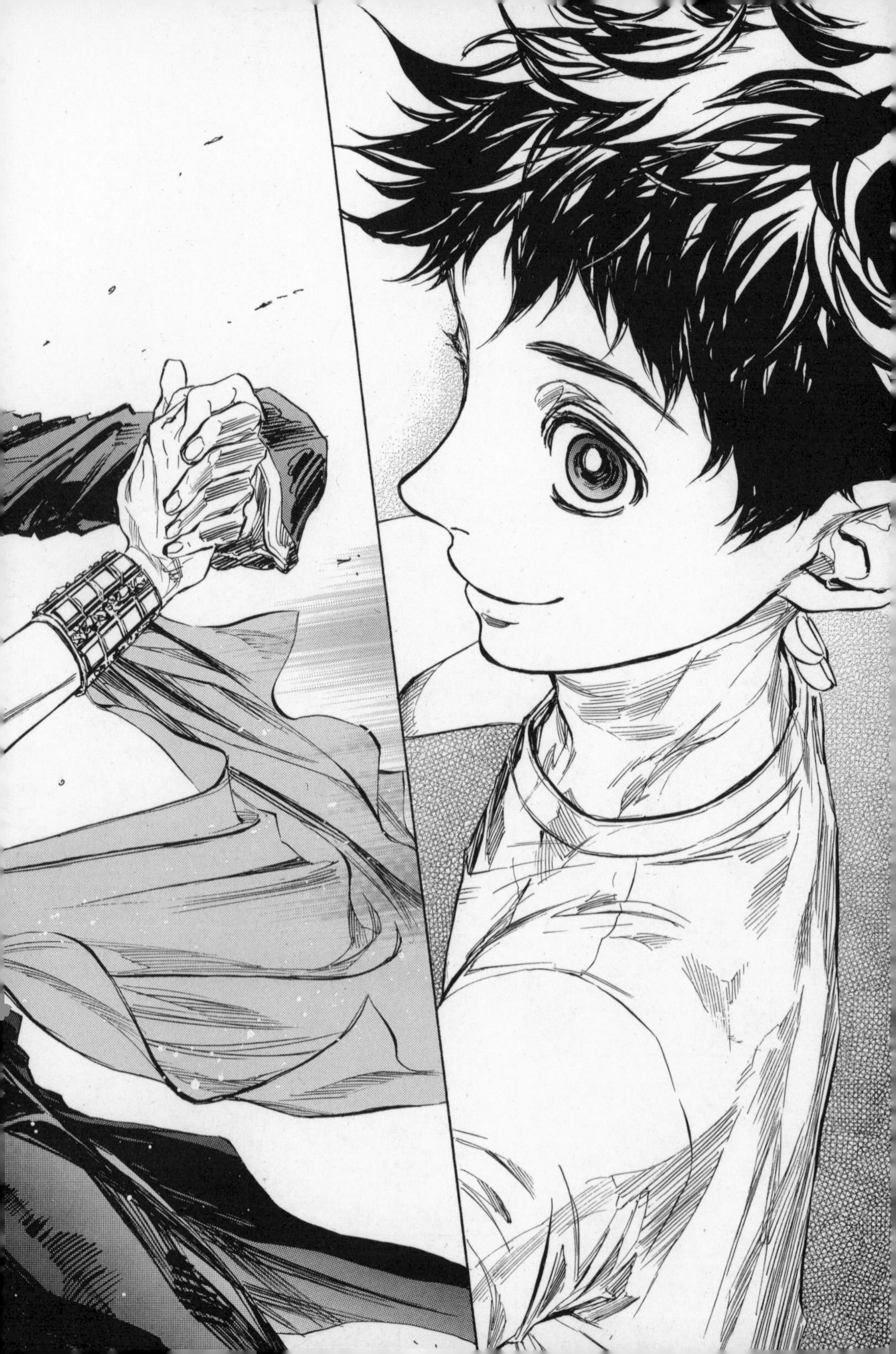

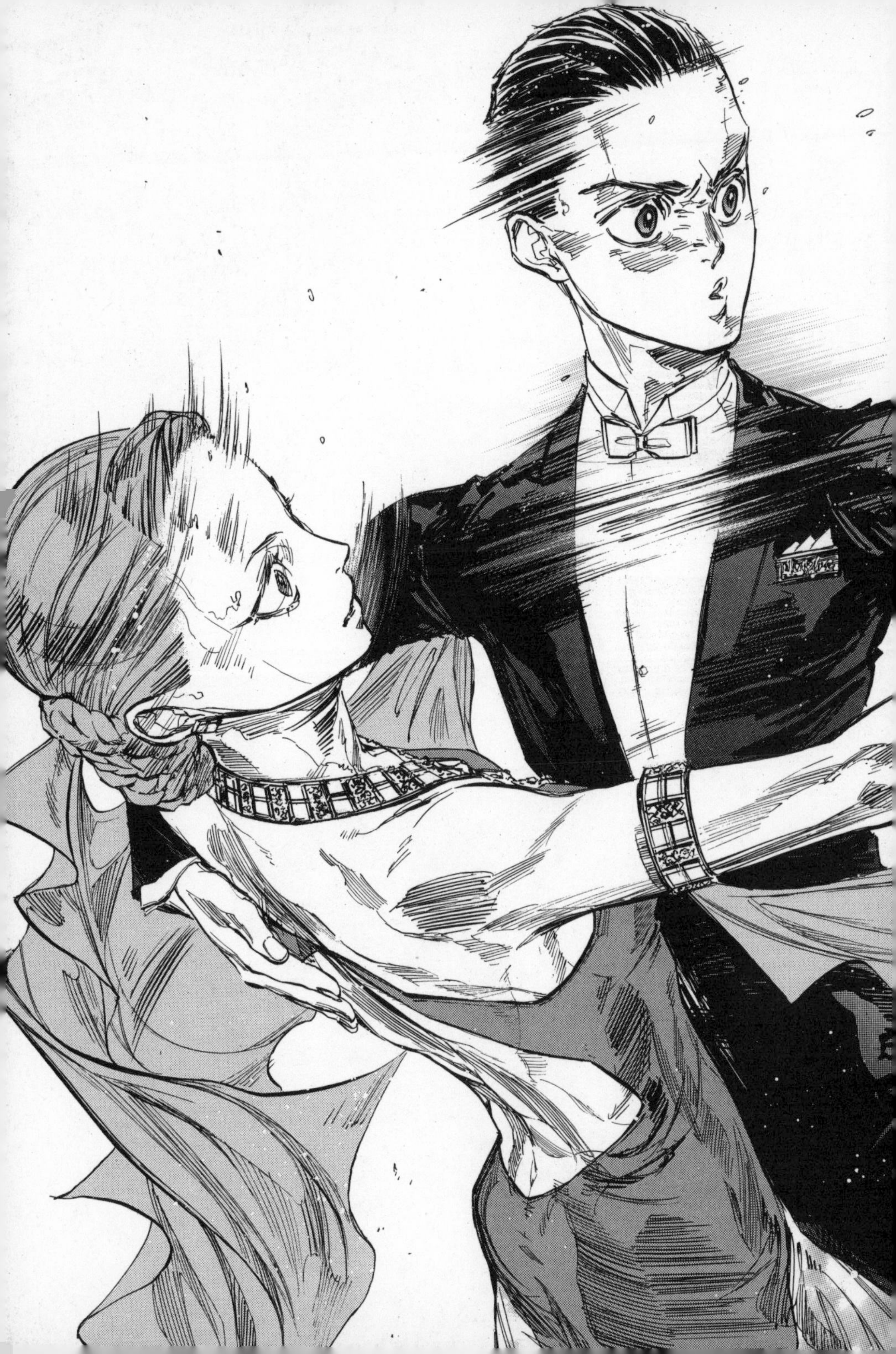

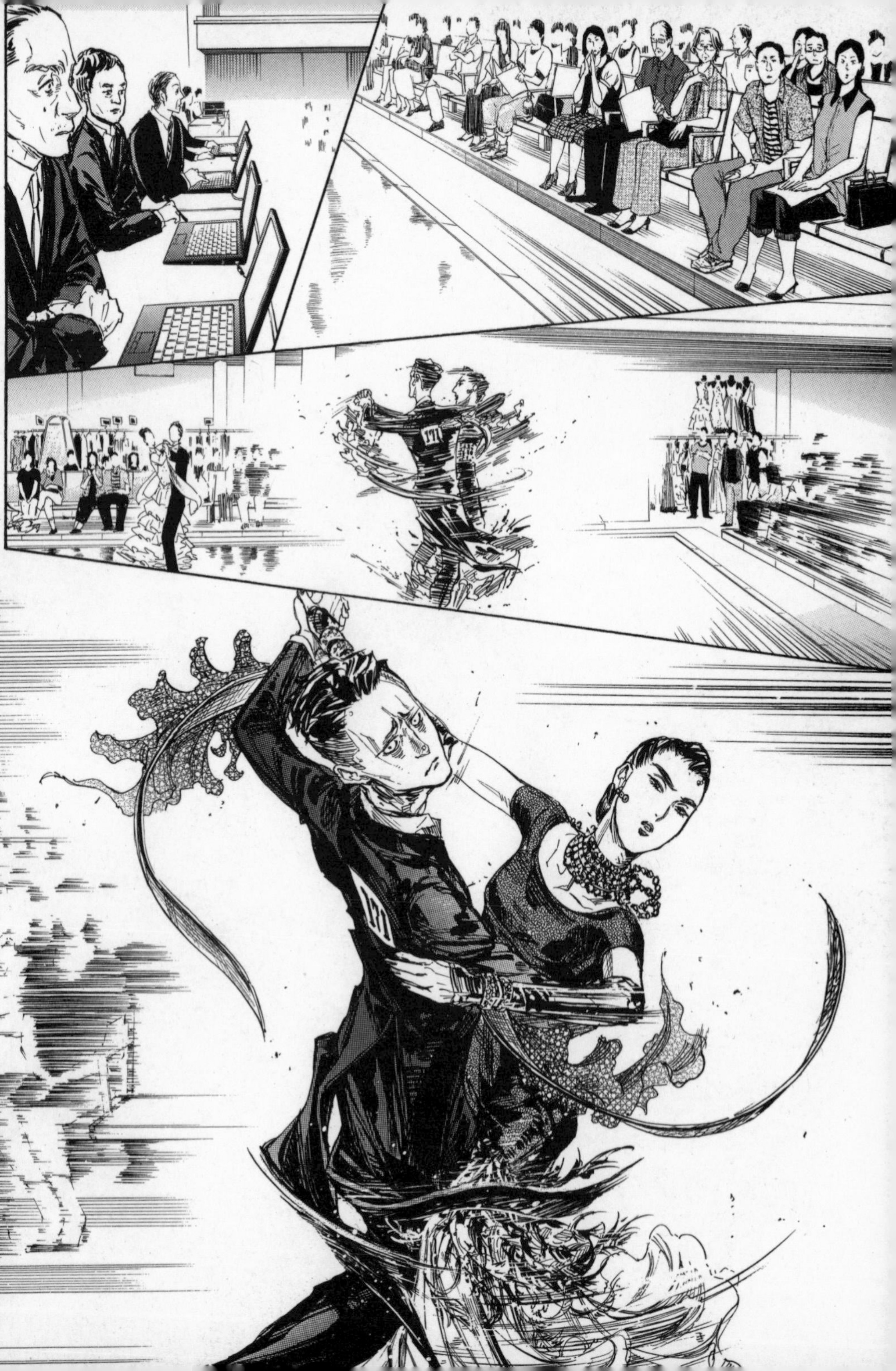
171

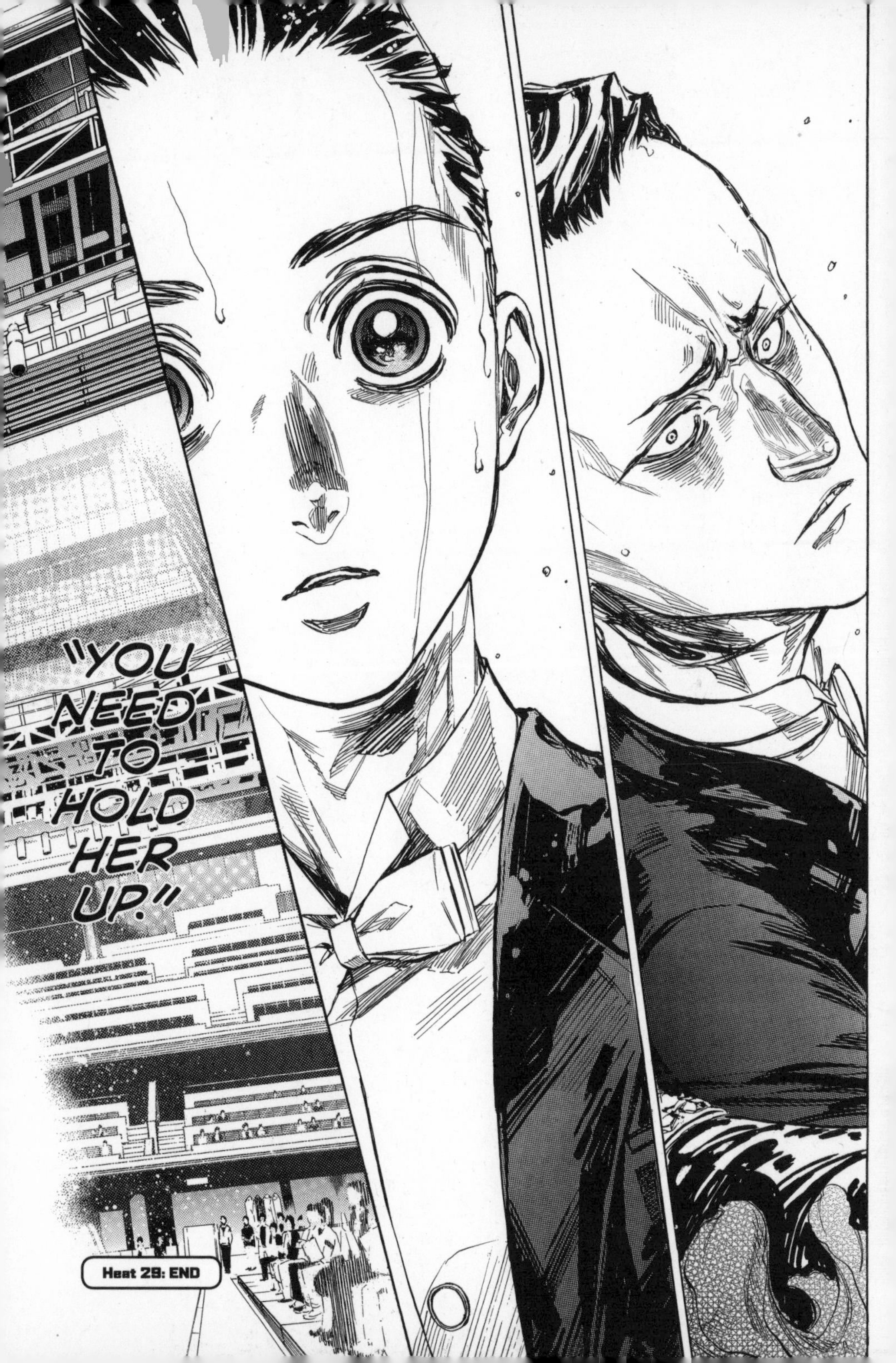
"YOU NEED TO HOLD HER UP."
Heat 29: END

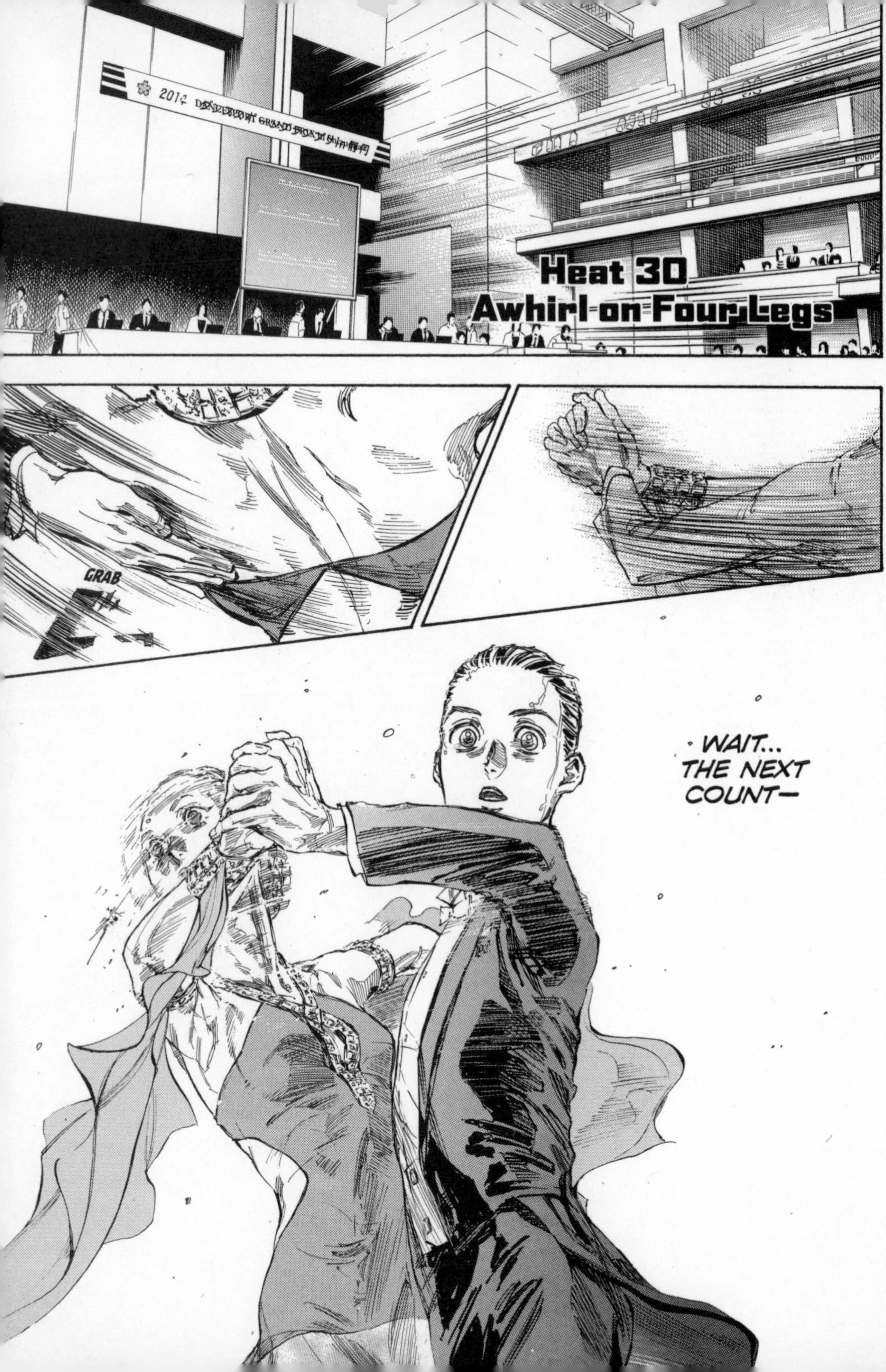
Heat 30
Awhirl on Four Legs
GRAB
WAIT... THE NEXT COUNT—

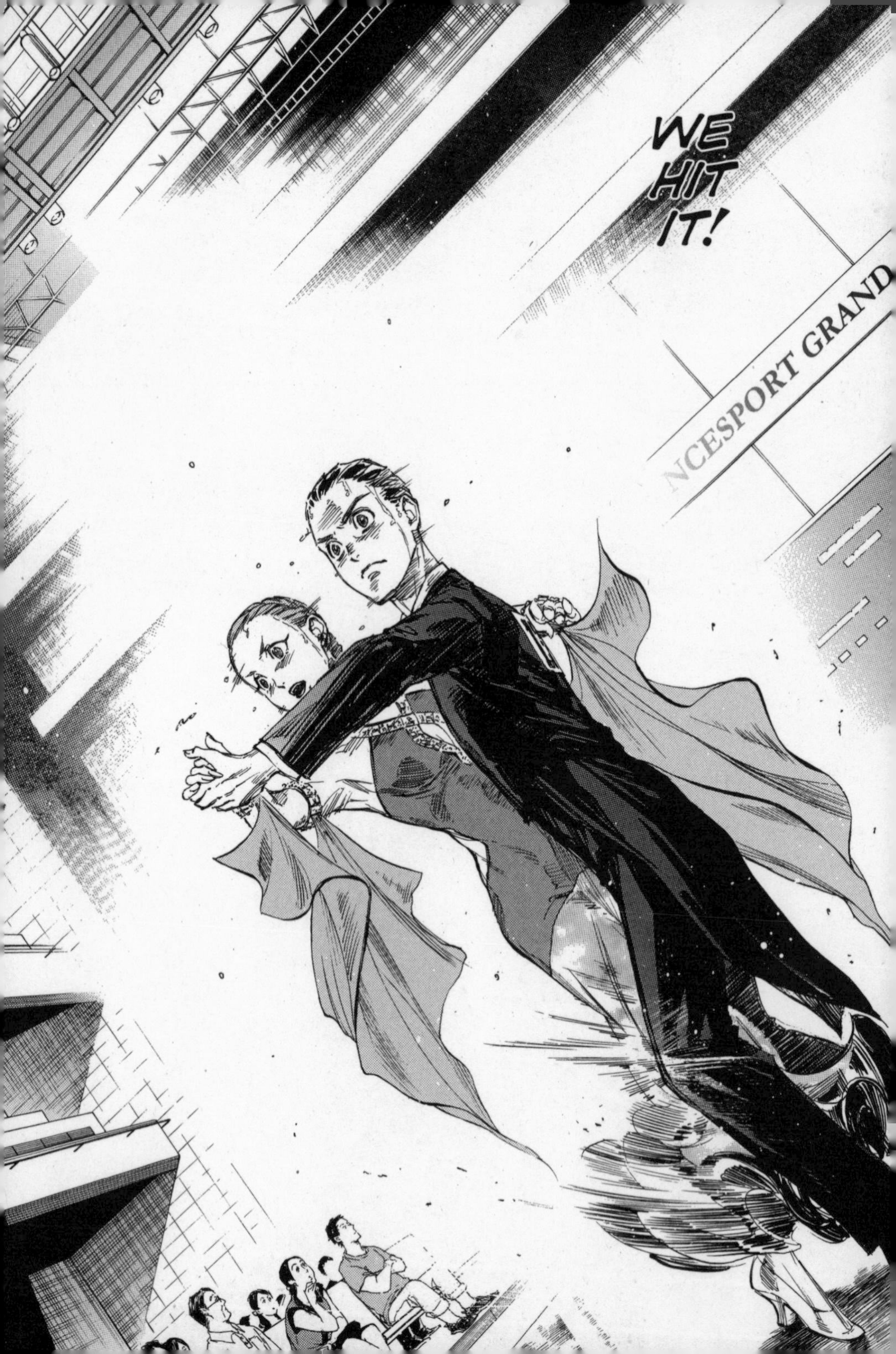
WE HIT IT!
NCESPORT GRAND

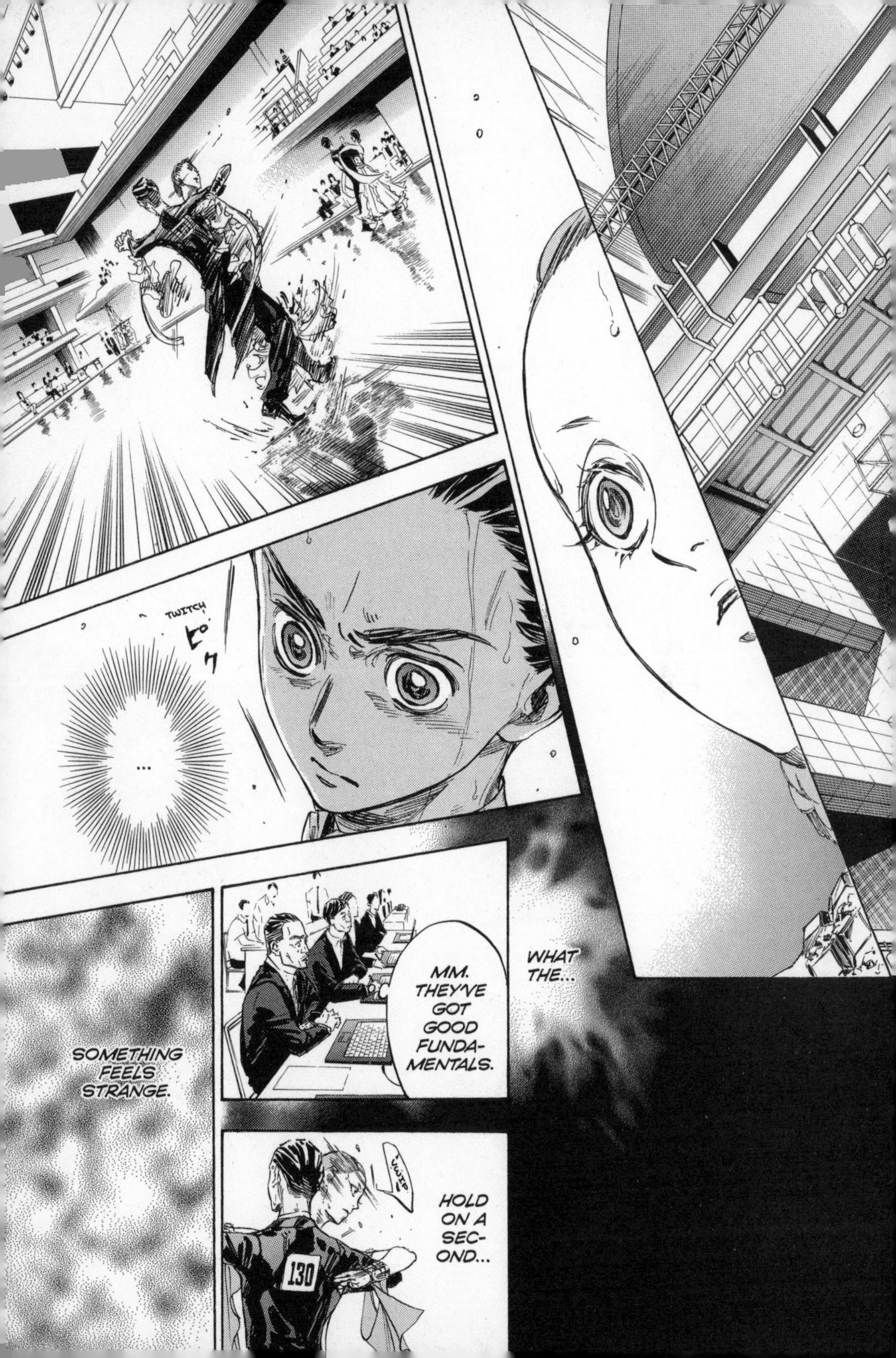
TWITCH
ピク
...
WHAT THE...
MM. THEY'VE GOT GOOD FUNDAMENTALS.
WHIP
130
HOLD ON A SECOND...
SOMETHING FEELS STRANGE.

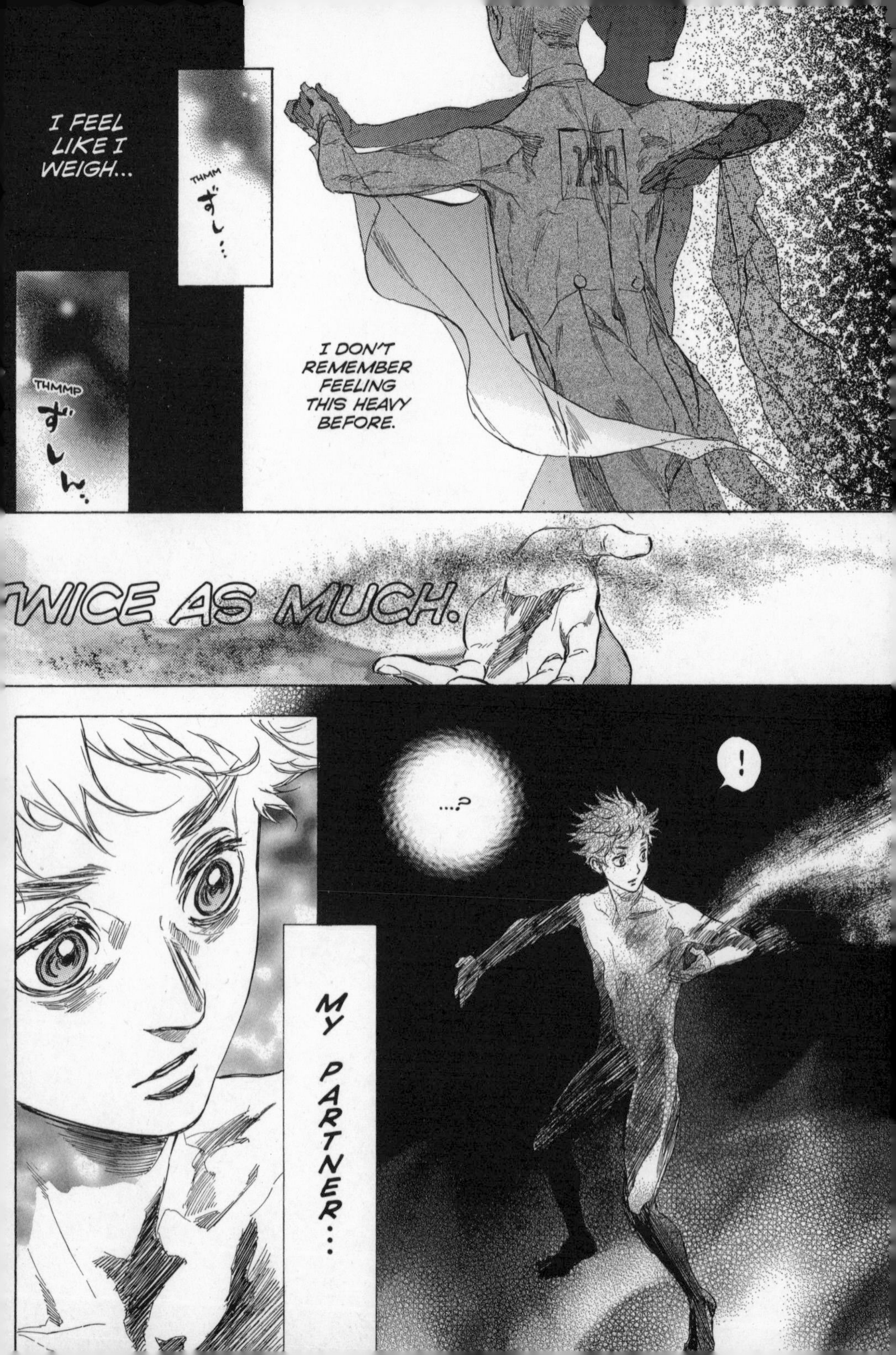
I DON'T REMEMBER FEELING THIS HEAVY BEFORE.
THMM
ずし…
I FEEL LIKE I WEIGH...
THMMP
ずしん…
TWICE AS MUCH.
!
...?
MY PARTNER...

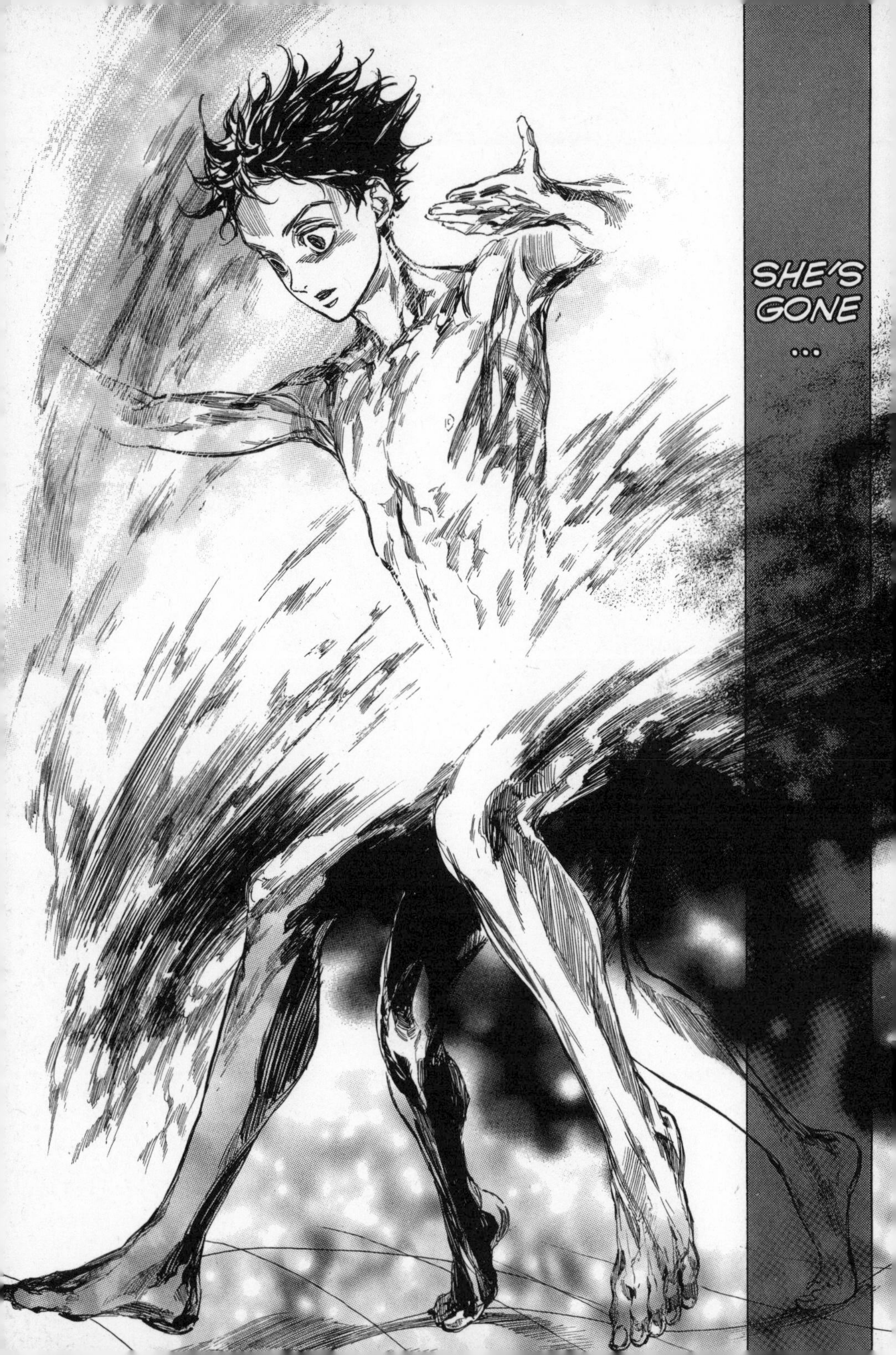
SHE'S GONE
...

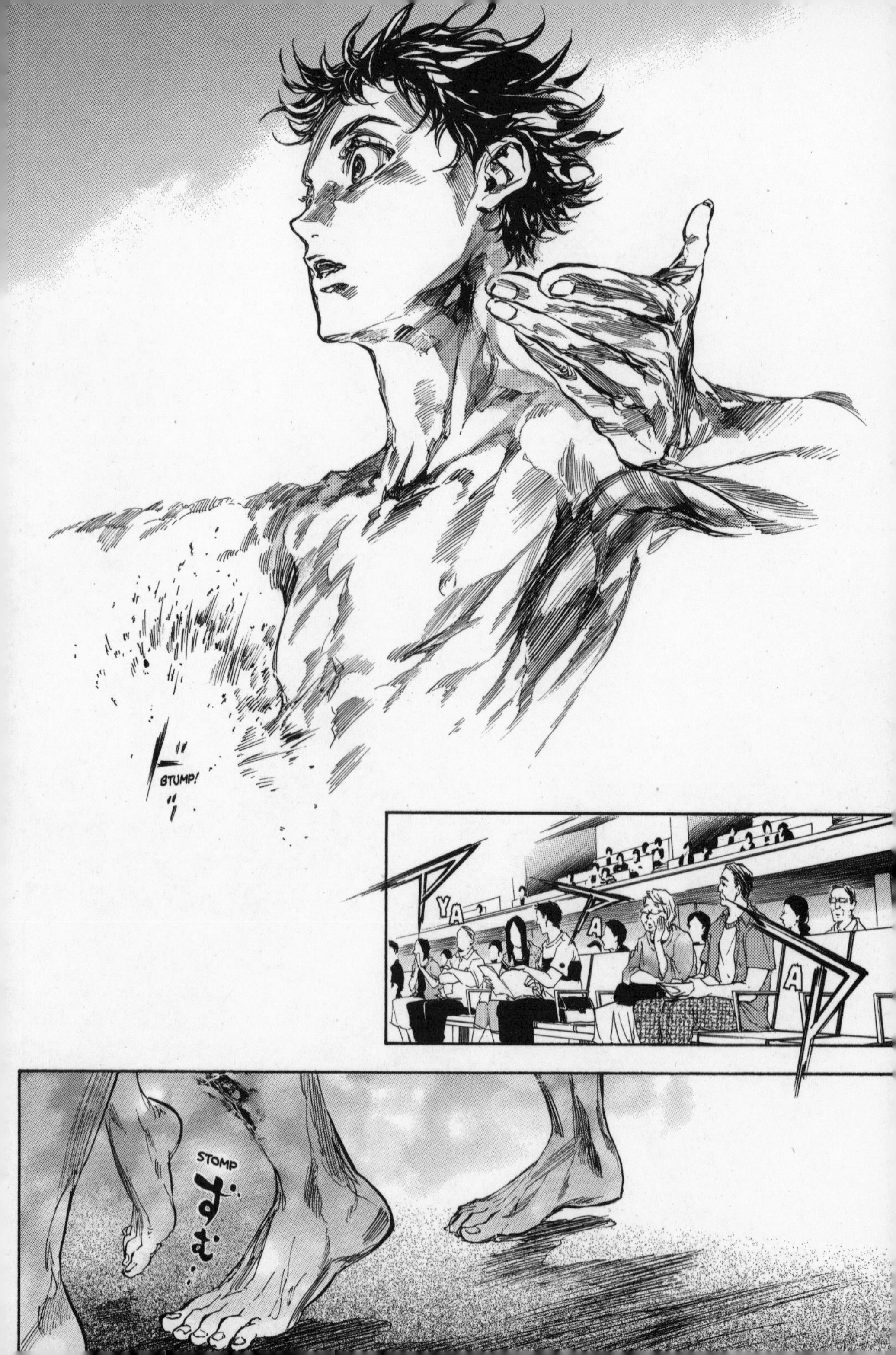
BTUMP!
YA
A
A
STOMP
ずむ..

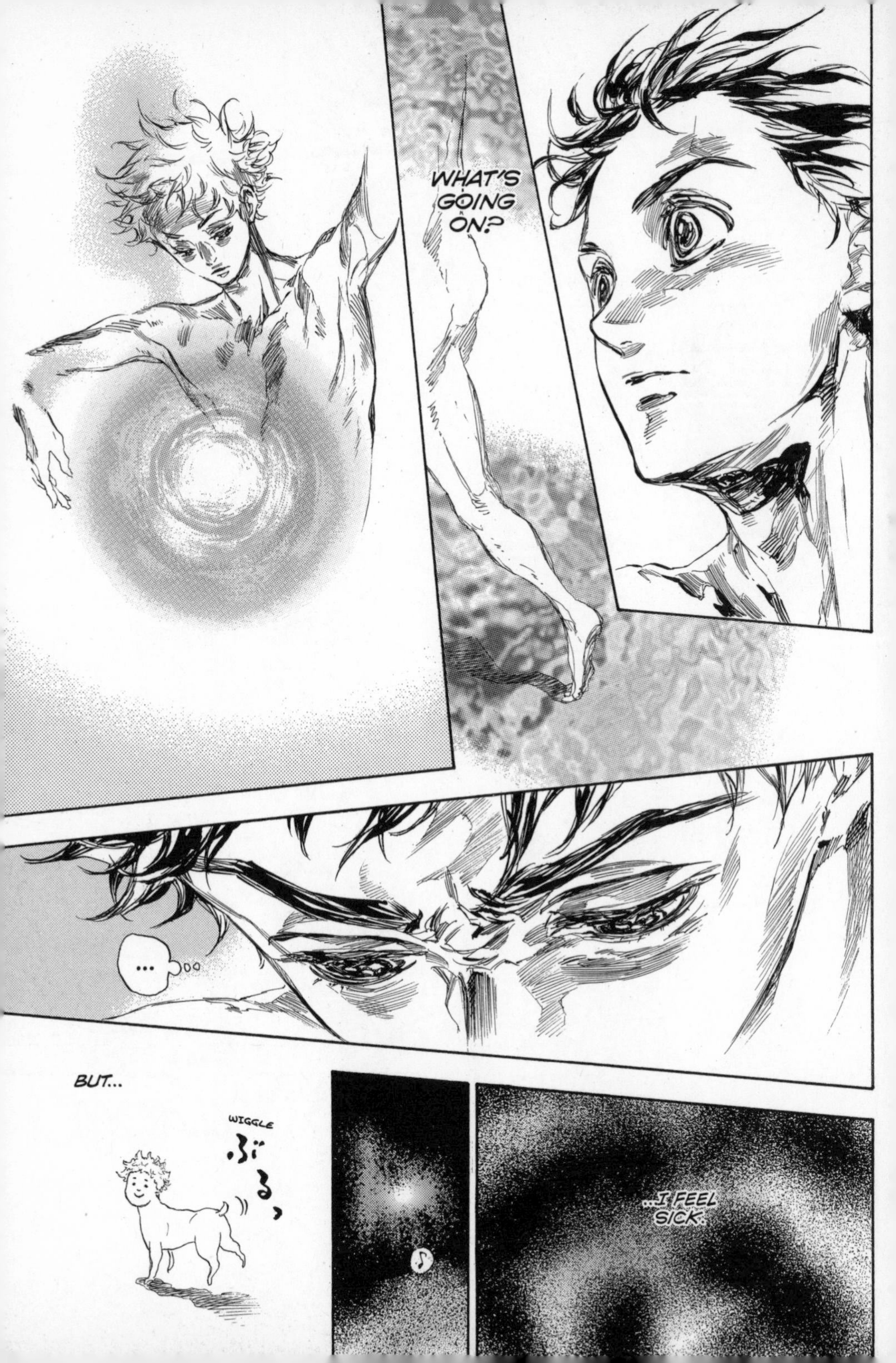
WHAT'S GOING ON?
...
...I FEEL SICK.
BUT...
WIGGLE
ぶるっ

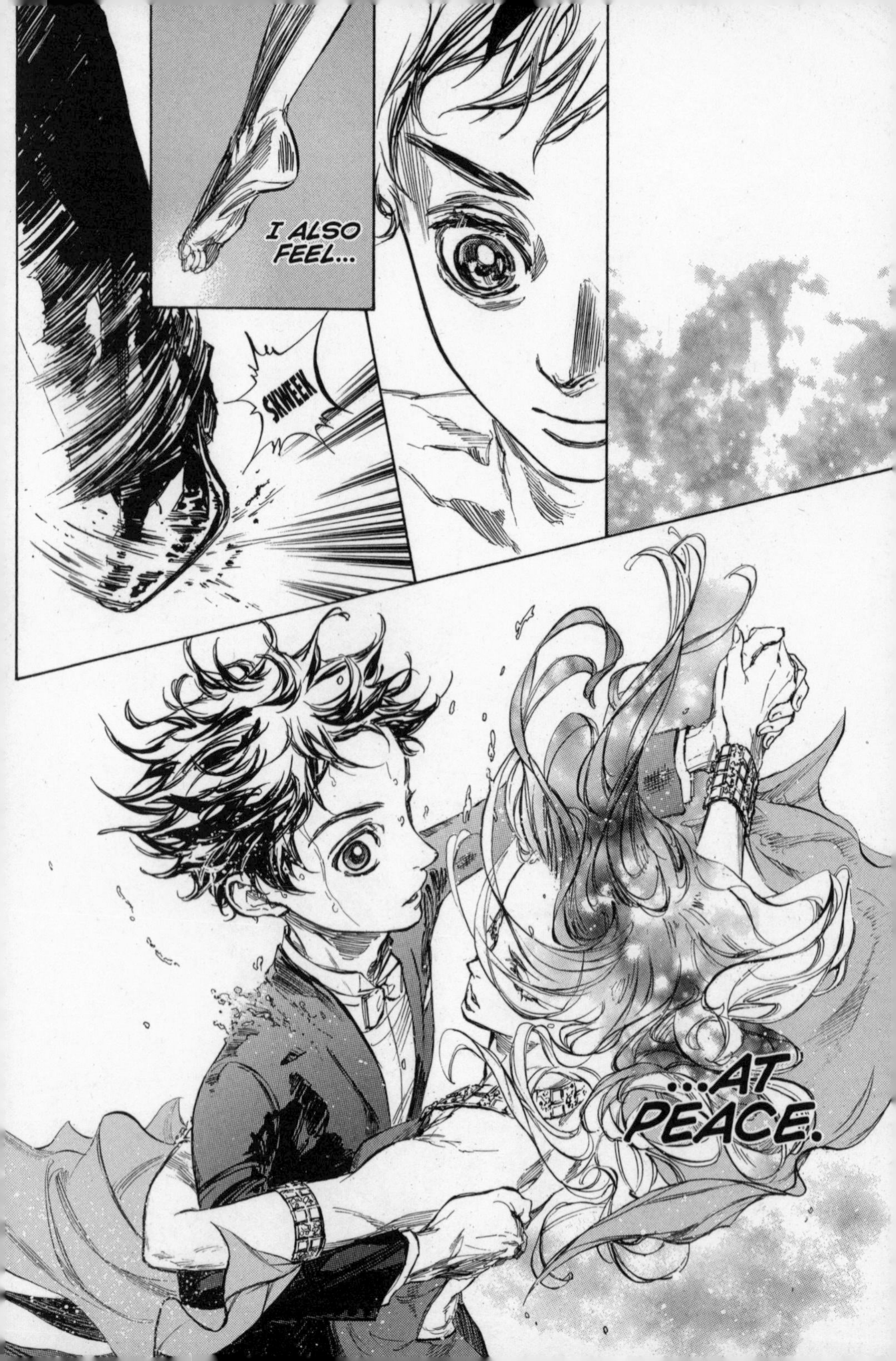
I ALSO FEEL...
SKWEEK
...AT PEACE.

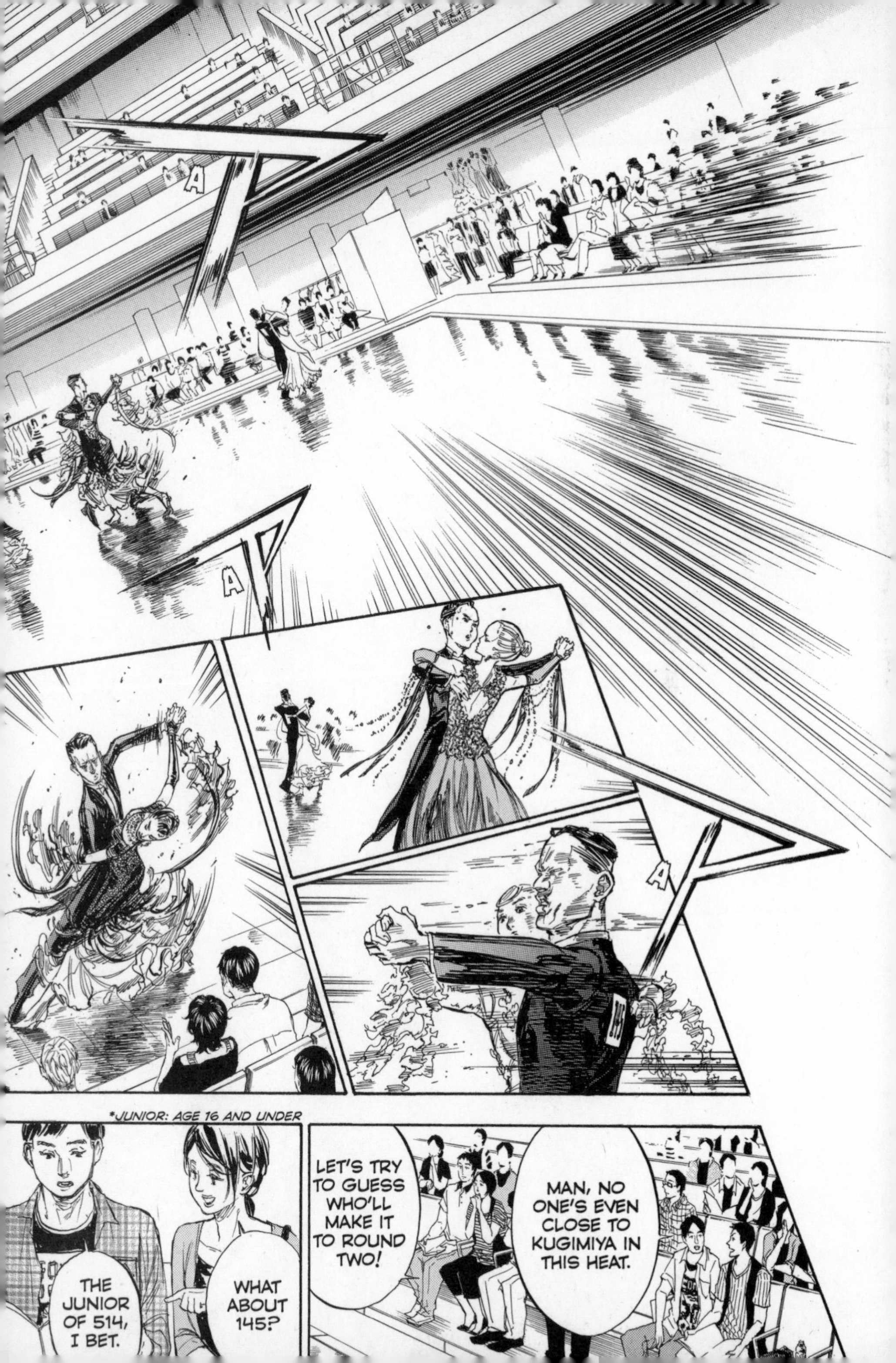
A
A
A
*JUNIOR: AGE 16 AND UNDER
MAN, NO ONE'S EVEN CLOSE TO KUGIMIYA IN THIS HEAT.
LET'S TRY TO GUESS WHO'LL MAKE IT TO ROUND TWO!
WHAT ABOUT 145?
THE JUNIOR OF 514, I BET.

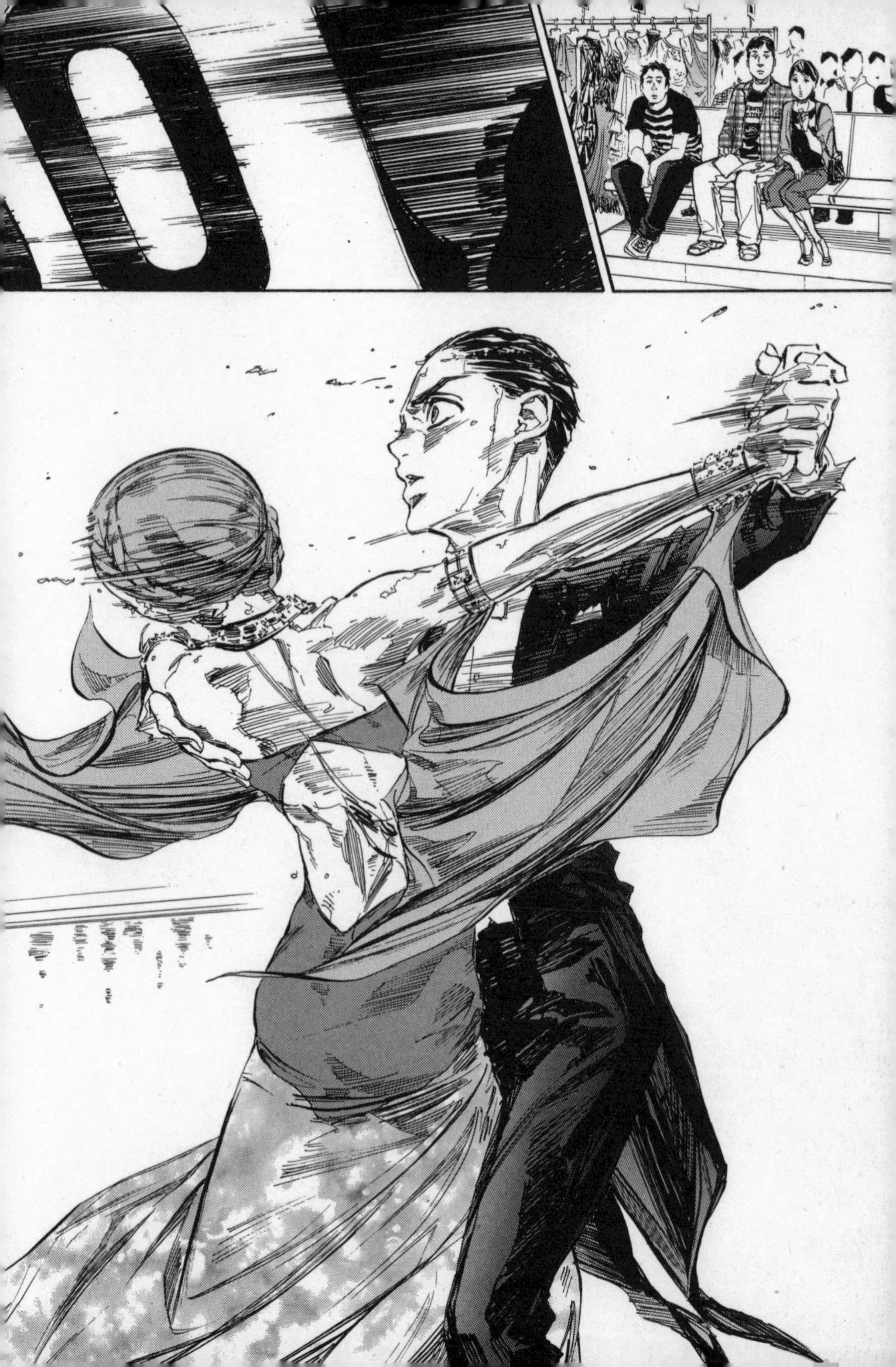

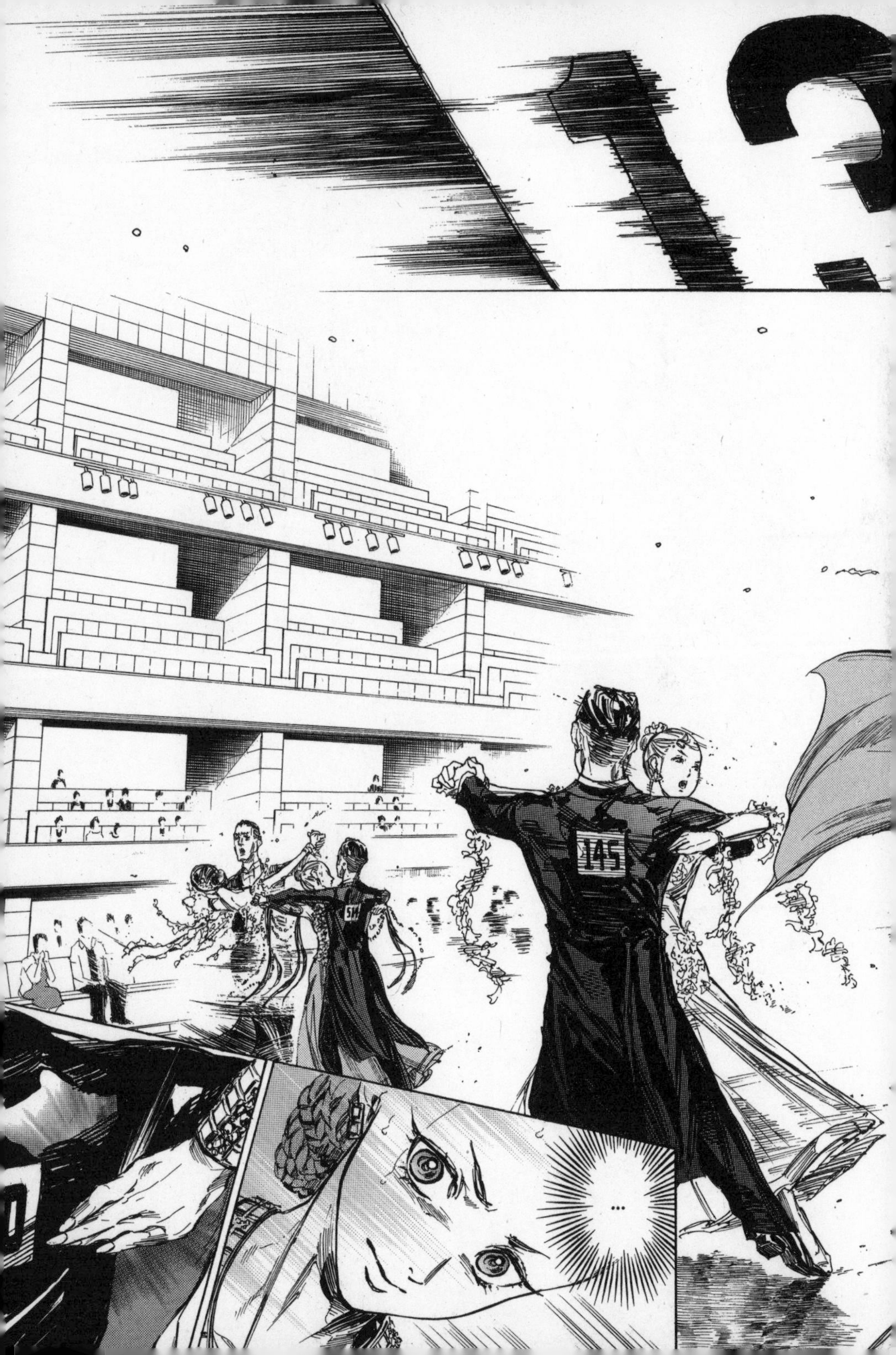
145
...

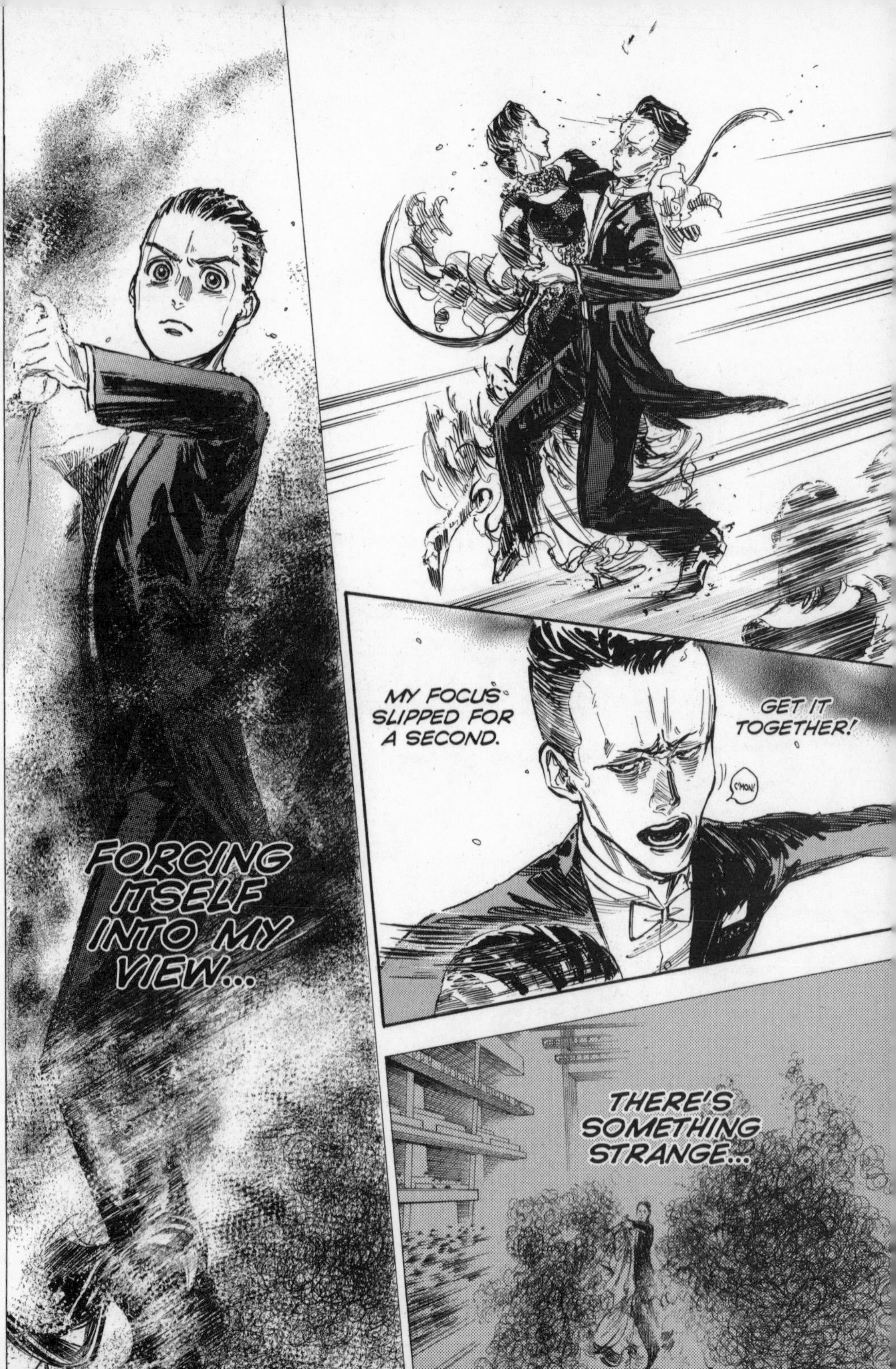
GET IT TOGETHER!
C'MON!
MY FOCUS SLIPPED FOR A SECOND.
THERE'S SOMETHING STRANGE...
FORCING ITSELF INTO MY VIEW...

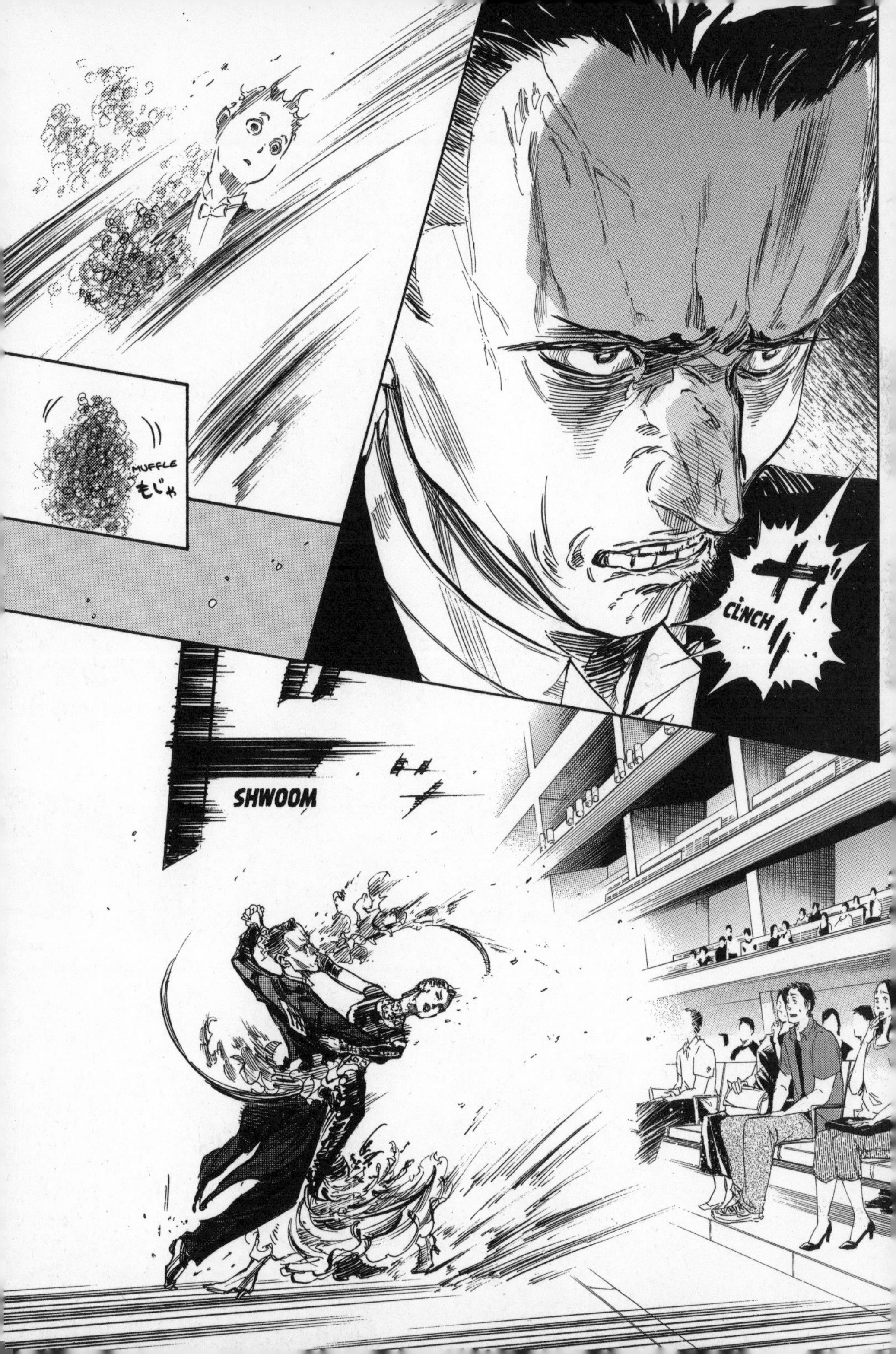
CLINCH
MUFFLE
もじゃ
SHWOOM

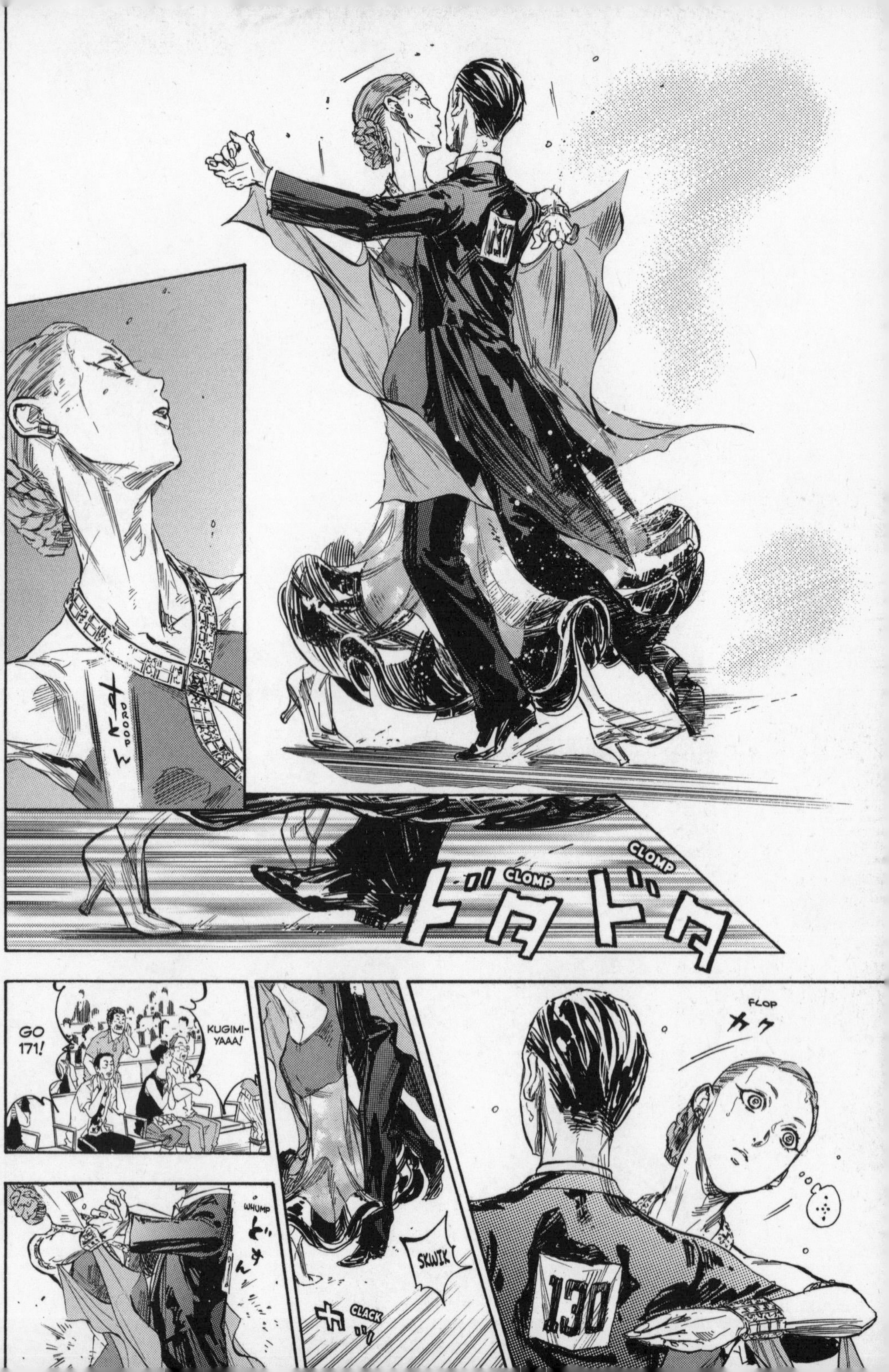
すとん
DROOP
トタドタ
CLOMP
CLOMP
カク
FLOP
SKWIK
カッ
CLACK
GO 171!
KUGIMI-YAAA!
どすん
WHUMP

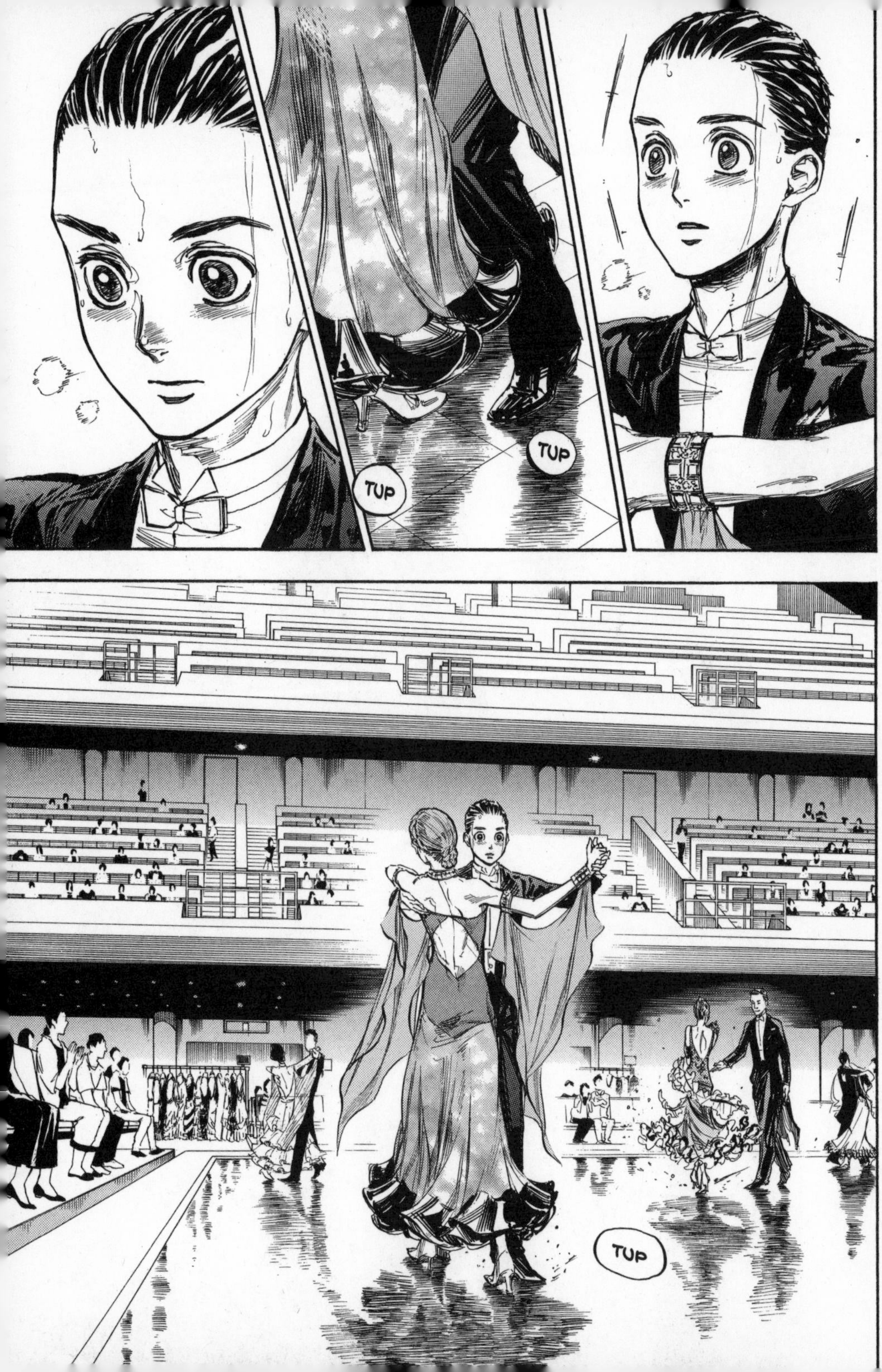
TUP
TUP
TUP

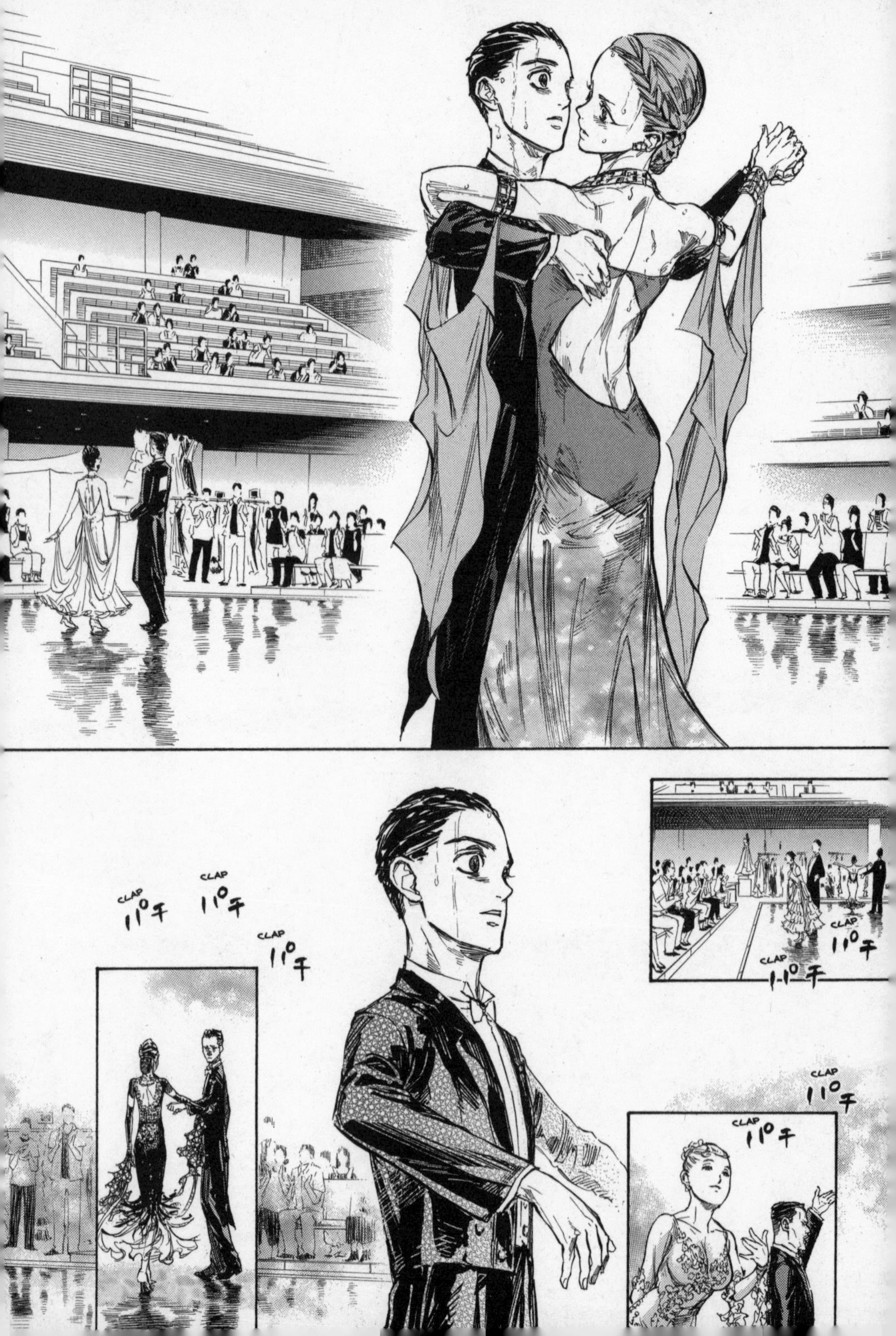
CLAP
CLAP
CLAP
CLAP
CLAP
CLAP
CLAP

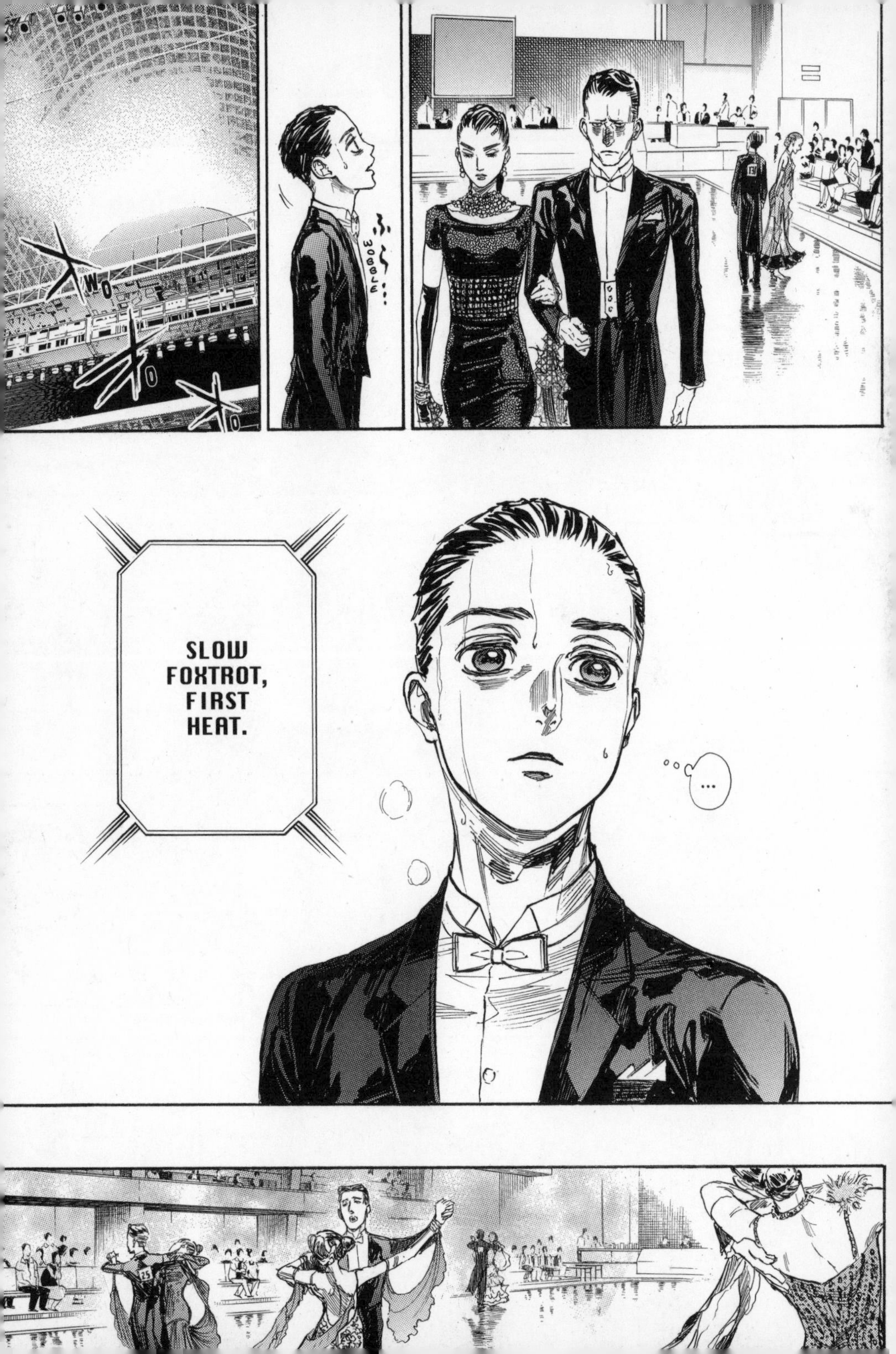
WOBBLE...
WO
O
O
SLOW FOXTROT, FIRST HEAT.
...

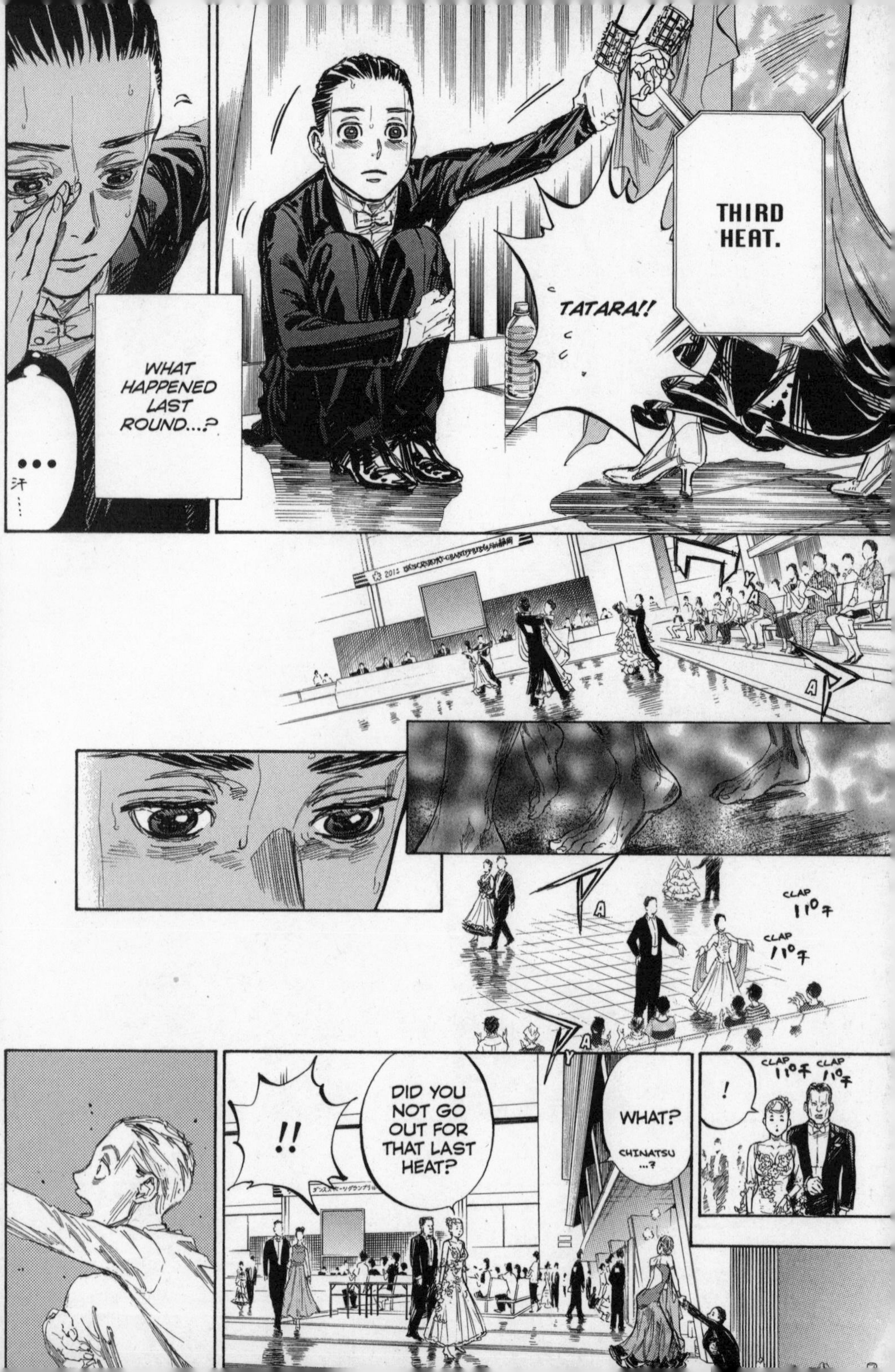

THIRD HEAT.
TATARA!!
WHAT HAPPENED LAST ROUND...?
•••
汗…
YA
A
A
A
CLAP パチ
CLAP パチ
YA A
!
CLAP パチ CLAP パチ
WHAT?
CHINATSU ...?
DID YOU NOT GO OUT FOR THAT LAST HEAT?
!!

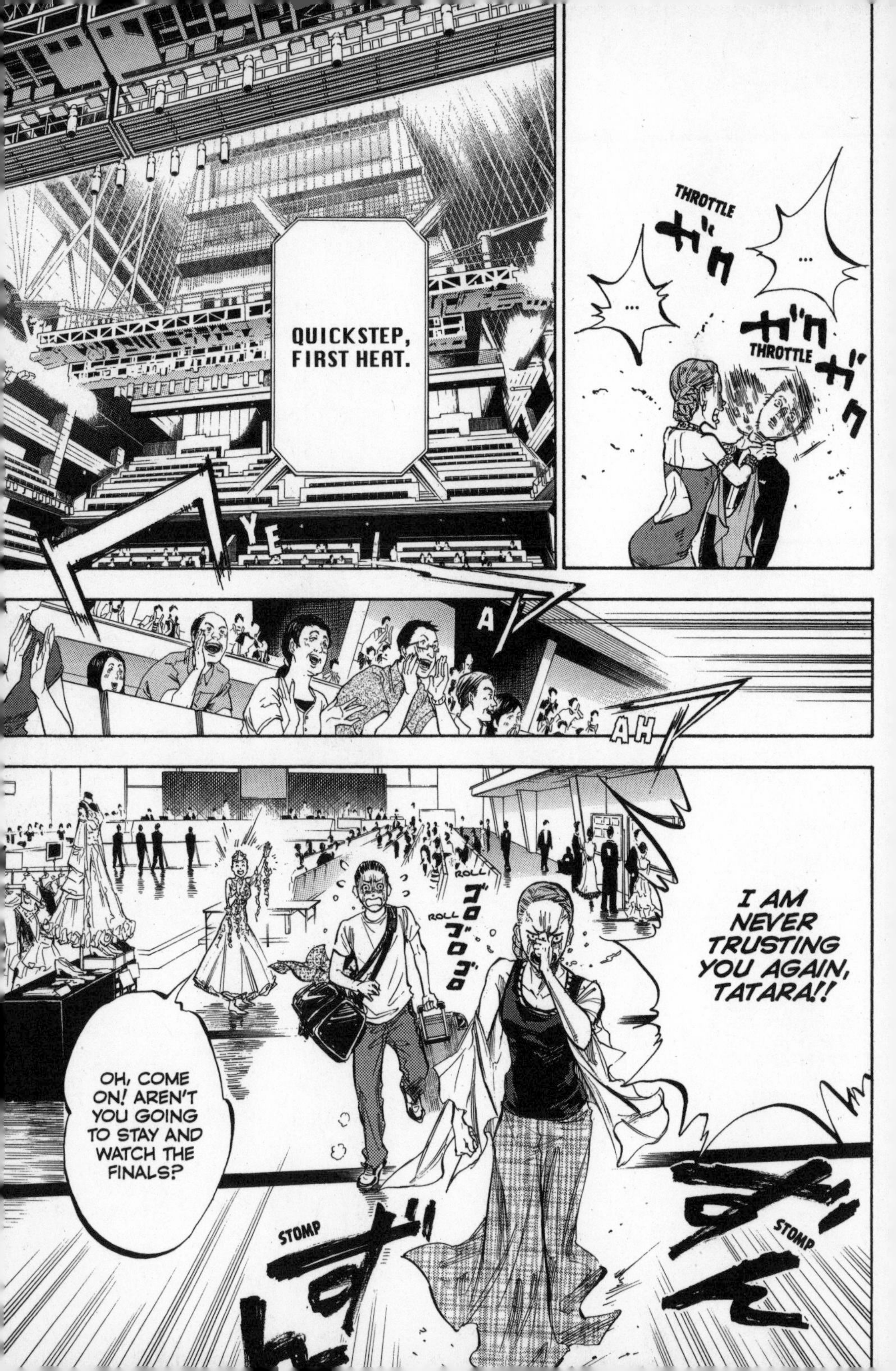
THROTTLE
ガク
...
...
ガクガク
THROTTLE
QUICKSTEP, FIRST HEAT.
YE
A
AH
I AM NEVER TRUSTING YOU AGAIN, TATARA!!
ROLL
ゴロゴロゴロ
ROLL
OH, COME ON! AREN'T YOU GOING TO STAY AND WATCH THE FINALS?
STOMP
STOMP

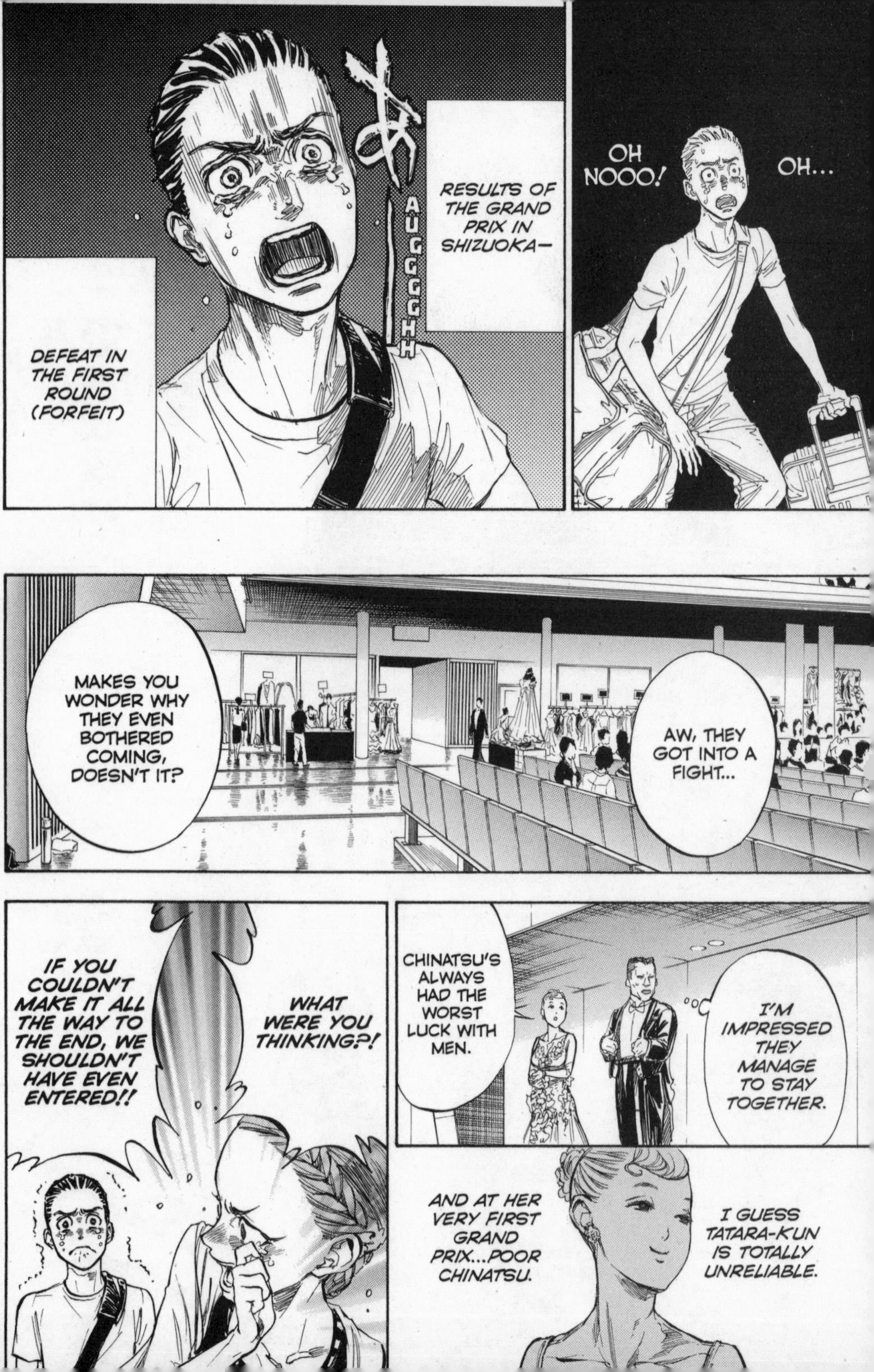
OH...
OH NOOO!
RESULTS OF THE GRAND PRIX IN SHIZUOKA—
AUGGGGHH
DEFEAT IN THE FIRST ROUND (FORFEIT)
AW, THEY GOT INTO A FIGHT...
MAKES YOU WONDER WHY THEY EVEN BOTHERED COMING, DOESN'T IT?
I'M IMPRESSED THEY MANAGE TO STAY TOGETHER.
CHINATSU'S ALWAYS HAD THE WORST LUCK WITH MEN.
I GUESS TATARA-KUN IS TOTALLY UNRELIABLE.
AND AT HER VERY FIRST GRAND PRIX...POOR CHINATSU.
WHAT WERE YOU THINKING?!
IF YOU COULDN'T MAKE IT ALL THE WAY TO THE END, WE SHOULDN'T HAVE EVEN ENTERED!!

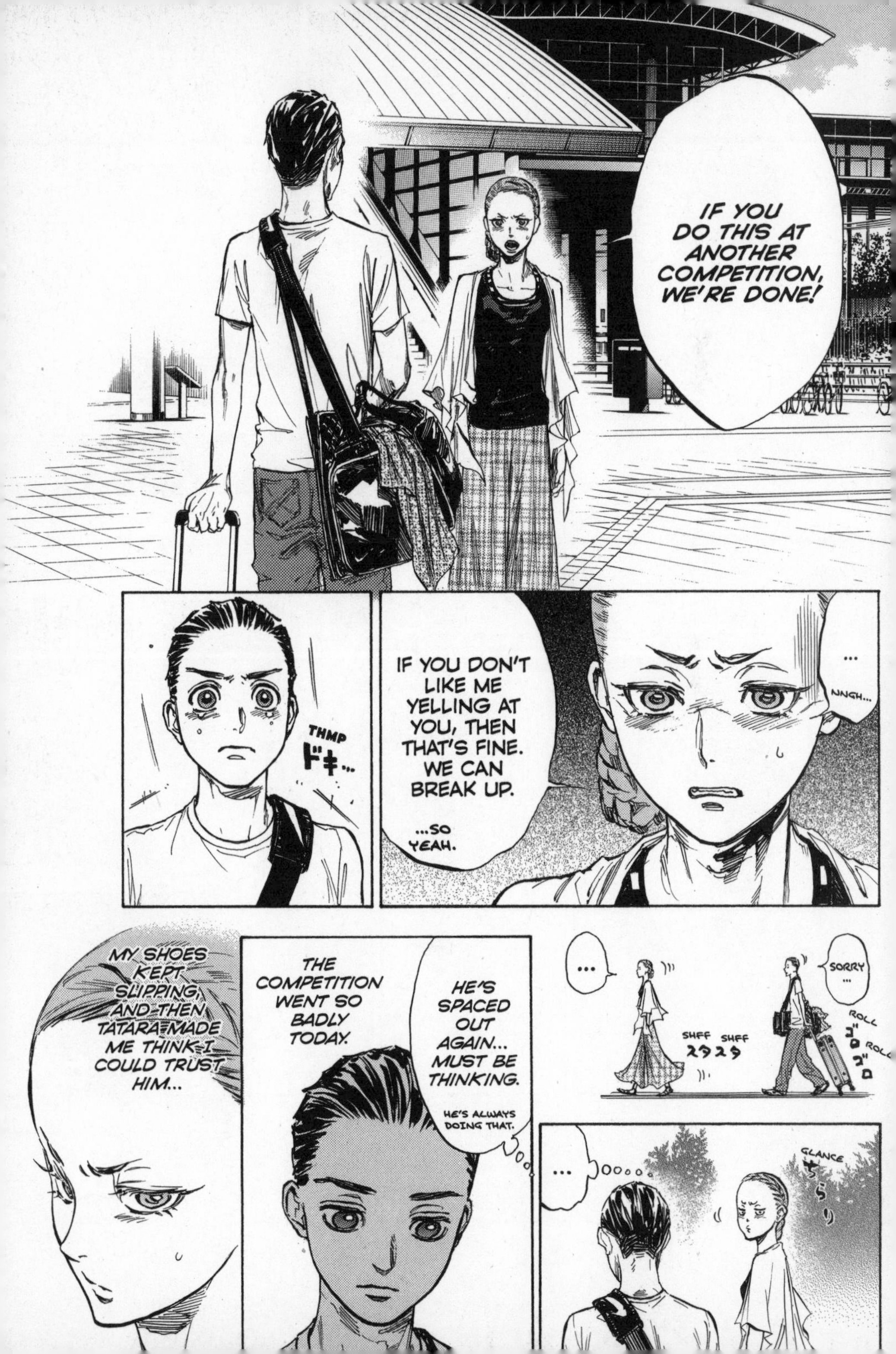
IF YOU DO THIS AT ANOTHER COMPETITION, WE'RE DONE!
...
NNGH...
IF YOU DON'T LIKE ME YELLING AT YOU, THEN THAT'S FINE. WE CAN BREAK UP.
...SO YEAH.
THMP
ドキ...
SORRY...
ROLL ゴロ
ROLL ゴロ
SHFF SHFF
スタスタ
...
...
GLANCE
ちらり
HE'S SPACED OUT AGAIN... MUST BE THINKING.
HE'S ALWAYS DOING THAT.
THE COMPETITION WENT SO BADLY TODAY.
MY SHOES KEPT SLIPPING, AND THEN TATARA MADE ME THINK I COULD TRUST HIM...

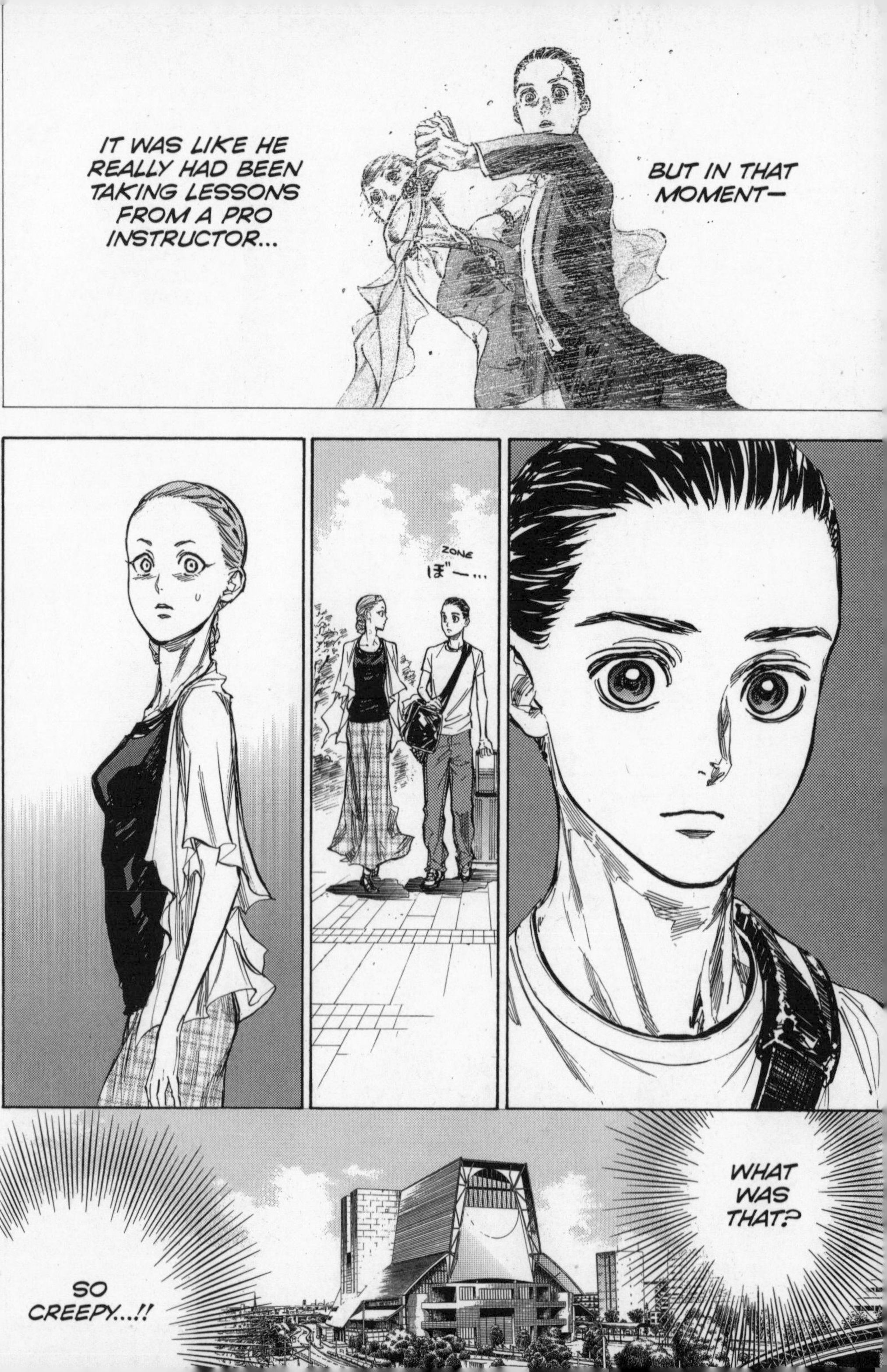
IT WAS LIKE HE REALLY HAD BEEN TAKING LESSONS FROM A PRO INSTRUCTOR...
BUT IN THAT MOMENT—
ZONE
ぼー...
WHAT WAS THAT?
SO CREEPY...!!

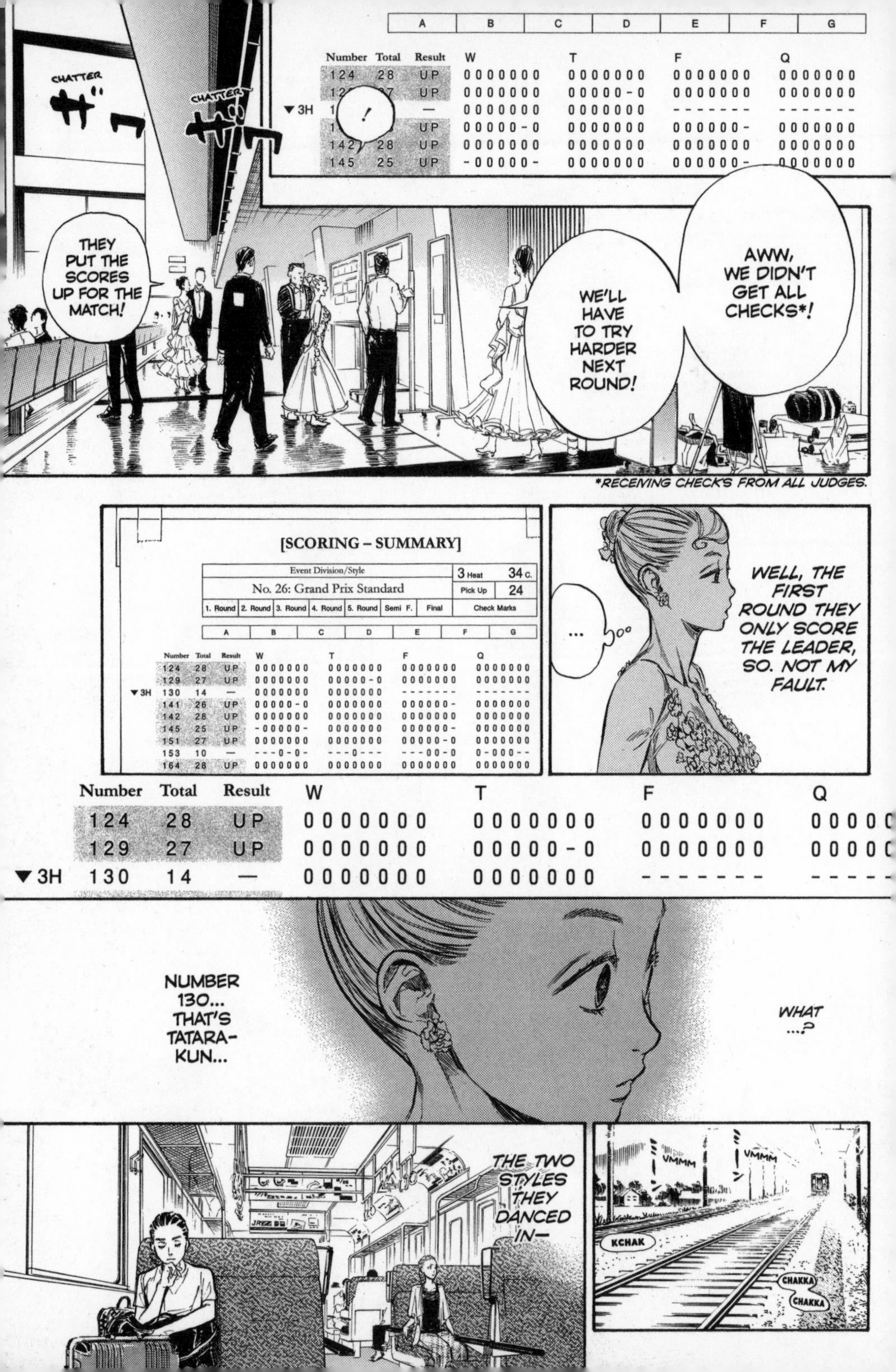
A B C D E F G
Number Total Result W T F Q
124 28 UP 0000000 0000000 0000000 0000000
UP 0000000 00000-0 0000000 0000000
▼3H — 0000000 0000000 ------- -------
UP 00000-0 0000000 000000- 0000000
142 28 UP 0000000 0000000 0000000 0000000
145 25 UP -00000- 0000000 000000- 0000000
!
CHATTER
CHATTER
THEY PUT THE SCORES UP FOR THE MATCH!
AWW, WE DIDN'T GET ALL CHECKS*!
WE'LL HAVE TO TRY HARDER NEXT ROUND!
*RECEIVING CHECKS FROM ALL JUDGES.
WELL, THE FIRST ROUND THEY ONLY SCORE THE LEADER, SO. NOT MY FAULT.
...
[SCORING – SUMMARY]
Event Division/Style
No. 26: Grand Prix Standard
3 Heat 34 c.
Pick Up 24
1. Round 2. Round 3. Round 4. Round 5. Round Semi F. Final Check Marks
A B C D E F G
Number Total Result W T F Q
124 28 UP 0000000 0000000 0000000 0000000
129 27 UP 0000000 00000-0 0000000 0000000
▼3H 130 14 — 0000000 0000000 ------- -------
141 26 UP 00000-0 0000000 000000- 0000000
142 28 UP 0000000 0000000 0000000 0000000
145 25 UP -00000- 0000000 000000- 0000000
151 27 UP 0000000 0000000 00000-0 0000000
153 10 — ---0-0- ---0--- ---00-0 0-000--
164 28 UP 0000000 0000000 0000000 0000000
Number Total Result W T F Q
124 28 UP 0000000 0000000 0000000 00000
129 27 UP 0000000 00000-0 0000000 00000
▼3H 130 14 — 0000000 0000000 ------- -----
WHAT ...?
NUMBER 130... THAT'S TATARA-KUN...
VMMM
VMMM
KCHAK
CHAKKA
CHAKKA
THE TWO STYLES THEY DANCED IN—

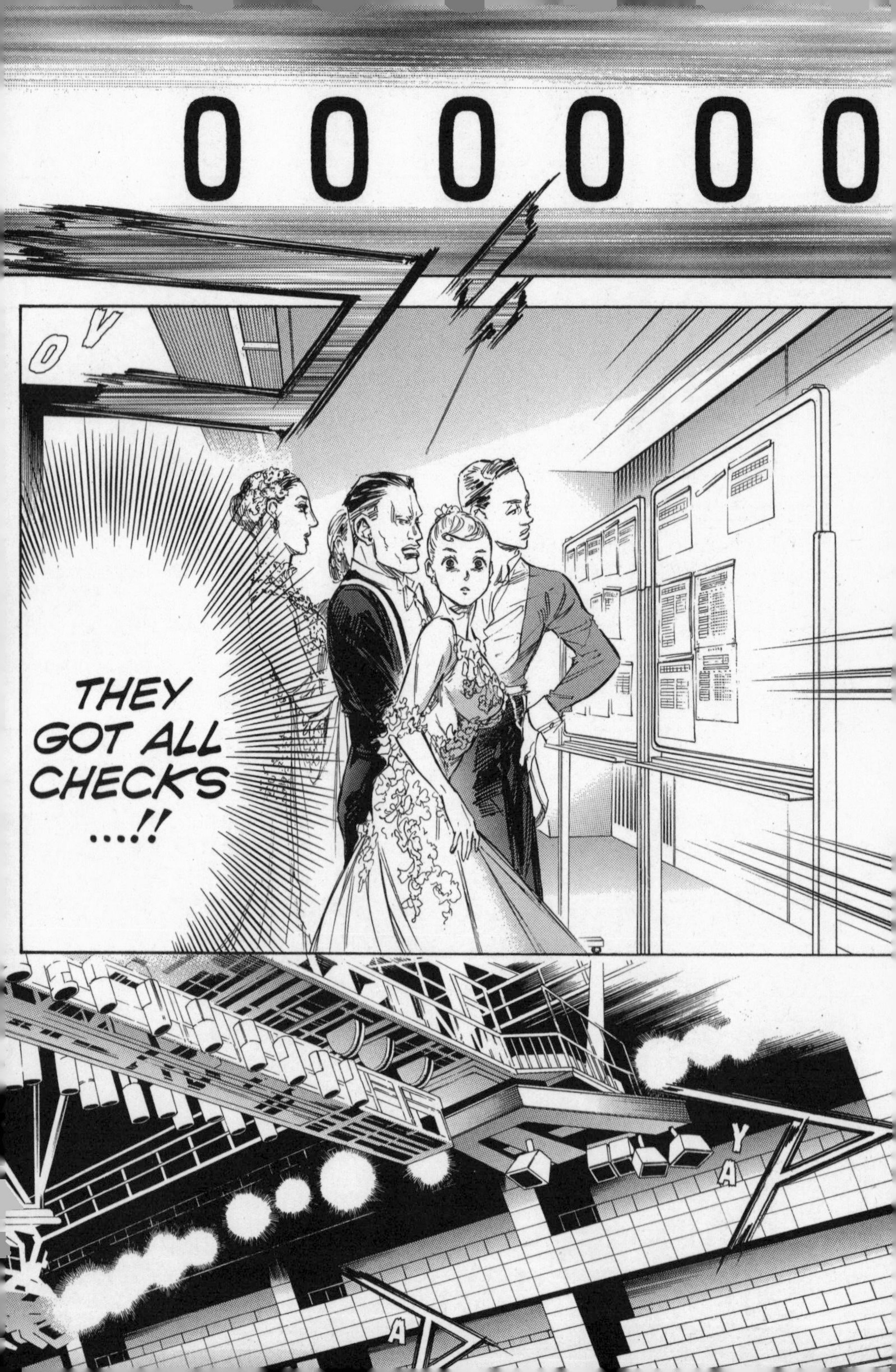
000000
THEY GOT ALL CHECKS ...!!

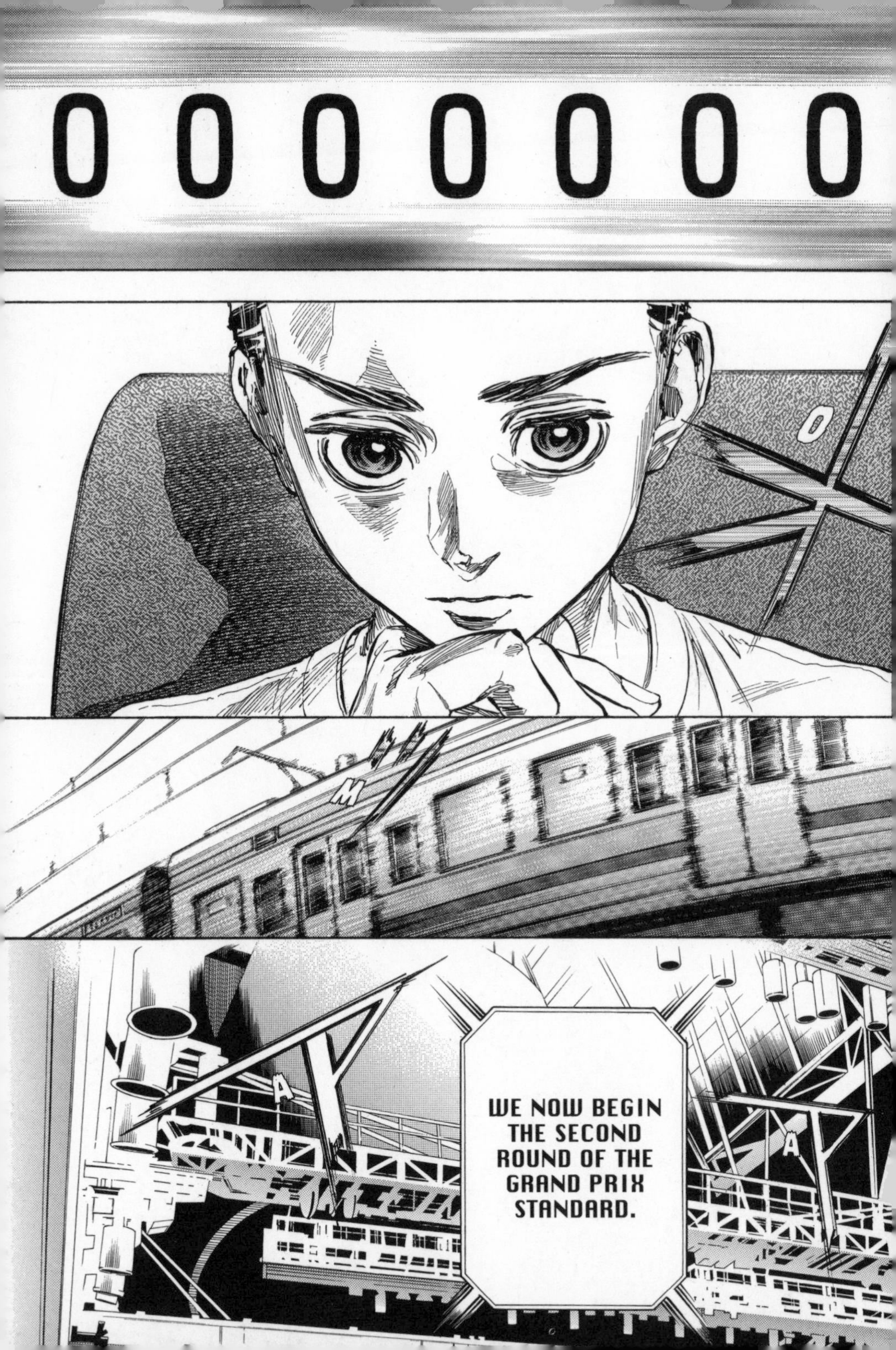
0000000
O
M
A
A
WE NOW BEGIN THE SECOND ROUND OF THE GRAND PRIX STANDARD.

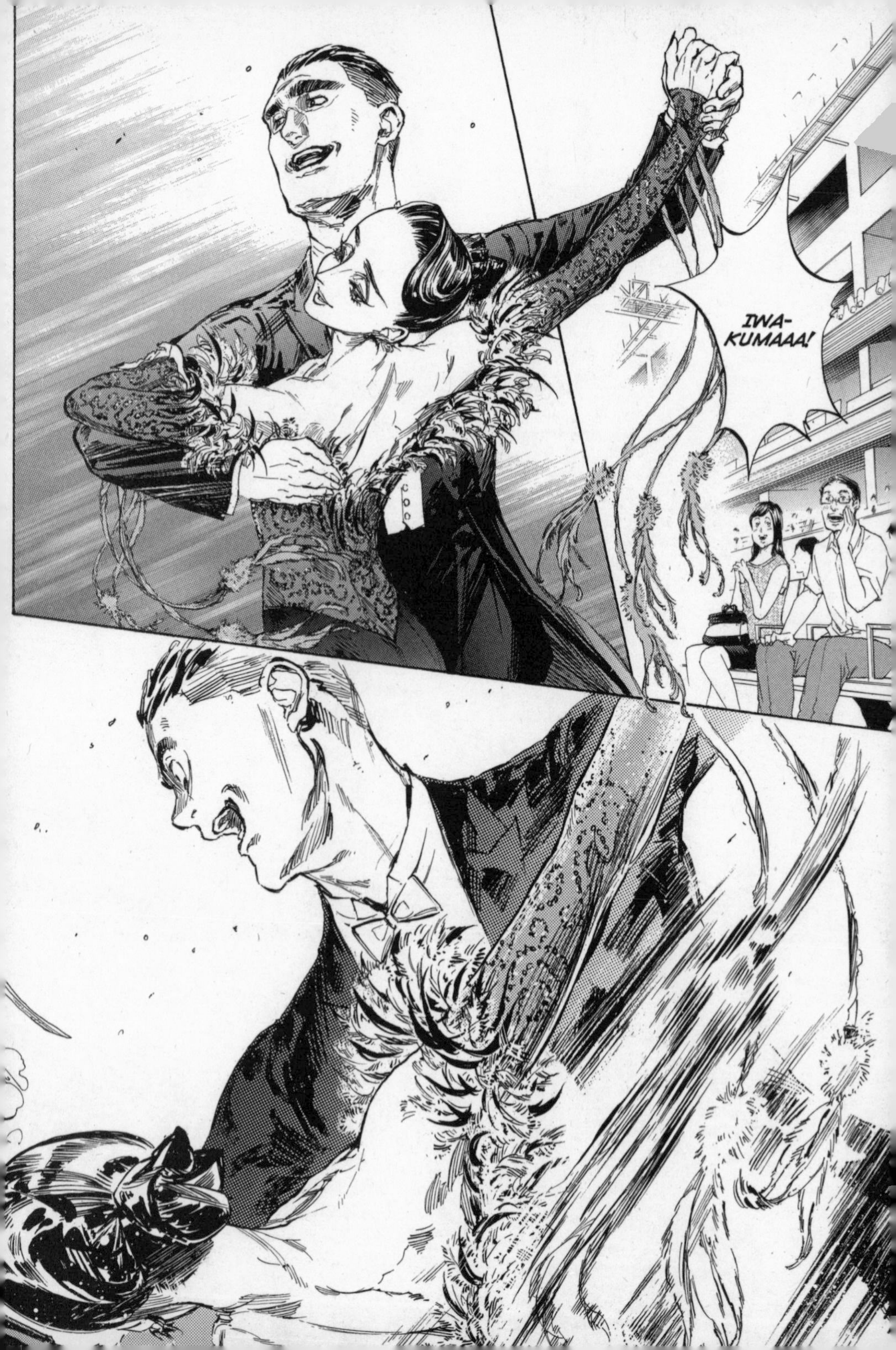
IWA-
KUMAAA!

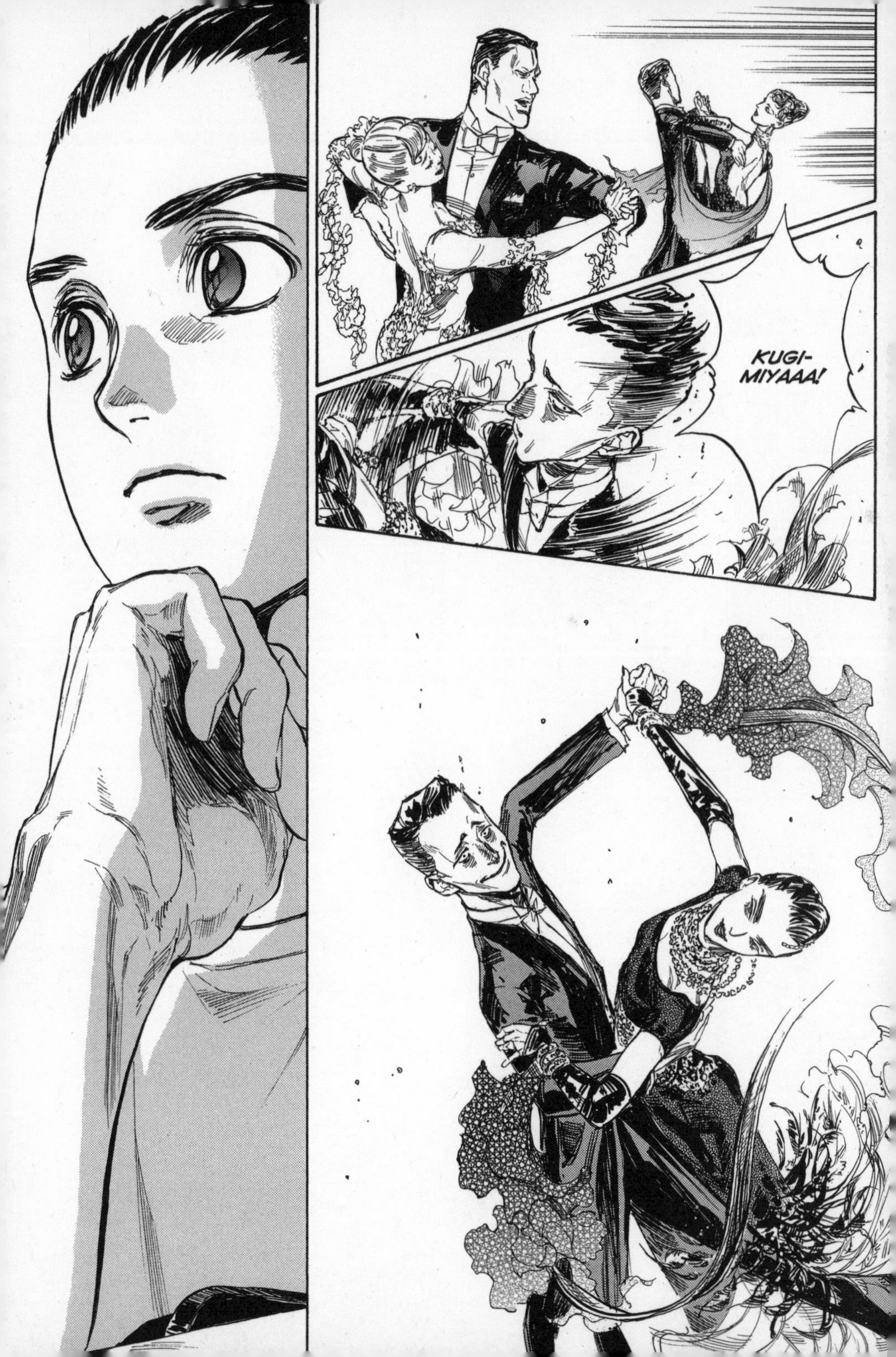
KUGI-
MIYAAA!

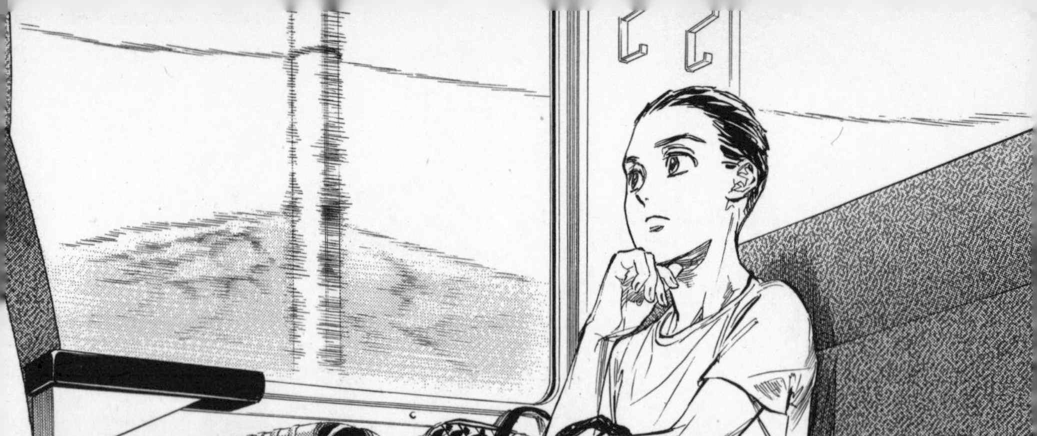

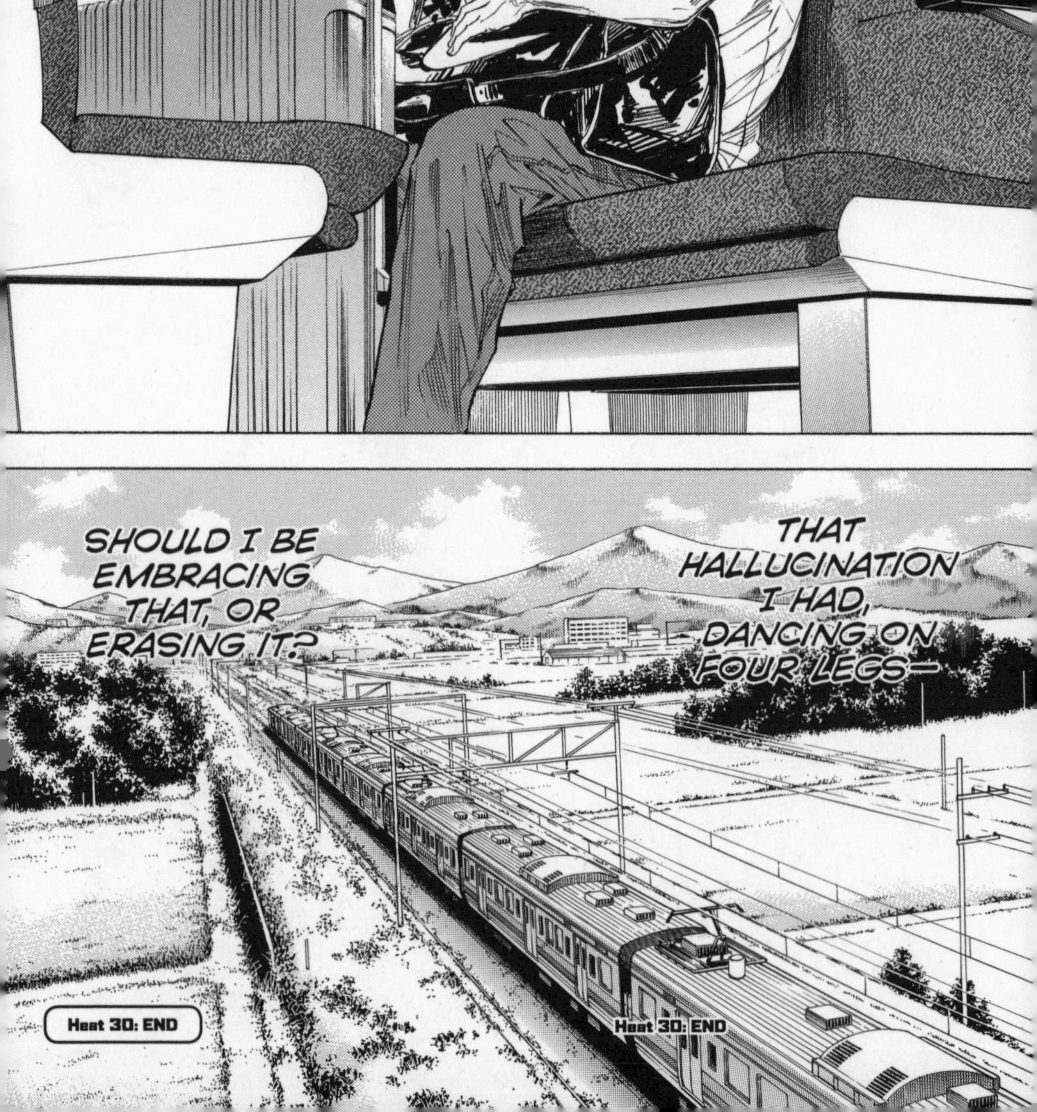
THAT HALLUCINATION I HAD, DANCING ON FOUR LEGS—
SHOULD I BE EMBRACING THAT, OR ERASING IT?
Heat 30: END
Heat 30: END

WELCOME TO THE BALLROOM

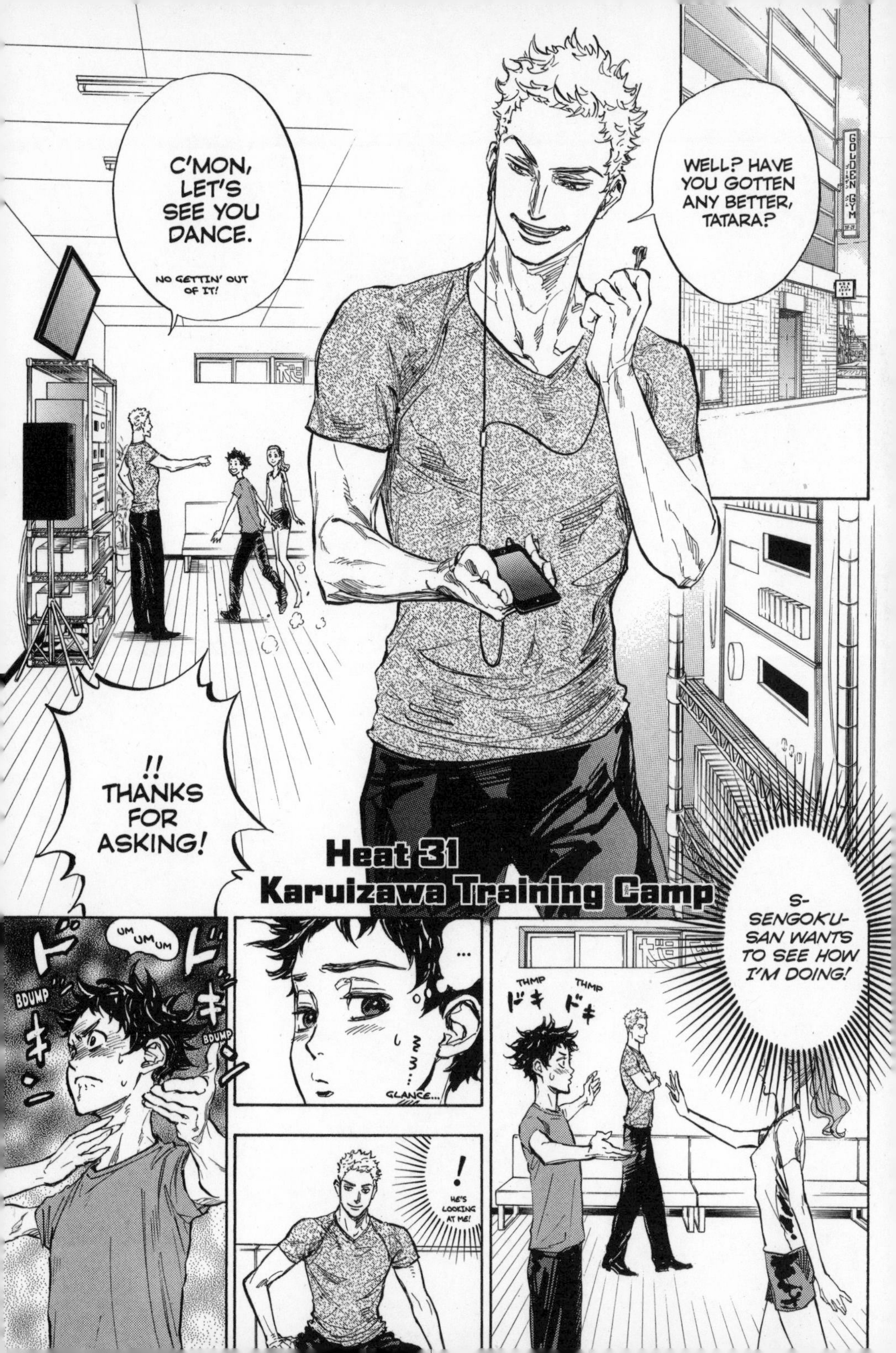

GOLDEN GYM
WELL? HAVE YOU GOTTEN ANY BETTER, TATARA?
C'MON, LET'S SEE YOU DANCE.
NO GETTIN' OUT OF IT!
!! THANKS FOR ASKING!
Heat 31
Karuizawa Training Camp
S-SENGOKU-SAN WANTS TO SEE HOW I'M DOING!
THMP THMP
...
GLANCE...
!
HE'S LOOKING AT ME!
UM UM UM
BDUMP
BDUMP

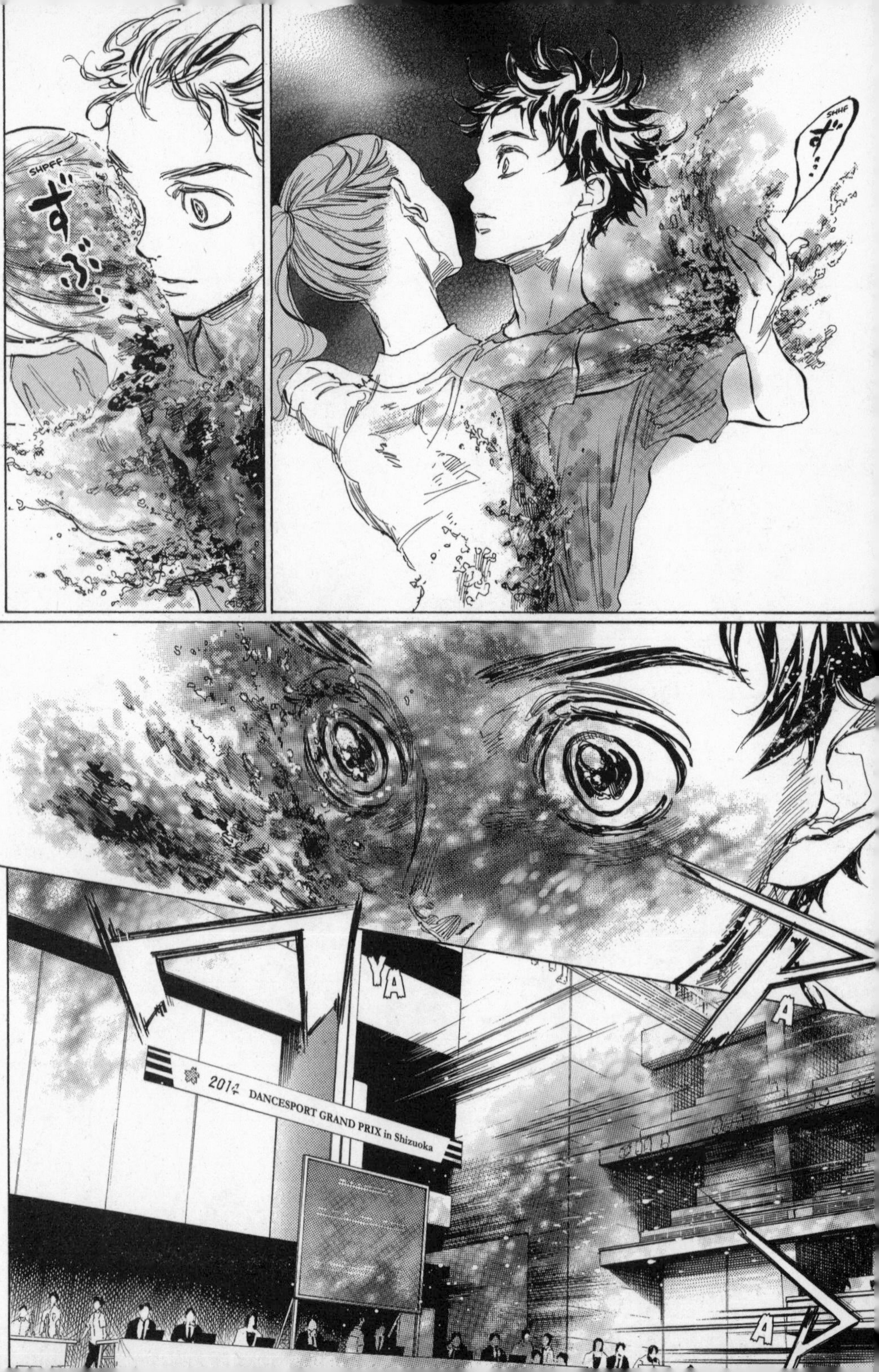
SHHF
ず…
SHPFF
ずぶ…
YA
A
A
2014 DANCESPORT GRAND PRIX in Shizuoka

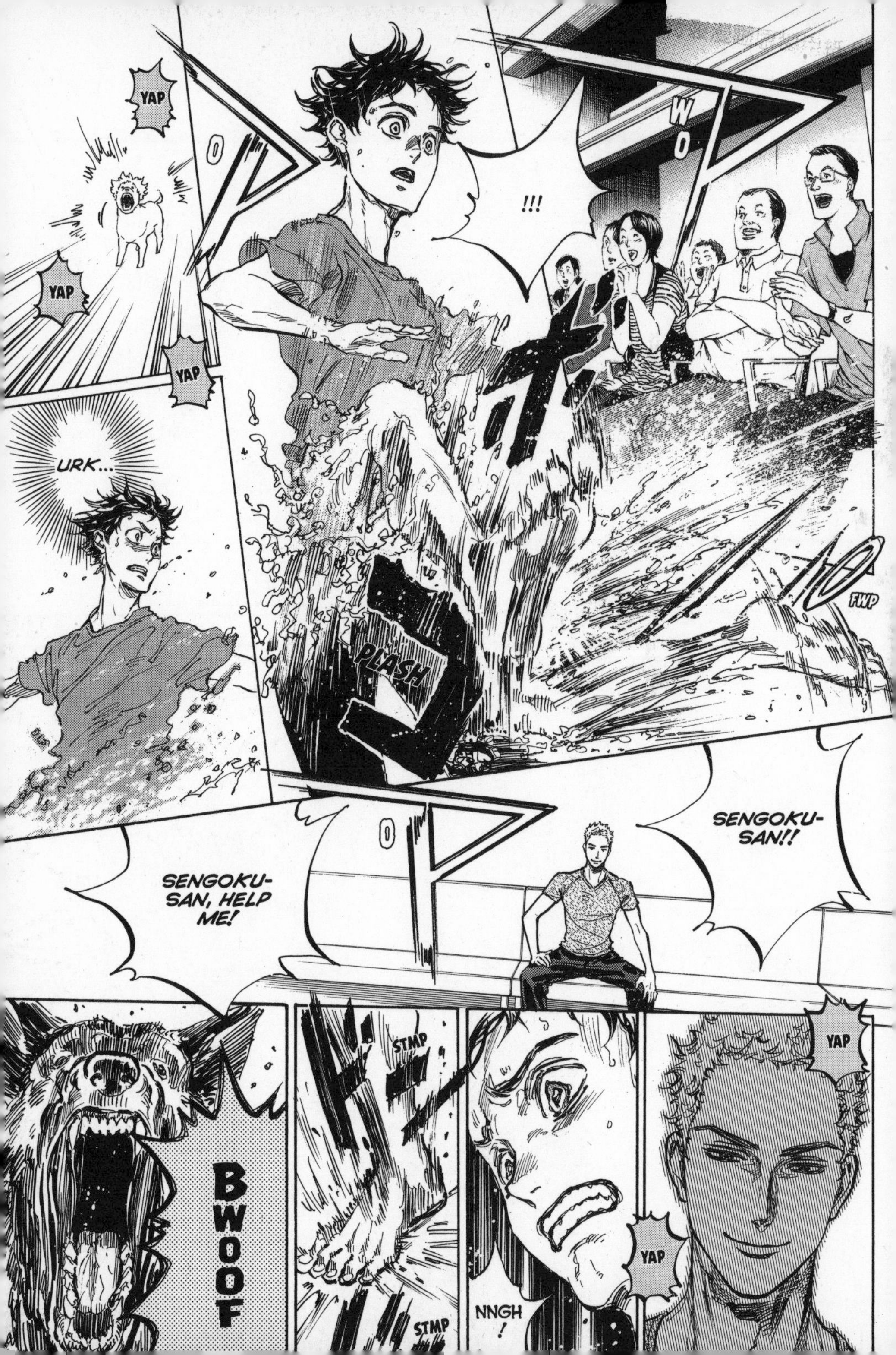
WO
!!!
O
FWP
PLASH
YAP
YAP
YAP
URK...
SENGOKU-SAN!!
O
SENGOKU-SAN, HELP ME!
YAP
YAP
NNGH!
STMP
STMP
BWOOF

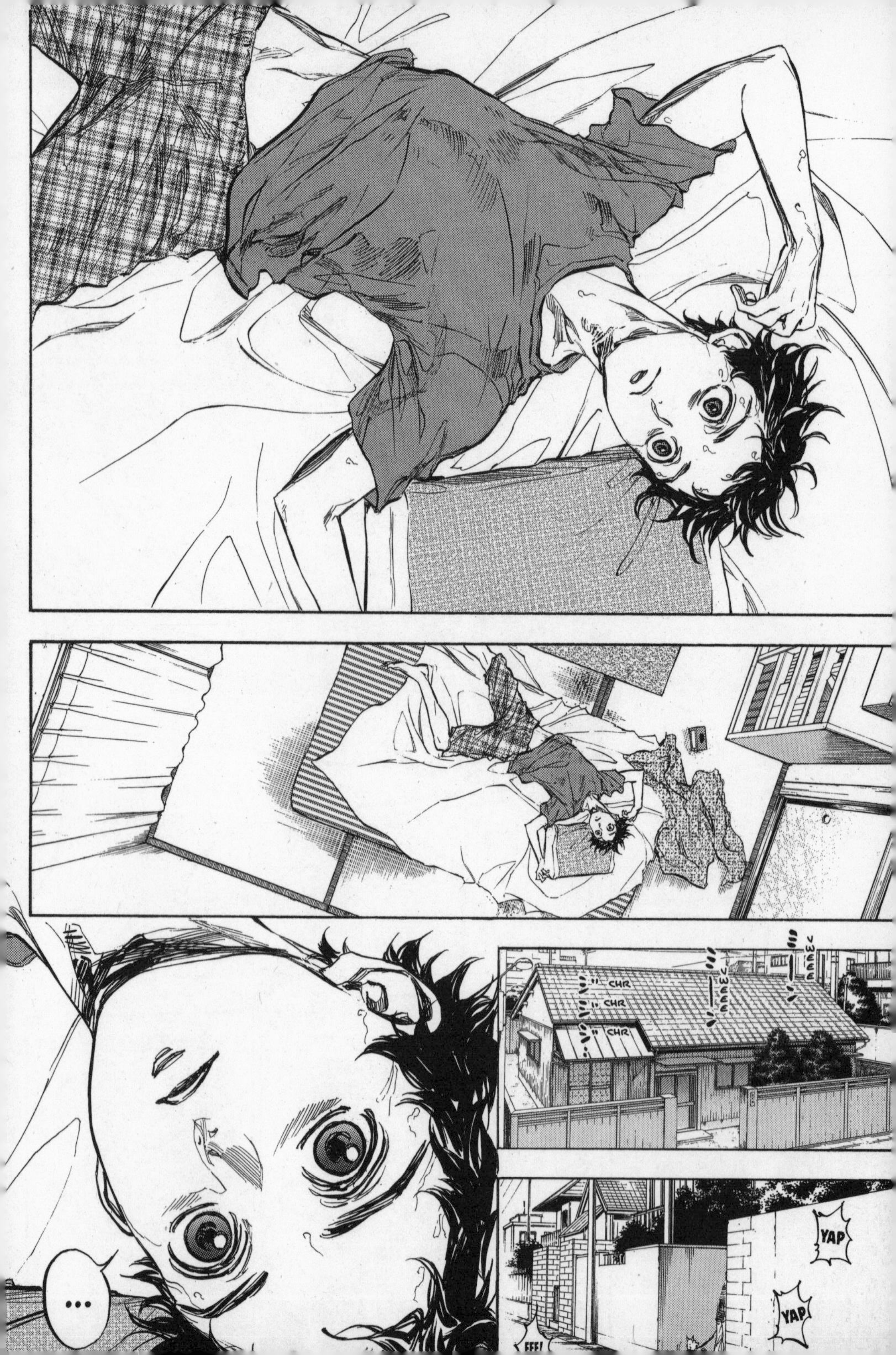
MEEE—!!
MEEE—!!
CHR
CHR
CHR
YAP
YAP
EEE!
...

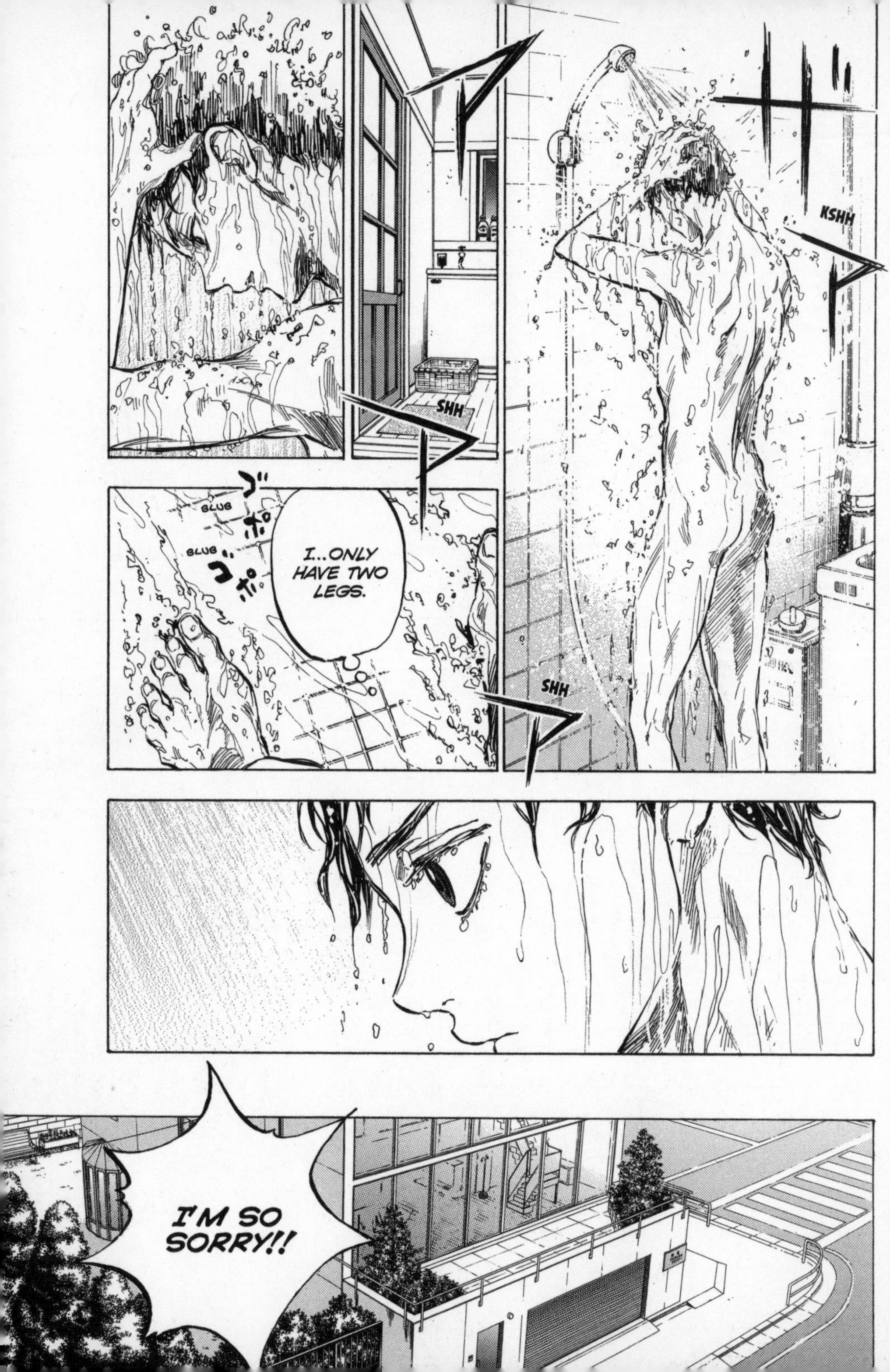
KSHH
SHH
SHH
BLUB
BLUB
I...ONLY HAVE TWO LEGS.
I'M SO SORRY!!

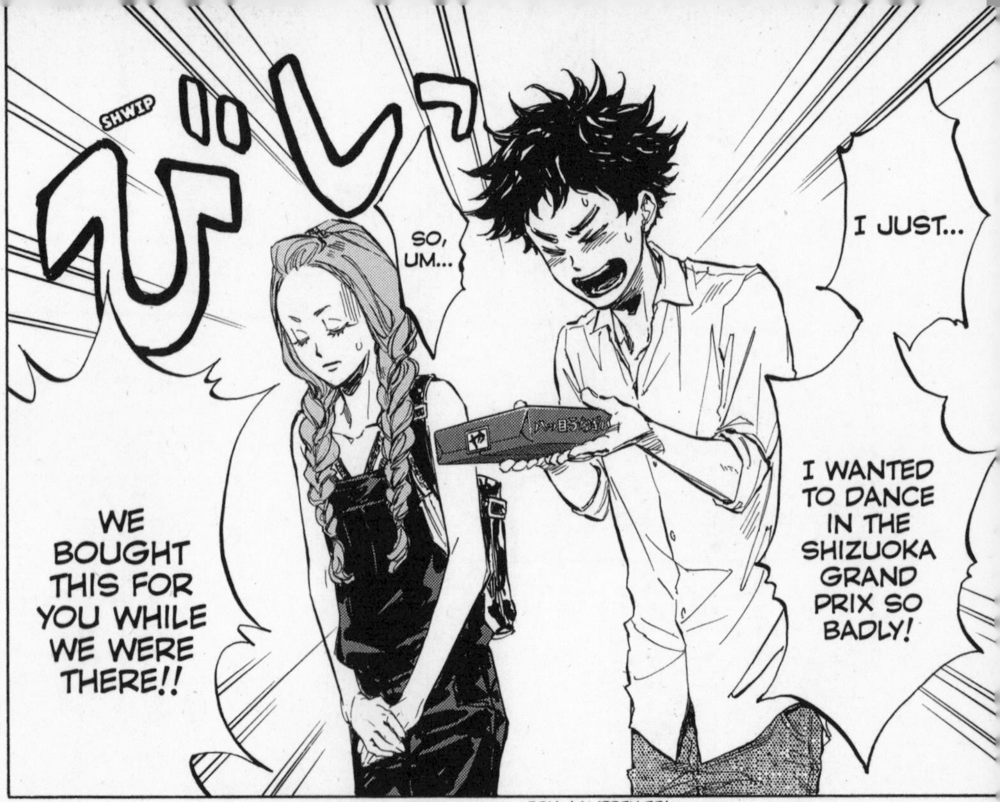
I JUST...
I WANTED TO DANCE IN THE SHIZUOKA GRAND PRIX SO BADLY!
SHWIP
びしっ
SO, UM...
WE BOUGHT THIS FOR YOU WHILE WE WERE THERE!!

BOX: LAMPREY EEL

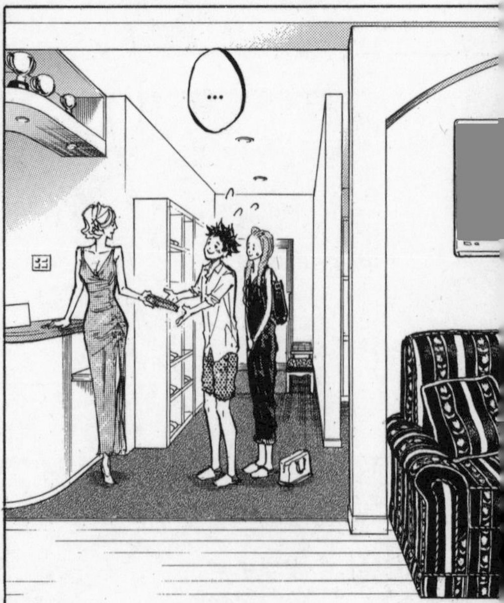
...
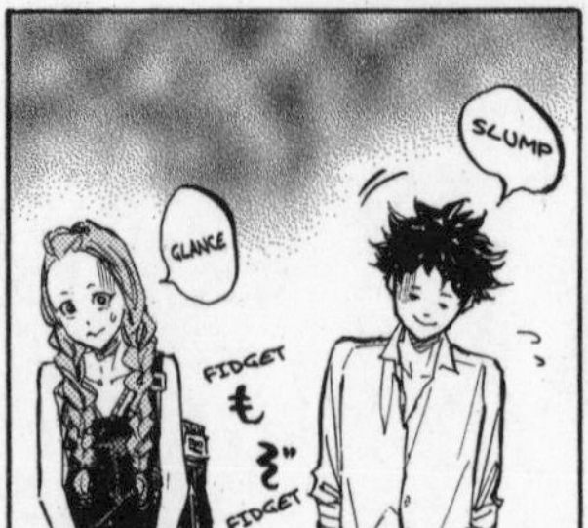
SLUMP
GLANCE
FIDGET
もぞ
FIDGET
もぞ
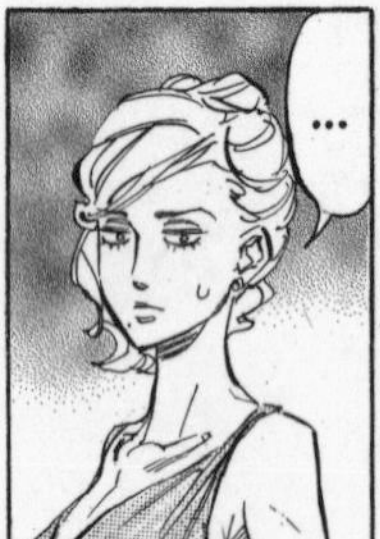
...
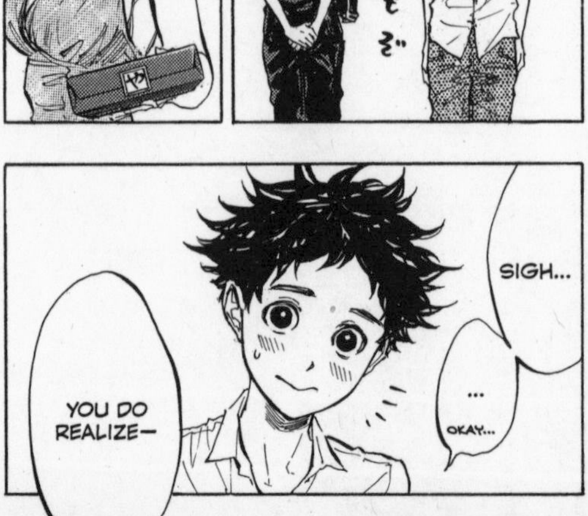
SIGH...
... OKAY...
YOU DO REALIZE—

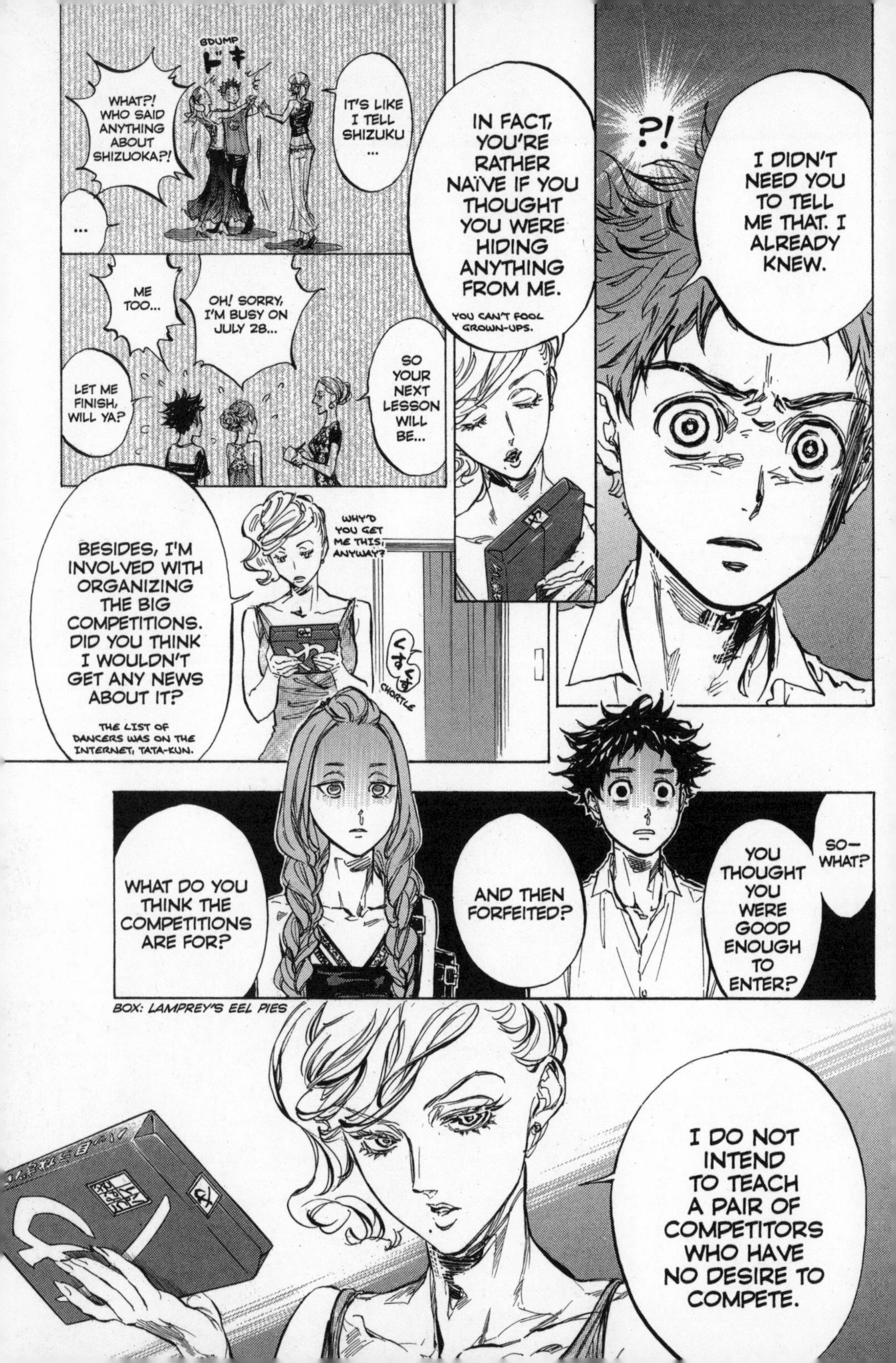
?!
I DIDN'T NEED YOU TO TELL ME THAT. I ALREADY KNEW.
IN FACT, YOU'RE RATHER NAÏVE IF YOU THOUGHT YOU WERE HIDING ANYTHING FROM ME.
YOU CAN'T FOOL GROWN-UPS.
IT'S LIKE I TELL SHIZUKU ...
BDUMP
ドキ
WHAT?! WHO SAID ANYTHING ABOUT SHIZUOKA?!
...
SO YOUR NEXT LESSON WILL BE...
OH! SORRY, I'M BUSY ON JULY 28...
ME TOO...
LET ME FINISH, WILL YA?
WHY'D YOU GET ME THIS, ANYWAY?
くすくす
CHORTLE
BESIDES, I'M INVOLVED WITH ORGANIZING THE BIG COMPETITIONS. DID YOU THINK I WOULDN'T GET ANY NEWS ABOUT IT?
THE LIST OF DANCERS WAS ON THE INTERNET, TATA-KUN.
SO— WHAT?
YOU THOUGHT YOU WERE GOOD ENOUGH TO ENTER?
AND THEN FORFEITED?
WHAT DO YOU THINK THE COMPETITIONS ARE FOR?
BOX: LAMPREY'S EEL PIES
I DO NOT INTEND TO TEACH A PAIR OF COMPETITORS WHO HAVE NO DESIRE TO COMPETE.

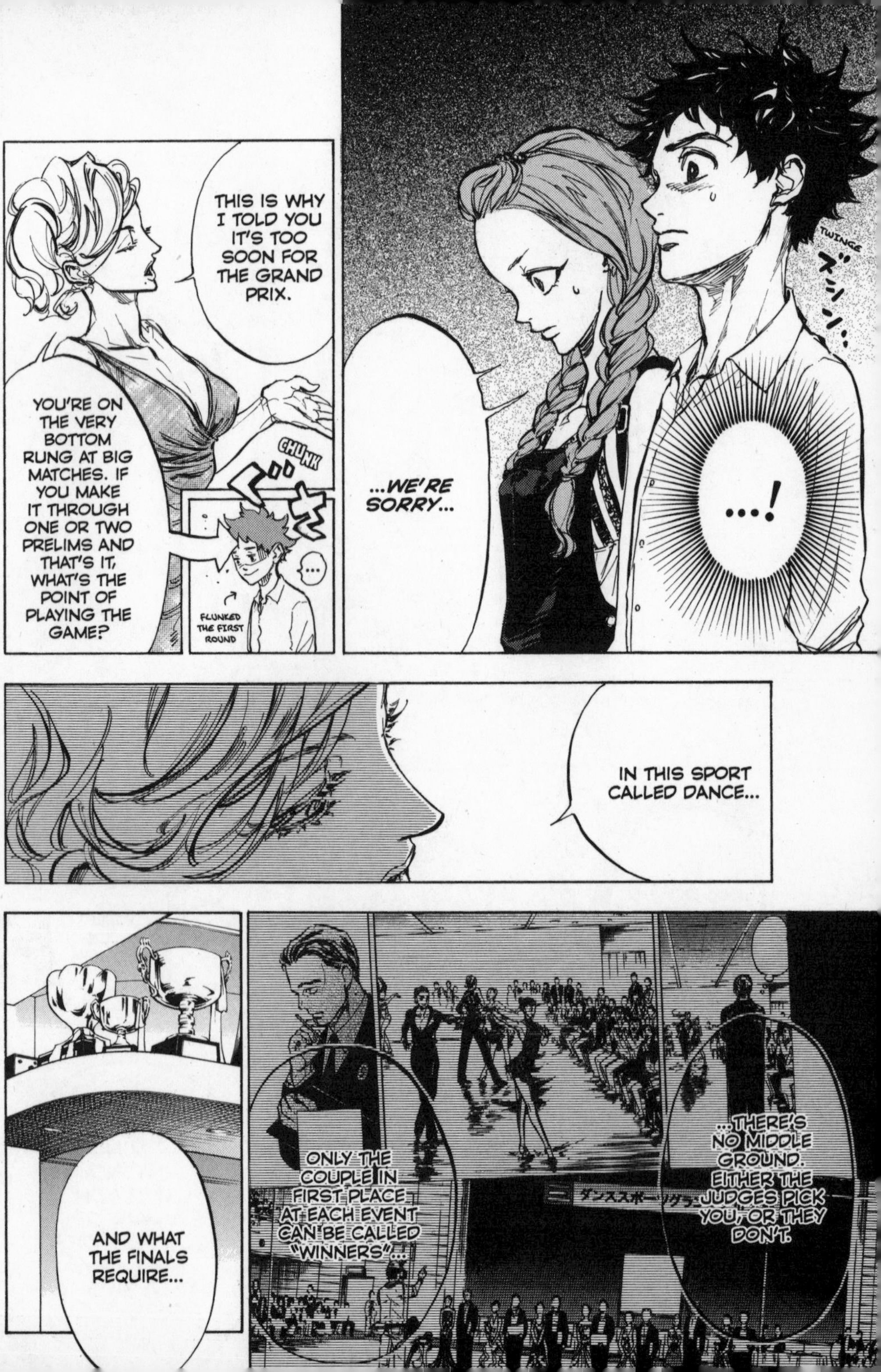
TWINGE
...!
...WE'RE SORRY...
THIS IS WHY I TOLD YOU IT'S TOO SOON FOR THE GRAND PRIX.
CHUNK
YOU'RE ON THE VERY BOTTOM RUNG AT BIG MATCHES. IF YOU MAKE IT THROUGH ONE OR TWO PRELIMS AND THAT'S IT, WHAT'S THE POINT OF PLAYING THE GAME?
...
FLUNKED THE FIRST ROUND
IN THIS SPORT CALLED DANCE...
...THERE'S NO MIDDLE GROUND. EITHER THE JUDGES PICK YOU, OR THEY DON'T.
ONLY THE COUPLE IN FIRST PLACE AT EACH EVENT CAN BE CALLED "WINNERS"...
AND WHAT THE FINALS REQUIRE...

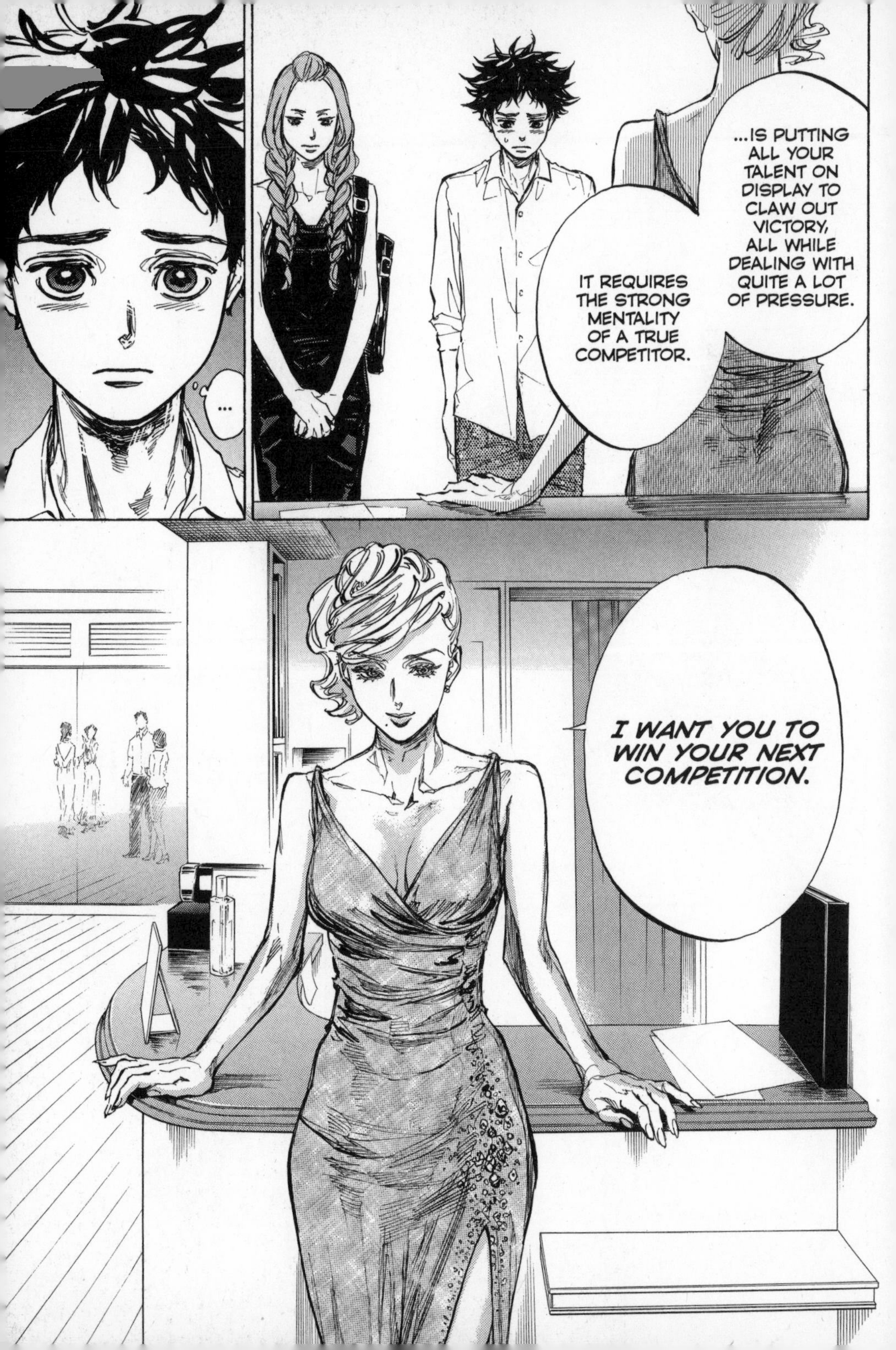

...IS PUTTING ALL YOUR TALENT ON DISPLAY TO CLAW OUT VICTORY, ALL WHILE DEALING WITH QUITE A LOT OF PRESSURE.
IT REQUIRES THE STRONG MENTALITY OF A TRUE COMPETITOR.
...
I WANT YOU TO WIN YOUR NEXT COMPETITION.

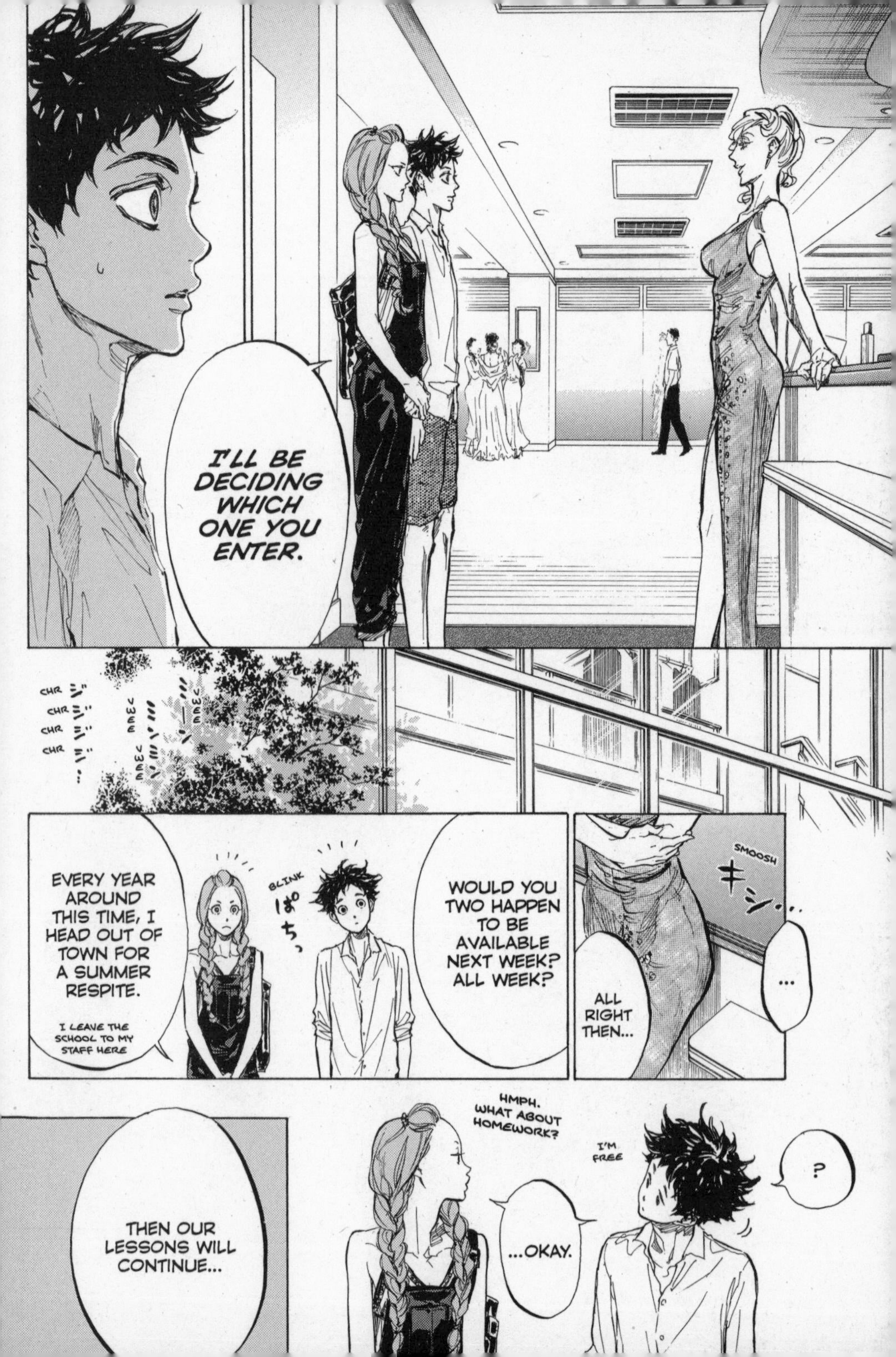

I'LL BE DECIDING WHICH ONE YOU ENTER.
CHR CHR CHR CHR
VWEE VWEE VWEE
...
ALL RIGHT THEN...
SMOOSH
WOULD YOU TWO HAPPEN TO BE AVAILABLE NEXT WEEK? ALL WEEK?
BLINK
EVERY YEAR AROUND THIS TIME, I HEAD OUT OF TOWN FOR A SUMMER RESPITE.
I LEAVE THE SCHOOL TO MY STAFF HERE
?
I'M FREE
HMPH. WHAT ABOUT HOMEWORK?
...OKAY.
THEN OUR LESSONS WILL CONTINUE...

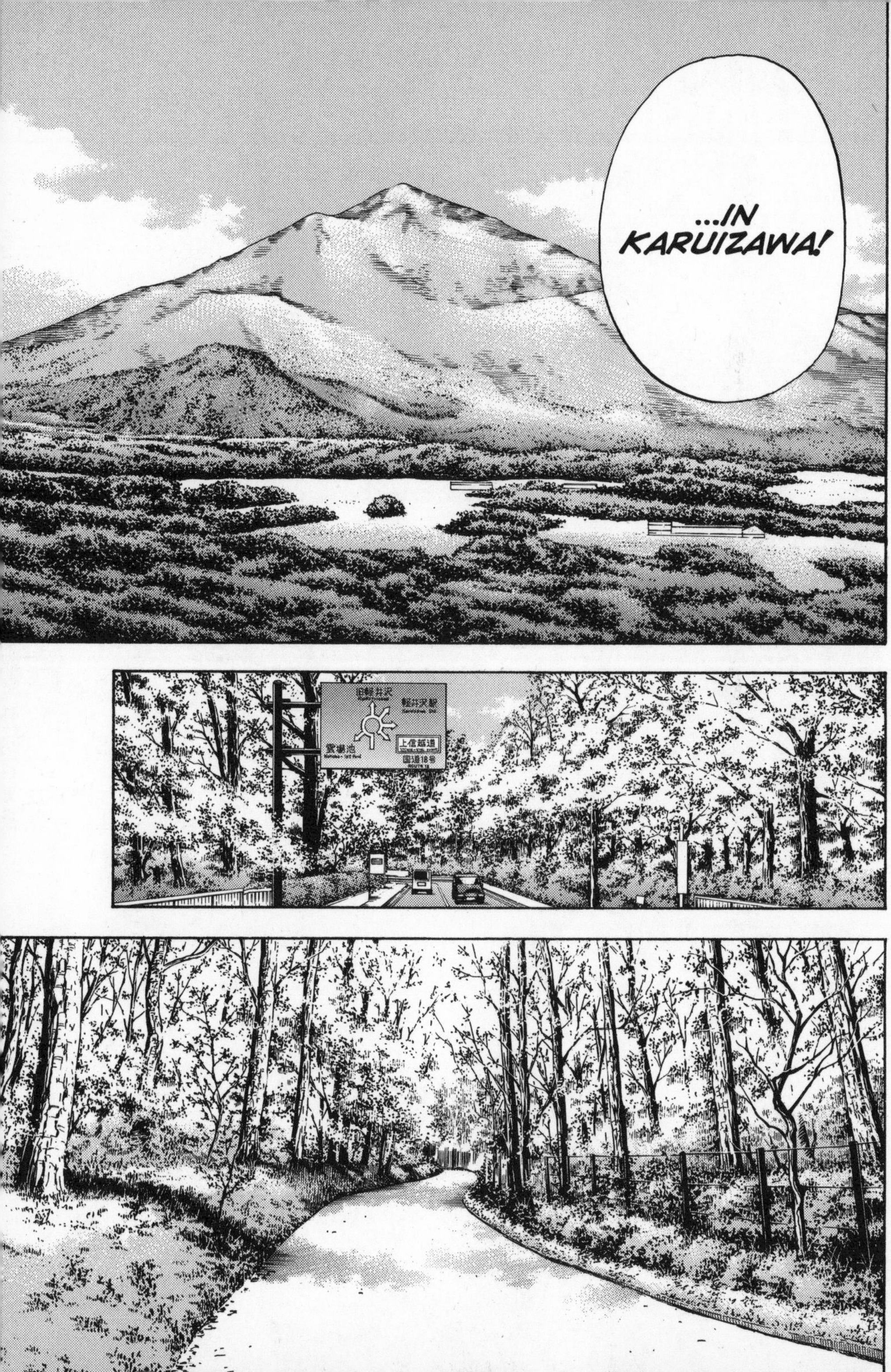
...IN KARUIZAWA!
旧軽井沢
軽井沢駅
雲場池
上信越道
国道18号

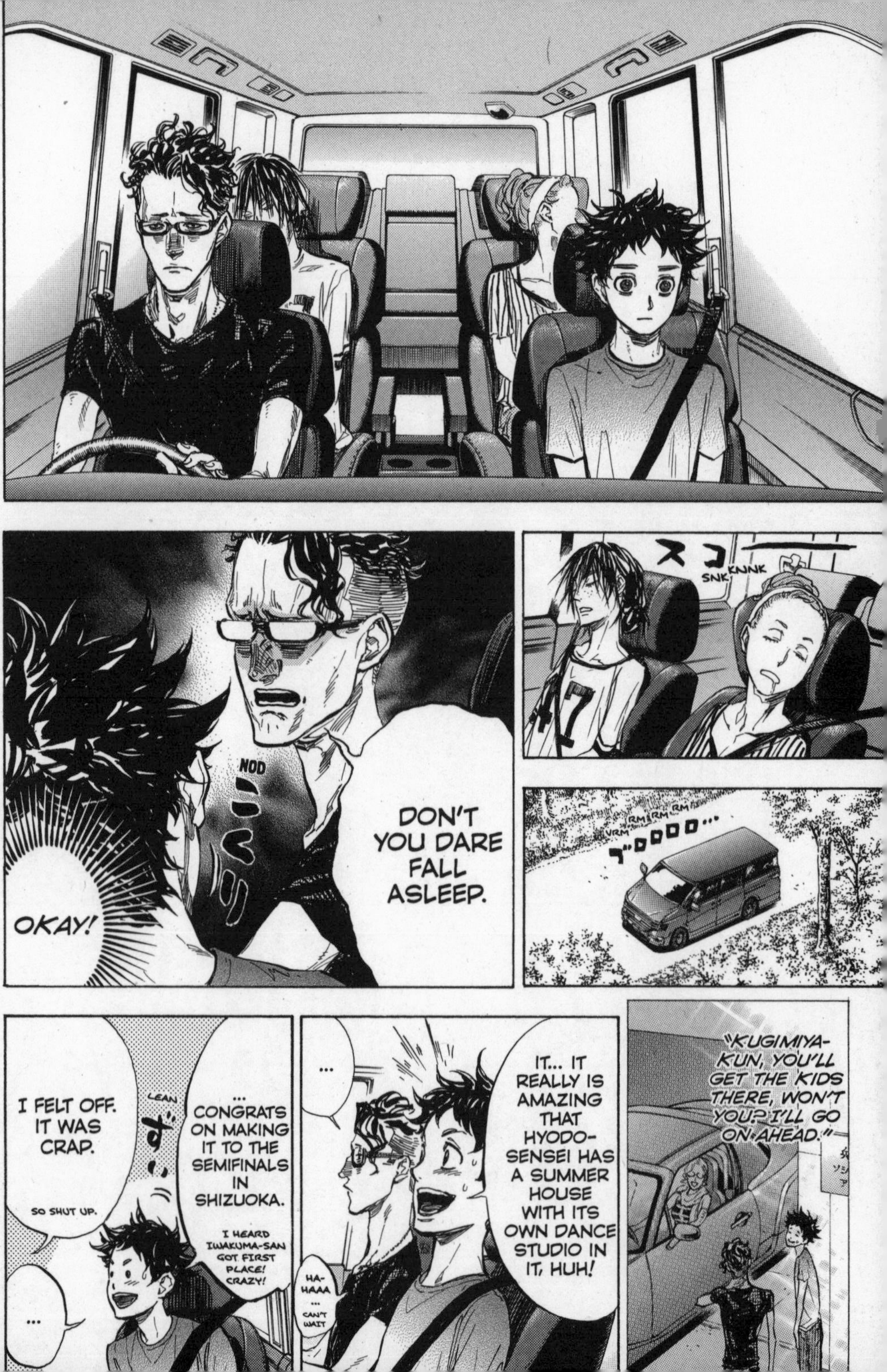

SNK KNNK
VRM RM RM RM
DON'T YOU DARE FALL ASLEEP.
NOD
OKAY!
"KUGIMIYA-KUN, YOU'LL GET THE KIDS THERE, WON'T YOU? I'LL GO ON AHEAD."
IT... IT REALLY IS AMAZING THAT HYODO-SENSEI HAS A SUMMER HOUSE WITH ITS OWN DANCE STUDIO IN IT, HUH!
...
HA-HAAA ...
CAN'T WAIT
... CONGRATS ON MAKING IT TO THE SEMIFINALS IN SHIZUOKA.
I HEARD IWAKUMA-SAN GOT FIRST PLACE! CRAZY!
LEAN
I FELT OFF. IT WAS CRAP.
SO SHUT UP.
...

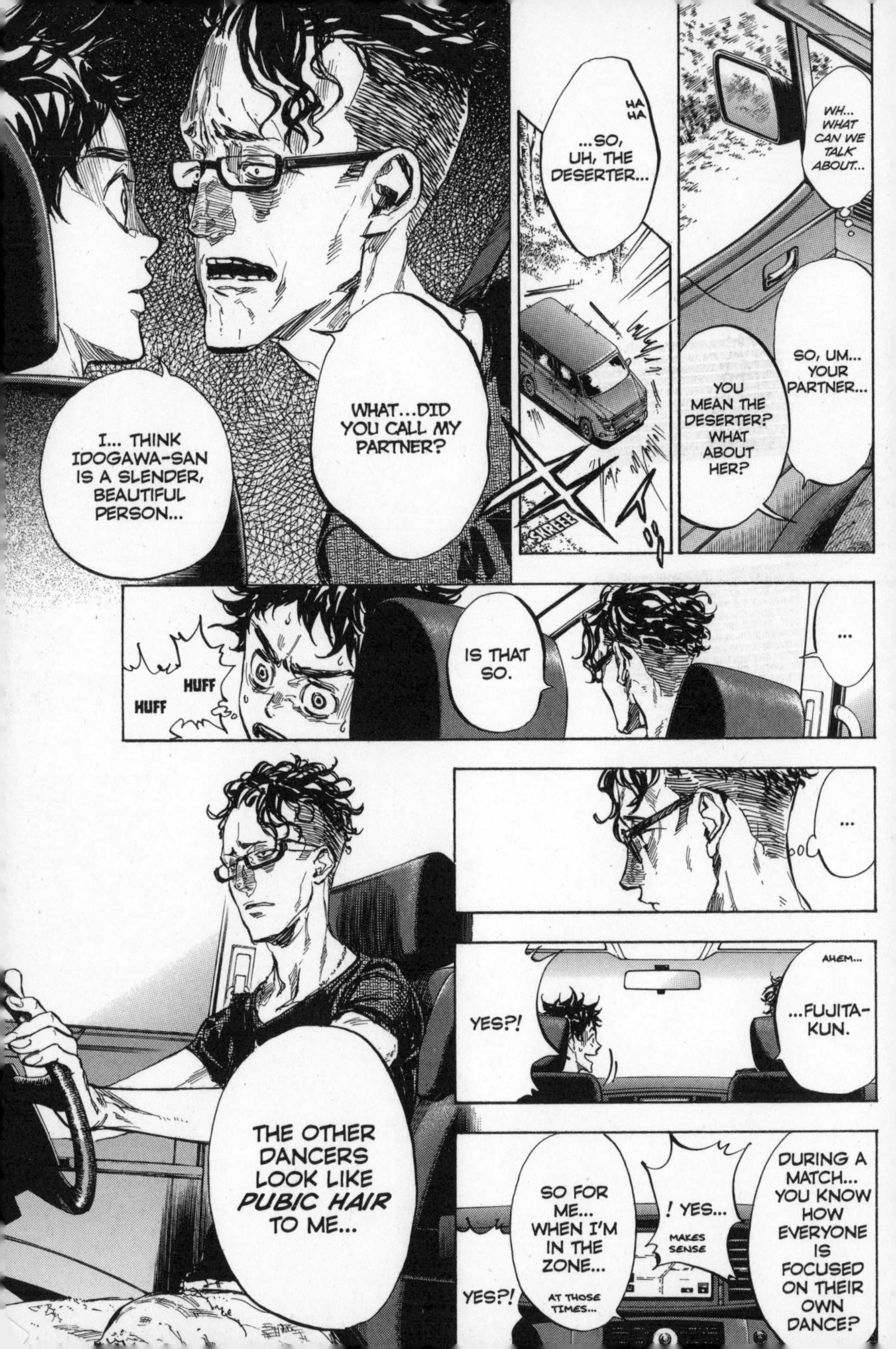
WH... WHAT CAN WE TALK ABOUT...
SO, UM... YOUR PARTNER...
YOU MEAN THE DESERTER? WHAT ABOUT HER?
HA HA
...SO, UH, THE DESERTER...
SKREEE
WHAT...DID YOU CALL MY PARTNER?
I... THINK IDOGAWA-SAN IS A SLENDER, BEAUTIFUL PERSON...
...
IS THAT SO.
HUFF
HUFF
...
AHEM...
...FUJITA-KUN.
YES?!
DURING A MATCH... YOU KNOW HOW EVERYONE IS FOCUSED ON THEIR OWN DANCE?
! YES...
MAKES SENSE
SO FOR ME... WHEN I'M IN THE ZONE...
AT THOSE TIMES...
YES?!
THE OTHER DANCERS LOOK LIKE *PUBIC HAIR* TO ME...

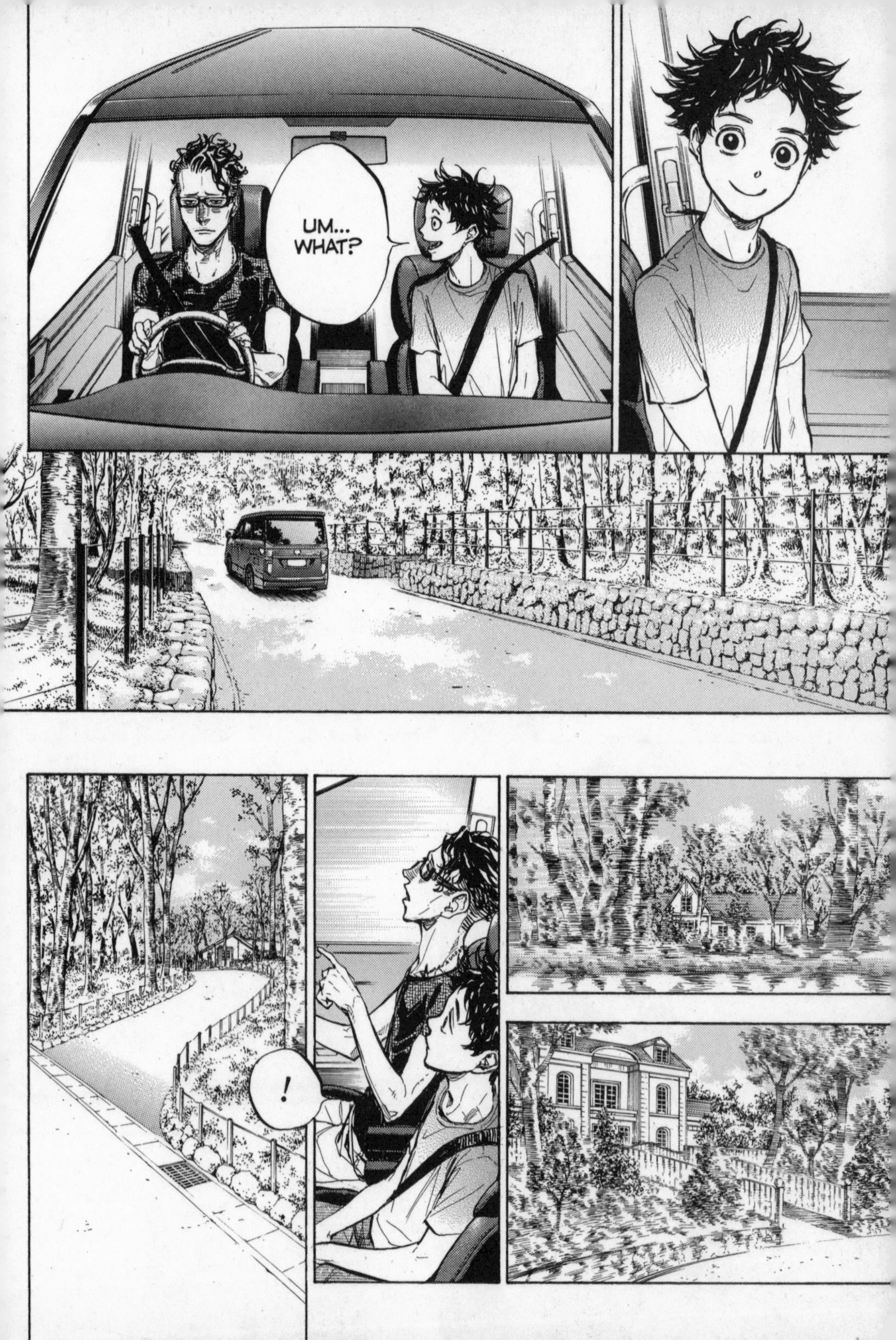
UM... WHAT?
!

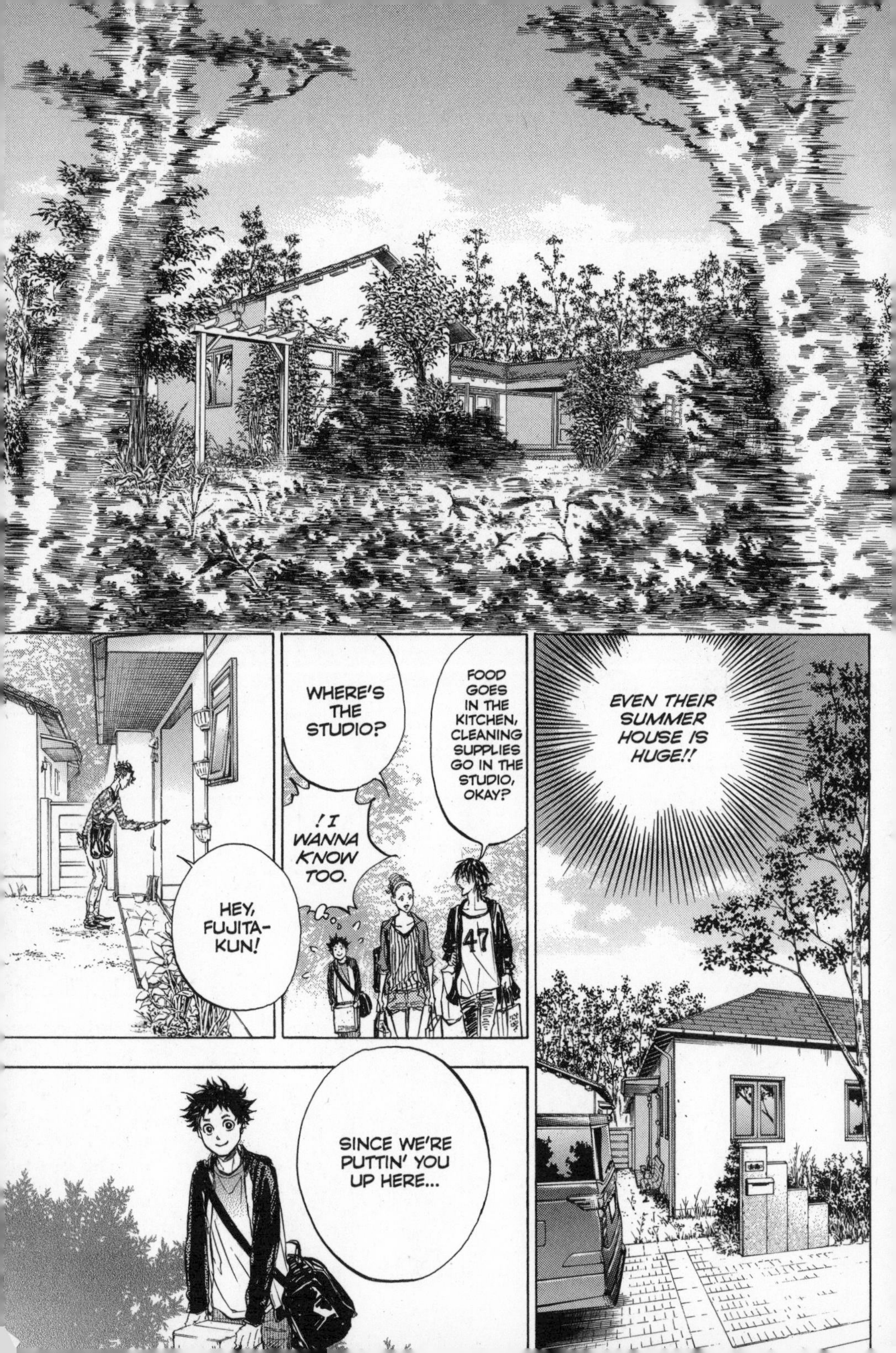
EVEN THEIR SUMMER HOUSE IS HUGE!!
FOOD GOES IN THE KITCHEN, CLEANING SUPPLIES GO IN THE STUDIO, OKAY?
WHERE'S THE STUDIO?
! I WANNA KNOW TOO.
HEY, FUJITA-KUN!
SINCE WE'RE PUTTIN' YOU UP HERE...

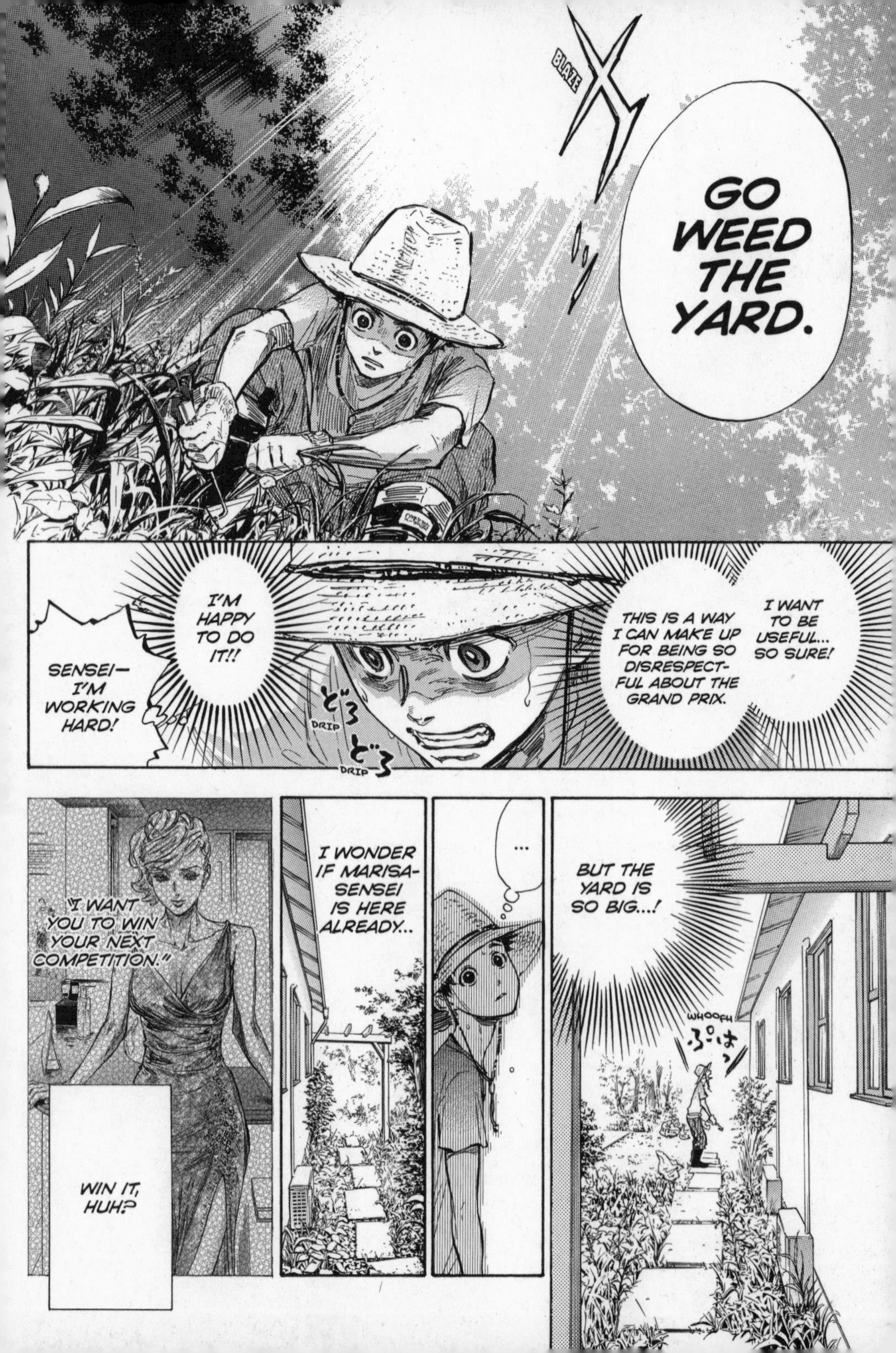
BLAZE
GO WEED THE YARD.
I WANT TO BE USEFUL... SO SURE!
THIS IS A WAY I CAN MAKE UP FOR BEING SO DISRESPECT-FUL ABOUT THE GRAND PRIX.
I'M HAPPY TO DO IT!!
SENSEI— I'M WORKING HARD!
どろ DRIP
どろ DRIP
WHOOFH ぷはっ
BUT THE YARD IS SO BIG...!
...
I WONDER IF MARISA-SENSEI IS HERE ALREADY...
"I WANT YOU TO WIN YOUR NEXT COMPETITION."
WIN IT, HUH?

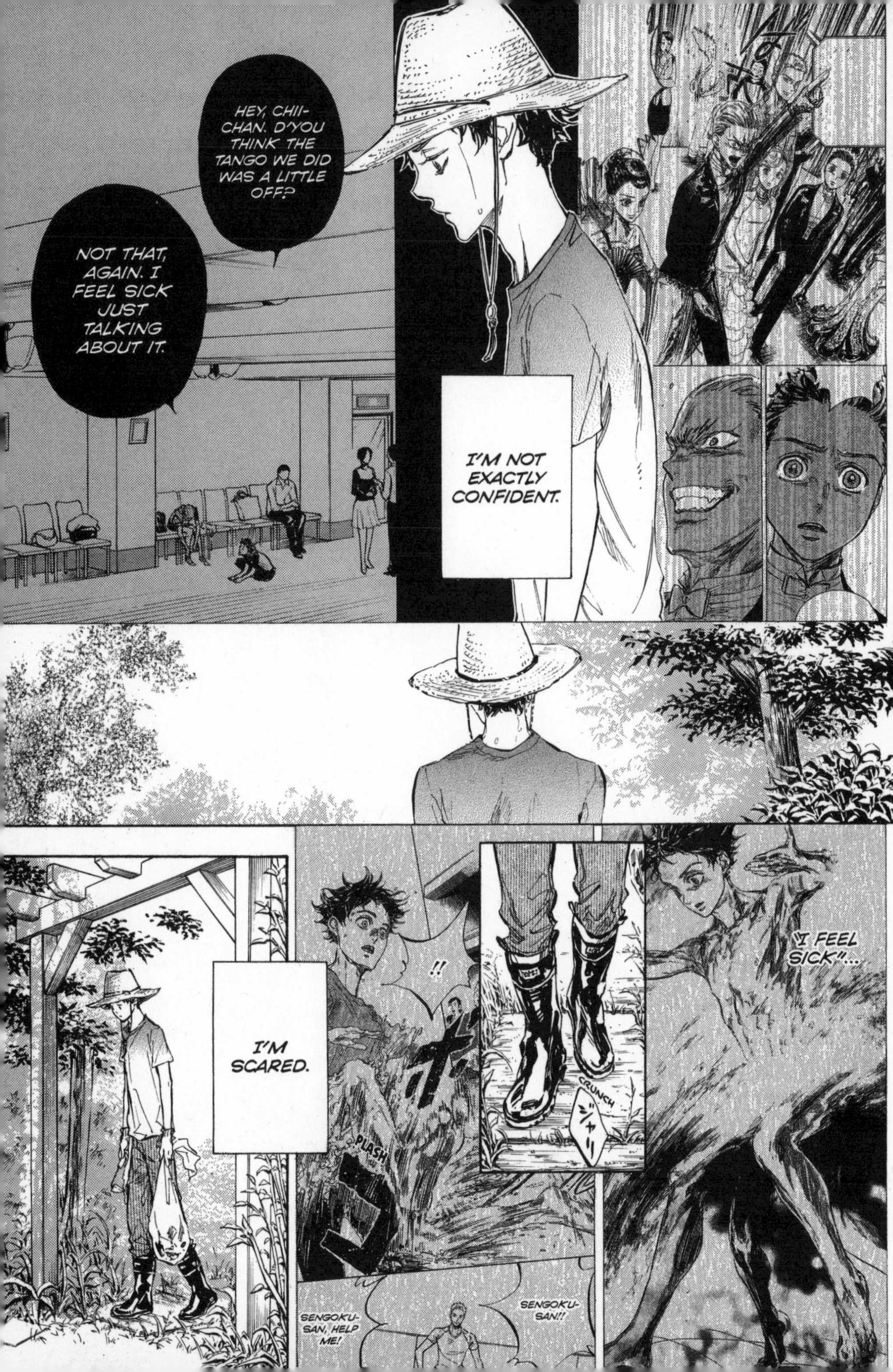
HEY, CHII-CHAN. D'YOU THINK THE TANGO WE DID WAS A LITTLE OFF?
NOT THAT, AGAIN. I FEEL SICK JUST TALKING ABOUT IT.
I'M NOT EXACTLY CONFIDENT.
"I FEEL SICK"...
CRUNCH
ジャリ
!!
PLASH
SENGOKU-SAN!!
SENGOKU-SAN, HELP ME!
I'M SCARED.

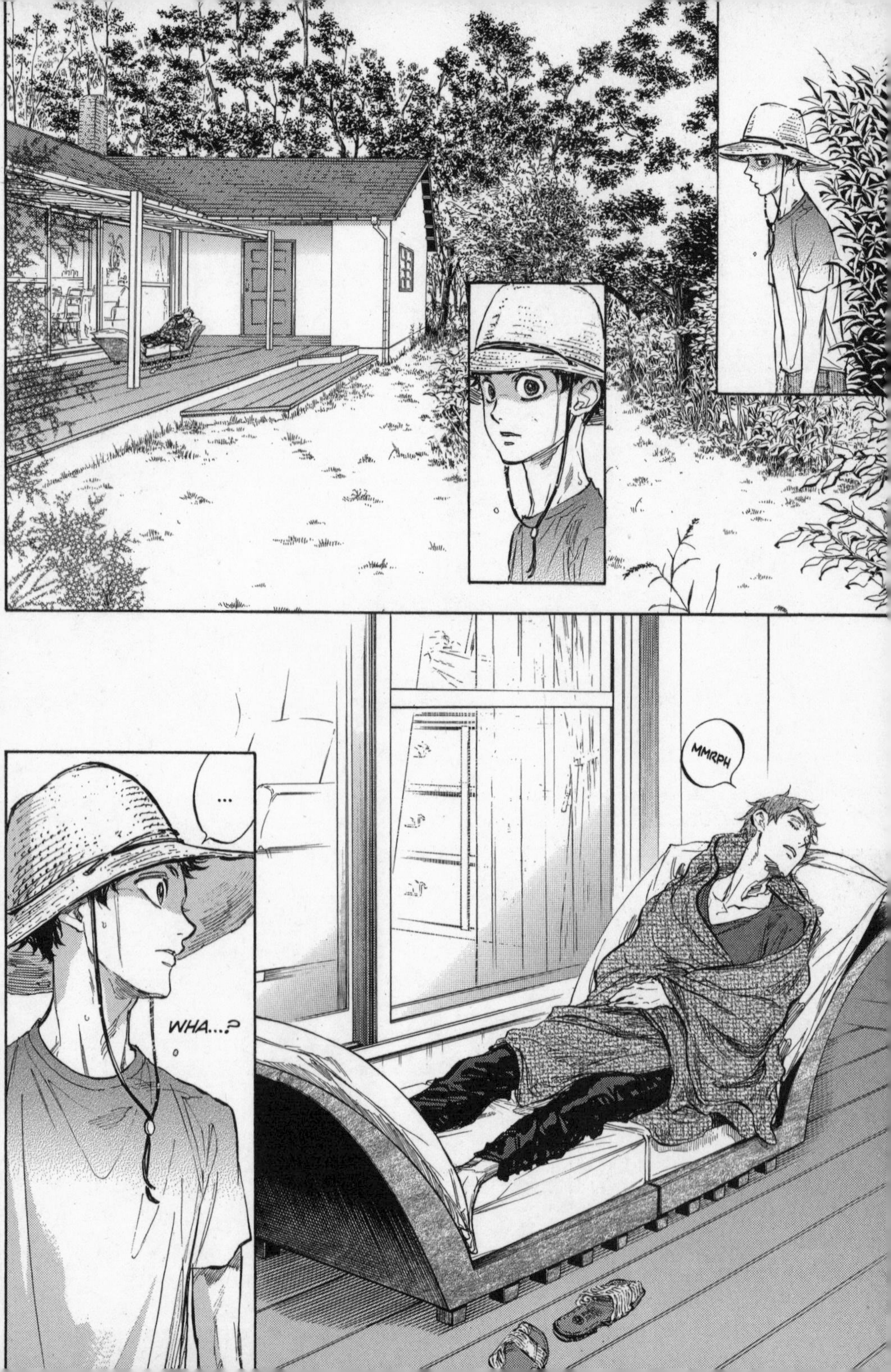
MMRPH
...
WHA...?

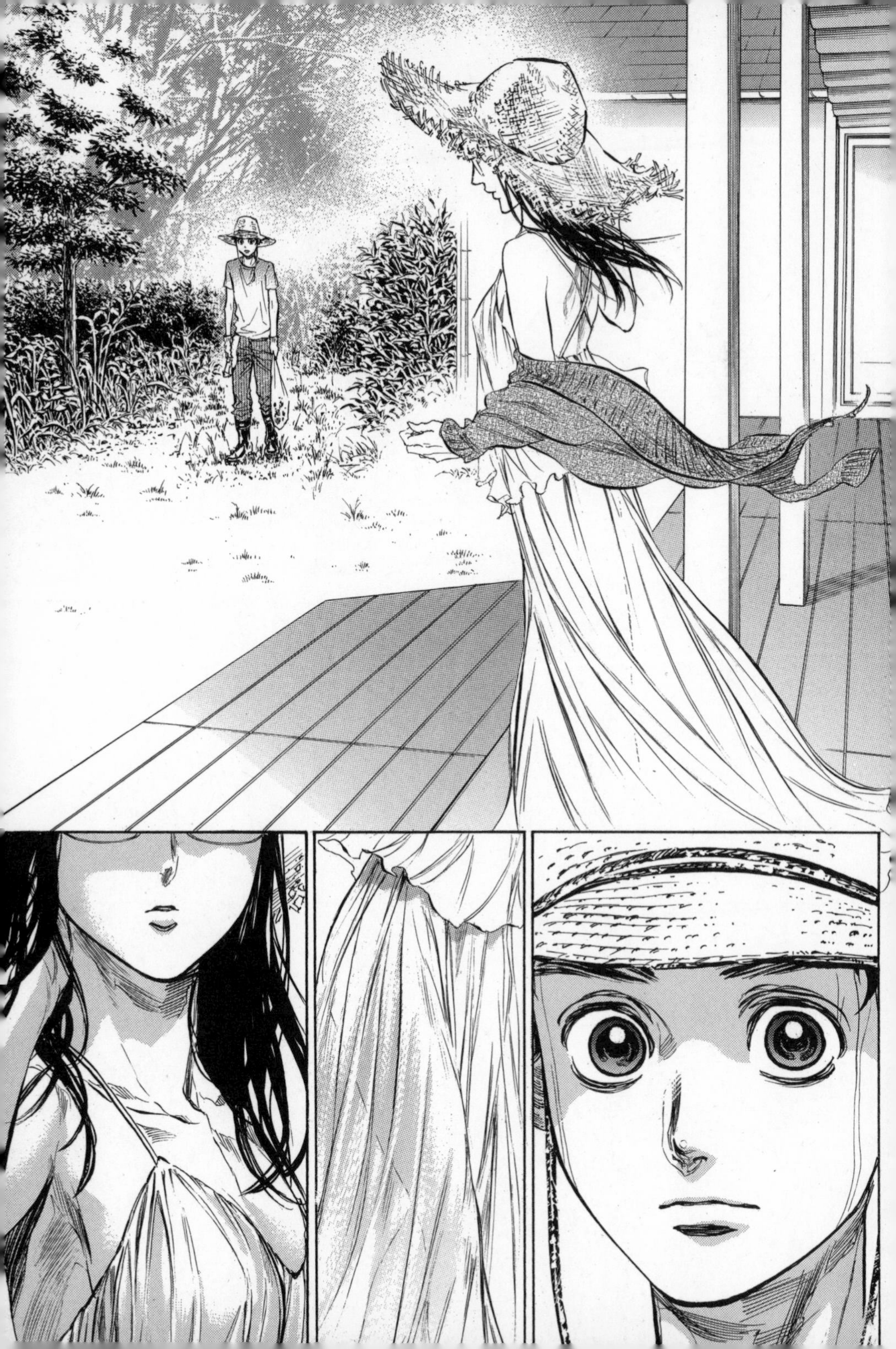

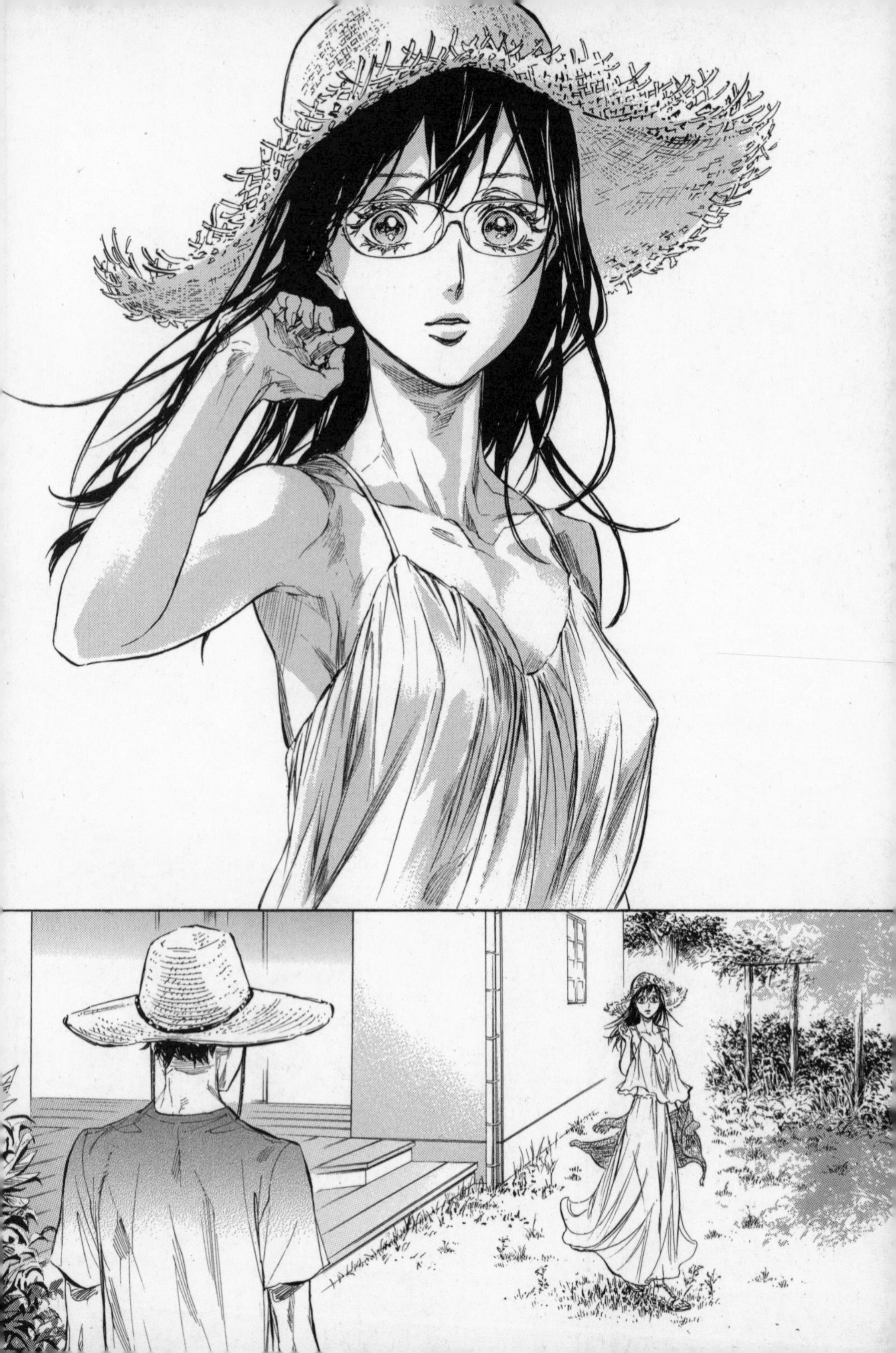

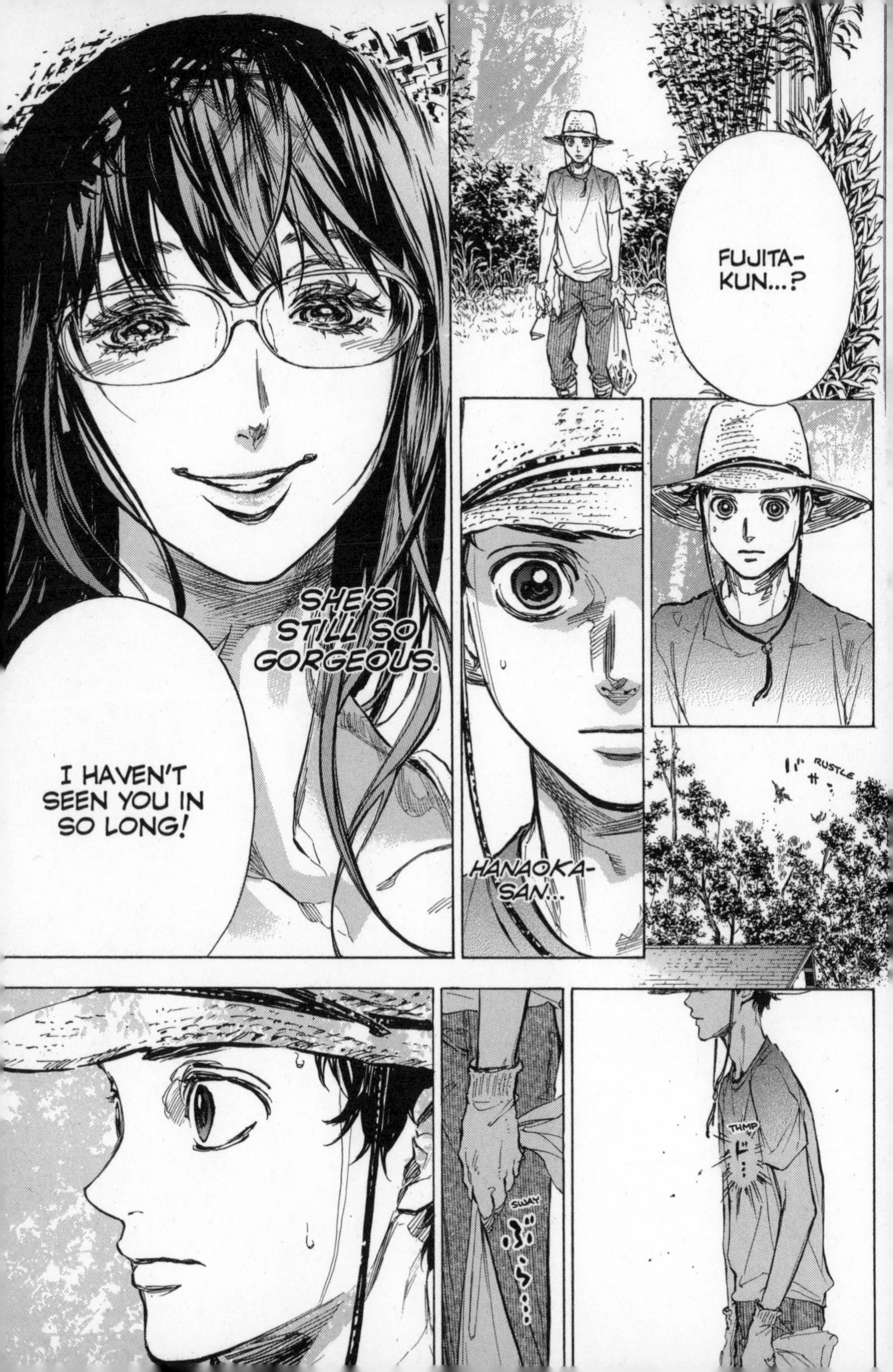
FUJITA-KUN...?
RUSTLE
HANAOKA-SAN...
SHE'S STILL SO GORGEOUS.
I HAVEN'T SEEN YOU IN SO LONG!
THMP
SWAY

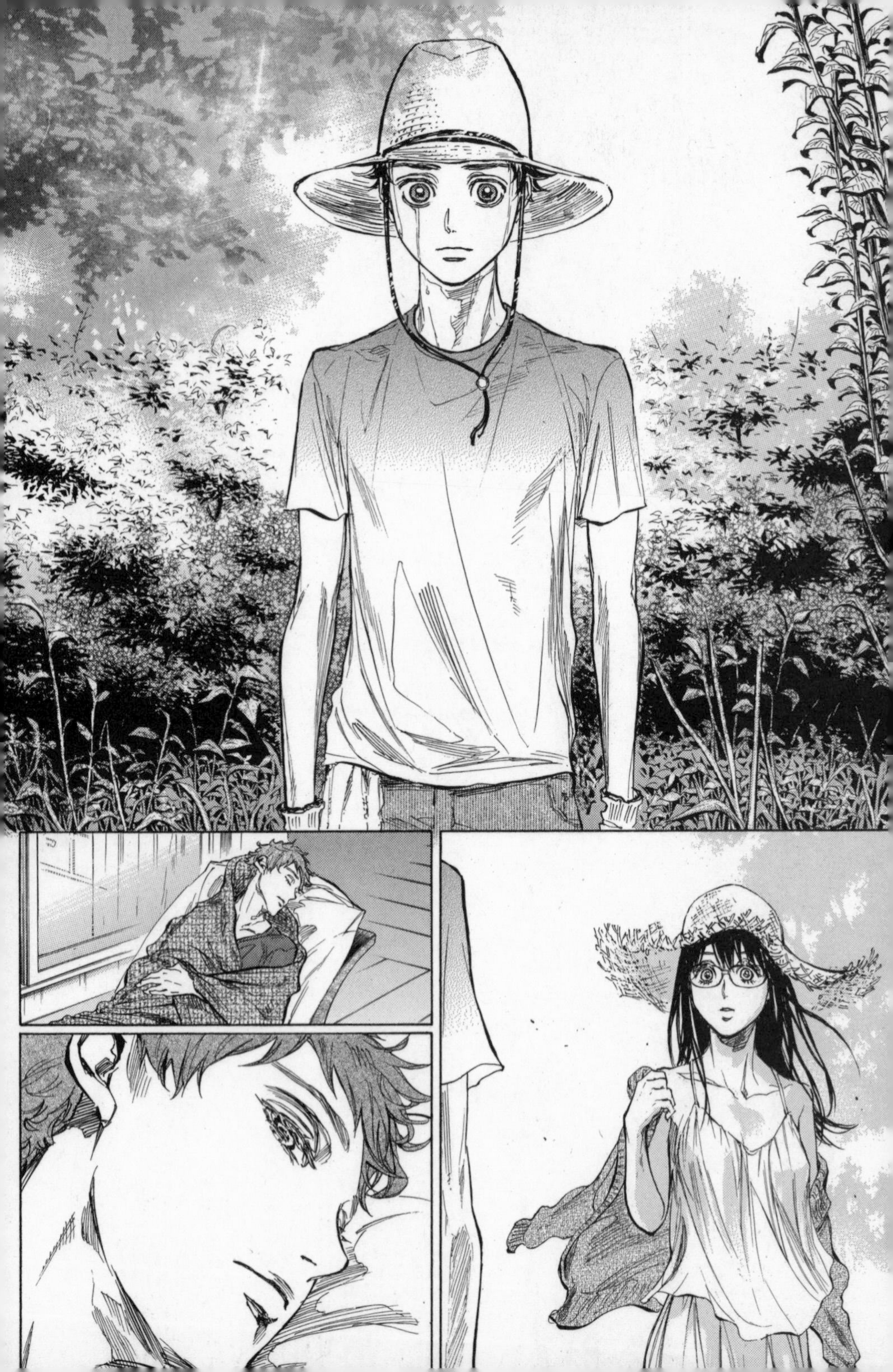

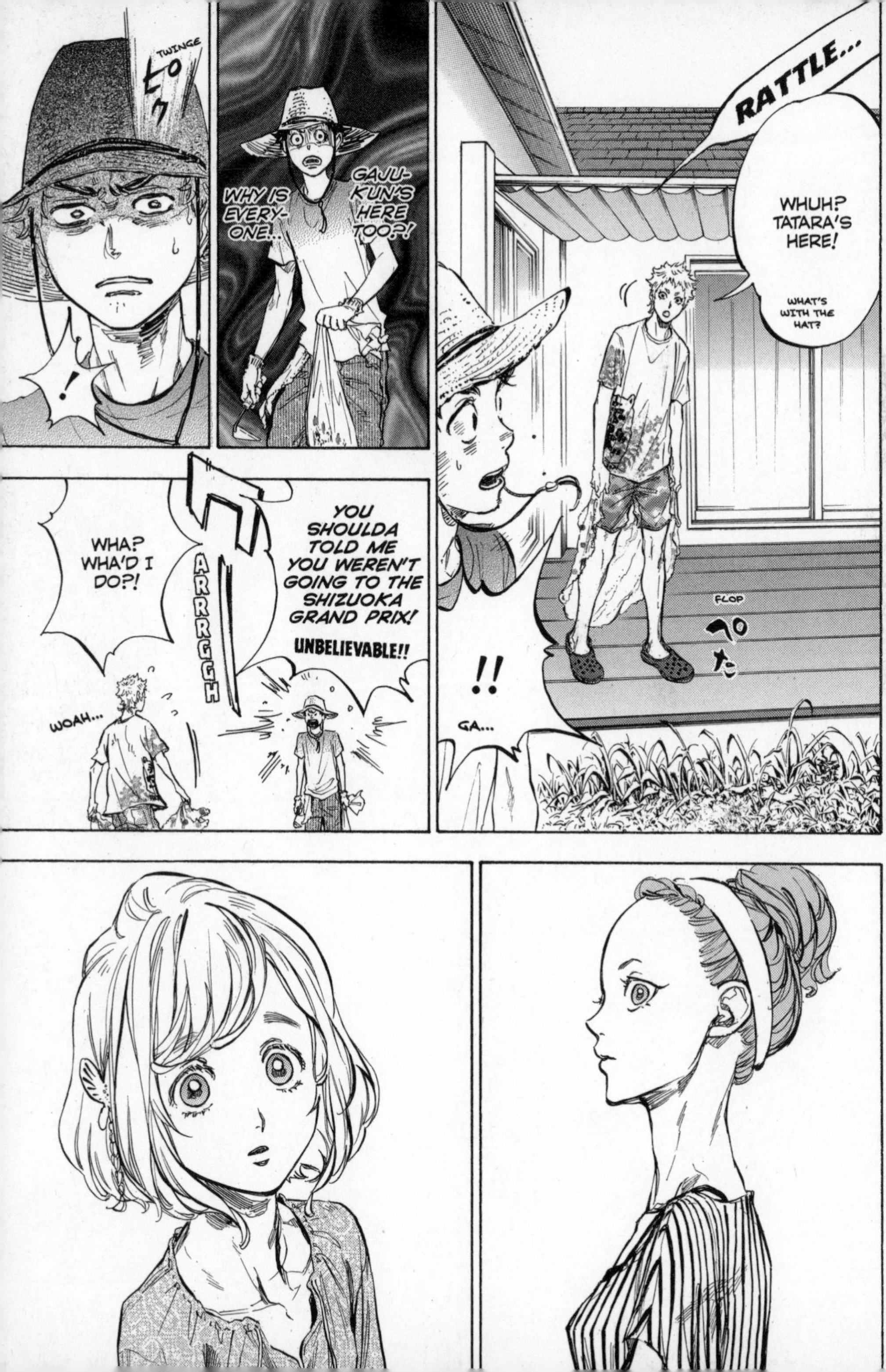
RATTLE...
WHUH? TATARA'S HERE!
WHAT'S WITH THE HAT?
FLOP
!!
GA...
GAJU-KUN'S HERE TOO?!
WHY IS EVERY-ONE...
TWINGE
!
YOU SHOULDA TOLD ME YOU WEREN'T GOING TO THE SHIZUOKA GRAND PRIX!
UNBELIEVABLE!!
ARRRGGH
WHA? WHA'D I DO?!
WOAH...

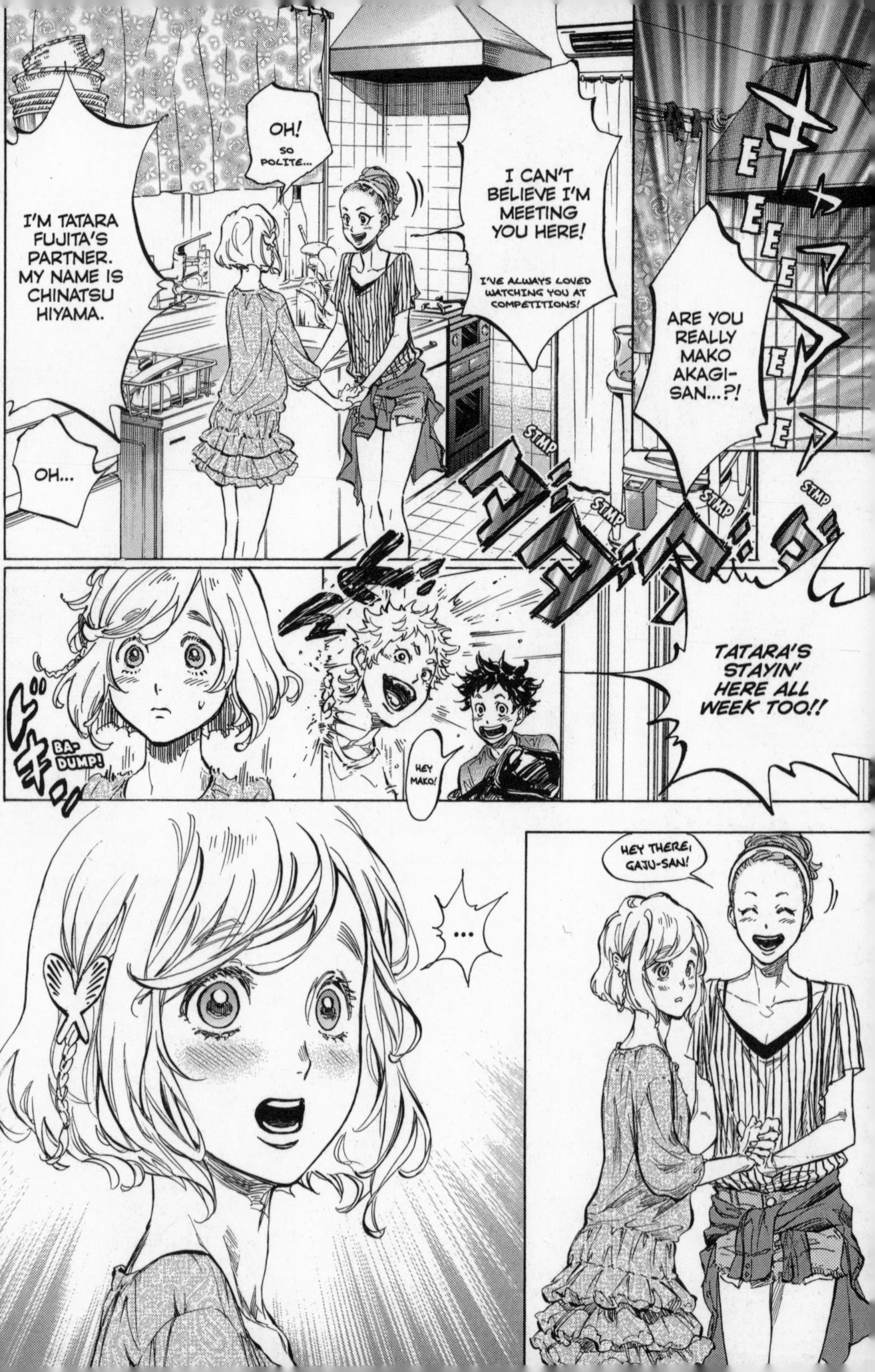

ARE YOU REALLY MAKO AKAGI-SAN...?!
STMP
STMP
STMP
STMP
I CAN'T BELIEVE I'M MEETING YOU HERE!
I'VE ALWAYS LOVED WATCHING YOU AT COMPETITIONS!
OH! SO POLITE...
I'M TATARA FUJITA'S PARTNER. MY NAME IS CHINATSU HIYAMA.
OH...
TATARA'S STAYIN' HERE ALL WEEK TOO!!
HEY MAKO!
BA-DUMP!
HEY THERE, GAJU-SAN!
...

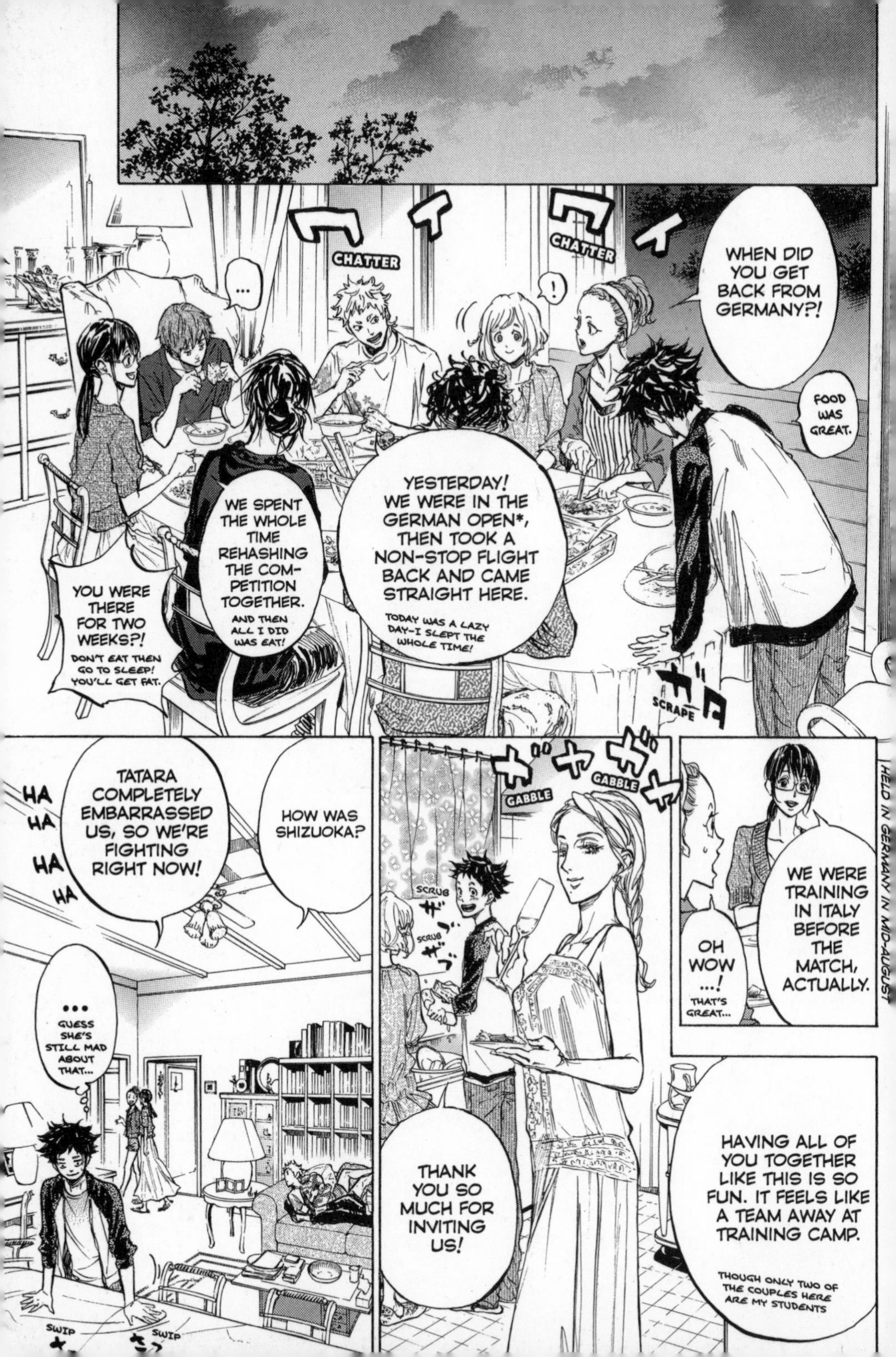
CHATTER
CHATTER
WHEN DID YOU GET BACK FROM GERMANY?!
!
FOOD WAS GREAT.
YESTERDAY! WE WERE IN THE GERMAN OPEN*, THEN TOOK A NON-STOP FLIGHT BACK AND CAME STRAIGHT HERE.
TODAY WAS A LAZY DAY–I SLEPT THE WHOLE TIME!
...
WE SPENT THE WHOLE TIME REHASHING THE COM-PETITION TOGETHER.
AND THEN ALL I DID WAS EAT!
YOU WERE THERE FOR TWO WEEKS?!
DON'T EAT THEN GO TO SLEEP! YOU'LL GET FAT.
SCRAPE
WE WERE TRAINING IN ITALY BEFORE THE MATCH, ACTUALLY.
OH WOW ...!
THAT'S GREAT...
HAVING ALL OF YOU TOGETHER LIKE THIS IS SO FUN. IT FEELS LIKE A TEAM AWAY AT TRAINING CAMP.
THOUGH ONLY TWO OF THE COUPLES HERE ARE MY STUDENTS
GABBLE
GABBLE
SCRUB
SCRUB
THANK YOU SO MUCH FOR INVITING US!
HOW WAS SHIZUOKA?
TATARA COMPLETELY EMBARRASSED US, SO WE'RE FIGHTING RIGHT NOW!
HA
HA
HA
HA
...
GUESS SHE'S STILL MAD ABOUT THAT...
SWIP
SWIP

*HELD IN GERMANY IN MID-AUGUST

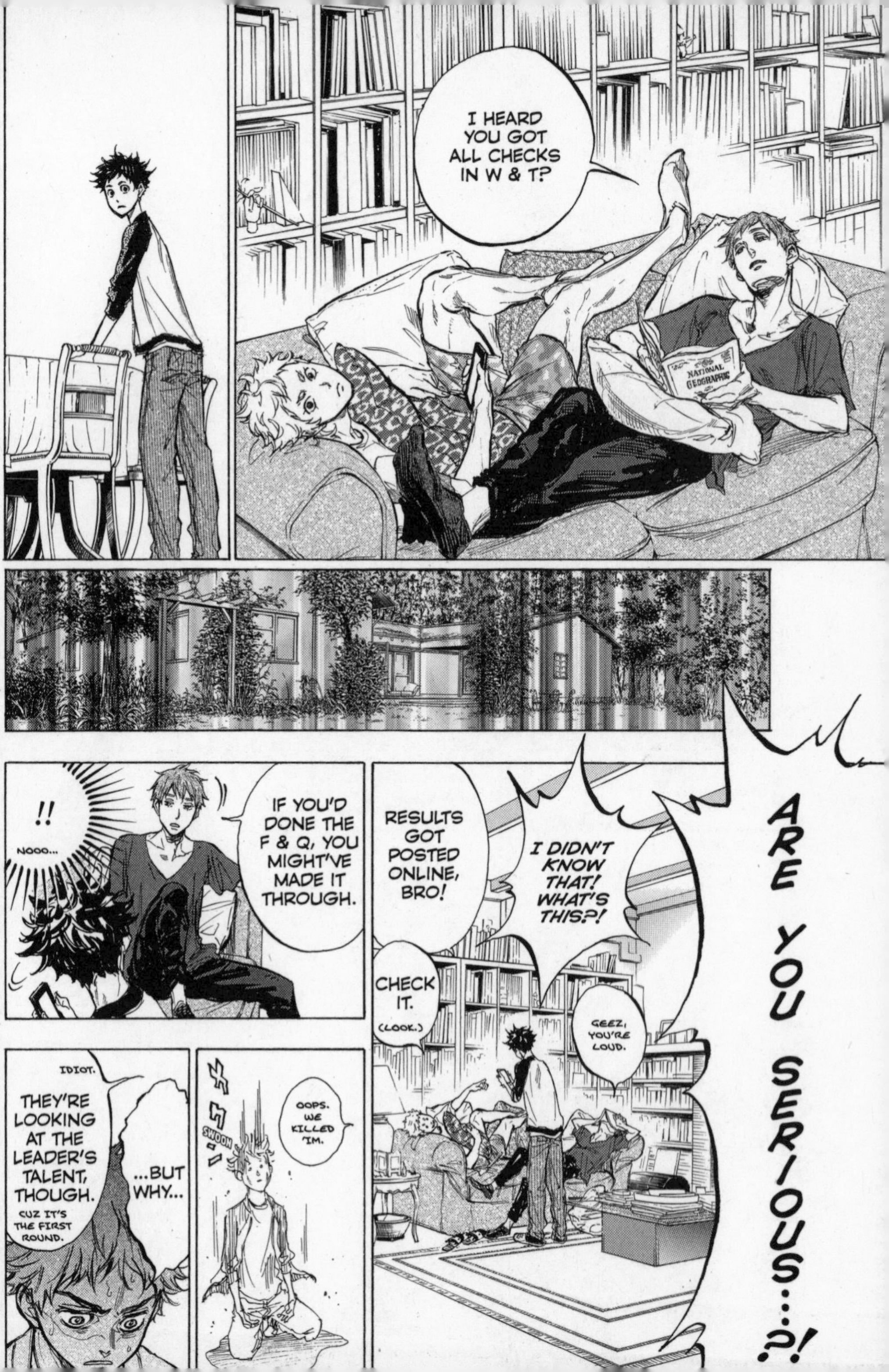
I HEARD YOU GOT ALL CHECKS IN W & T?
ARE YOU SERIOUS...?!
I DIDN'T KNOW THAT! WHAT'S THIS?!
RESULTS GOT POSTED ONLINE, BRO!
CHECK IT.
(LOOK.)
GEEZ, YOU'RE LOUD.
IF YOU'D DONE THE F & Q, YOU MIGHT'VE MADE IT THROUGH.
!!
NOOO...
OOPS. WE KILLED 'IM.
SWOON
...BUT WHY...
IDIOT.
THEY'RE LOOKING AT THE LEADER'S TALENT, THOUGH.
CUZ IT'S THE FIRST ROUND.

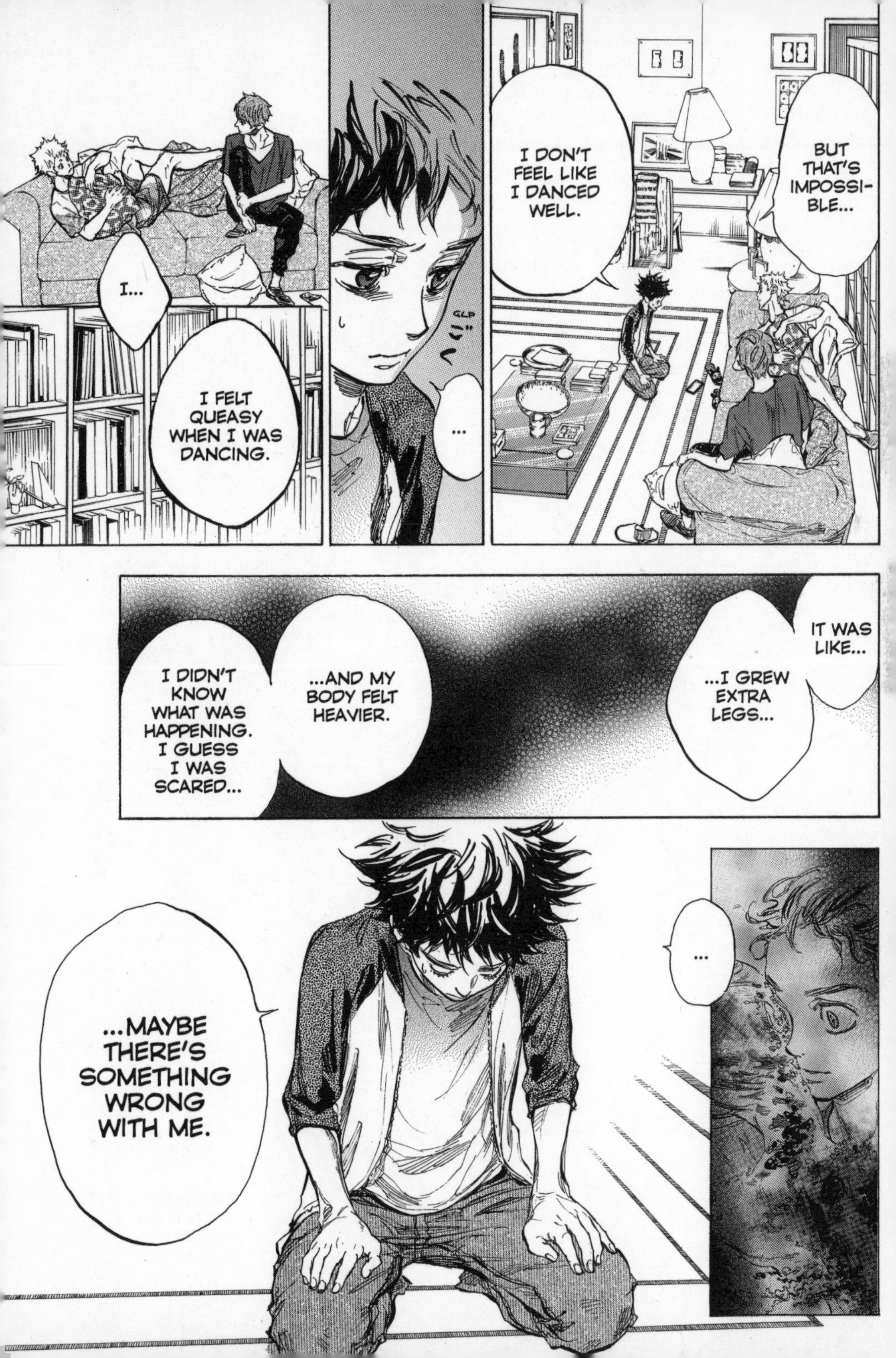
BUT THAT'S IMPOSSIBLE...
I DON'T FEEL LIKE I DANCED WELL.
GLP
...
I...
I FELT QUEASY WHEN I WAS DANCING.
IT WAS LIKE...
...I GREW EXTRA LEGS...
...AND MY BODY FELT HEAVIER.
I DIDN'T KNOW WHAT WAS HAPPENING. I GUESS I WAS SCARED...
...
...MAYBE THERE'S SOMETHING WRONG WITH ME.

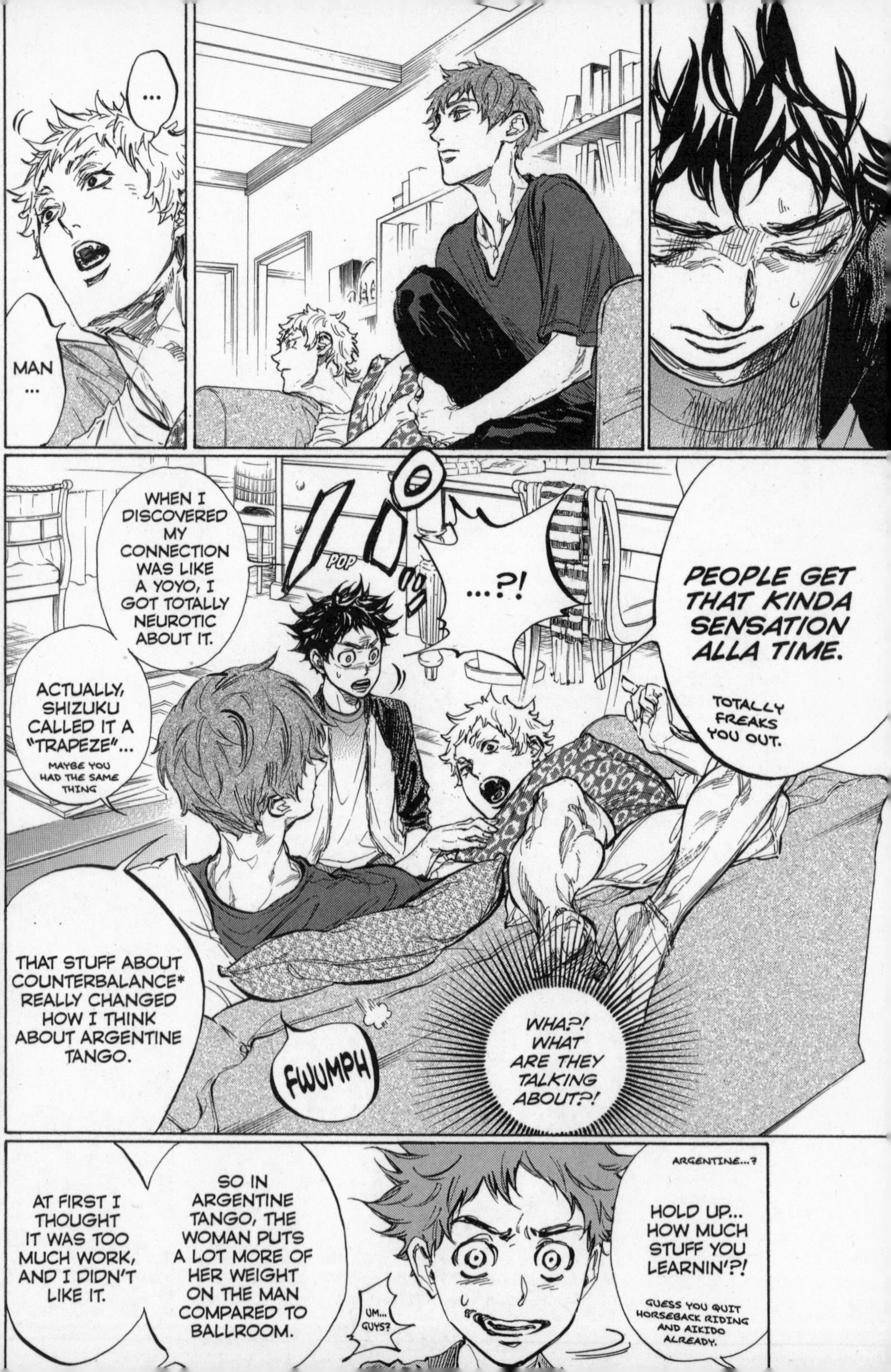
...
MAN ...
PEOPLE GET THAT KINDA SENSATION ALLA TIME.
TOTALLY FREAKS YOU OUT.
...?!
POP
WHEN I DISCOVERED MY CONNECTION WAS LIKE A YOYO, I GOT TOTALLY NEUROTIC ABOUT IT.
ACTUALLY, SHIZUKU CALLED IT A "TRAPEZE"...
MAYBE YOU HAD THE SAME THING
WHA?! WHAT ARE THEY TALKING ABOUT?!
FWUMPH
THAT STUFF ABOUT COUNTERBALANCE* REALLY CHANGED HOW I THINK ABOUT ARGENTINE TANGO.
ARGENTINE...?
HOLD UP... HOW MUCH STUFF YOU LEARNIN'?!
GUESS YOU QUIT HORSEBACK RIDING AND AIKIDO ALREADY.
UM... GUYS?
SO IN ARGENTINE TANGO, THE WOMAN PUTS A LOT MORE OF HER WEIGHT ON THE MAN COMPARED TO BALLROOM.
AT FIRST I THOUGHT IT WAS TOO MUCH WORK, AND I DIDN'T LIKE IT.

*COUNTERBALANCE... THE BALANCE ONE HOLDS SO

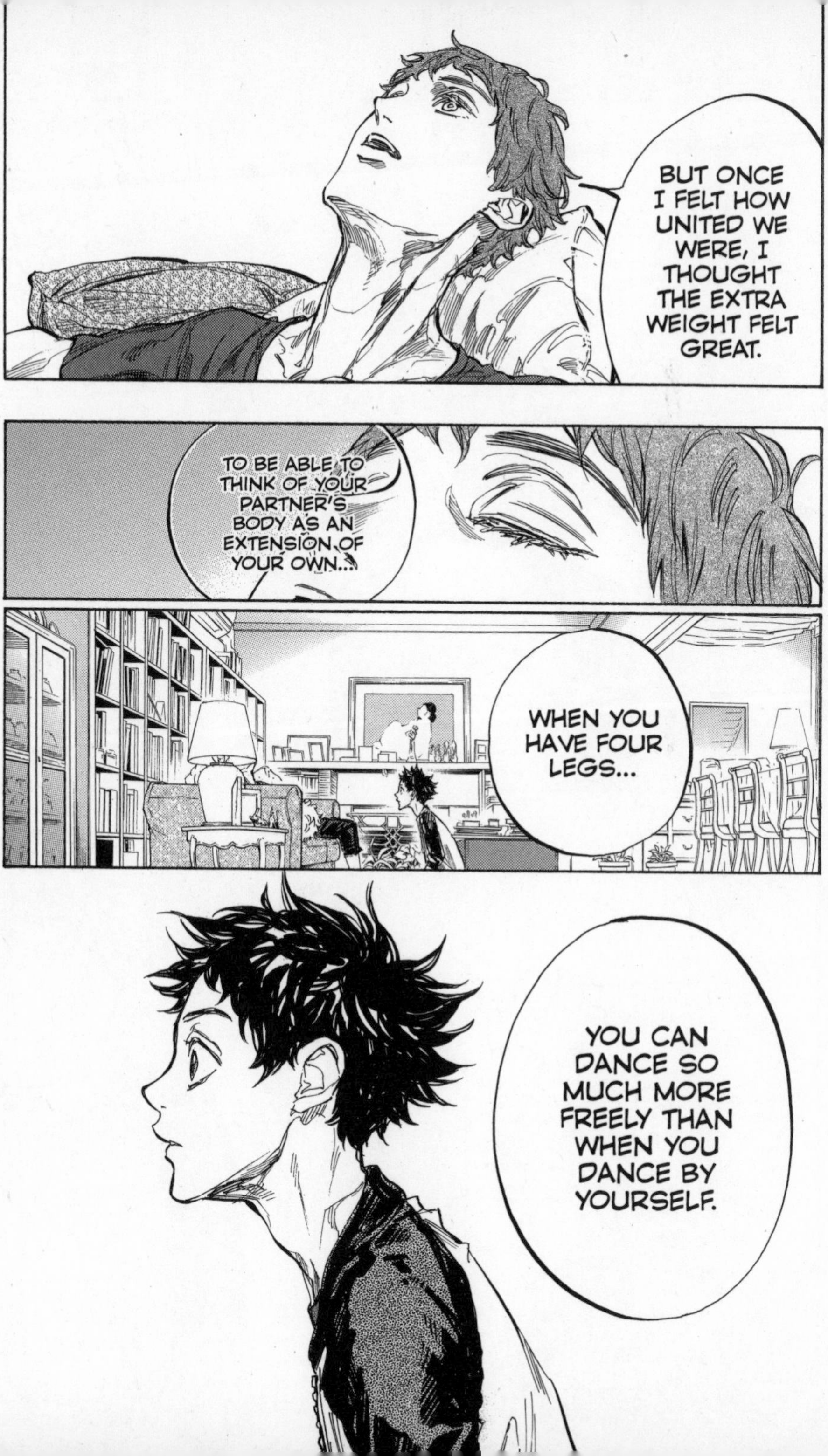
BUT ONCE I FELT HOW UNITED WE WERE, I THOUGHT THE EXTRA WEIGHT FELT GREAT.
TO BE ABLE TO THINK OF YOUR PARTNER'S BODY AS AN EXTENSION OF YOUR OWN...
WHEN YOU HAVE FOUR LEGS...
YOU CAN DANCE SO MUCH MORE FREELY THAN WHEN YOU DANCE BY YOURSELF.

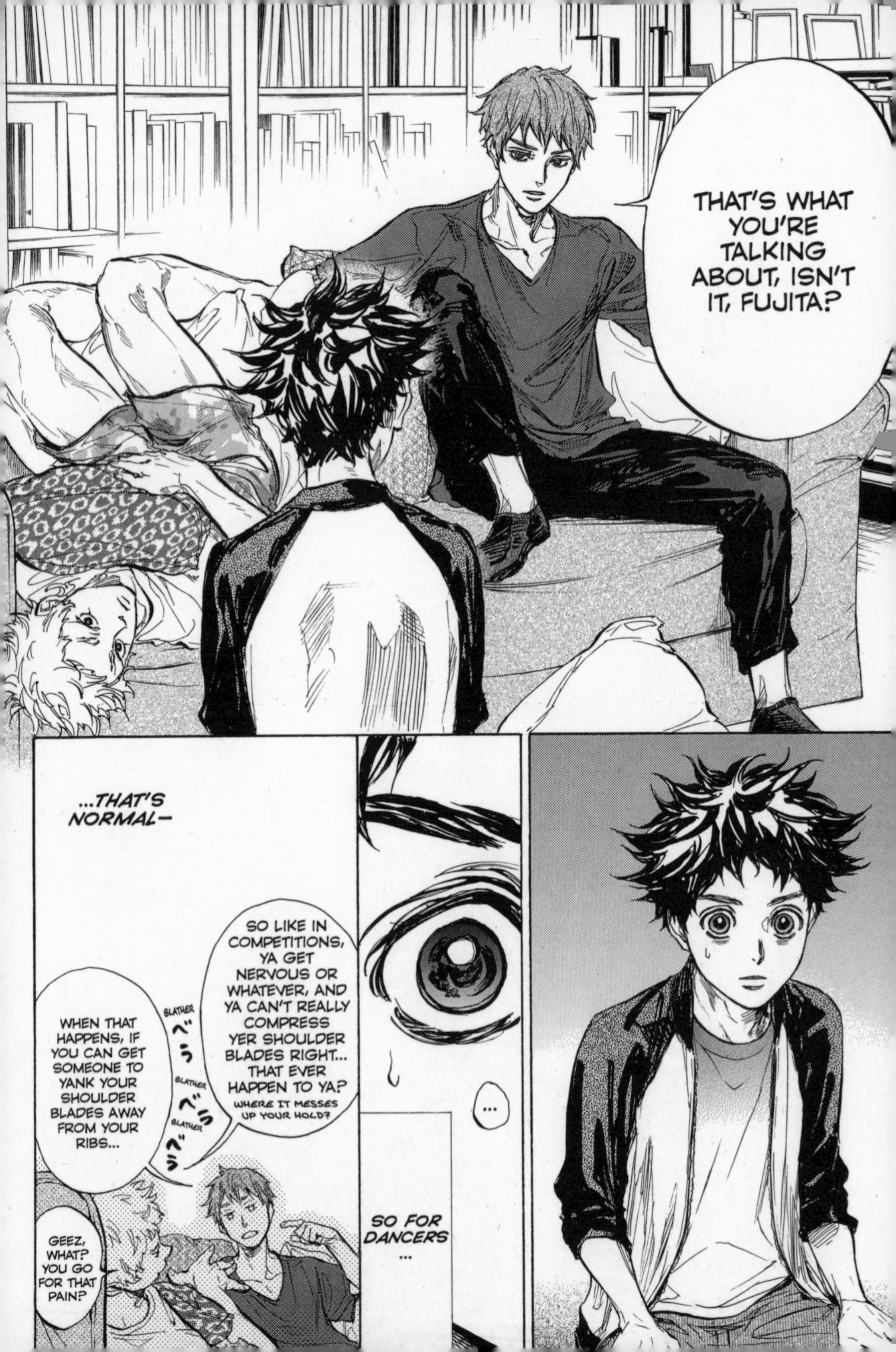
THAT'S WHAT YOU'RE TALKING ABOUT, ISN'T IT, FUJITA?
...
SO FOR DANCERS ...
...THAT'S NORMAL—
SO LIKE IN COMPETITIONS, YA GET NERVOUS OR WHATEVER, AND YA CAN'T REALLY COMPRESS YER SHOULDER BLADES RIGHT... THAT EVER HAPPEN TO YA?
WHERE IT MESSES UP YOUR HOLD?
BLATHER
BLATHER
BLATHER
WHEN THAT HAPPENS, IF YOU CAN GET SOMEONE TO YANK YOUR SHOULDER BLADES AWAY FROM YOUR RIBS...
GEEZ, WHAT? YOU GO FOR THAT PAIN?

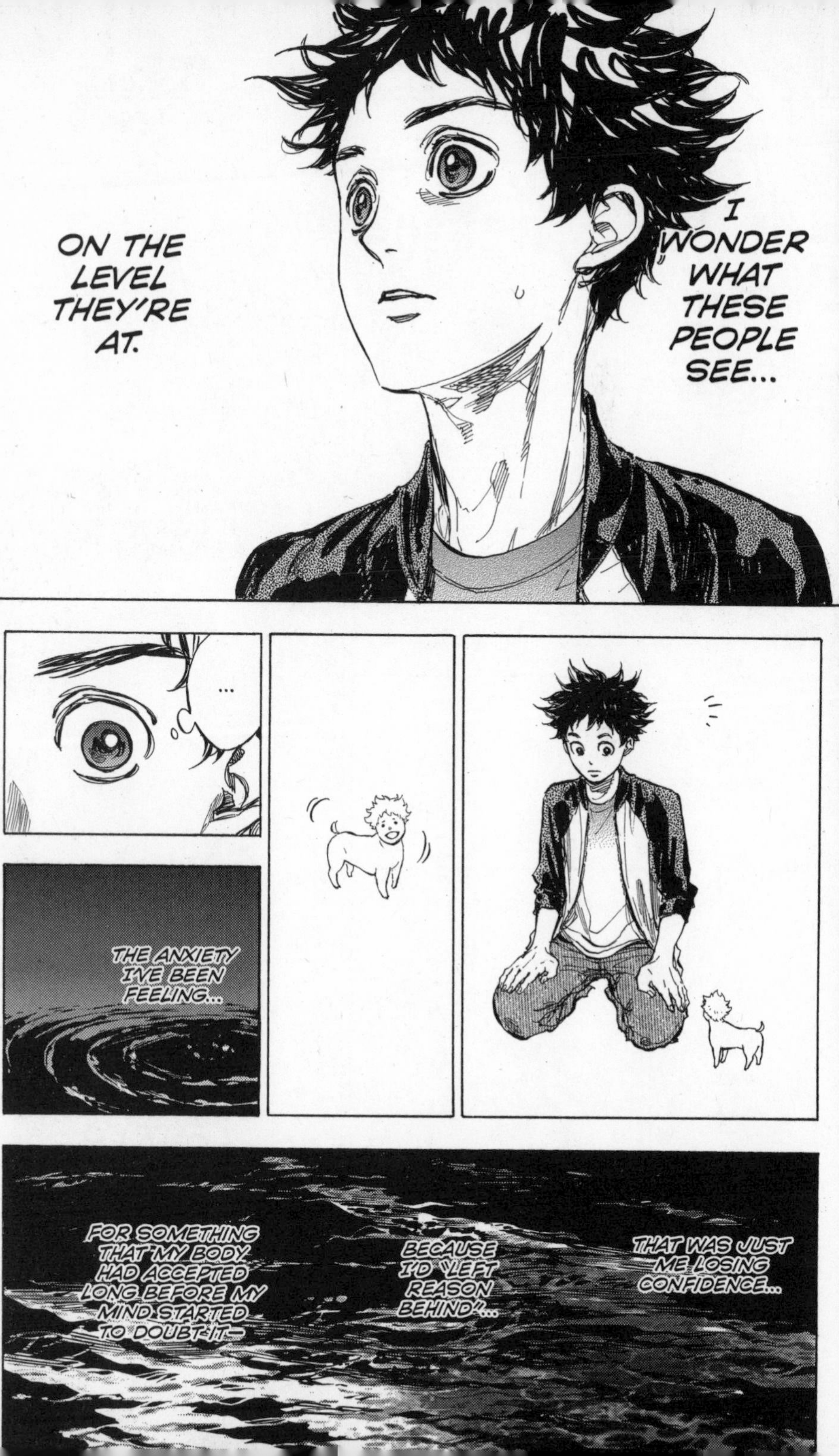
I WONDER WHAT THESE PEOPLE SEE...
ON THE LEVEL THEY'RE AT.
...
THE ANXIETY I'VE BEEN FEELING...
THAT WAS JUST ME LOSING CONFIDENCE...
BECAUSE I'D "LEFT REASON BEHIND"...
FOR SOMETHING THAT MY BODY HAD ACCEPTED LONG BEFORE MY MIND STARTED TO DOUBT IT—

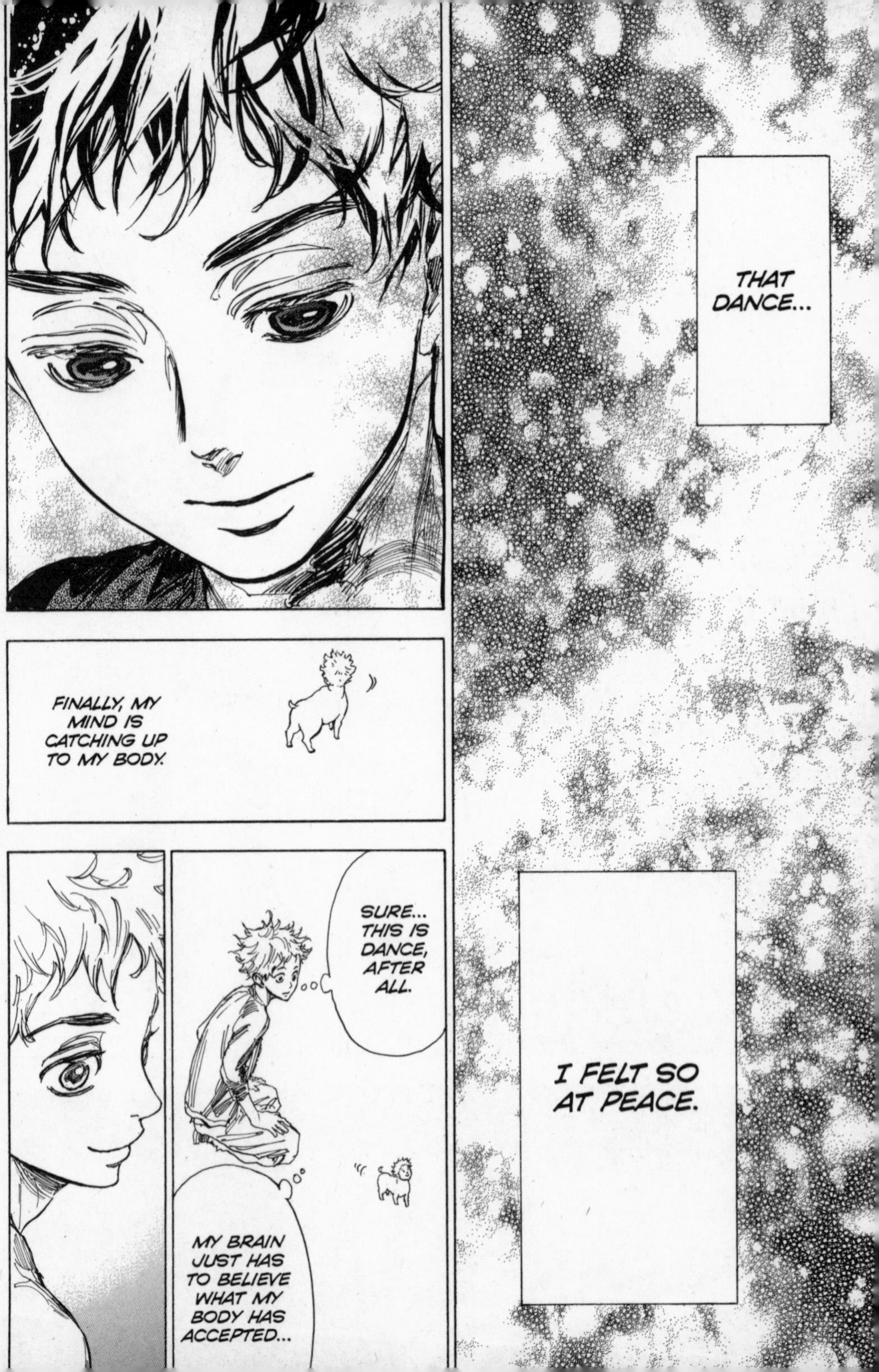
THAT DANCE...
I FELT SO AT PEACE.
FINALLY, MY MIND IS CATCHING UP TO MY BODY.
SURE... THIS IS DANCE, AFTER ALL.
MY BRAIN JUST HAS TO BELIEVE WHAT MY BODY HAS ACCEPTED...

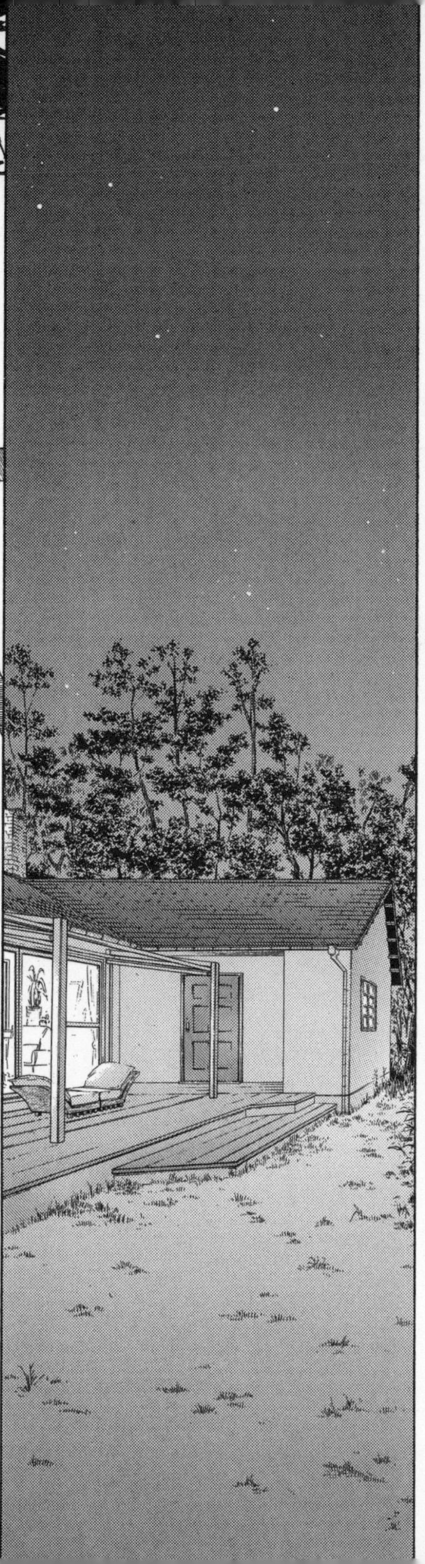

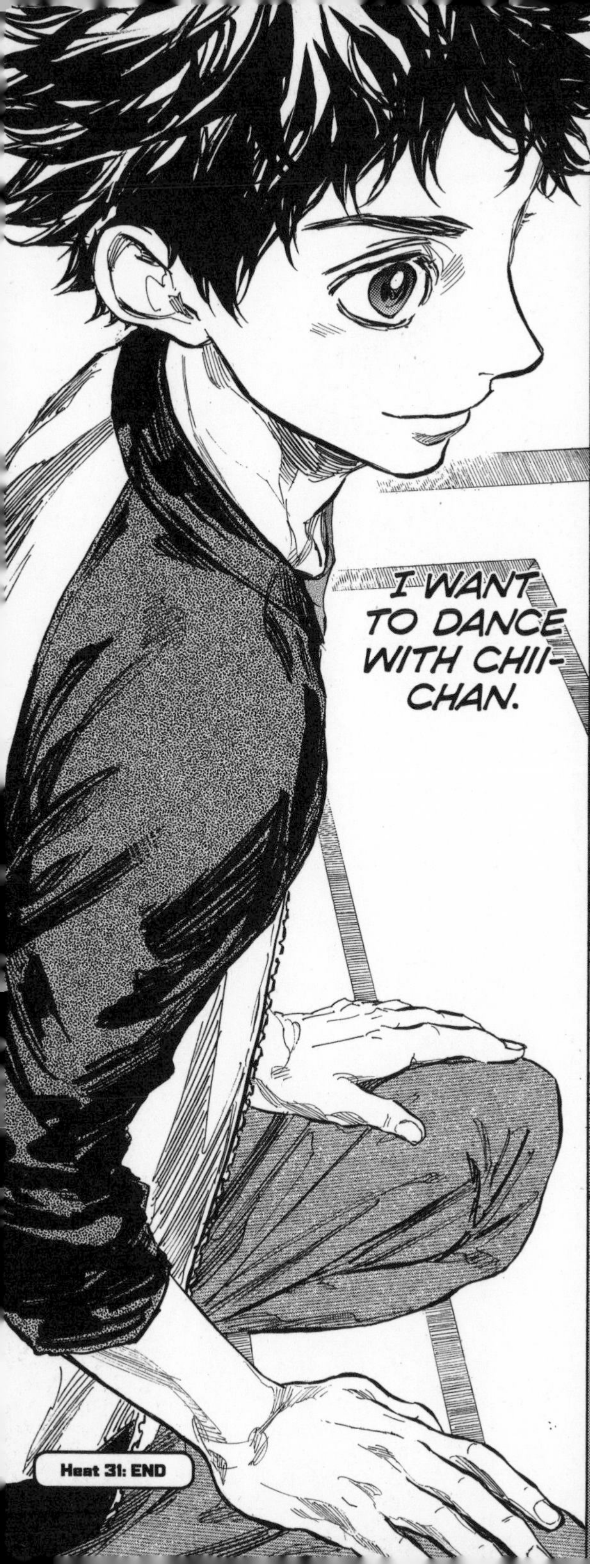
I WANT TO DANCE WITH CHII-CHAN.
Heat 31: END

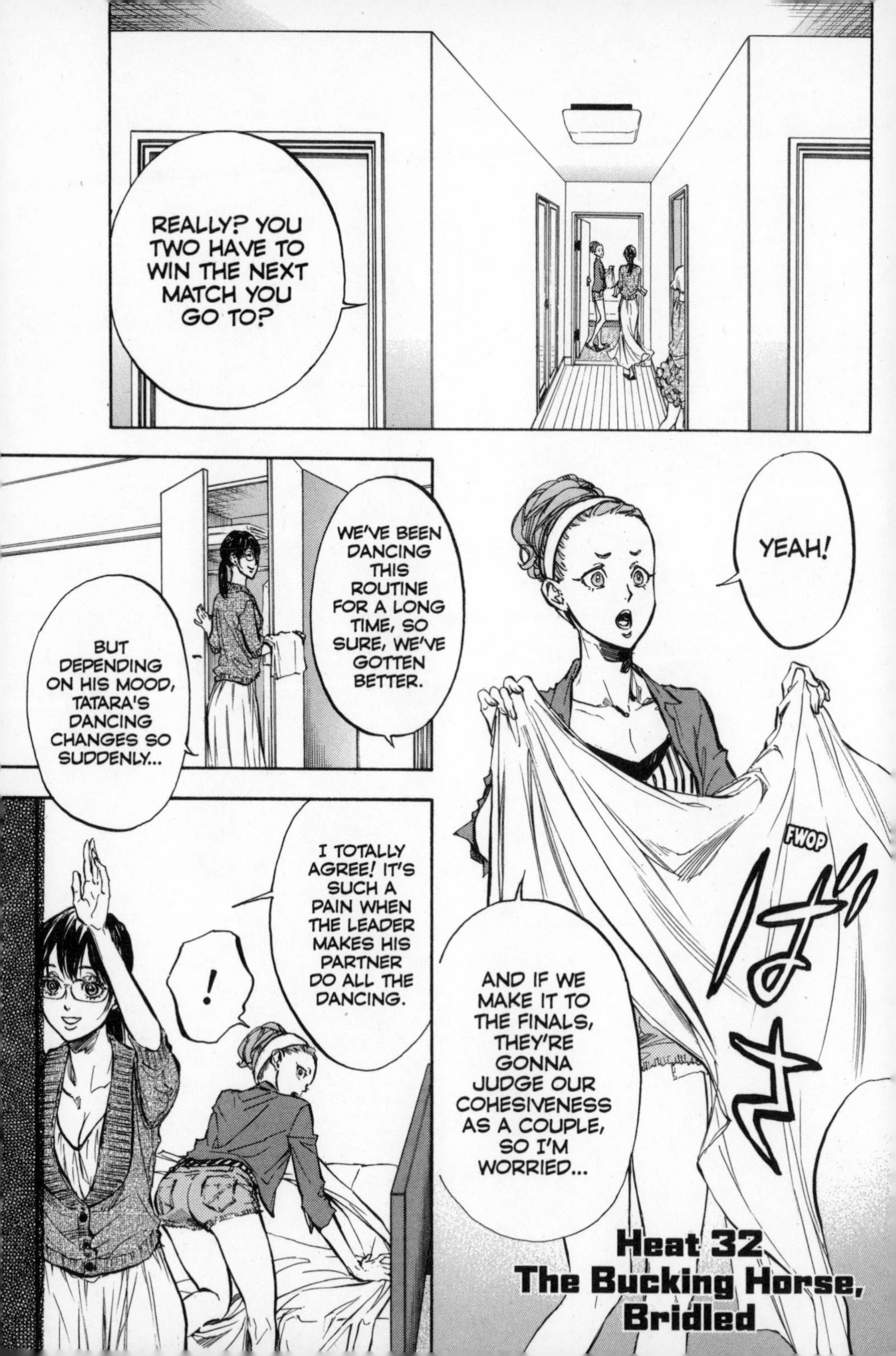
REALLY? YOU TWO HAVE TO WIN THE NEXT MATCH YOU GO TO?
YEAH!
FWOP
ばさ
AND IF WE MAKE IT TO THE FINALS, THEY'RE GONNA JUDGE OUR COHESIVENESS AS A COUPLE, SO I'M WORRIED...
WE'VE BEEN DANCING THIS ROUTINE FOR A LONG TIME, SO SURE, WE'VE GOTTEN BETTER.
BUT DEPENDING ON HIS MOOD, TATARA'S DANCING CHANGES SO SUDDENLY...
I TOTALLY AGREE! IT'S SUCH A PAIN WHEN THE LEADER MAKES HIS PARTNER DO ALL THE DANCING.
!
Heat 32
The Bucking Horse, Bridled

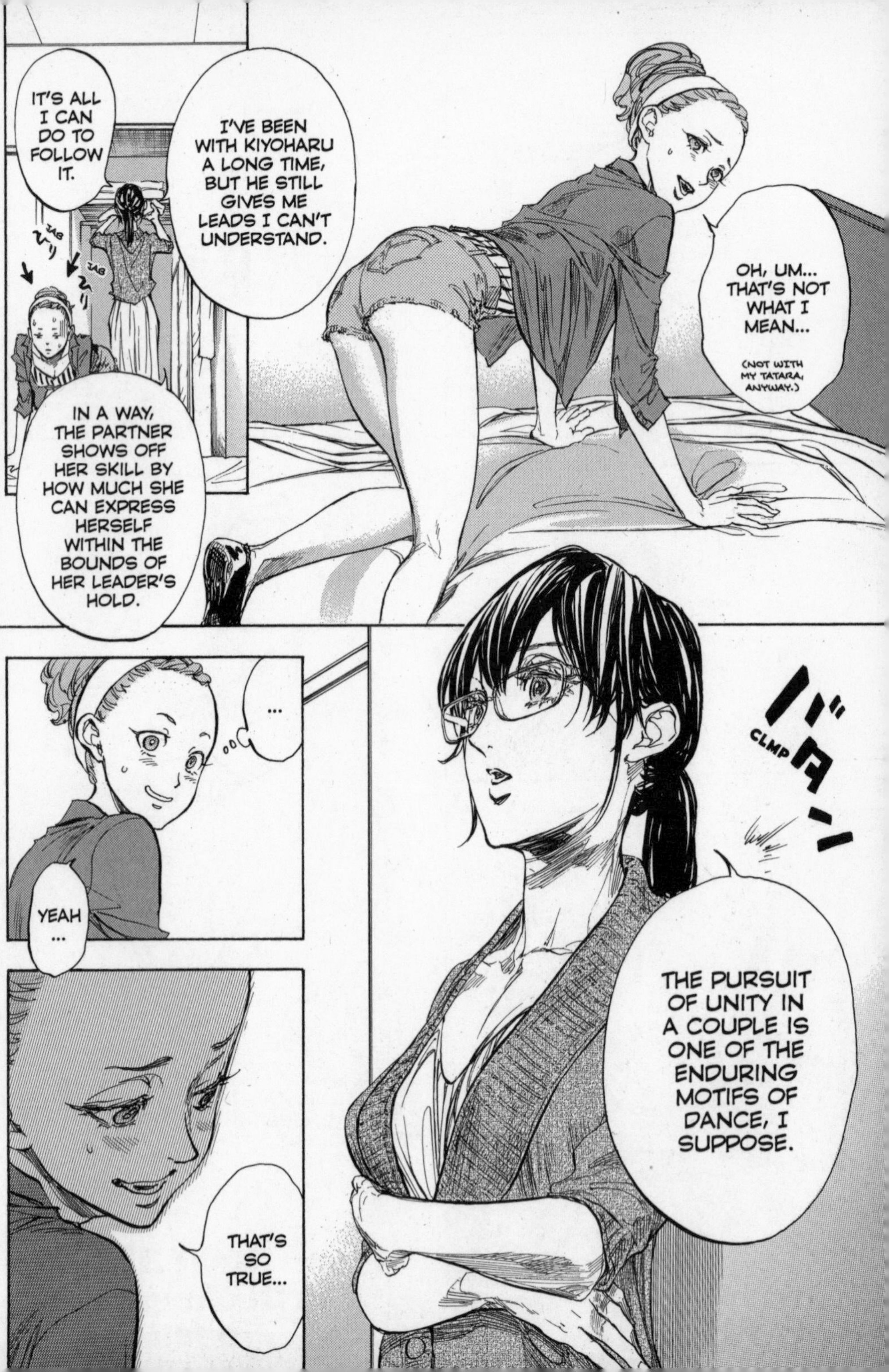
OH, UM... THAT'S NOT WHAT I MEAN...
(NOT WITH MY TATARA, ANYWAY.)
I'VE BEEN WITH KIYOHARU A LONG TIME, BUT HE STILL GIVES ME LEADS I CAN'T UNDERSTAND.
IT'S ALL I CAN DO TO FOLLOW IT.
JAB
JAB
IN A WAY, THE PARTNER SHOWS OFF HER SKILL BY HOW MUCH SHE CAN EXPRESS HERSELF WITHIN THE BOUNDS OF HER LEADER'S HOLD.
CLMP
THE PURSUIT OF UNITY IN A COUPLE IS ONE OF THE ENDURING MOTIFS OF DANCE, I SUPPOSE.
...
YEAH...
THAT'S SO TRUE...

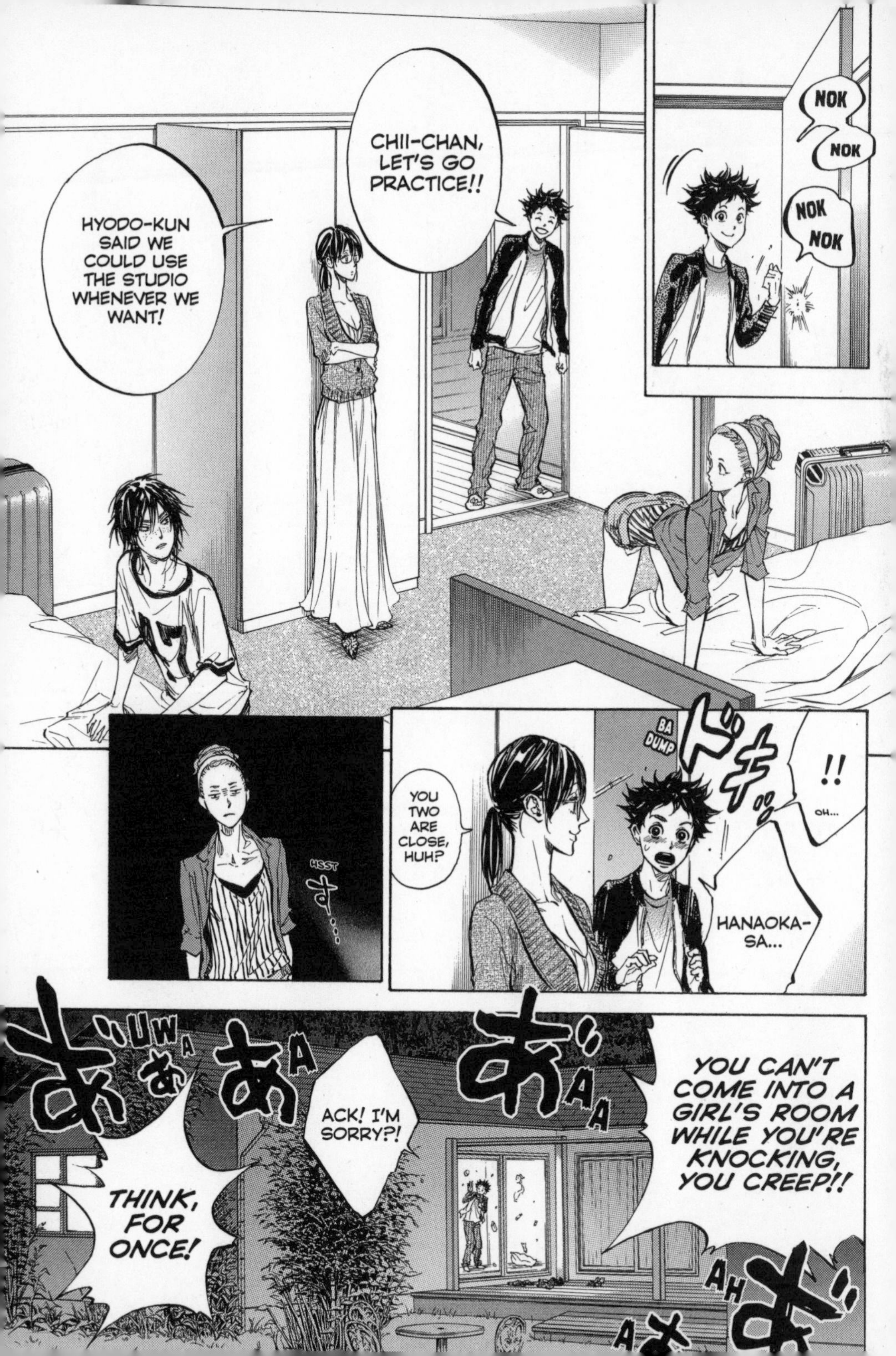

NOK
NOK
NOK NOK
CHII-CHAN, LET'S GO PRACTICE!!
HYODO-KUN SAID WE COULD USE THE STUDIO WHENEVER WE WANT!
BA DUMP
ドキッ
!!
OH...
HANAOKA-SA...
YOU TWO ARE CLOSE, HUH?
HSST
す…
YOU CAN'T COME INTO A GIRL'S ROOM WHILE YOU'RE KNOCKING, YOU CREEP!!
AH
ACK! I'M SORRY?!
UWA
THINK, FOR ONCE!

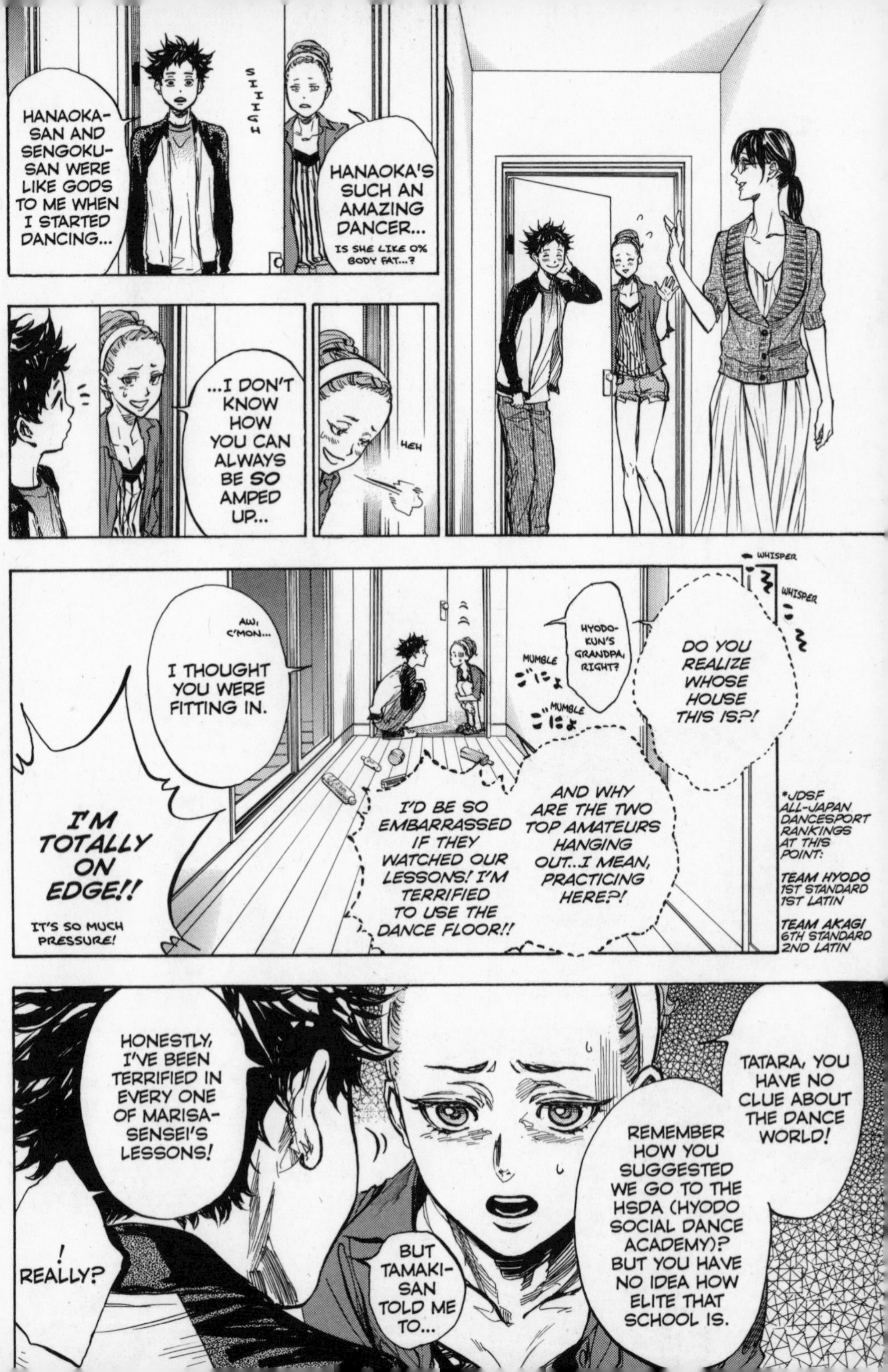
HANAOKA'S SUCH AN AMAZING DANCER...
IS SHE LIKE 0% BODY FAT...?
SIIIGH
HANAOKA-SAN AND SENGOKU-SAN WERE LIKE GODS TO ME WHEN I STARTED DANCING...
HEH
...I DON'T KNOW HOW YOU CAN ALWAYS BE SO AMPED UP...
WHISPER
WHISPER
DO YOU REALIZE WHOSE HOUSE THIS IS?!
HYODO-KUN'S GRANDPA, RIGHT?
MUMBLE
ごにょ
MUMBLE
ごにょ
AND WHY ARE THE TWO TOP AMATEURS HANGING OUT...I MEAN, PRACTICING HERE?!
I'D BE SO EMBARRASSED IF THEY WATCHED OUR LESSONS! I'M TERRIFIED TO USE THE DANCE FLOOR!!
AW, C'MON...
I THOUGHT YOU WERE FITTING IN.
I'M TOTALLY ON EDGE!!
IT'S SO MUCH PRESSURE!
*JDSF ALL-JAPAN DANCESPORT RANKINGS AT THIS POINT:
TEAM HYODO 1ST STANDARD 1ST LATIN
TEAM AKAGI 6TH STANDARD 2ND LATIN
TATARA, YOU HAVE NO CLUE ABOUT THE DANCE WORLD!
REMEMBER HOW YOU SUGGESTED WE GO TO THE HSDA (HYODO SOCIAL DANCE ACADEMY)? BUT YOU HAVE NO IDEA HOW ELITE THAT SCHOOL IS.
BUT TAMAKI-SAN TOLD ME TO...
HONESTLY, I'VE BEEN TERRIFIED IN EVERY ONE OF MARISA-SENSEI'S LESSONS!
!
REALLY?

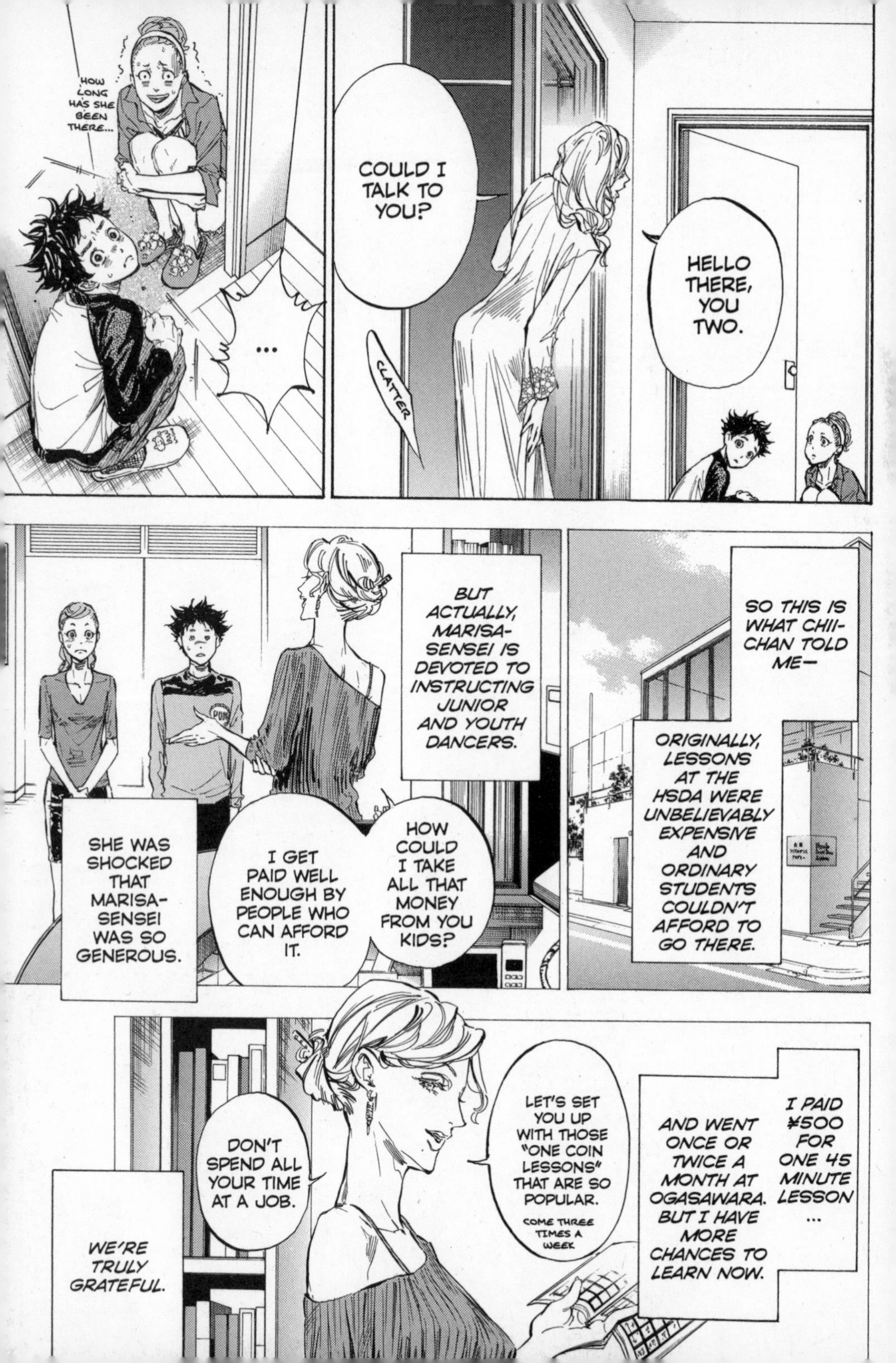
HELLO THERE, YOU TWO.
COULD I TALK TO YOU?
CLATTER
HOW LONG HAS SHE BEEN THERE...
...
SO THIS IS WHAT CHII-CHAN TOLD ME—
ORIGINALLY, LESSONS AT THE HSDA WERE UNBELIEVABLY EXPENSIVE AND ORDINARY STUDENTS COULDN'T AFFORD TO GO THERE.
BUT ACTUALLY, MARISA-SENSEI IS DEVOTED TO INSTRUCTING JUNIOR AND YOUTH DANCERS.
HOW COULD I TAKE ALL THAT MONEY FROM YOU KIDS?
I GET PAID WELL ENOUGH BY PEOPLE WHO CAN AFFORD IT.
SHE WAS SHOCKED THAT MARISA-SENSEI WAS SO GENEROUS.
I PAID ¥500 FOR ONE 45 MINUTE LESSON...
AND WENT ONCE OR TWICE A MONTH AT OGASAWARA. BUT I HAVE MORE CHANCES TO LEARN NOW.
LET'S SET YOU UP WITH THOSE "ONE COIN LESSONS" THAT ARE SO POPULAR.
COME THREE TIMES A WEEK
DON'T SPEND ALL YOUR TIME AT A JOB.
WE'RE TRULY GRATEFUL.

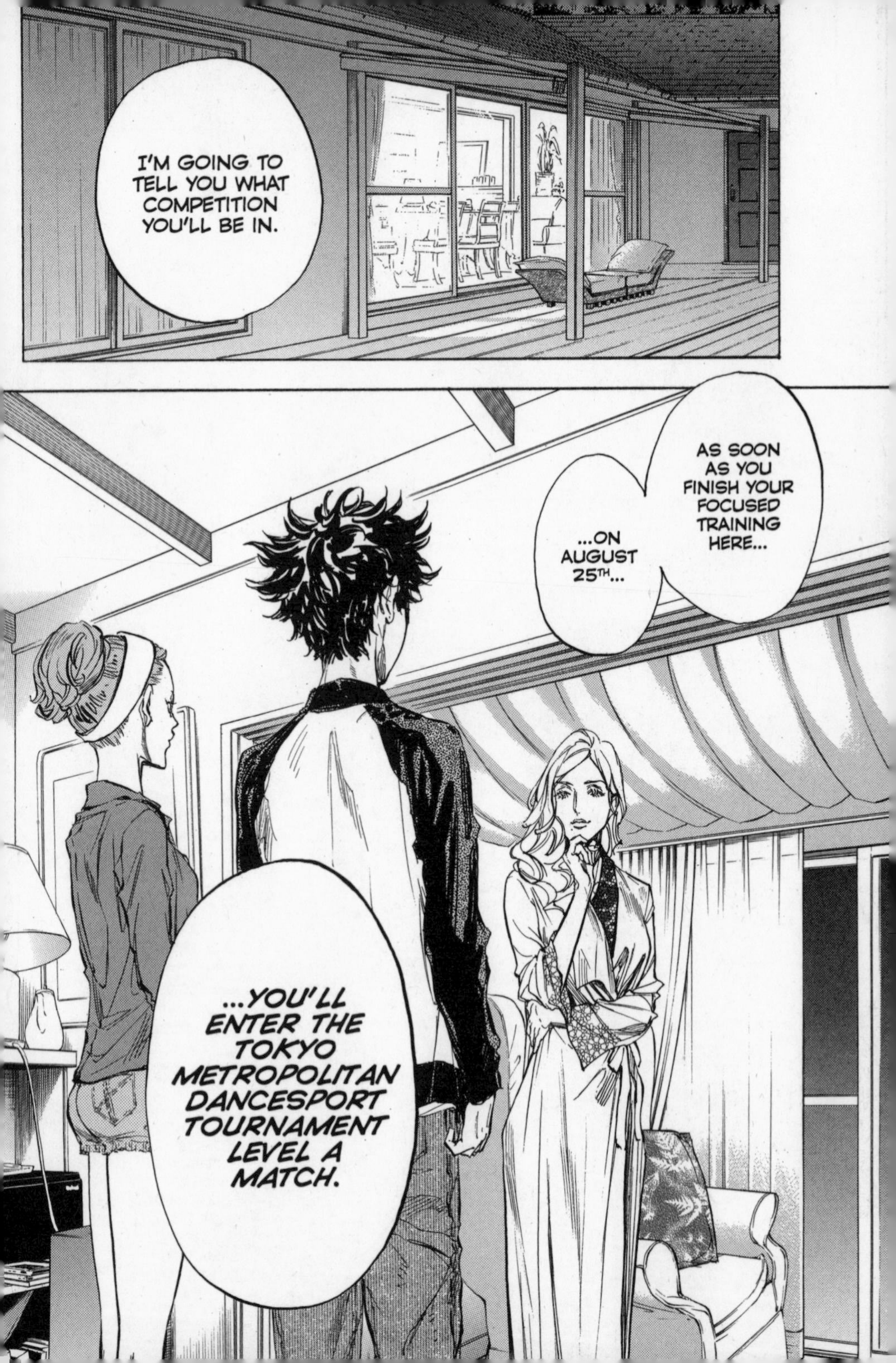
I'M GOING TO TELL YOU WHAT COMPETITION YOU'LL BE IN.
AS SOON AS YOU FINISH YOUR FOCUSED TRAINING HERE...
...ON AUGUST 25TH...
...YOU'LL ENTER THE TOKYO METROPOLITAN DANCESPORT TOURNAMENT LEVEL A MATCH.

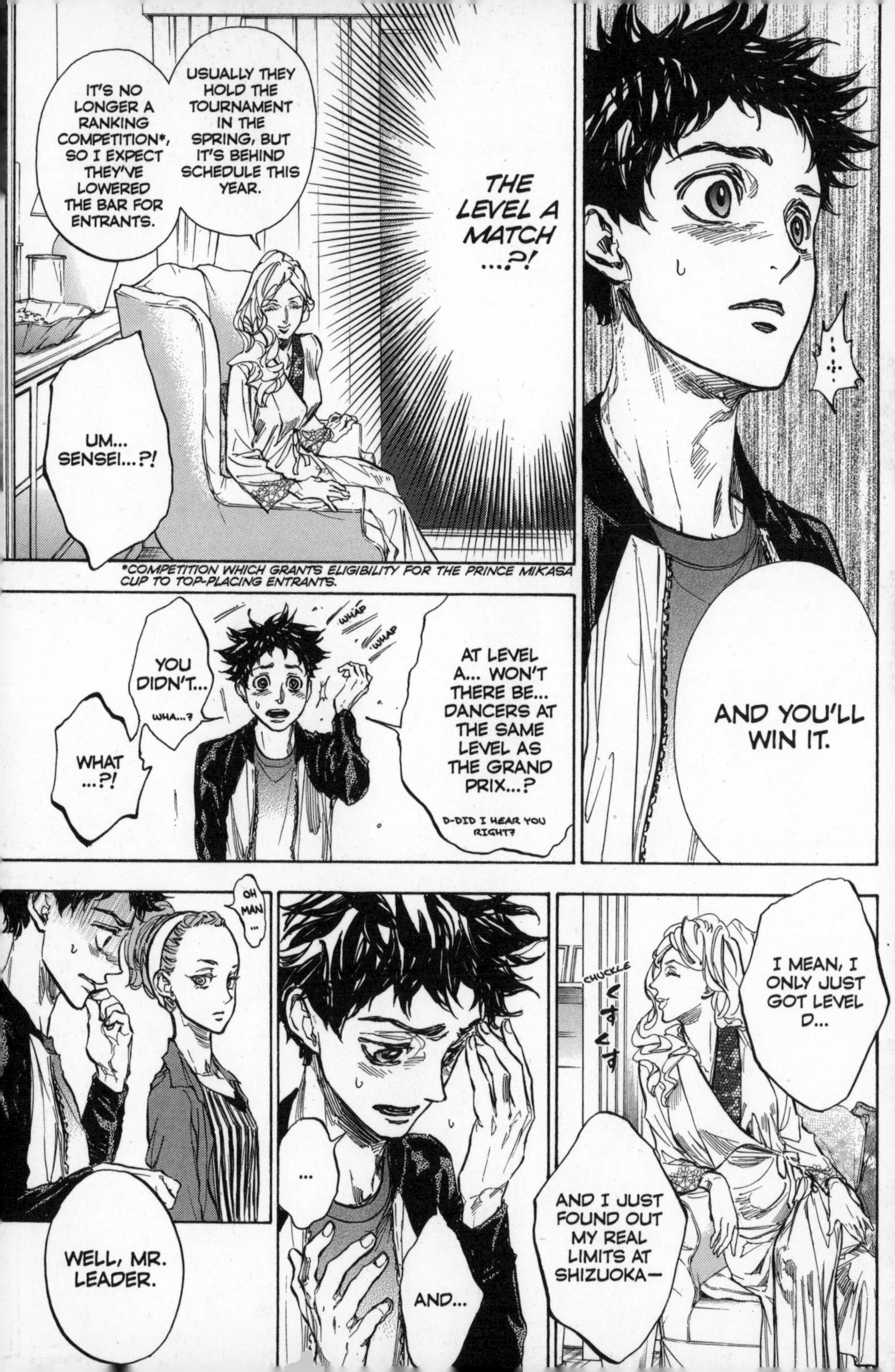
...!
AND YOU'LL WIN IT.
THE LEVEL A MATCH ...?!
USUALLY THEY HOLD THE TOURNAMENT IN THE SPRING, BUT IT'S BEHIND SCHEDULE THIS YEAR.
IT'S NO LONGER A RANKING COMPETITION*, SO I EXPECT THEY'VE LOWERED THE BAR FOR ENTRANTS.
UM... SENSEI...?!
WHAP
WHAP
AT LEVEL A... WON'T THERE BE... DANCERS AT THE SAME LEVEL AS THE GRAND PRIX...?
D-DID I HEAR YOU RIGHT?
YOU DIDN'T...
WHA...?
WHAT ...?!
I MEAN, I ONLY JUST GOT LEVEL D...
CHUCKLE
くすくす
AND I JUST FOUND OUT MY REAL LIMITS AT SHIZUOKA—
...
AND...
OH MAN ...
WELL, MR. LEADER.

*COMPETITION WHICH GRANTS ELIGIBILITY FOR THE PRINCE MIKASA CUP TO TOP-PLACING ENTRANTS.

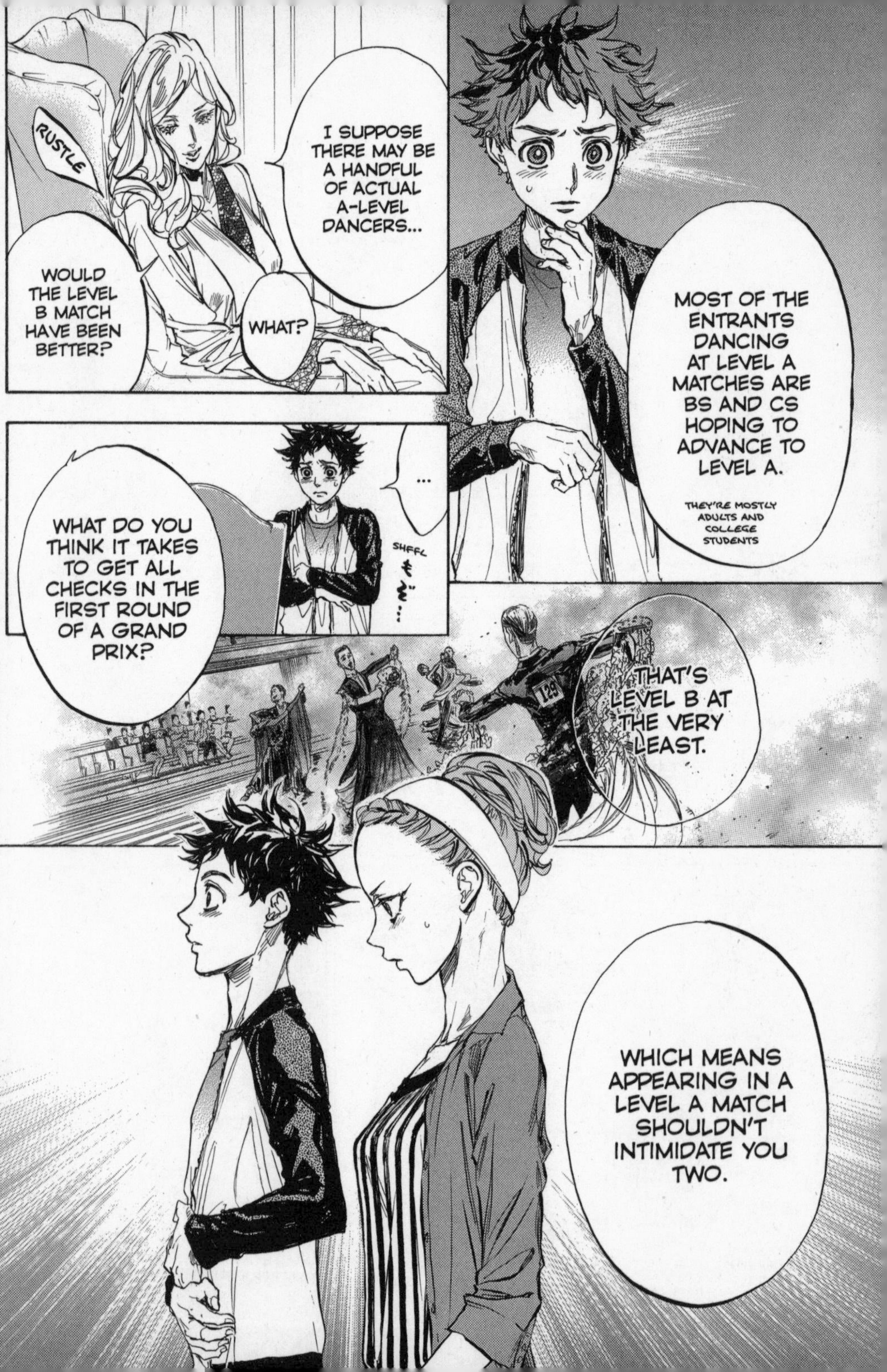
MOST OF THE ENTRANTS DANCING AT LEVEL A MATCHES ARE BS AND CS HOPING TO ADVANCE TO LEVEL A.
THEY'RE MOSTLY ADULTS AND COLLEGE STUDENTS
I SUPPOSE THERE MAY BE A HANDFUL OF ACTUAL A-LEVEL DANCERS...
RUSTLE
WHAT?
WOULD THE LEVEL B MATCH HAVE BEEN BETTER?
...
SHFFL
もぞ…
WHAT DO YOU THINK IT TAKES TO GET ALL CHECKS IN THE FIRST ROUND OF A GRAND PRIX?
129
THAT'S LEVEL B AT THE VERY LEAST.
WHICH MEANS APPEARING IN A LEVEL A MATCH SHOULDN'T INTIMIDATE YOU TWO.

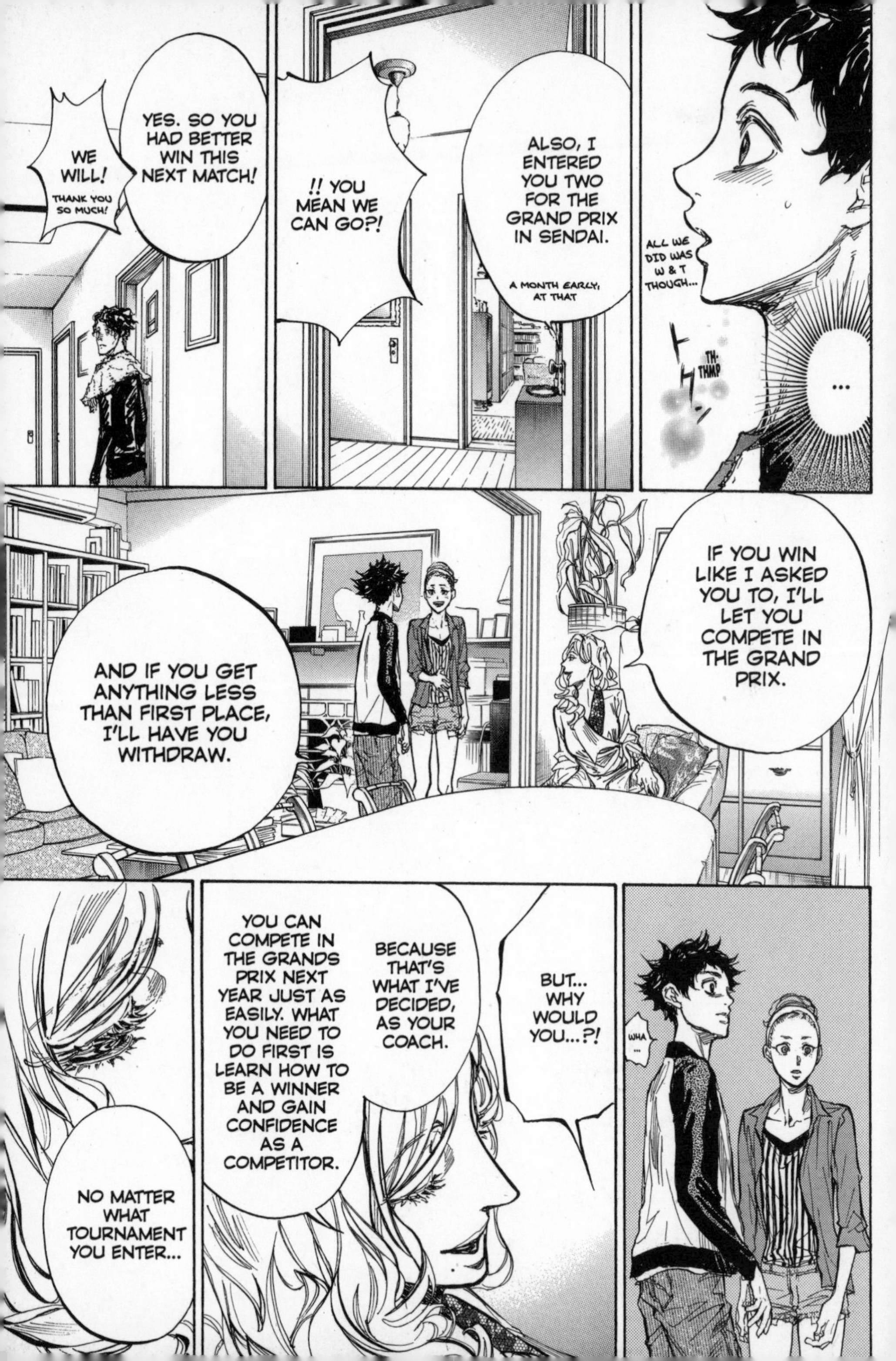

ALL WE DID WAS W & T THOUGH...
TH-THMP
...
ALSO, I ENTERED YOU TWO FOR THE GRAND PRIX IN SENDAI.
A MONTH EARLY, AT THAT
!! YOU MEAN WE CAN GO?!
YES. SO YOU HAD BETTER WIN THIS NEXT MATCH!
WE WILL!
THANK YOU SO MUCH!
IF YOU WIN LIKE I ASKED YOU TO, I'LL LET YOU COMPETE IN THE GRAND PRIX.
AND IF YOU GET ANYTHING LESS THAN FIRST PLACE, I'LL HAVE YOU WITHDRAW.
WHA...
BUT... WHY WOULD YOU...?!
BECAUSE THAT'S WHAT I'VE DECIDED, AS YOUR COACH.
YOU CAN COMPETE IN THE GRANDS PRIX NEXT YEAR JUST AS EASILY. WHAT YOU NEED TO DO FIRST IS LEARN HOW TO BE A WINNER AND GAIN CONFIDENCE AS A COMPETITOR.
NO MATTER WHAT TOURNAMENT YOU ENTER...

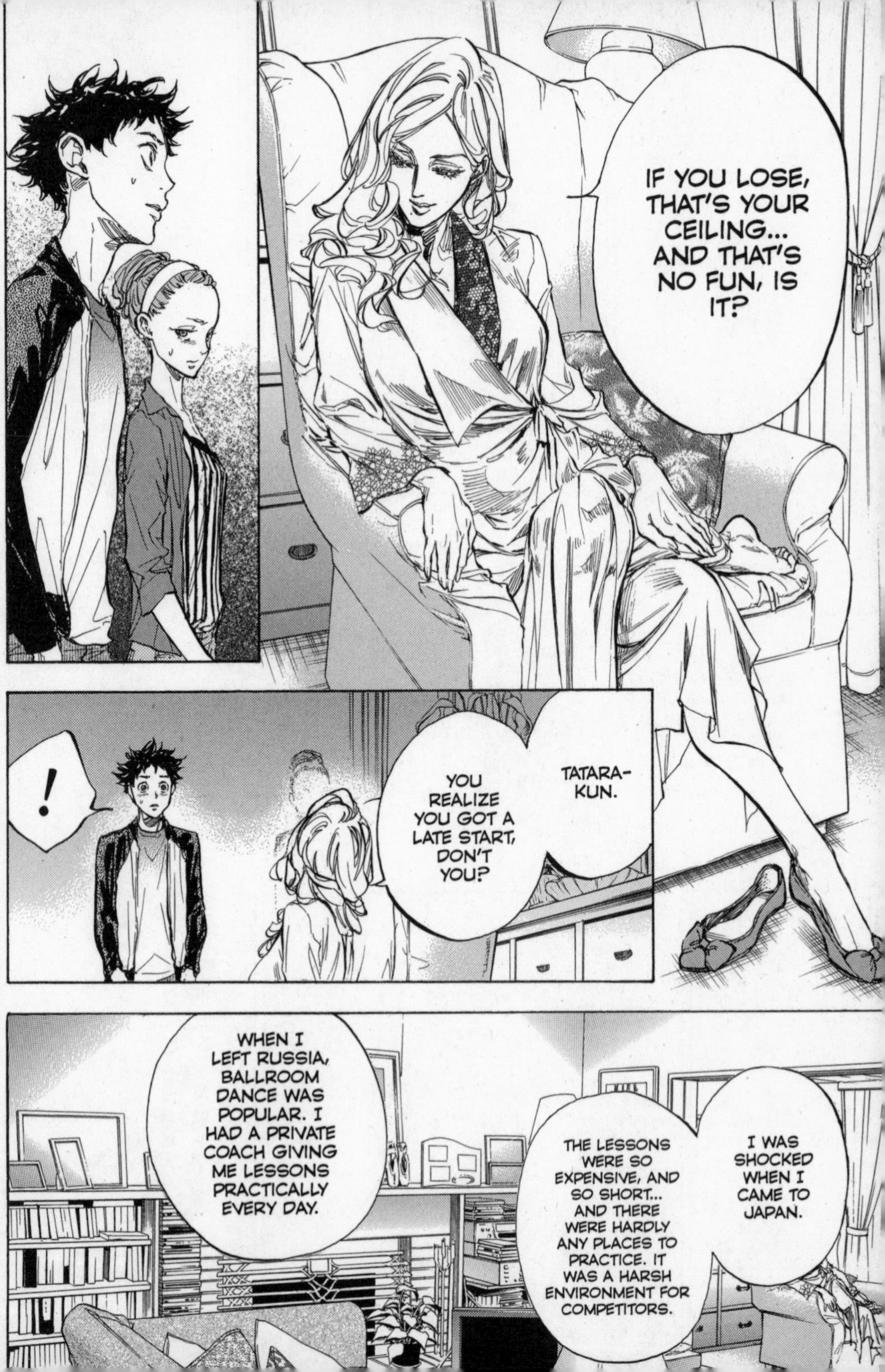
IF YOU LOSE, THAT'S YOUR CEILING... AND THAT'S NO FUN, IS IT?
TATARA-KUN.
YOU REALIZE YOU GOT A LATE START, DON'T YOU?
!
I WAS SHOCKED WHEN I CAME TO JAPAN.
THE LESSONS WERE SO EXPENSIVE, AND SO SHORT... AND THERE WERE HARDLY ANY PLACES TO PRACTICE. IT WAS A HARSH ENVIRONMENT FOR COMPETITORS.
WHEN I LEFT RUSSIA, BALLROOM DANCE WAS POPULAR. I HAD A PRIVATE COACH GIVING ME LESSONS PRACTICALLY EVERY DAY.

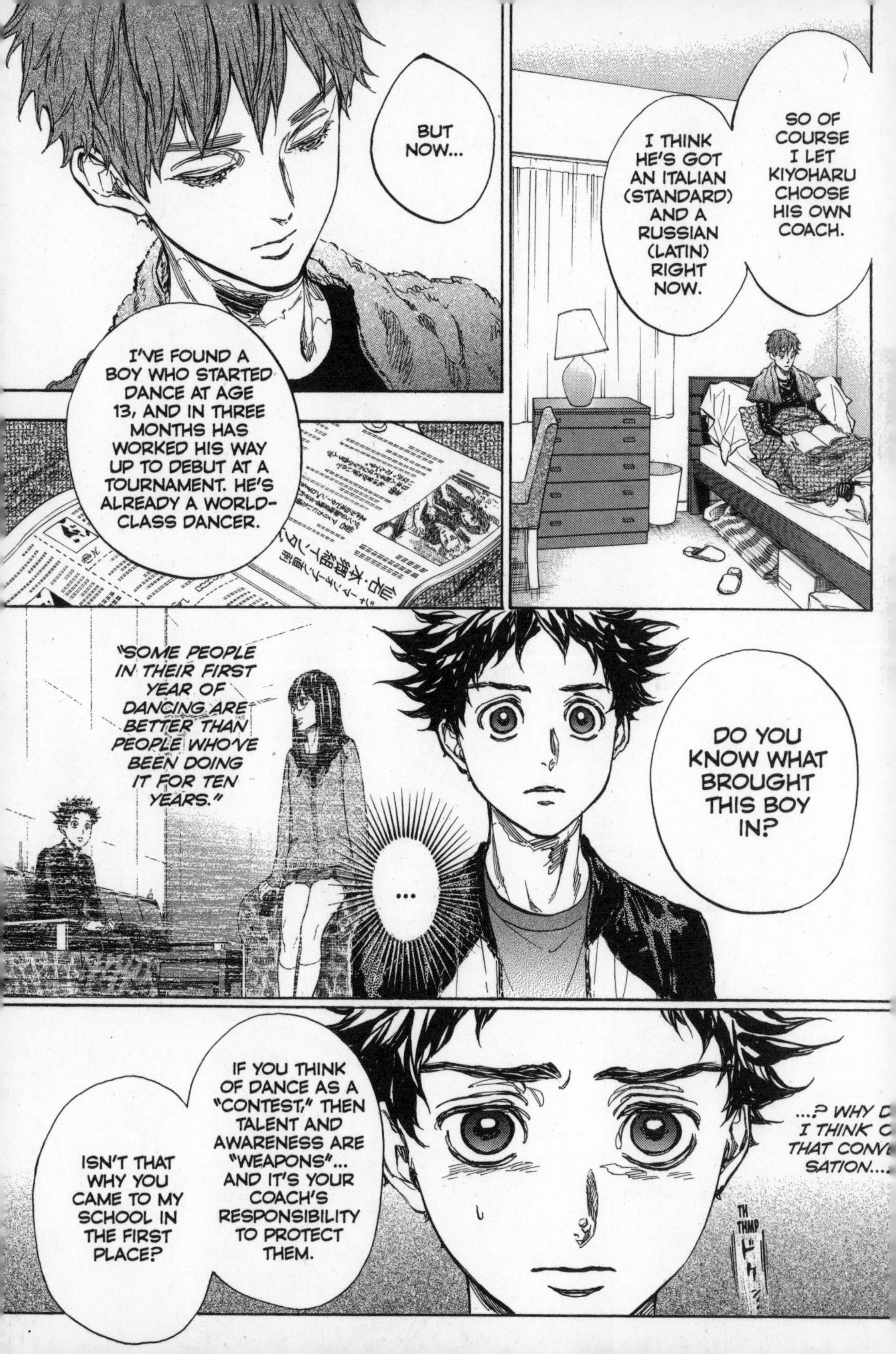
SO OF COURSE I LET KIYOHARU CHOOSE HIS OWN COACH.
I THINK HE'S GOT AN ITALIAN (STANDARD) AND A RUSSIAN (LATIN) RIGHT NOW.
BUT NOW...
I'VE FOUND A BOY WHO STARTED DANCE AT AGE 13, AND IN THREE MONTHS HAS WORKED HIS WAY UP TO DEBUT AT A TOURNAMENT. HE'S ALREADY A WORLD-CLASS DANCER.
DO YOU KNOW WHAT BROUGHT THIS BOY IN?
...
"SOME PEOPLE IN THEIR FIRST YEAR OF DANCING ARE BETTER THAN PEOPLE WHO'VE BEEN DOING IT FOR TEN YEARS."
...? WHY D I THINK O THAT CONV SATION...
TH THMP
IF YOU THINK OF DANCE AS A "CONTEST," THEN TALENT AND AWARENESS ARE "WEAPONS"... AND IT'S YOUR COACH'S RESPONSIBILITY TO PROTECT THEM.
ISN'T THAT WHY YOU CAME TO MY SCHOOL IN THE FIRST PLACE?

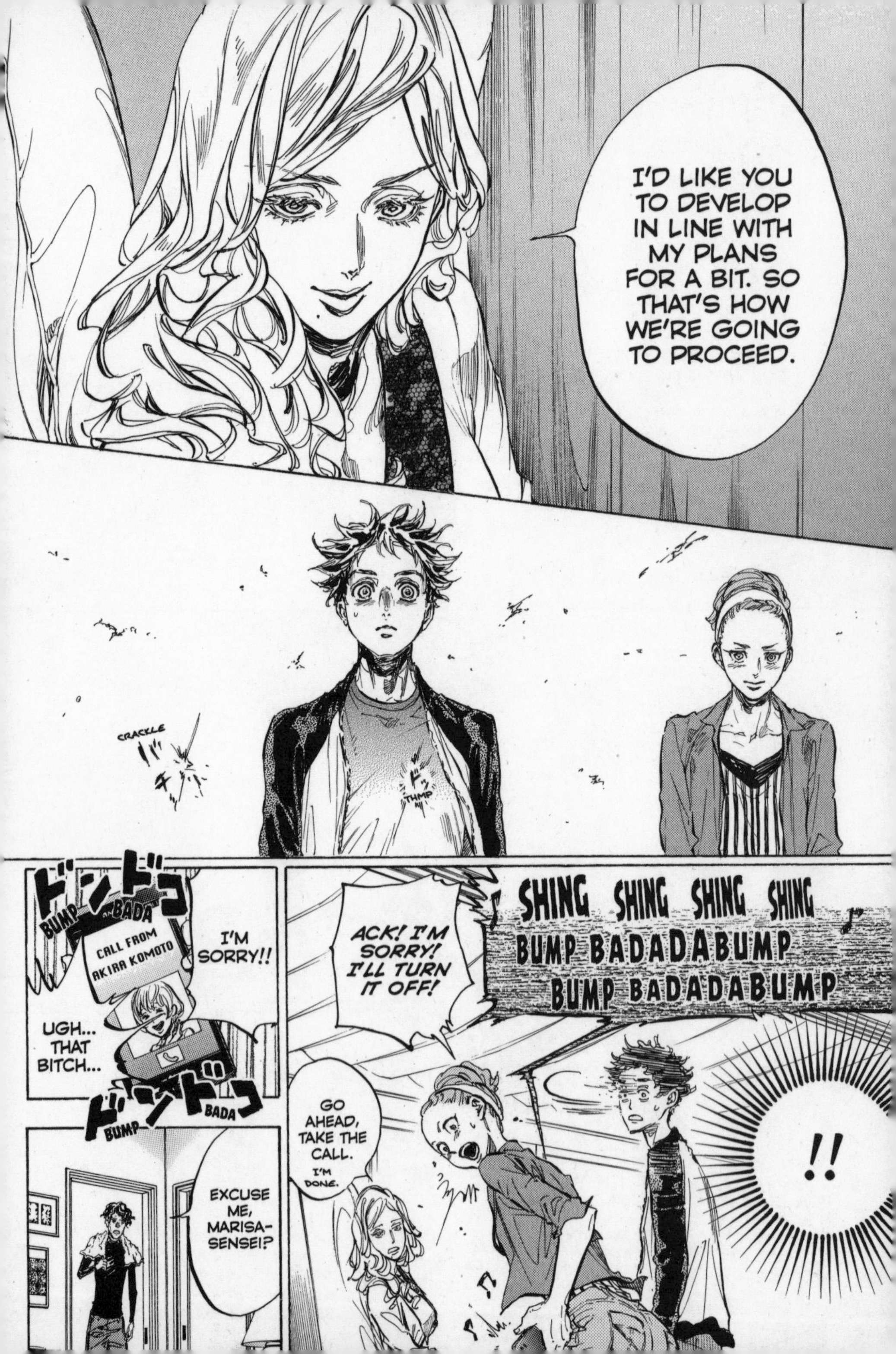
I'D LIKE YOU TO DEVELOP IN LINE WITH MY PLANS FOR A BIT. SO THAT'S HOW WE'RE GOING TO PROCEED.
CRACKLE
THMP
SHING SHING SHING SHING
BUMP BADADABUMP
BUMP BADADABUMP
ACK! I'M SORRY! I'LL TURN IT OFF!
!!
GO AHEAD, TAKE THE CALL.
I'M DONE.
BUMP BADA
CALL FROM AKIRA KOMOTO
I'M SORRY!!
UGH... THAT BITCH...
BUMP BADA
EXCUSE ME, MARISA-SENSEI?

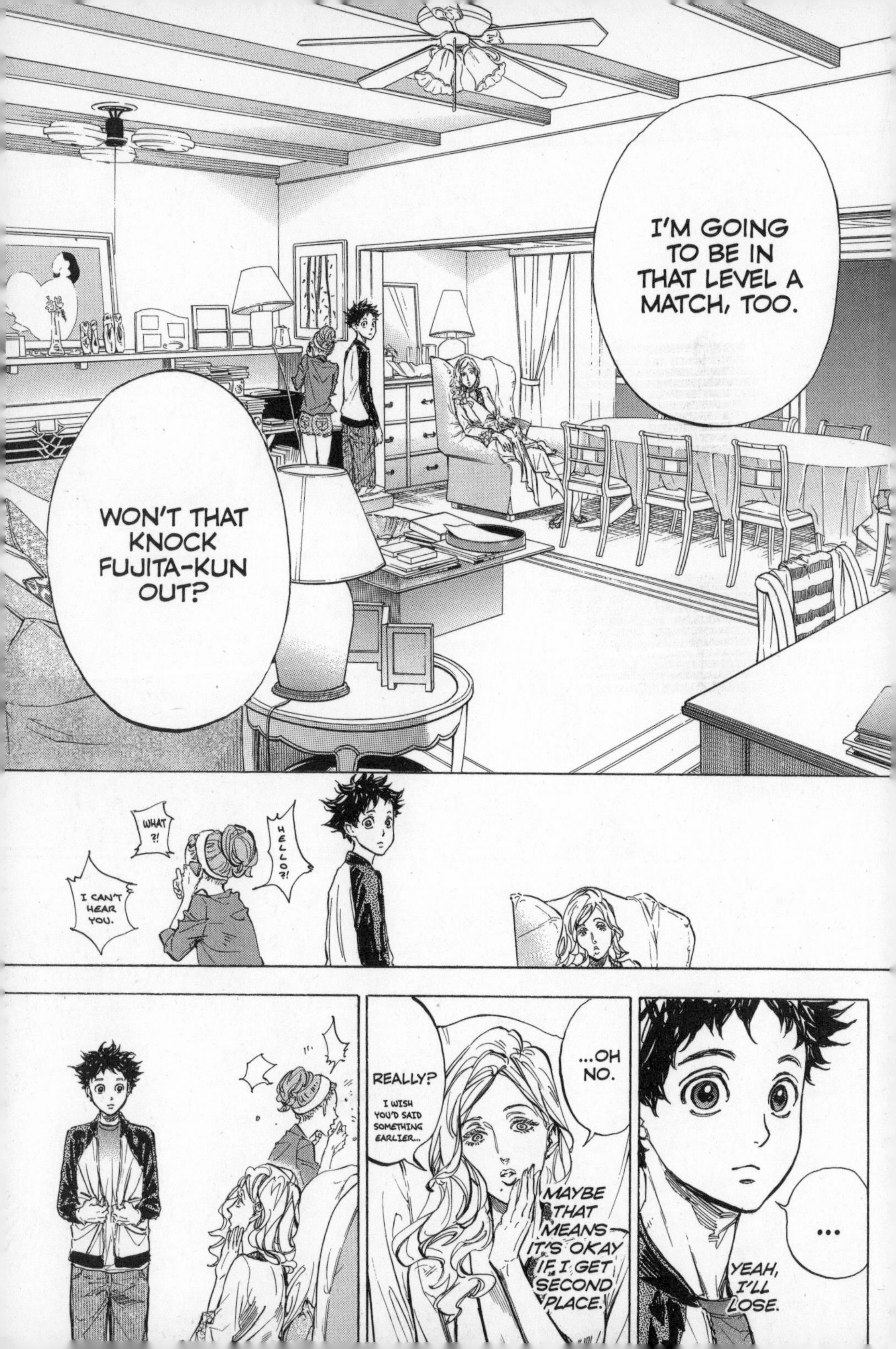
I'M GOING TO BE IN THAT LEVEL A MATCH, TOO.
WON'T THAT KNOCK FUJITA-KUN OUT?
HELLO?!
WHAT?!
I CAN'T HEAR YOU.
...
YEAH, I'LL LOSE.
...OH NO.
REALLY?
I WISH YOU'D SAID SOMETHING EARLIER...
MAYBE THAT MEANS IT'S OKAY IF I GET SECOND PLACE.

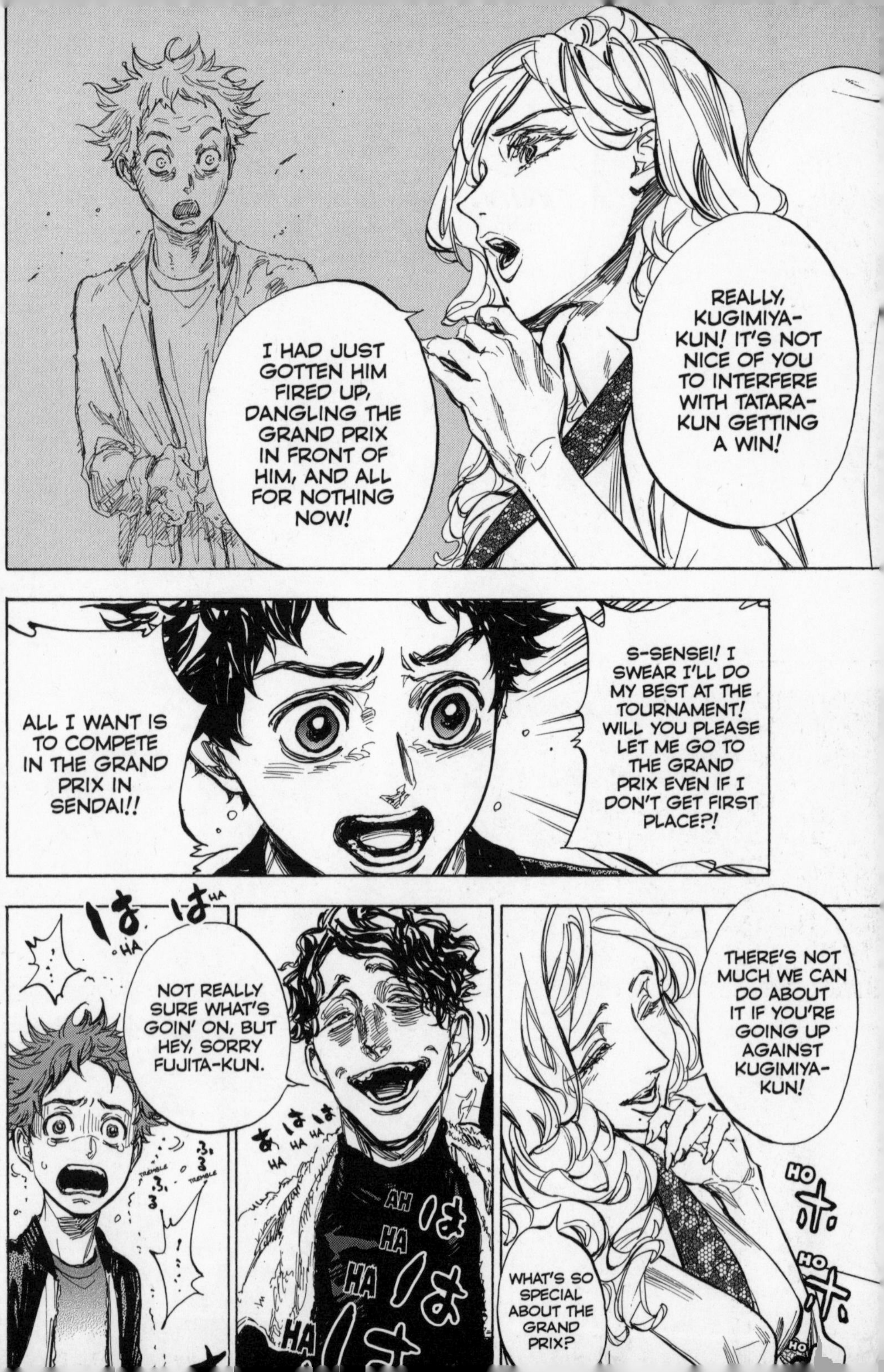
REALLY, KUGIMIYA-KUN! IT'S NOT NICE OF YOU TO INTERFERE WITH TATARA-KUN GETTING A WIN!
I HAD JUST GOTTEN HIM FIRED UP, DANGLING THE GRAND PRIX IN FRONT OF HIM, AND ALL FOR NOTHING NOW!
S-SENSEI! I SWEAR I'LL DO MY BEST AT THE TOURNAMENT! WILL YOU PLEASE LET ME GO TO THE GRAND PRIX EVEN IF I DON'T GET FIRST PLACE?!
ALL I WANT IS TO COMPETE IN THE GRAND PRIX IN SENDAI!!
THERE'S NOT MUCH WE CAN DO ABOUT IT IF YOU'RE GOING UP AGAINST KUGIMIYA-KUN!
HO HO HO
WHAT'S SO SPECIAL ABOUT THE GRAND PRIX?
AH HA HA HA
HA HA HA HA
HA HA
NOT REALLY SURE WHAT'S GOIN' ON, BUT HEY, SORRY FUJITA-KUN.
TREMBLE TREMBLE

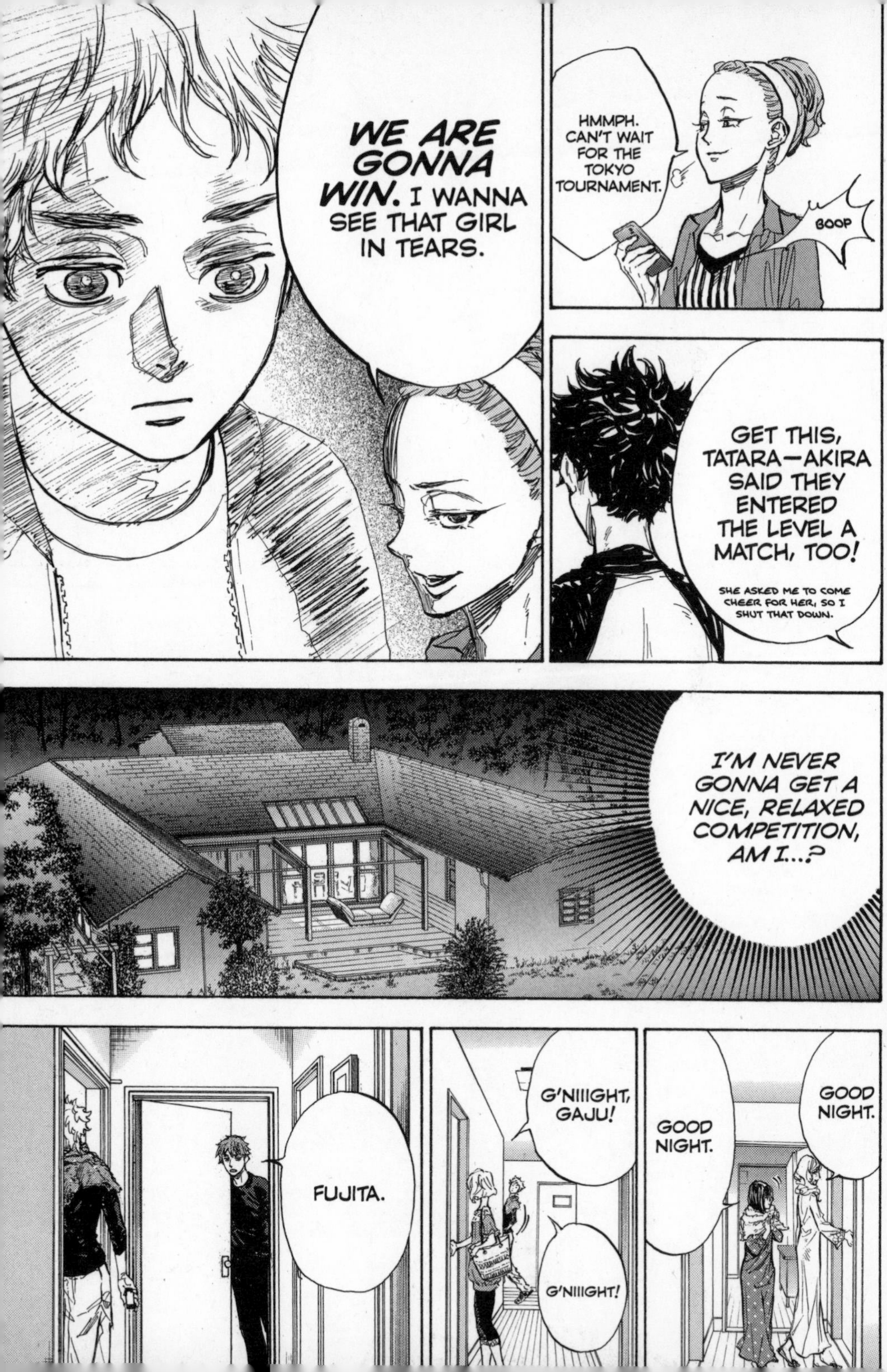
HMMPH. CAN'T WAIT FOR THE TOKYO TOURNAMENT.
BOOP
GET THIS, TATARA—AKIRA SAID THEY ENTERED THE LEVEL A MATCH, TOO!
SHE ASKED ME TO COME CHEER FOR HER, SO I SHUT THAT DOWN.
WE ARE GONNA WIN. I WANNA SEE THAT GIRL IN TEARS.
I'M NEVER GONNA GET A NICE, RELAXED COMPETITION, AM I...?
GOOD NIGHT.
GOOD NIGHT.
G'NIIIGHT, GAJU!
G'NIIIGHT!
FUJITA.

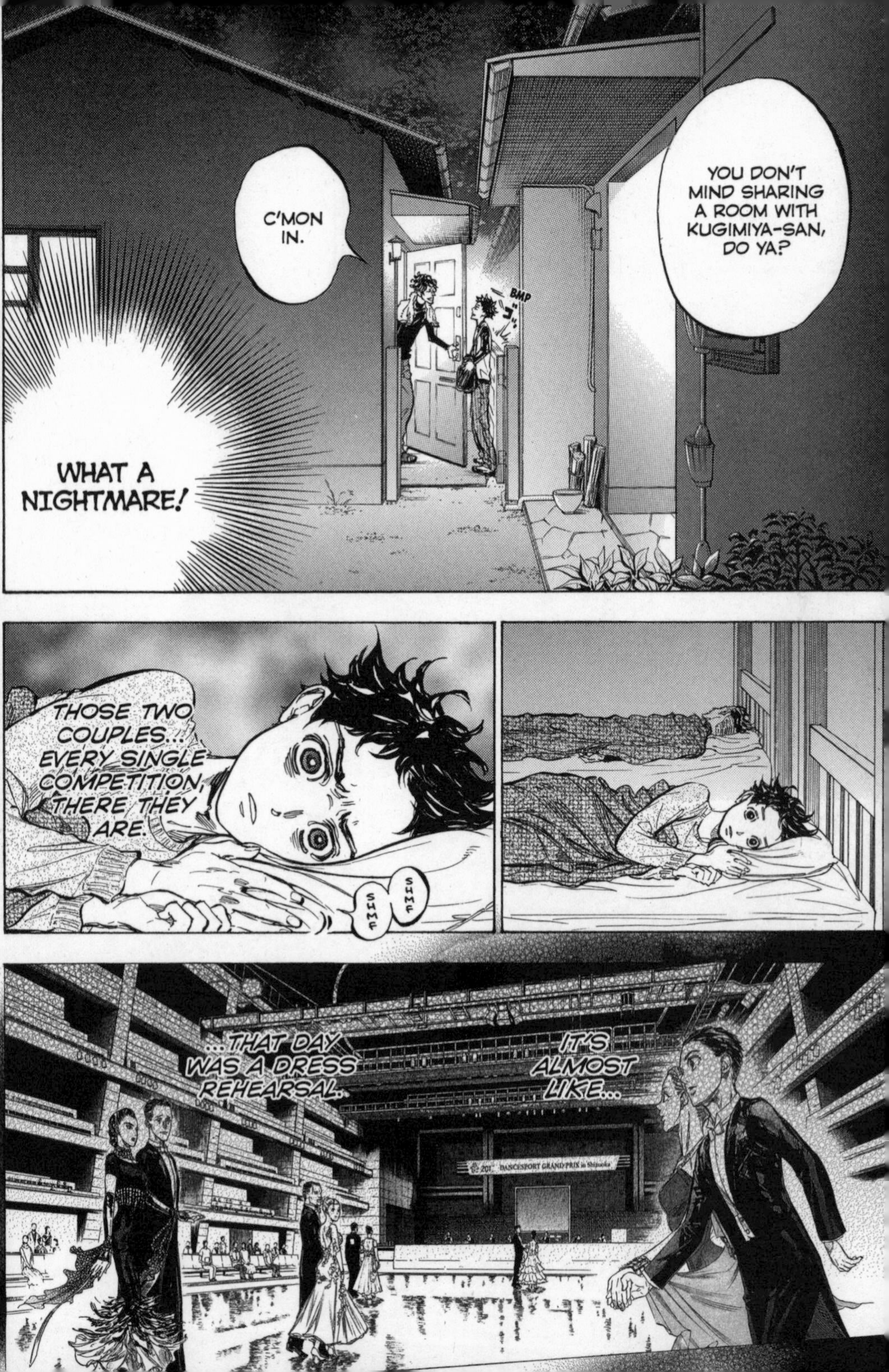
YOU DON'T MIND SHARING A ROOM WITH KUGIMIYA-SAN, DO YA?
C'MON IN.
BMP
WHAT A NIGHTMARE!
THOSE TWO COUPLES... EVERY SINGLE COMPETITION, THERE THEY ARE.
SHMF
SHMF
IT'S ALMOST LIKE...
...THAT DAY WAS A DRESS REHEARSAL.
DANCESPORT GRAND PRIX in Shizuoka

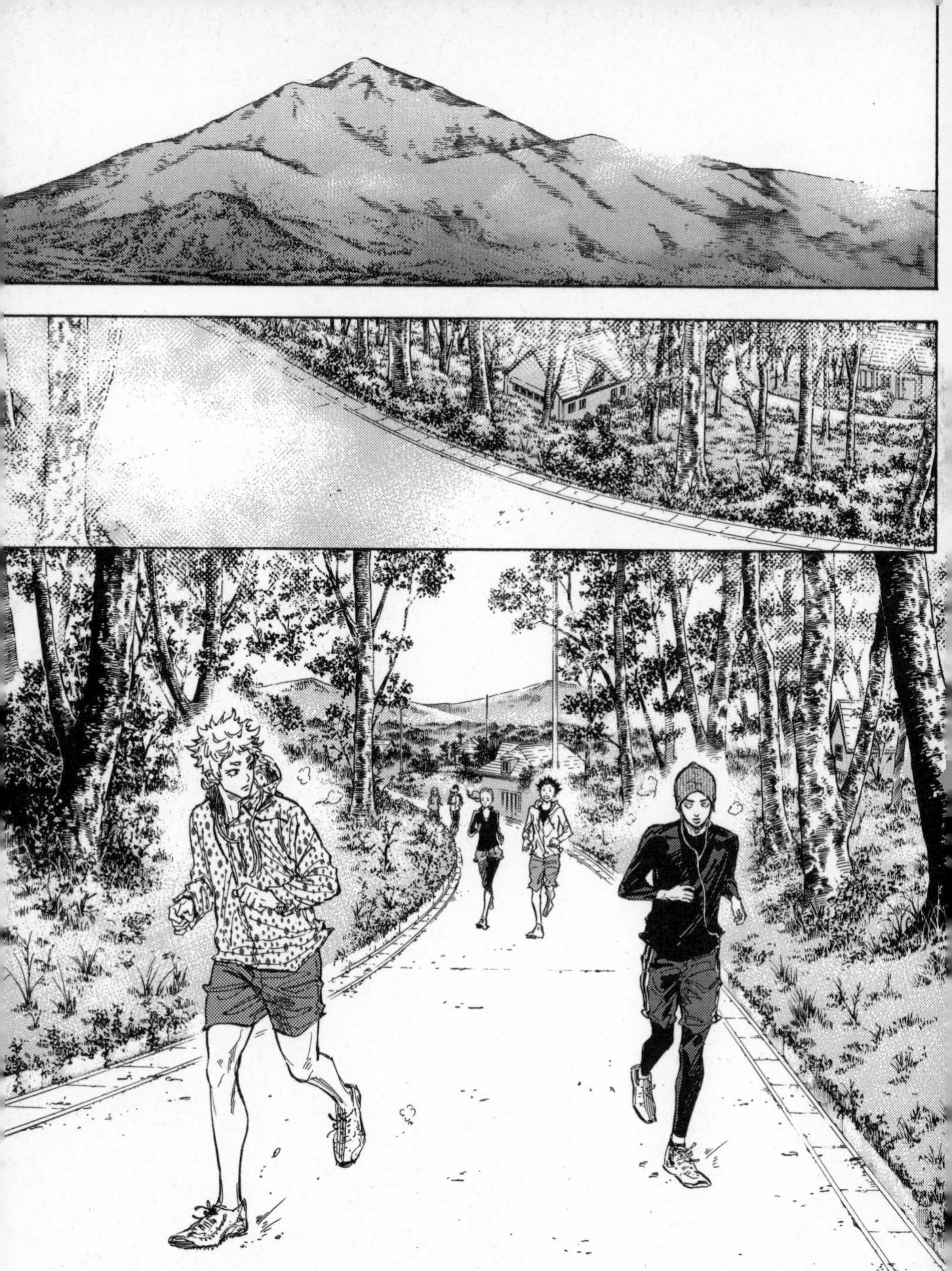

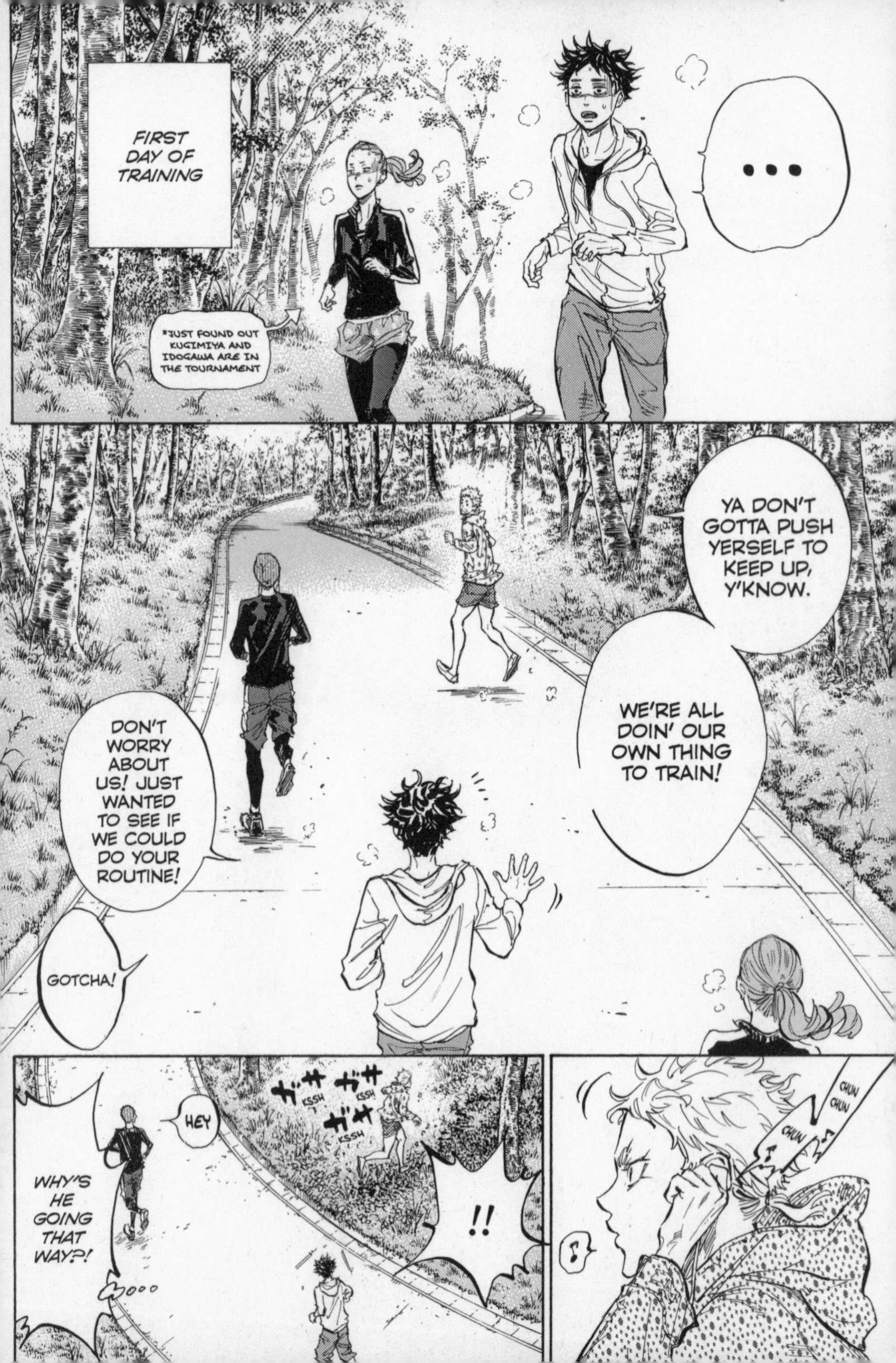
...
FIRST DAY OF TRAINING
*JUST FOUND OUT KUGIMIYA AND IDOGAWA ARE IN THE TOURNAMENT
YA DON'T GOTTA PUSH YERSELF TO KEEP UP, Y'KNOW.
WE'RE ALL DOIN' OUR OWN THING TO TRAIN!
DON'T WORRY ABOUT US! JUST WANTED TO SEE IF WE COULD DO YOUR ROUTINE!
GOTCHA!
CHUN CHUN
CHUN
KSSH KSSH
KSSH
HEY
!!
WHY'S HE GOING THAT WAY?!

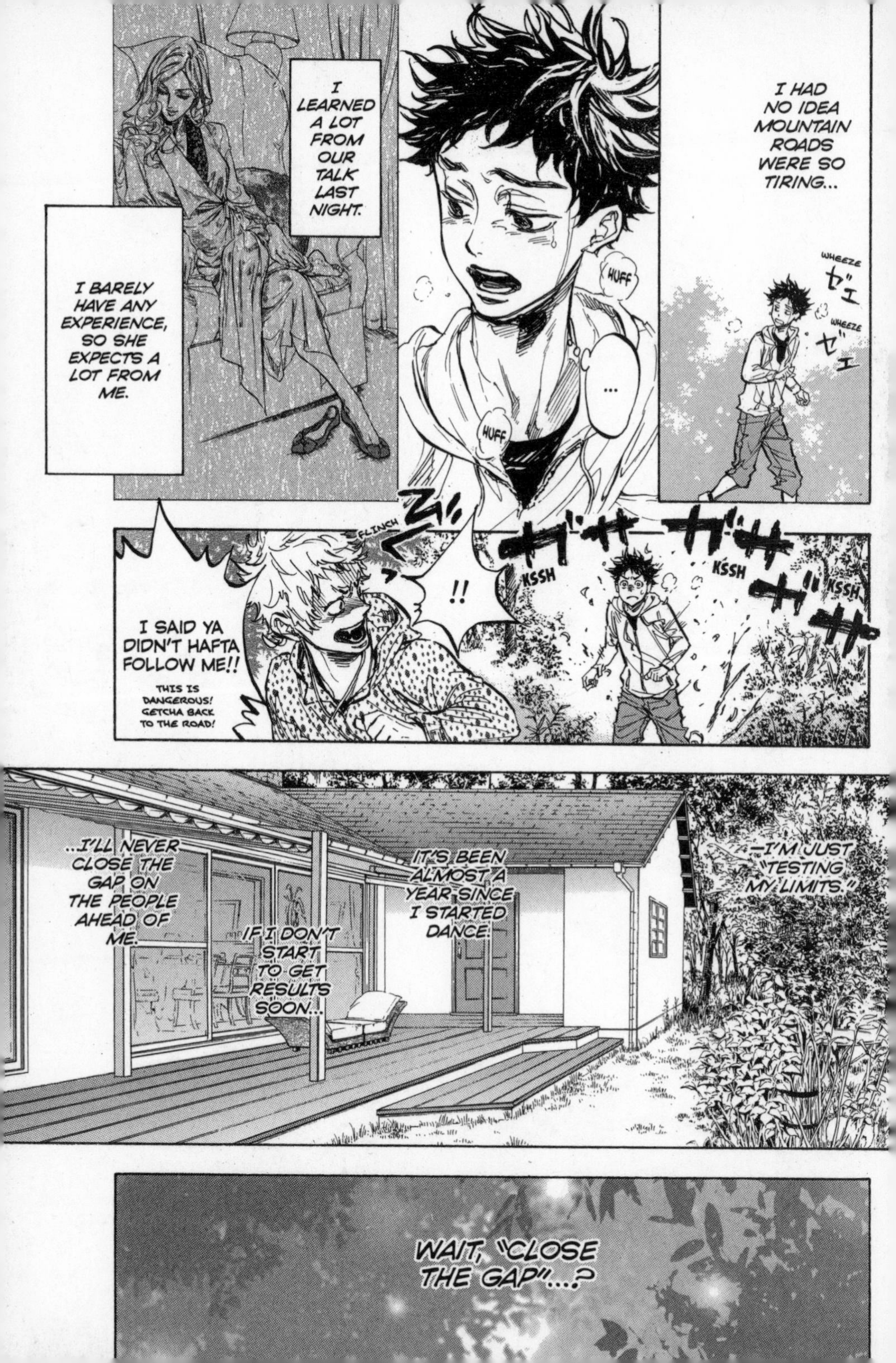
I HAD NO IDEA MOUNTAIN ROADS WERE SO TIRING...
WHEEZE ゼェ
WHEEZE ゼェ
HUFF
...
HUFF
I LEARNED A LOT FROM OUR TALK LAST NIGHT.
I BARELY HAVE ANY EXPERIENCE, SO SHE EXPECTS A LOT FROM ME.
KSSH
KSSH
KSSH
!!
FLINCH
I SAID YA DIDN'T HAFTA FOLLOW ME!!
THIS IS DANGEROUS! GETCHA BACK TO THE ROAD!
—I'M JUST "TESTING MY LIMITS."
IT'S BEEN ALMOST A YEAR SINCE I STARTED DANCE.
IF I DON'T START TO GET RESULTS SOON...
...I'LL NEVER CLOSE THE GAP ON THE PEOPLE AHEAD OF ME.
WAIT, "CLOSE THE GAP"...?

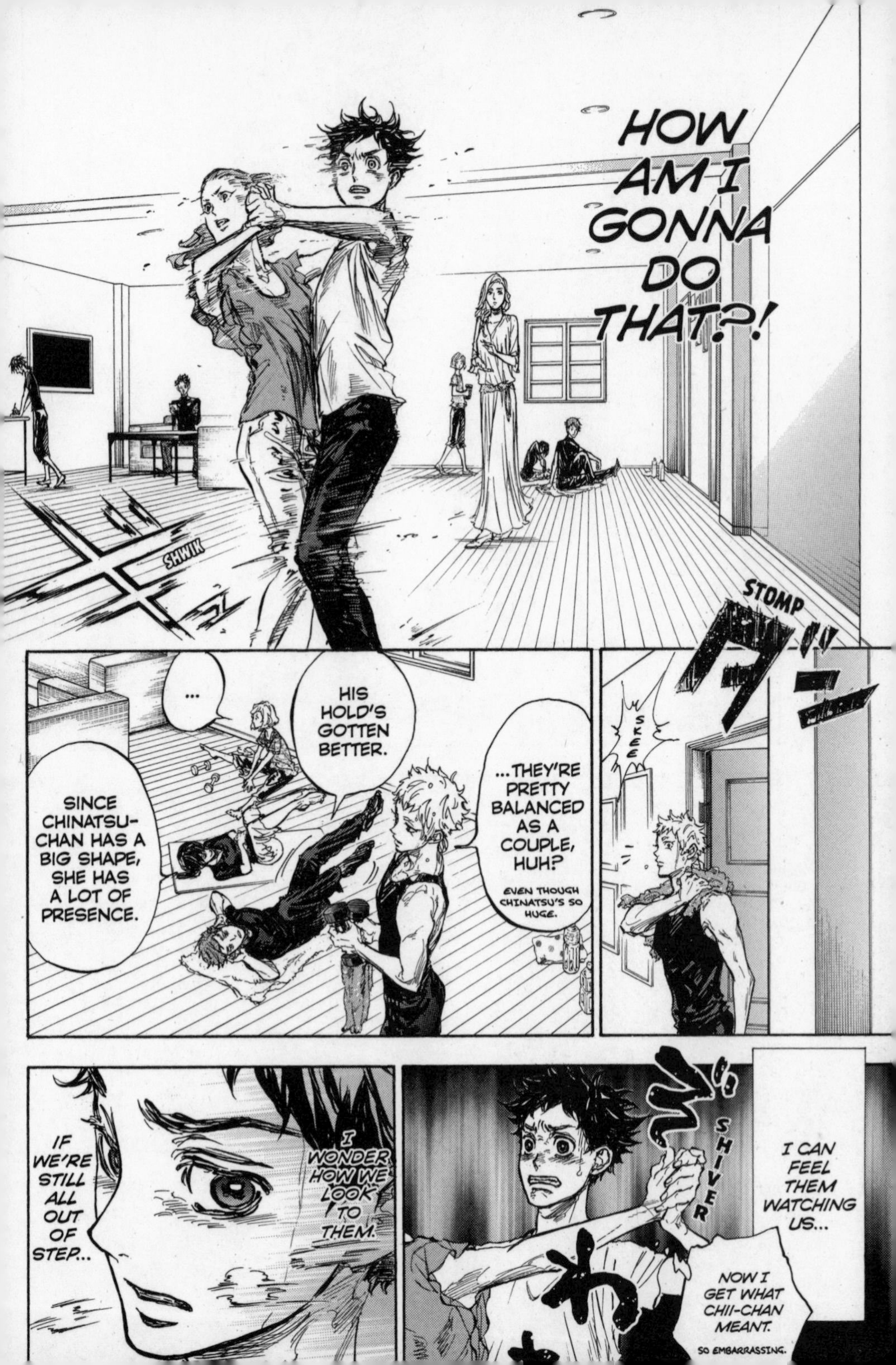
HOW AM I GONNA DO THAT?!
SHWIK
STOMP
SKEE
HIS HOLD'S GOTTEN BETTER.
...
...THEY'RE PRETTY BALANCED AS A COUPLE, HUH?
EVEN THOUGH CHINATSU'S SO HUGE.
SINCE CHINATSU-CHAN HAS A BIG SHAPE, SHE HAS A LOT OF PRESENCE.
SHIVER
I CAN FEEL THEM WATCHING US...
NOW I GET WHAT CHII-CHAN MEANT.
SO EMBARRASSING.
I WONDER HOW WE LOOK TO THEM.
IF WE'RE STILL ALL OUT OF STEP...

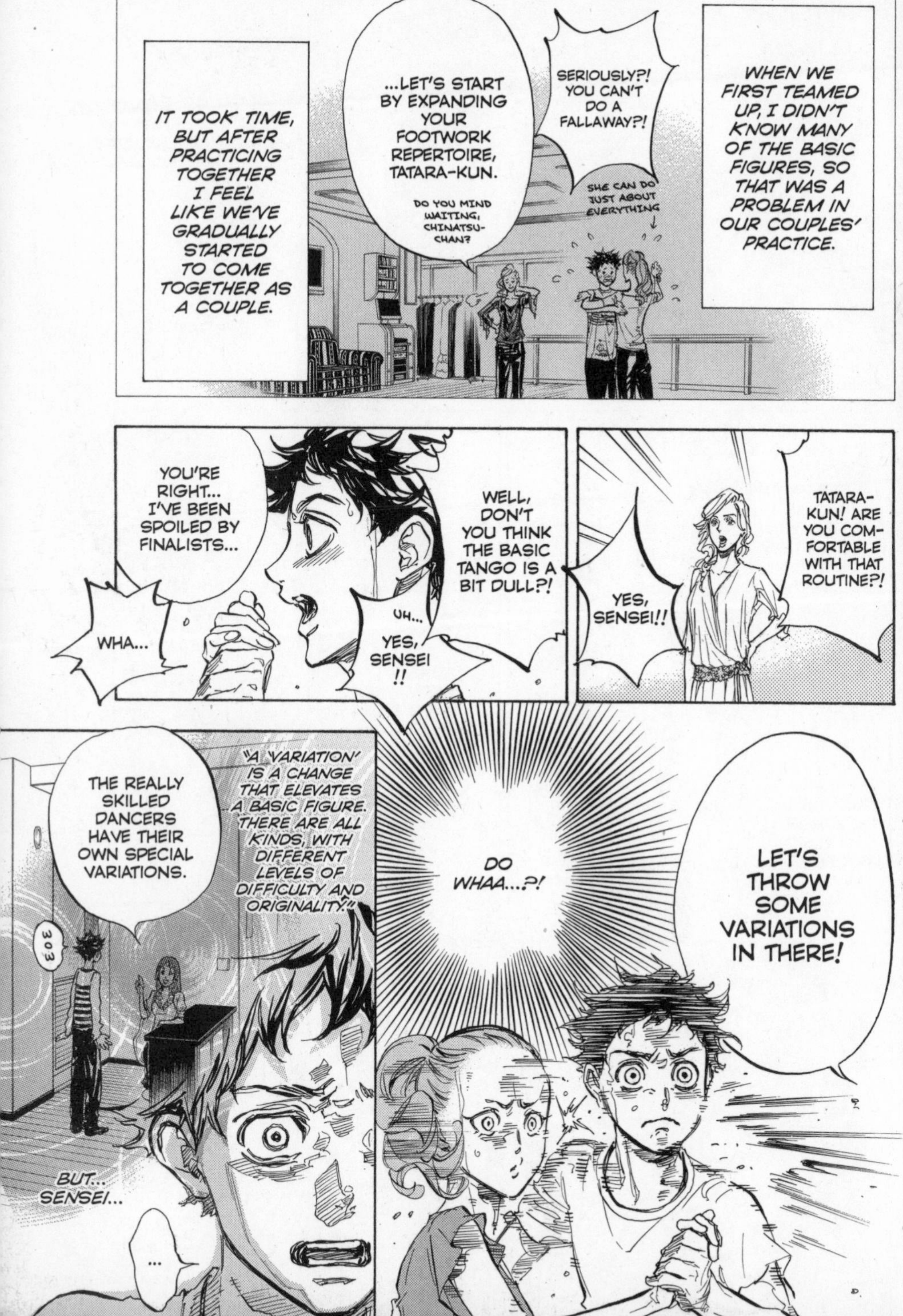
WHEN WE FIRST TEAMED UP, I DIDN'T KNOW MANY OF THE BASIC FIGURES, SO THAT WAS A PROBLEM IN OUR COUPLES' PRACTICE.
SERIOUSLY?! YOU CAN'T DO A FALLAWAY?!
SHE CAN DO JUST ABOUT EVERYTHING
...LET'S START BY EXPANDING YOUR FOOTWORK REPERTOIRE, TATARA-KUN.
DO YOU MIND WAITING, CHINATSU-CHAN?
IT TOOK TIME, BUT AFTER PRACTICING TOGETHER I FEEL LIKE WE'VE GRADUALLY STARTED TO COME TOGETHER AS A COUPLE.
TATARA-KUN! ARE YOU COMFORTABLE WITH THAT ROUTINE?!
YES, SENSEI!!
WELL, DON'T YOU THINK THE BASIC TANGO IS A BIT DULL?!
UH...
YES, SENSEI !!
YOU'RE RIGHT... I'VE BEEN SPOILED BY FINALISTS...
WHA...
LET'S THROW SOME VARIATIONS IN THERE!
DO WHAA...?!
"A 'VARIATION' IS A CHANGE THAT ELEVATES A BASIC FIGURE. THERE ARE ALL KINDS, WITH DIFFERENT LEVELS OF DIFFICULTY AND ORIGINALITY."
THE REALLY SKILLED DANCERS HAVE THEIR OWN SPECIAL VARIATIONS.
BUT... SENSEI...
...

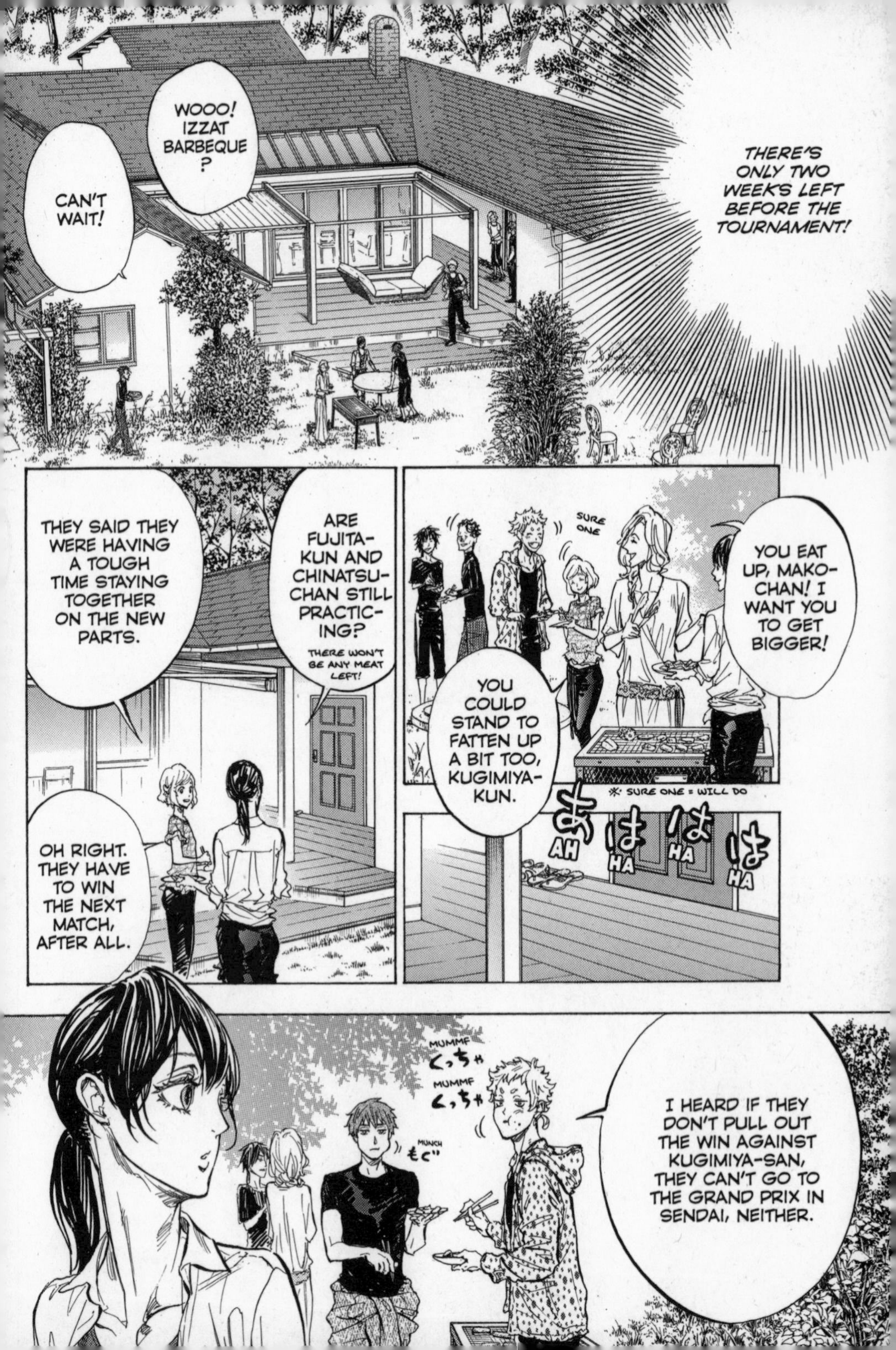
THERE'S ONLY TWO WEEKS LEFT BEFORE THE TOURNAMENT!
WOOO! IZZAT BARBEQUE?
CAN'T WAIT!
YOU EAT UP, MAKO-CHAN! I WANT YOU TO GET BIGGER!
SURE ONE
YOU COULD STAND TO FATTEN UP A BIT TOO, KUGIMIYA-KUN.
※ SURE ONE = WILL DO
あはははは
AH HA HA HA
ARE FUJITA-KUN AND CHINATSU-CHAN STILL PRACTICING?
THERE WON'T BE ANY MEAT LEFT!
THEY SAID THEY WERE HAVING A TOUGH TIME STAYING TOGETHER ON THE NEW PARTS.
OH RIGHT. THEY HAVE TO WIN THE NEXT MATCH, AFTER ALL.
I HEARD IF THEY DON'T PULL OUT THE WIN AGAINST KUGIMIYA-SAN, THEY CAN'T GO TO THE GRAND PRIX IN SENDAI, NEITHER.
MUMMF くっちゃ
MUMMF くっちゃ
MUNCH もぐ

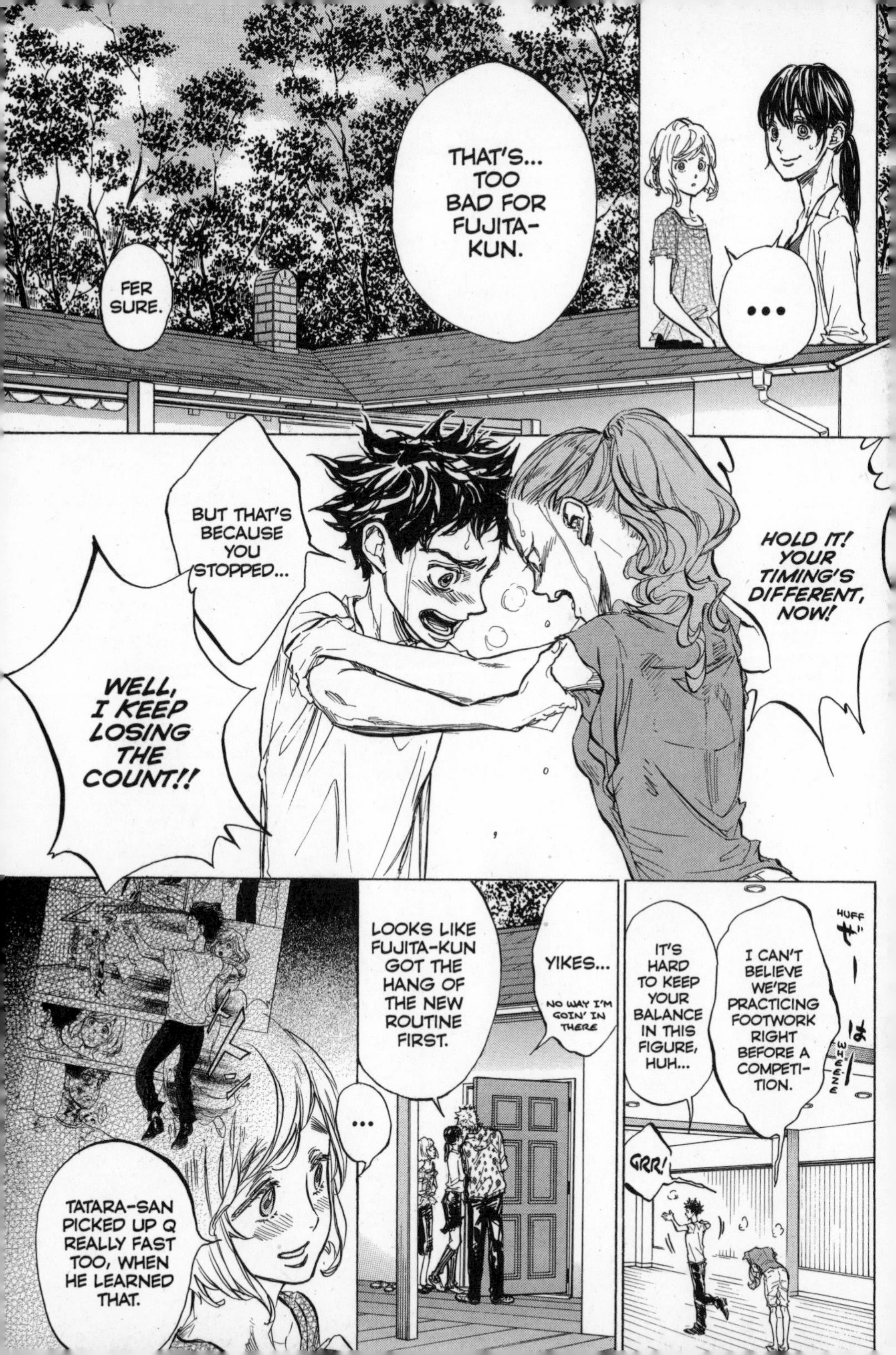
...
THAT'S... TOO BAD FOR FUJITA-KUN.
FER SURE.
HOLD IT! YOUR TIMING'S DIFFERENT, NOW!
BUT THAT'S BECAUSE YOU STOPPED...
WELL, I KEEP LOSING THE COUNT!!
HUFF
WHEEZE
I CAN'T BELIEVE WE'RE PRACTICING FOOTWORK RIGHT BEFORE A COMPETITION.
IT'S HARD TO KEEP YOUR BALANCE IN THIS FIGURE, HUH...
GRR!
YIKES...
NO WAY I'M GOIN' IN THERE
LOOKS LIKE FUJITA-KUN GOT THE HANG OF THE NEW ROUTINE FIRST.
...
TATARA-SAN PICKED UP Q REALLY FAST TOO, WHEN HE LEARNED THAT.

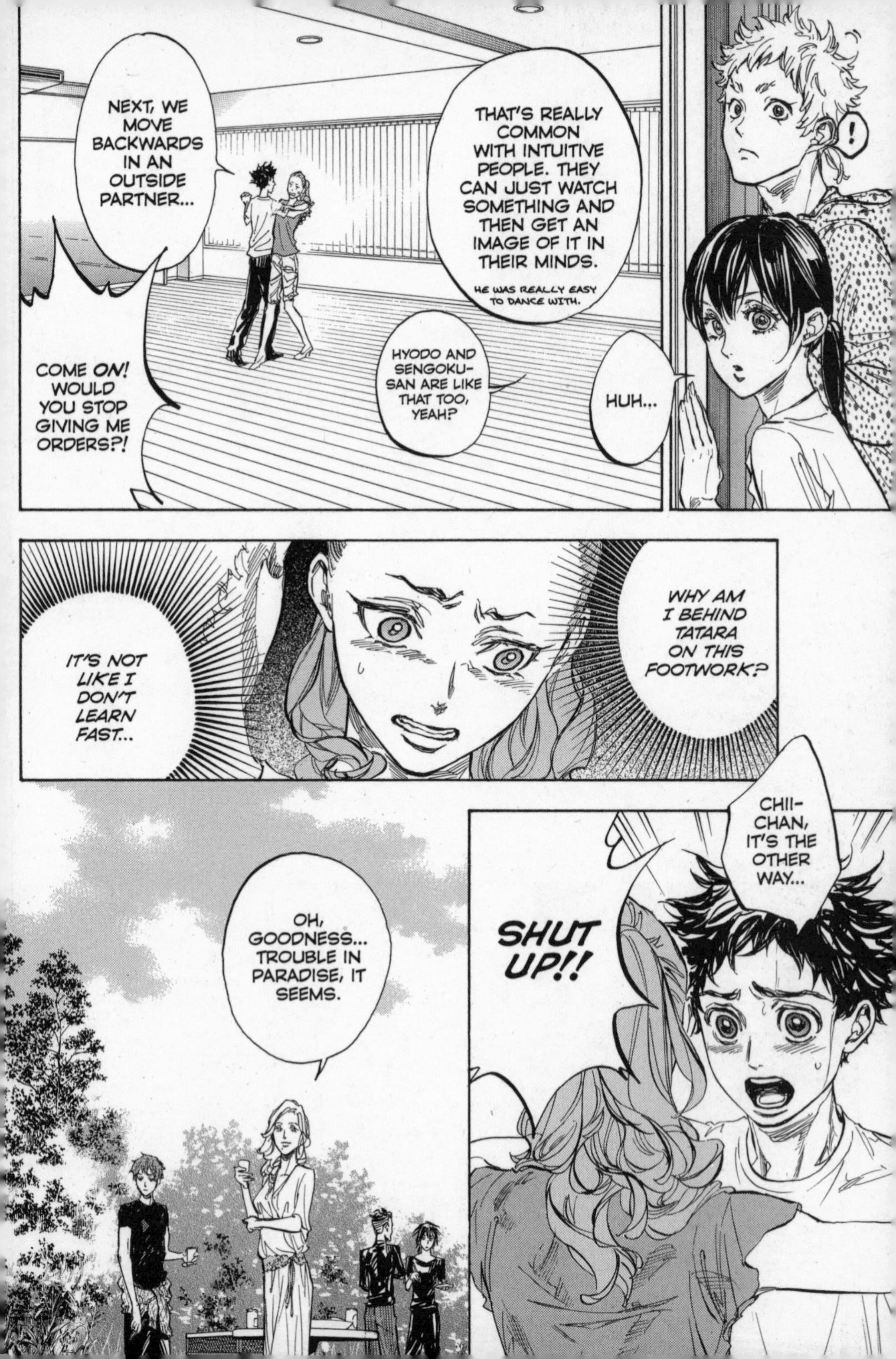
HUH...
THAT'S REALLY COMMON WITH INTUITIVE PEOPLE. THEY CAN JUST WATCH SOMETHING AND THEN GET AN IMAGE OF IT IN THEIR MINDS.
HE WAS REALLY EASY TO DANCE WITH.
HYODO AND SENGOKU-SAN ARE LIKE THAT TOO, YEAH?
NEXT, WE MOVE BACKWARDS IN AN OUTSIDE PARTNER...
COME ON! WOULD YOU STOP GIVING ME ORDERS?!
WHY AM I BEHIND TATARA ON THIS FOOTWORK?
IT'S NOT LIKE I DON'T LEARN FAST...
CHII-CHAN, IT'S THE OTHER WAY...
SHUT UP!!
OH, GOODNESS... TROUBLE IN PARADISE, IT SEEMS.

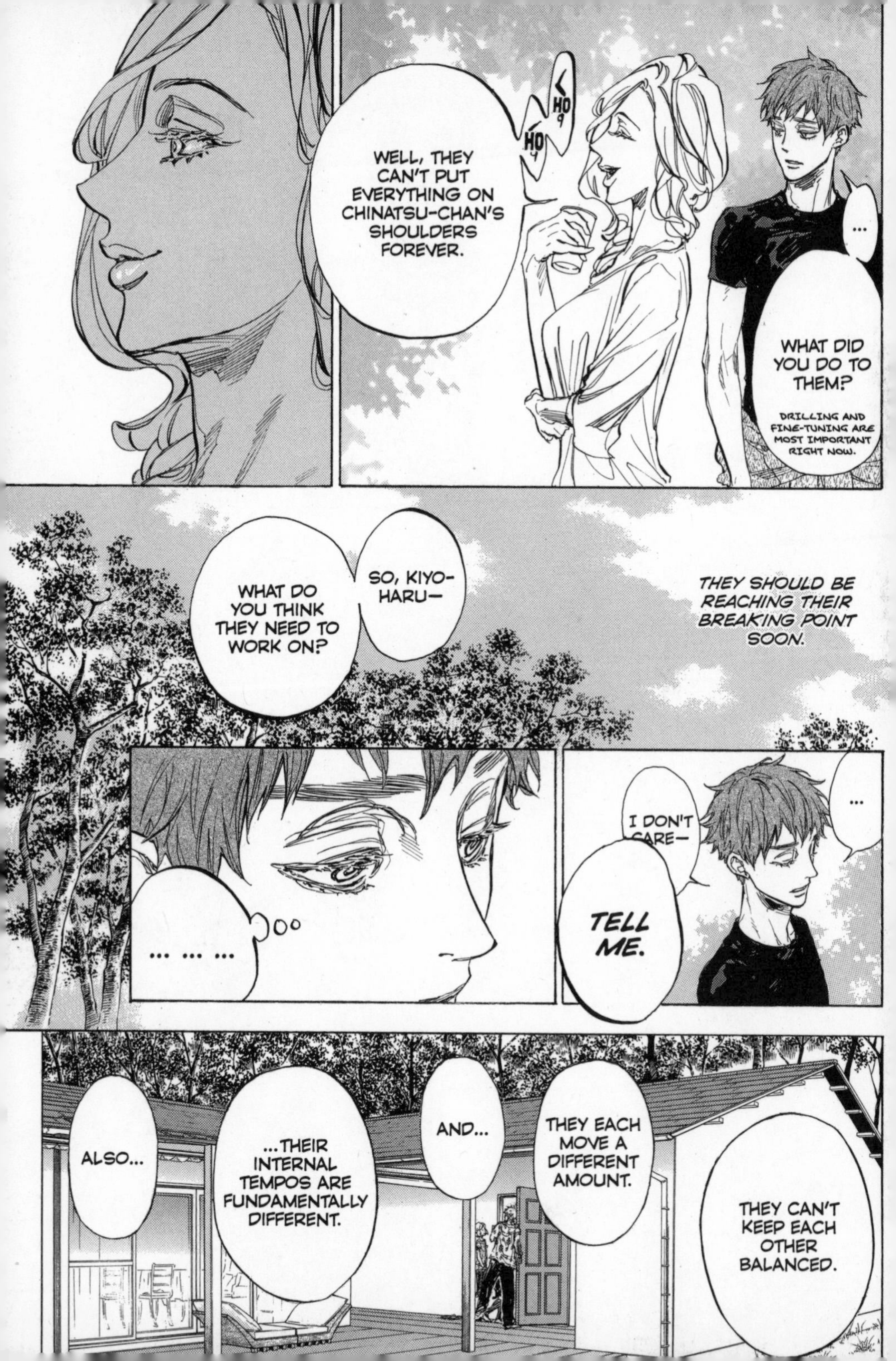
...
WHAT DID YOU DO TO THEM?
DRILLING AND FINE-TUNING ARE MOST IMPORTANT RIGHT NOW.
HO HO
WELL, THEY CAN'T PUT EVERYTHING ON CHINATSU-CHAN'S SHOULDERS FOREVER.
THEY SHOULD BE REACHING THEIR BREAKING POINT SOON.
SO, KIYO-HARU—
WHAT DO YOU THINK THEY NEED TO WORK ON?
...
I DON'T CARE—
TELL ME.
... ...
THEY CAN'T KEEP EACH OTHER BALANCED.
THEY EACH MOVE A DIFFERENT AMOUNT.
AND...
...THEIR INTERNAL TEMPOS ARE FUNDAMENTALLY DIFFERENT.
ALSO...

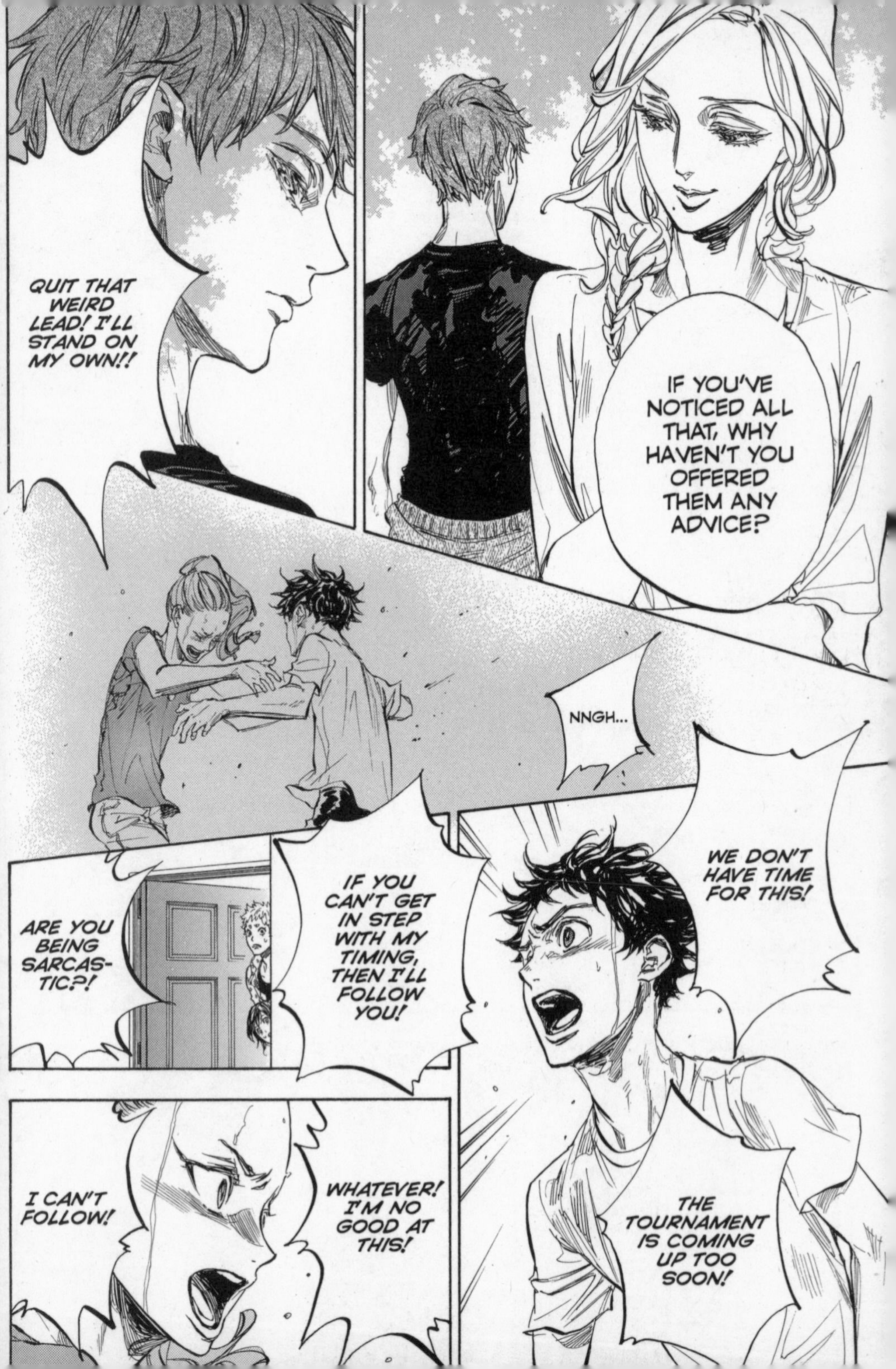
IF YOU'VE NOTICED ALL THAT, WHY HAVEN'T YOU OFFERED THEM ANY ADVICE?
QUIT THAT WEIRD LEAD! I'LL STAND ON MY OWN!!
NNGH...
WE DON'T HAVE TIME FOR THIS!
IF YOU CAN'T GET IN STEP WITH MY TIMING, THEN I'LL FOLLOW YOU!
THE TOURNAMENT IS COMING UP TOO SOON!
ARE YOU BEING SARCAS-TIC?!
WHATEVER! I'M NO GOOD AT THIS!
I CAN'T FOLLOW!

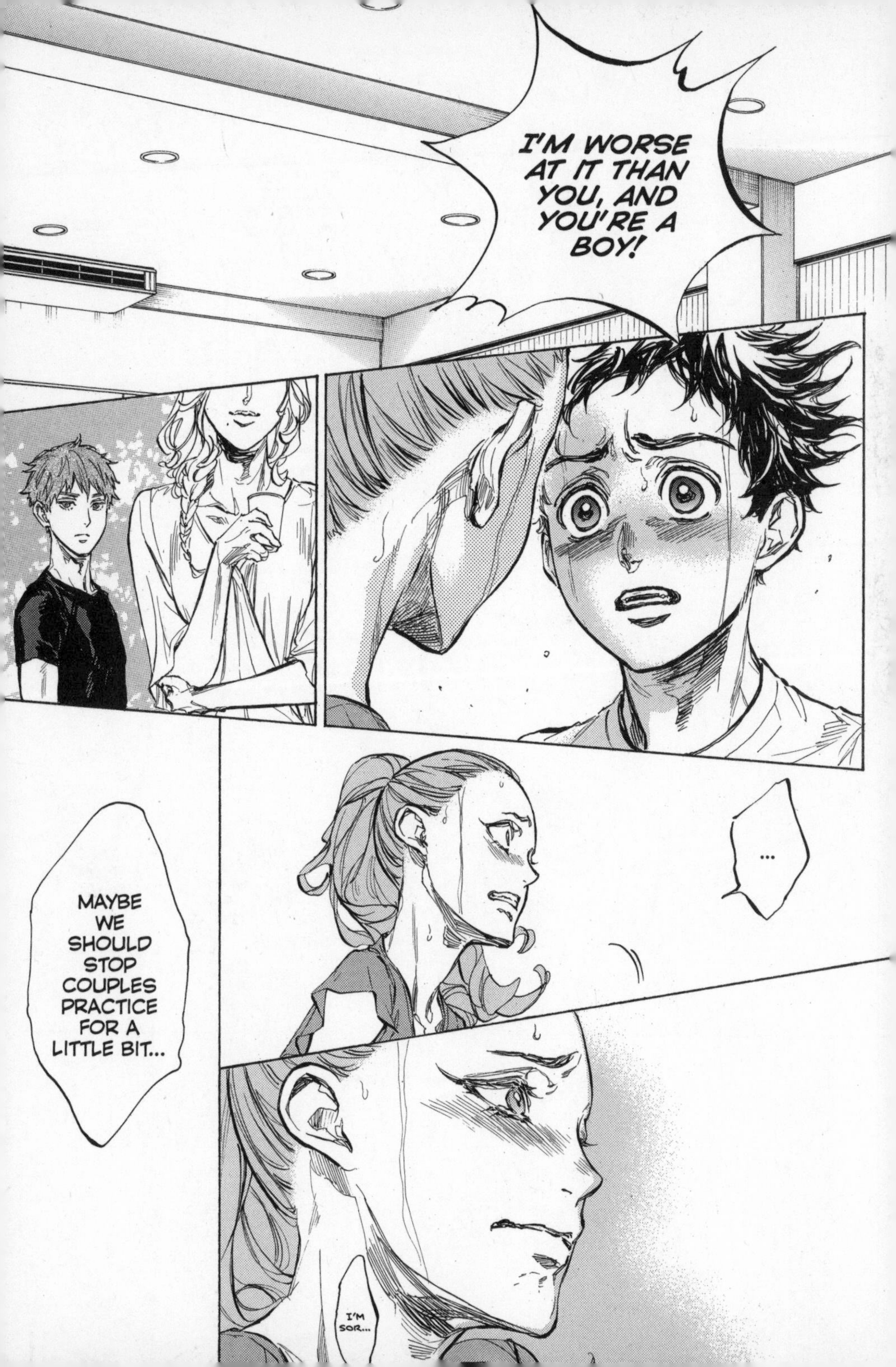
I'M WORSE AT IT THAN YOU, AND YOU'RE A BOY!
...
MAYBE WE SHOULD STOP COUPLES PRACTICE FOR A LITTLE BIT...
I'M SOR...

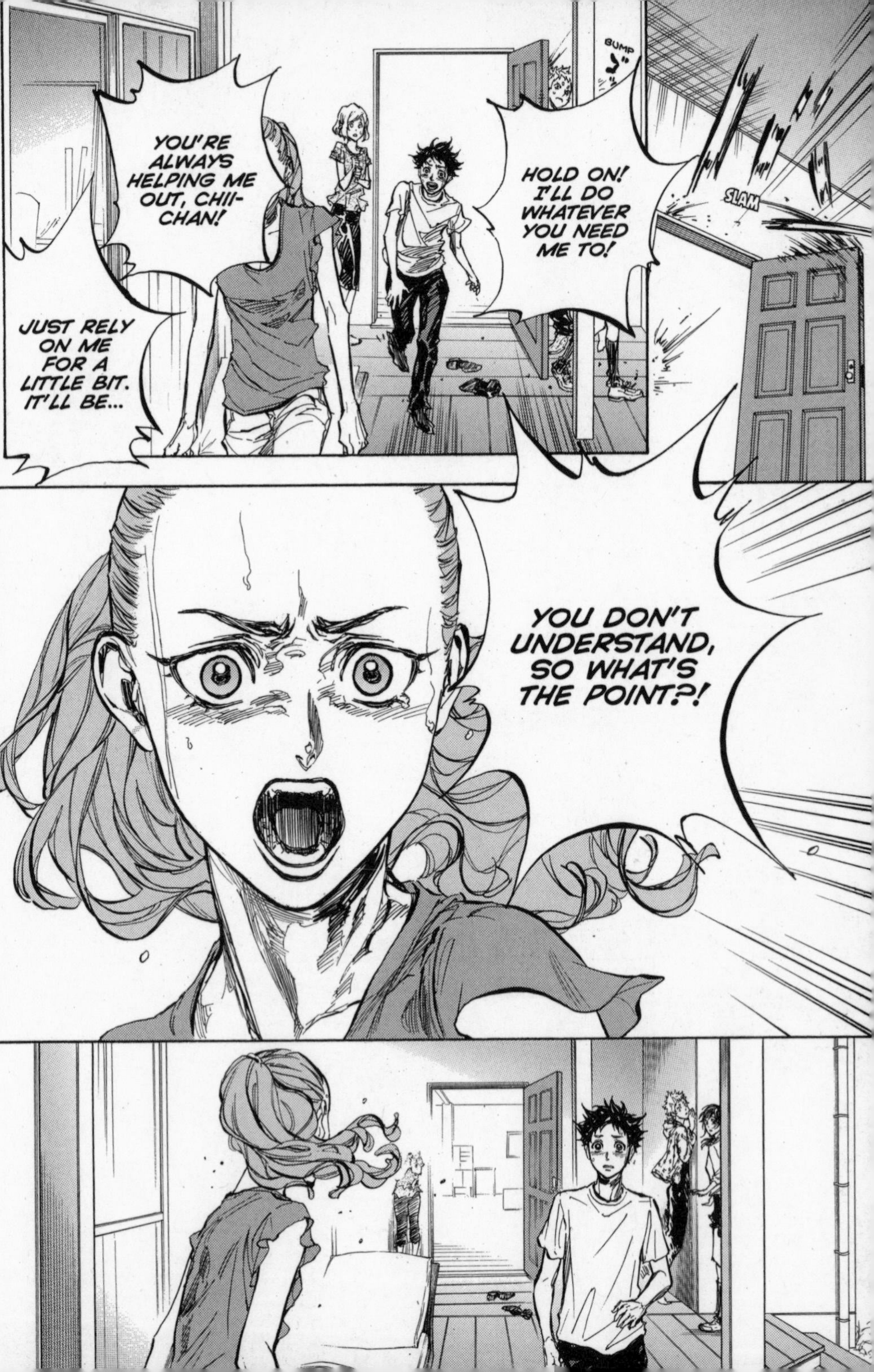
SLAM
BUMP
HOLD ON! I'LL DO WHATEVER YOU NEED ME TO!
YOU'RE ALWAYS HELPING ME OUT, CHII-CHAN!
JUST RELY ON ME FOR A LITTLE BIT. IT'LL BE...
YOU DON'T UNDERSTAND, SO WHAT'S THE POINT?!

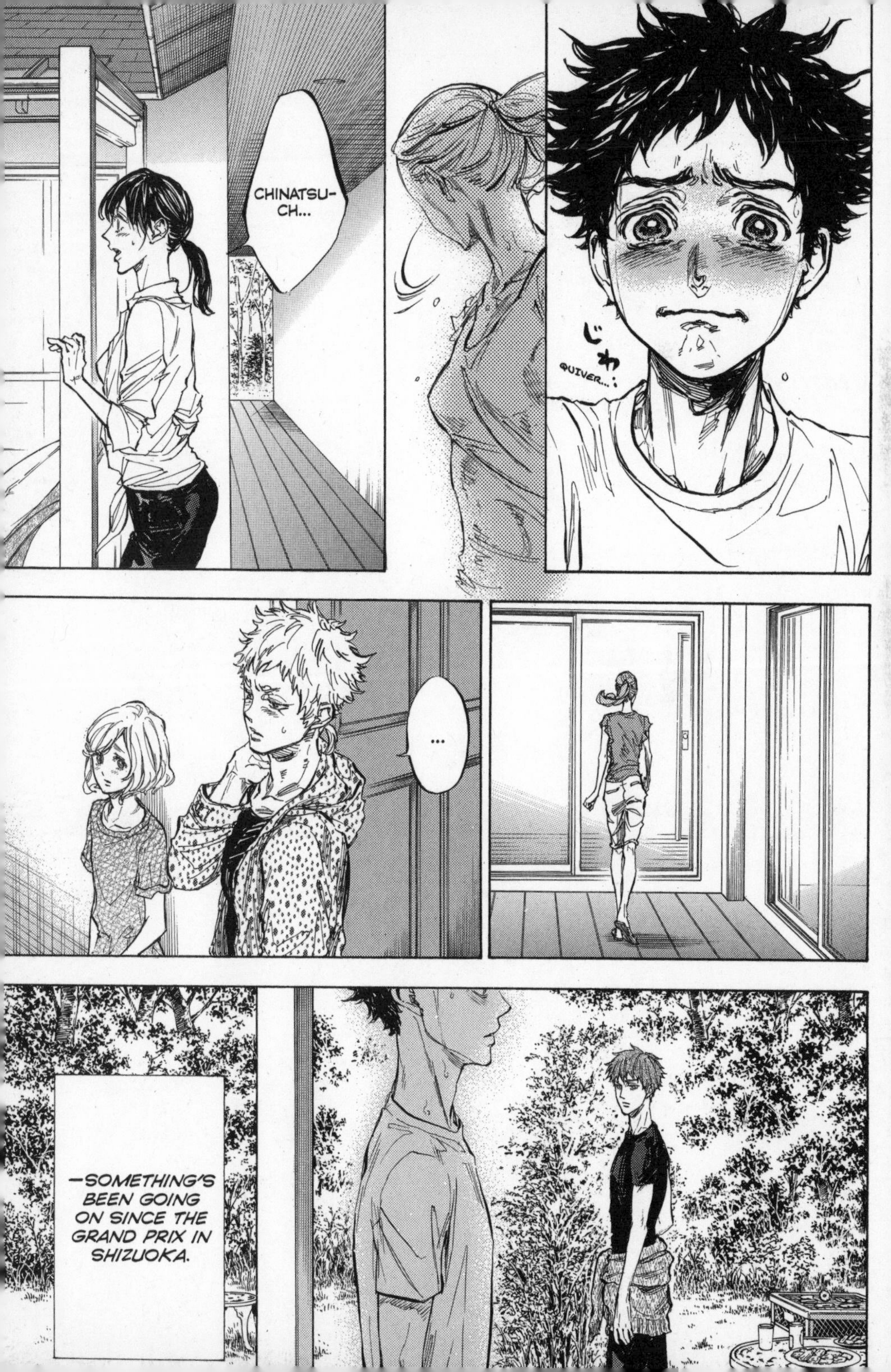
じわ
QUIVER...
CHINATSU-CH...
...
—SOMETHING'S BEEN GOING ON SINCE THE GRAND PRIX IN SHIZUOKA.

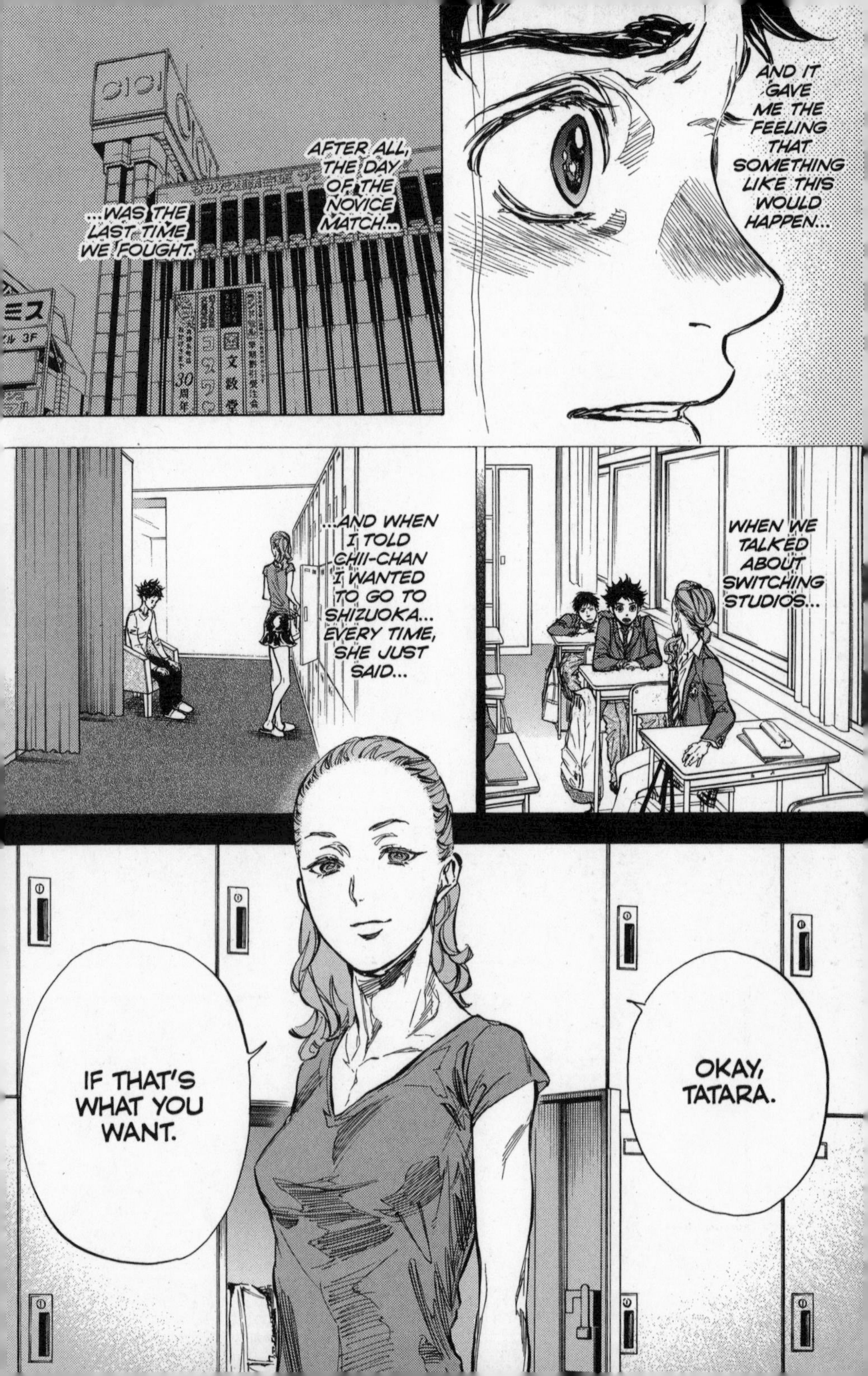
AND IT GAVE ME THE FEELING THAT SOMETHING LIKE THIS WOULD HAPPEN...
AFTER ALL, THE DAY OF THE NOVICE MATCH...
...WAS THE LAST TIME WE FOUGHT.
WHEN WE TALKED ABOUT SWITCHING STUDIOS...
...AND WHEN I TOLD CHII-CHAN I WANTED TO GO TO SHIZUOKA... EVERY TIME, SHE JUST SAID...
OKAY, TATARA.
IF THAT'S WHAT YOU WANT.

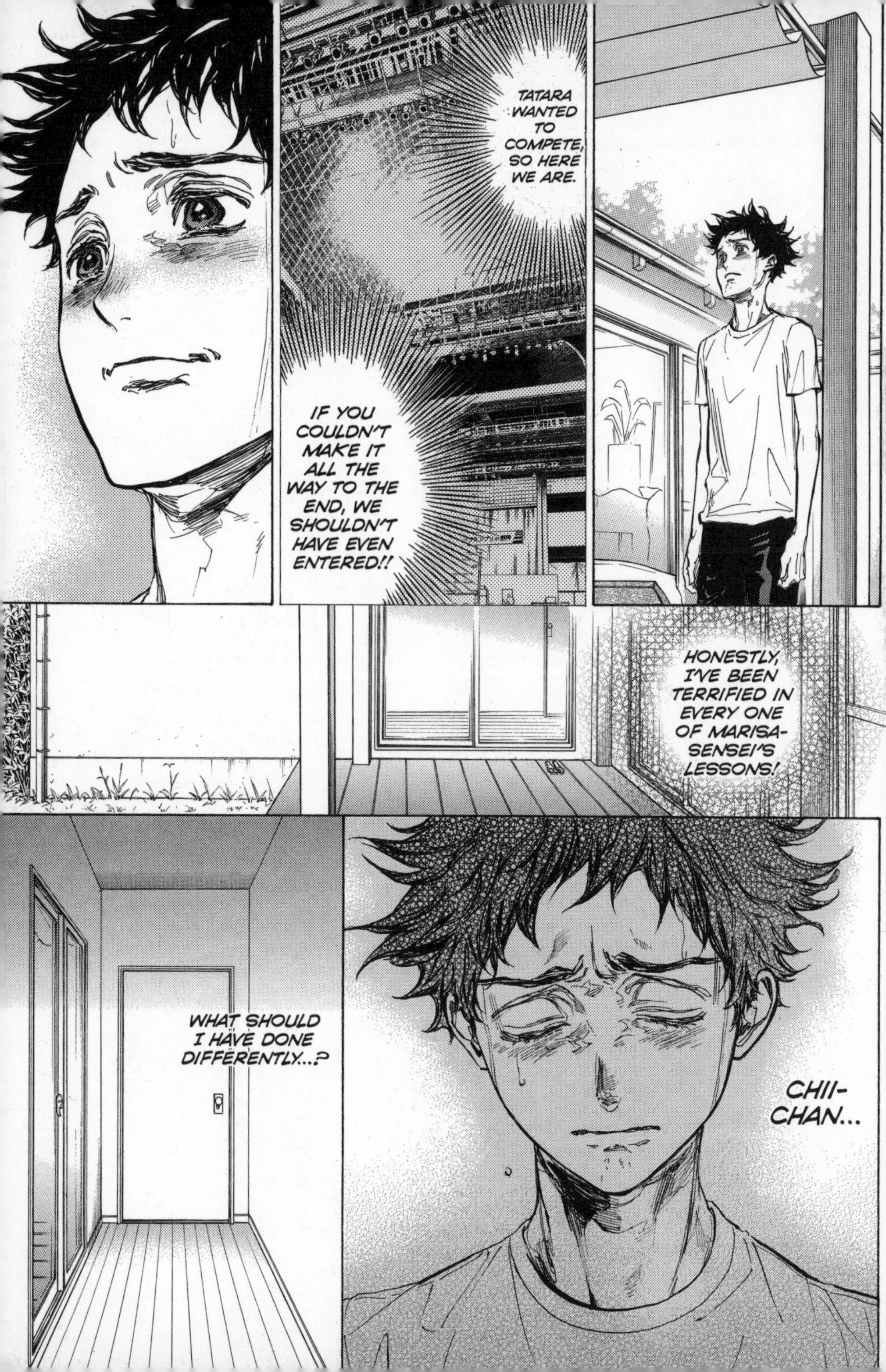
TATARA WANTED TO COMPETE, SO HERE WE ARE.
IF YOU COULDN'T MAKE IT ALL THE WAY TO THE END, WE SHOULDN'T HAVE EVEN ENTERED!!
HONESTLY, I'VE BEEN TERRIFIED IN EVERY ONE OF MARISA-SENSEI'S LESSONS!
CHII-CHAN...
WHAT SHOULD I HAVE DONE DIFFERENTLY...?

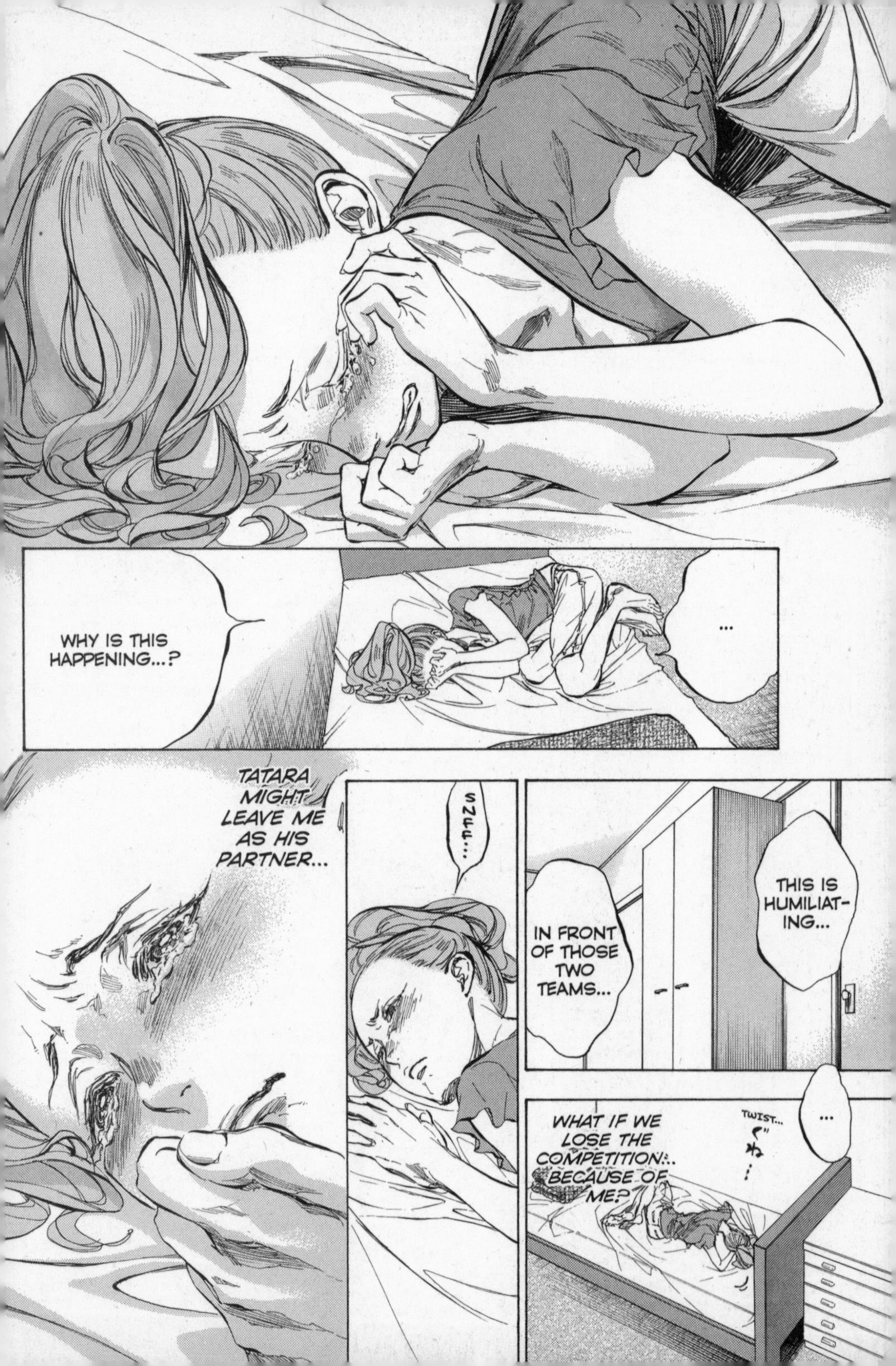
...
WHY IS THIS HAPPENING...?
THIS IS HUMILIAT-ING...
IN FRONT OF THOSE TWO TEAMS...
...
TWIST...
WHAT IF WE LOSE THE COMPETITION... BECAUSE OF ME?
SNFF...
TATARA MIGHT LEAVE ME AS HIS PARTNER...

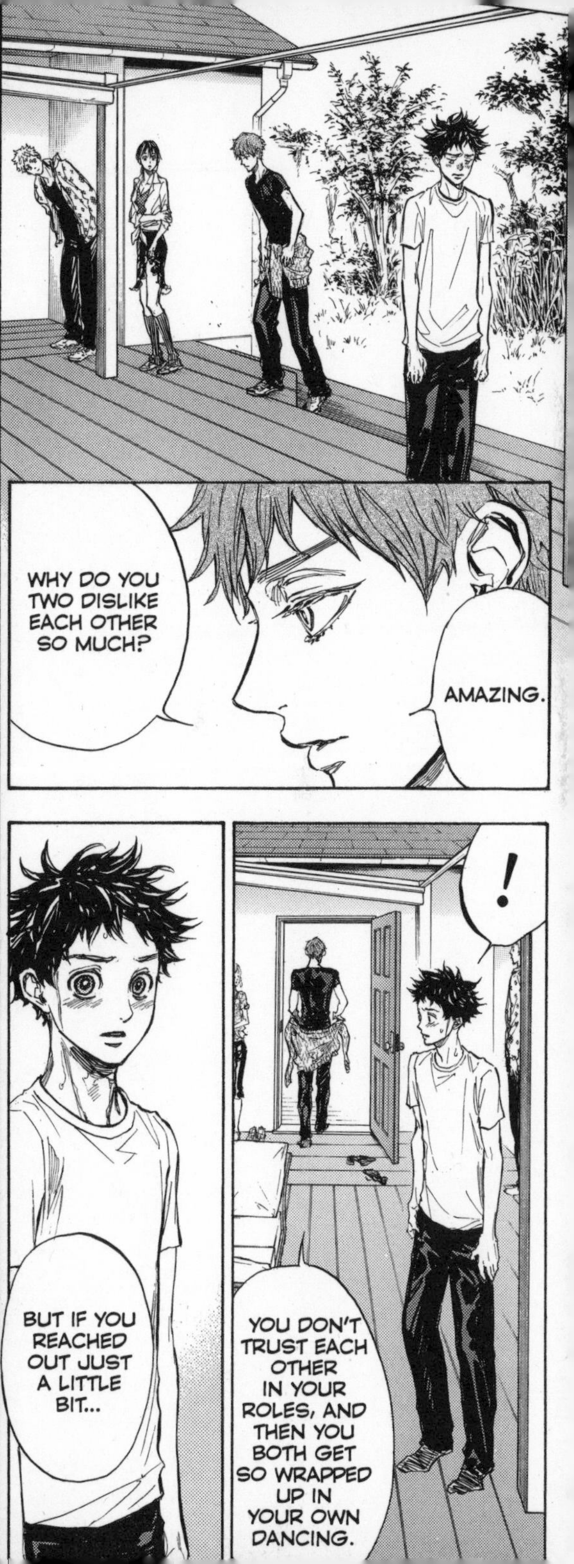
AMAZING.
WHY DO YOU TWO DISLIKE EACH OTHER SO MUCH?
!
YOU DON'T TRUST EACH OTHER IN YOUR ROLES, AND THEN YOU BOTH GET SO WRAPPED UP IN YOUR OWN DANCING.
BUT IF YOU REACHED OUT JUST A LITTLE BIT...
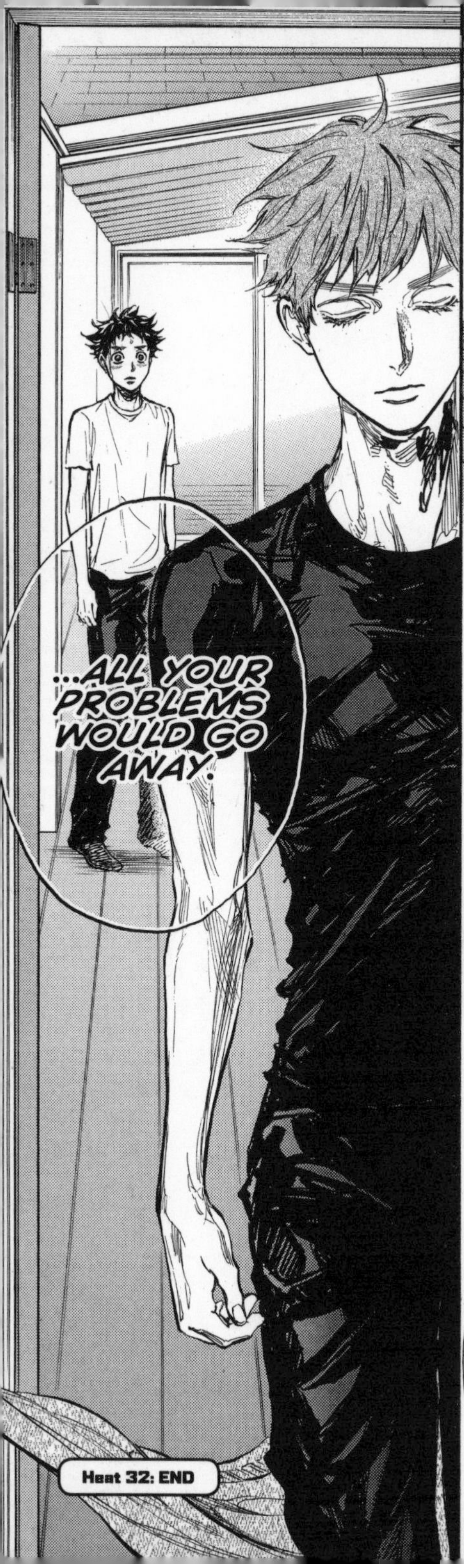
...ALL YOUR PROBLEMS WOULD GO AWAY.
Heat 32: END

Extra Heat

"What if We Genderswap the Leaders and Partners?!"

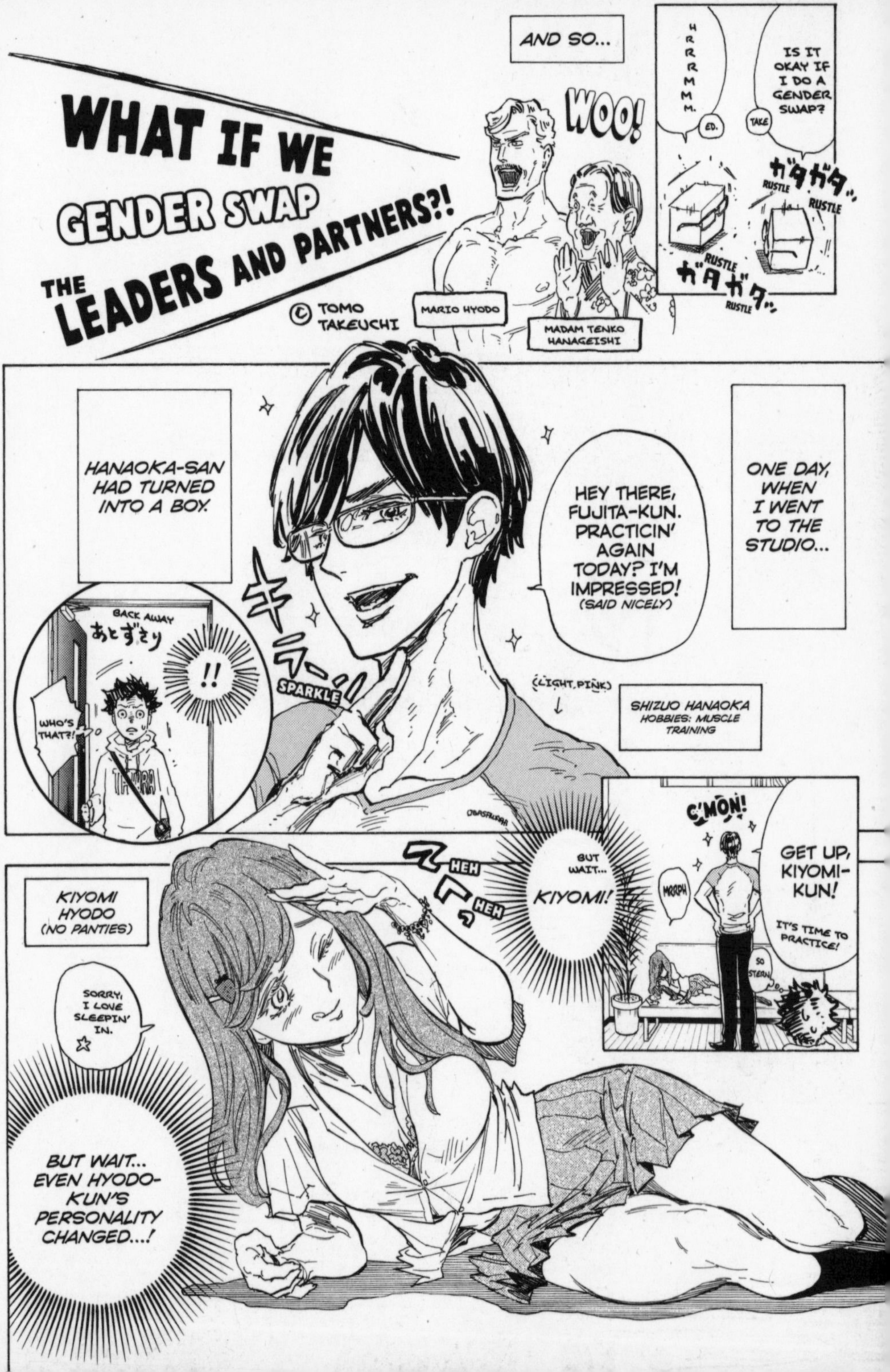
IS IT OKAY IF I DO A GENDER SWAP?
TAKE
HRRRMMM.
ED.
ガタガタッ RUSTLE RUSTLE
ガタガタッ RUSTLE RUSTLE
AND SO...
WOO!
MARIO HYODO
MADAM TENKO HANAGEISHI
WHAT IF WE GENDER SWAP THE LEADERS AND PARTNERS?!
© TOMO TAKEUCHI
ONE DAY, WHEN I WENT TO THE STUDIO...
HEY THERE, FUJITA-KUN. PRACTICIN' AGAIN TODAY? I'M IMPRESSED! (SAID NICELY)
HANAOKA-SAN HAD TURNED INTO A BOY.
キラーン SPARKLE
(LIGHT PINK)
SHIZUO HANAOKA HOBBIES: MUSCLE TRAINING
BACK AWAY あとずさり
!!
WHO'S THAT?!
GET UP, KIYOMI-KUN! IT'S TIME TO PRACTICE!
C'MON!
MRRPH
SO STERN
BUT WAIT... KIYOMI!
HEH HEH
KIYOMI HYODO (NO PANTIES)
SORRY, I LOVE SLEEPIN' IN. ☆
BUT WAIT... EVEN HYODO-KUN'S PERSONALITY CHANGED...!

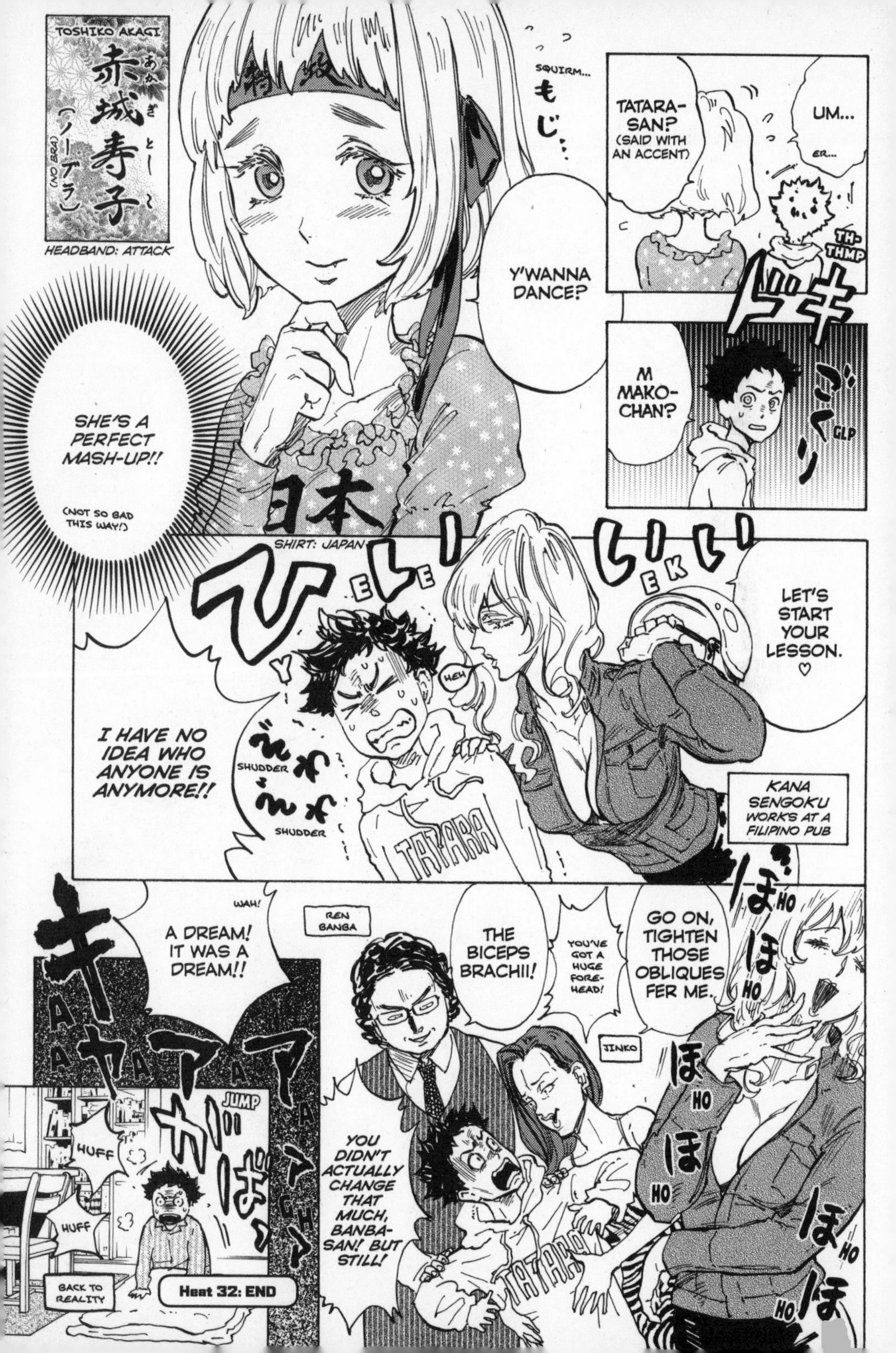
UM...
ER...
TATARA-SAN? (SAID WITH AN ACCENT)
TH-THMP
ドキ
ごくン GLP
M MAKO-CHAN?
SQUIRM... もじ...
Y'WANNA DANCE?
TOSHIKO AKAGI
赤城寿子 (あかぎとし~) (ノーブラ) (NO BRA)
HEADBAND: ATTACK
SHE'S A PERFECT MASH-UP!!
(NOT SO BAD THIS WAY!)
日本
SHIRT: JAPAN
LET'S START YOUR LESSON. ♡
ひ YEEEE EEKII
HEH
KANA SENGOKU WORKS AT A FILIPINO PUB
SHUDDER
SHUDDER
I HAVE NO IDEA WHO ANYONE IS ANYMORE!!
ほほほほほほ HO HO HO HO HO HO
GO ON, TIGHTEN THOSE OBLIQUES FER ME.
YOU'VE GOT A HUGE FORE-HEAD!
JINKO
THE BICEPS BRACHII!
REN BANBA
WAH!
YOU DIDN'T ACTUALLY CHANGE THAT MUCH, BANBA-SAN! BUT STILL!
A DREAM! IT WAS A DREAM!!
キャアアア AAAAAAGH
がばっ JUMP
HUFF
HUFF
BACK TO REALITY
Heat 32: END

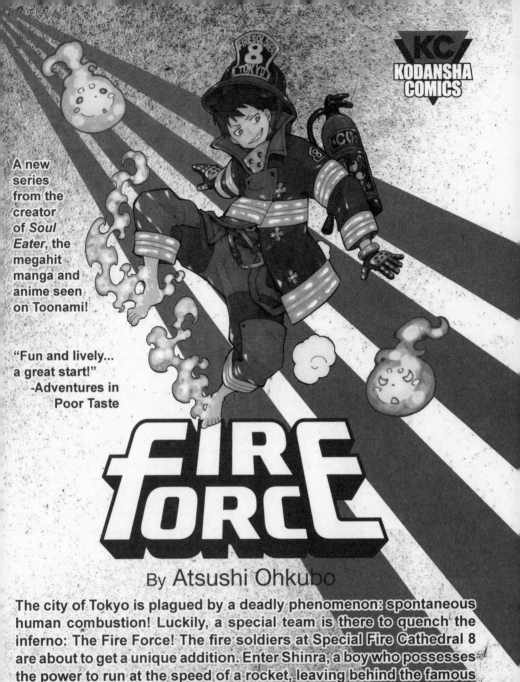

A new series from the creator of *Soul Eater*, the megahit manga and anime seen on Toonami!

"Fun and lively... a great start!"
-Adventures in Poor Taste

FIRE FORCE

By Atsushi Ohkubo

The city of Tokyo is plagued by a deadly phenomenon: spontaneous human combustion! Luckily, a special team is there to quench the inferno: The Fire Force! The fire soldiers at Special Fire Cathedral 8 are about to get a unique addition. Enter Shinra, a boy who possesses the power to run at the speed of a rocket, leaving behind the famous "devil's footprints" (and destroying his shoes in the process). Can Shinra and his colleagues discover the source of this strange epidemic before the city burns to ashes?

The award-winning manga about what happens inside you!

"Far more entertaining than it ought to be... what kid doesn't want to think that every time they sneeze a torpedo shoots out their nose?"
–Anime News Network

Strep throat! Hay fever! Influenza! The world is a dangerous place for a red blood cell just trying to get her deliveries finished. Fortunately, she's not alone…she's got a whole human body's worth of cells ready to help out! The mysterious white blood cells, the buff and brash killer T cells, even the cute little platelets— everyone's got to come together if they want to keep you healthy!

Cells at Work!

はたらく細胞

By Akane Shimizu

KC
KODANSHA COMICS

> **New action series from Hiroyuki Takei, creator of the classic shonen franchise Shaman King!**

In medieval Japan, a bell hanging on the collar is a sign that a cat has a master. Norachiyo's bell hangs from his katana sheath, but he is nonetheless a stray — a ronin. This one-eyed cat samurai travels across a dishonest world, cutting through pretense and deception with his blade.

NeKoGaHara

STRAY CAT SAMURAI

By

Hiroyuki Takei

KC
KODANSHA
COMICS

Japan's most powerful spirit medium delves into the ghost world's greatest mysteries!

Story by Kyo Shirodaira, famed author of mystery fiction and creator of *Spiral*, *Blast of Tempest*, and *The Record of a Fallen Vampire*.

Both touched by spirits called yôkai, Kotoko and Kurô have gained unique superhuman powers. But to gain her powers Kotoko has given up an eye and a leg, and Kurô's personal life is in shambles. So when Kotoko suggests they team up to deal with renegades from the spirit world, Kurô doesn't have many other choices, but Kotoko might just have a few ulterior motives...

IN/SPECTRE

STORY BY **KYO SHIRODAIRA**
ART BY **CHASHIBA KATASE**

Welcome to the Ballroom volume 7 is a work of fiction. Names, characters, places, and incidents are the products of the author's imagination or are used fictitiously. Any resemblance to actual events, locales, or persons, living or dead, is entirely coincidental.

A Kodansha Comics Trade Paperback Original.

Welcome to the Ballroom volume 7 copyright © 2014 Tomo Takeuchi
English translation copyright © 2017 Tomo Takeuchi

All rights reserved.

Published in the United States by Kodansha Comics, an imprint of Kodansha USA Publishing, LLC, New York.

Publication rights for this English edition arranged through Kodansha Ltd., Tokyo.

First published in Japan in 2014 by Kodansha Ltd., Tokyo, as *Booruruumu e Youkoso* volume 7.

ISBN 978-1-63236-520-0

Printed in the United States of America.

www.kodanshacomics.com

9 8 7 6 5 4 3 2 1

Translator: Karen McGillicuddy
Lettering: Brndn Blakeslee
Editing: Paul Starr
Kodansha Comics edition cover design by Phil Balsman